STUDY GU

for

Financial Markets and Institutions

EIGHTH EDITION

Frederic S. Mishkin   Stanley G. Eakins

William Gerken

Auburn University

PEARSON

Boston Columbus Indianapolis New York San Francisco Upper Saddle River
Amsterdam Cape Town Dubai London Madrid Milan Munich Paris Montreal Toronto
Delhi Mexico City Sao Paulo Sydney Hong Kong Seoul Singapore Taipei Tokyo

Executive Acquisitions Editor: Adrienne D'Ambrosio
Editorial Project Manager: Erin McDonagh
Production Project Manager: Alison Eusden

10 9 8 7 6 5 4 3 2 1

www.pearsonhighered.com

ISBN-10:   0-13-342707-2
ISBN-13: 978-0-13-342707-3

PEARSON

Contents

Chapter 1
Why Study Financial Markets and Institutions?

■ Chapter Learning Goals

By the end of this chapter, you should

1. Be able to describe the three main financial markets and their importance to investors and businesses.
2. Know why intermediaries exist.
3. Be able to list the main intermediaries.
4. Know how to define monetary policy and know how changes in the policy impact the financial markets.

■ Chapter Summary

Chapter 1 introduces the material you will study in this course and establishes the scope of the topics covered by *Financial Markets and Institutions*.

The Major Financial Markets

The first major topic of this book is financial markets. In general, a **financial market** is where financial assets (also called **securities**) are exchanged, much like a product market is where assets such as clothes and automobiles are bought and sold. In the financial markets, people with excess funds transfer use of those funds to people who have a shortage of funds. Transactions in the financial markets are often completed through financial intermediaries. **Financial intermediaries** are organizations that serve as "middlemen" and transfer funds from those with excess to those with a shortage. The three financial markets we encounter are **bond markets, stock markets,** and **foreign exchange markets.**

A bond is a security that represents a debt obligation of the borrower. The owner of the bond is the lender. The bond market is where debt transactions are completed. An important outcome of the bond market is the establishment of interest rates. **Interest rates** are what borrowers pay for the use of the money they obtain from lenders. Interest rates in the last 30 years have been more volatile than at any other time in U.S. history. We study interest rate fluctuations because changes in interest rates have important effects on individuals, financial institutions, and the overall economy. Short-term rates tend to fluctuate more and be lower than long-term rates. In addition, the rates paid on corporate bonds with lower ratings tend to be higher than rates on less risky bonds.

Debt and interest rates play such an important role in the economy that the role of debt is covered in Chapters 2, 11, 12, and 14. Expanded coverage on interest rates occurs in Chapters 3 through 5.

The **stock market** is where transactions are completed for financial assets that represent claims on the earnings and assets of a corporation. Ownership of a company is accomplished through purchasing **common stock.** The action of buying a common stock is typically referred to as buying a stock. The stock market has also been extremely volatile in recent years. For example, on October 19, 1987 (referred to as Black Monday), the Dow Jones Industrial Average lost more than 500 points, a 22% decline. From then until 2000, the stock market experienced one of the great bull markets in its history, with the Dow climbing to a peak of more than 11,000. With the collapse of the high-tech bubble in 2000, the stock market fell sharply, dropping by more than 30% by late 2002. It then rose to an all–time high above the 14,000 level in 2007, only to fall by more than 50% of its value to a low below 7,000 in 2009. Then another bull market began, with the Dow reaching new highs above the 15,000 level in 2013. In addition to affecting investor wealth, conditions in the stock market affect the ability of businesses to raise funds for expansion and growth. The role of the stock market is covered in Chapters 2, 6, and 13.

The **foreign exchange markets** establish the rate at which money in one country can be traded for money in another country. The amount of money that can be received in the foreign currency (for example, **euros**) for one unit of the domestic currency (say, U.S. dollars) is referred to as the **foreign exchange rate.** For example, at the time this study guide is being written in the beginning of 2013, 1 U.S. dollar can be exchanged for about 0.74 euros, and conversely 1 euro can be exchanged for $1.36. The exchange rate changes over time. A change in the foreign exchange rate has a direct impact on American consumers because it affects the cost of foreign goods. A **weak dollar** leads to more expensive foreign goods while making American goods cheaper abroad. A **strong dollar** has just the opposite impact. More on the foreign exchange market is covered in Chapter 15.

Examining Financial Institutions

The second major topic of this book is **financial institutions.** Financial institutions function as financial intermediaries. They play an important role in transferring funds from those with an excess to those with a shortage. The most important financial institution in a financial system is the **central bank,** which is responsible for the conduct of monetary policy. The central bank in the United States is the Federal Reserve System. Other important financial institutions are commercial banks, insurance companies, mutual funds, finance companies, mutual savings banks, credit unions, savings and loans, pension funds, and investment banks. Of these, **banks** are the largest financial intermediary and are the most familiar to individuals. Individuals often save money in a bank by putting money into a savings account and borrow money from banks for loans to purchase items such as cars and houses. Other institutions that accept deposits and make loans to individuals are mutual savings banks, credit unions, and savings and loans. At times, this normally well-functioning system of financial intermediaries may seize up and produce a **financial crisis,** which is a major disruption in financial markets that is characterized by sharp declines in assets prices and failures of many financial and non-financial firms. Improved technology, deregulation, and increased competition among intermediaries have led financial institutions to become more innovative in providing services and controlling costs. Information technology advances in particular have led to **e-finance,** a new means of delivering financial services electronically. Financial innovation has led to more investment opportunities for investors and additional sources of funds for businesses.

What Determines Interest Rates?

The third major topic of this book is the study of interest rates. A change in the **money supply** directly changes expected **inflation.** As the money supply increases, the rate of inflation tends to increase as well. As the rate of inflation increases, interest rates increase to compensate investors for the reduced spending power of the dollar. Changes in the money supply also play an important role in generating **business cycles,** which are the upward and downward movements of aggregate output in the economy. Because of the important relationship between the money supply, inflation, and interest rates, the study of the money supply is covered extensively in this book.

■ Exercises

Exercise 1: Definitions and Terminology

Match the terms in the right-hand column with the definition or description in the left-hand column. Place the letter of the term in the blank provided next to the appropriate definition.

____ 1. A financial asset that represents ownership of a corporation

____ 2. Anything generally accepted in payment for goods and services

____ 3. Helps with the transfer of funds from those with excess to those with a shortage

____ 4. A debt security that promises to make periodic payments for a specified period of time

____ 5. Price paid for the rental of borrowed funds

____ 6. A claim on the issuer's future income or assets

____ 7. Markets where those with excess funds transact with those who have a shortage of funds

____ 8. The financial institution in the United States that exercises control over monetary policy

____ 9. How the quantity of money and interest rates are managed

____ 10. The price of one country's currency relative to another currency

____ 11. The place where currencies are traded

____ 12. Financial institutions that accept deposits and make loans

____ 13. Major disruption in financial markets characterized by sharp declines in asset prices and failures of financial and non-financial firms

____ 14. New means of delivering financial services electronically

a.   money (money supply)

b.   stocks

c.   security

d.   Federal Reserve

e.   financial intermediary

f.   financial markets

g.   interest rate

h.   bond

i.   foreign exchange rate

j.   monetary policy

k.   e-finance

l.   the foreign exchange market

m.   banks

n.   financial crisis

Exercise 2: Money and Business Cycles

1.   Financial markets are an important part of the United States financial system. Why is a well functioning financial market important for the economic growth of a country and its citizens?

_____

_____

_____

2.   How do rising interest rates affect financial institutions and businesses?

_____

_____

_____

Exercise 3: Bond, Stock, and Foreign Exchange Markets

Some of the most important financial markets are discussed briefly in Chapter 1. The statements below refer to three of these markets in the United States: the bond market, the stock market, and the foreign exchange market. Indicate to which of the three markets the statement refers. Let B = bond market, S = stock market, and F = foreign exchange market.

_____   1.   The market where interest rates are determined.

_____   2.   The market where claims on the earnings of corporations are traded.

_____   3.   The market that made major news when the Dow Jones industrial average fell about 22% on October 19, 1987.

_____   4.   Individuals trying to decide how much a trip to France will cost might be influenced by the outcomes in this market.

_____   5.   The most widely followed financial market by individual investors in America.

_____   6.   The price of Japanese DVD players sold in the United States is affected by trading in this market.

_____   7.   The market where U.S. government Treasury securities are traded.

_____   8.   The market where residual owners exchange ownership claims on companies.

_____   9.   The main market that offers fixed-rate securities that have finite lives.

■ Self-Test

Part A: Fill in the Blanks

1. _____, the condition of rising price levels, which has exhibited a close relation to the money supply.

2. Evidence indicates that those countries with the highest rates of inflation are also the ones with the _____ money growth rates.

3. The flow of funds in financial markets will affect_____ _____, the production of _____ and _____, and the economic well-being of other countries.

4. Changes in interest rates affect the prices of _____ and _____.

5. Short-term interest rates are typically _____ volatile than long-term rates and are generally _____ in value.

6. Except for the period between 1963 and 1981, _____ on long-term Treasury bonds have been relatively stable around 5%.

7. The largest percentage decline in the history of the stock market occurred on _____, which is referred to as "Black Monday."

8. Financial intermediaries play an important role in transferring funds from those who wish to _____ to those who wish to borrow, thereby ensuring that resources are put to more productive uses.

9. The process of channeling funds by way of an intermediary or middleman is known as _____.

10. _____ markets, such as the bond market, the stock market, and foreign exchange market have become increasingly important areas of study.

11. Changes in _____, which represent the price of one country's currency in terms of another's, not only affect those individuals involved in international trade, but all consumers and producers.

12. The bond market is important because _____ rates are determined in this market.

13. The _____ market is the most widely followed financial market by individual investors in the United States.

14. A(n) _____ dollar means that the value of the dollar rises relative to foreign currencies and foreign goods become less expensive to Americans—good news for consumers.

15. A stronger dollar means that goods produced in the United States become more _____ to foreign purchasers, who are now likely to purchase fewer U.S. goods—bad news for *American* producers.

16. A new means of delivering financial services electronically is called _____.

17. The central bank in the United States is the _____.

18. The worst one-day decline in the history of the DJIA is referred to as _____.

Part B: True-False Questions

Circle whether the following statements are true (T) or false (F).

T   F   1.   Empirical evidence suggests that the price level and the money supply move together over long periods of time.

T   F   2.   Money is defined as anything that is generally accepted in payment for goods or services or in the repayment of debts.

T   F   3.   The condition of rising price levels is known as a recession.

T   F   4.   Economists frequently talk about "the interest rate" because *generally* most interest rates move up and down together.

T   F   5.   Monetary policy involves the management of money and interest rates.

T   F   6.   Financial intermediaries are essentially unproductive middlemen.

T   F   7.   Financial intermediation is an important activity because it allows funds to be channeled to those who can put them to productive use.

T   F   8.   Financial intermediaries should not exist unless they provided services that people valued.

T   F   9.   The foreign exchange market is likely to be of interest to those corporations that do a lot of overseas business.

T   F 10.   Economists tend to disregard events in the stock market because stock prices tend to be extremely stable and are therefore of little interest.

T   F 11.   The price of one country's currency in terms of another is called the concentration ratio.

T   F 12.   A stronger dollar means that American goods will likely become more expensive in foreign countries, and so foreigners will buy fewer of them.

T   F 13.   Financial intermediaries are important to the economy and are among the most highly regulated businesses in the economy.

T   F 14.   The central bank in the United States is the largest commercial bank in the United States.

T   F 15.   Two special features of this text that enhance the learning process are "Following the Financial News" and "Reading the *Wall Street Journal*."

T   F 16.   Following Black Monday, the DJIA experienced one of the greatest bull markets in history.

T   F 17.   Changes in interest rates only affect the bond market.

T   F 18.   Technological innovation largely has not affected financial intermediaries.

T   F 19.   Exchange rates do not vary much through time.

Part C: Multiple-Choice Questions

Circle the appropriate answer.

1. Changes in the money supply appear to have a major influence on
   (a) inflation.
   (b) the business cycle.
   (c) interest rates.
   (d) each of the above.
   (e) only (a) and (c) of the above.

2. The Federal Reserve is the government organization responsible for
   (a) monetary policy.
   (b) interest rates.
   (c) controlling the deficit.
   (d) all of the above.
   (e) (a) and (b) of the above.

3. Banks are an important part of the study of financial markets because
   (a) banks are the largest financial intermediary.
   (b) banks have been important in the rapid pace of financial innovation.
   (c) Both (a) and (b) are correct.
   (d) Neither (a) nor (b) is correct.

4. An increase in interest rates is likely to cause borrowing on houses to
   (a) fall.
   (b) rise.
   (c) rise in the short run if interest rates are expected to fall in the future.
   (d) remain unchanged.

5. An increase in the value of the dollar relative to all foreign currencies means that the price of foreign goods purchased by Americans
   (a) increases.
   (b) falls.
   (c) remains unchanged.
   (d) There is not enough information to answer.

6. Money is defined as
   (a) bills of exchange.
   (b) anything that is generally accepted in payment for goods and services or in the repayment of debt.
   (c) a riskless repository of spending power.
   (d) the unrecognized liability of governments.

7. Which of the following is *not* a claim on the assets or future income of a company?
   (a) A security
   (b) Stocks
   (c) Interest rate
   (d) Bonds
   (e) Both (b) and (c) are correct.

8. Which of the following is true about banks?
   (a) Banks are subject to little regulation.
   (b) Banks are the largest financial intermediary in the U.S. economy.

(c)   Banks set the level of interest rates in the economy.

(d)   Most Americans keep only a small proportion of their financial wealth in banks.

(e)   Both (b) and (c) are correct.

9.   Which of the following is *not* a major topic covered in this textbook?

(a)   Monetary policy

(b)   Personal investment

(c)   Financial markets

(d)   Financial institutions

(e)   Both (c) and (d) are correct.

10.   Which of the following firms is *not* considered an example of a financial intermediary?

(a)   Commercial banks

(b)   Insurance companies

(c)   Mutual funds

(d)   The Federal Reserve System

11.   The highest level of interest rates in the United States since 1950 occurred during the period

(a)   1980–1985.

(b)   1970–1975.

(c)   1990–1995.

(d)   1950–1955.

12.   The most important asset underlying the financial system is

(a)   money.

(b)   income.

(c)   stocks.

(d)   bonds.

13.   Which of the following groups of securities normally has the highest interest rate?

(a)   U.S. government long-term bonds

(b)   Three-month Treasury bills

(c)   Long-term corporate bonds

(d)   The rates on these securities vary too much to classify any one as having the highest rate.

14.   Since 1970, the exchange rate of the U.S. dollar relative to a basket of major foreign currency was at its strongest (highest appreciation) around the year

(a)   1970.

(b)   1980.

(c)   1985.

(d)   1995.

15. Which of the following is true regarding financial crises?
    (a) Modern financial innovations have completely eliminated financial crises.
    (b) Crises are characterized by large increases in asset prices.
    (c) Only financial firms are affected by financial crises.
    (d) Financial crises have been a feature of capitalist economies for centuries.

16. The most important financial institutions in the financial system are
    (a) savings and loan associations.
    (b) credit unions.
    (c) the central bank.
    (d) insurance companies.

17. Companies raise funds or capital for new projects through which of the following markets?
    (a) Foreign exchange market
    (b) Bond markets
    (c) Stock markets
    (d) Both (b) and (c)

18. Improvements in technology have led to
    (a) an increase in financial innovation by financial intermediaries.
    (b) e-finance.
    (c) reduced need for the Federal Reserve.
    (d) Both (a) and (b).
    (e) none of the above.

Part D: Short Answer Questions

1. The study of interest rates makes up a major segment of study in this text. Why is so much emphasis placed on interest rates?

   _____

   _____

2. The term "Black Monday" will appear on numerous occasions throughout the text. When was "Black Monday," and what happened on that day that generates this interest?

   _____

   _____

3. How has the extent of risk faced by individuals, businesses, and government changed in recent years from earlier segments of the century?

   _____

   _____

4. Describe what role financial intermediaries serve in the economy.

   _____

   _____

5.   Explain how changes in interest rates can affect personal and corporate expenditures and investment.

_____

_____

6.   How do financial markets contribute to the economy?

_____

_____

Part E: Problems

1.   You are considering traveling to Europe and plan to visit those countries that have adopted the euro as their home currency. Your budget for the trip is $10,000. How many euros can you purchase if the current exchange rate is 0.95 euros per U.S. dollar?

2.   Suppose you are forced to delay your trip due to temporary financial issues. Three months later, you are ready to take the trip. You go to exchange your U.S. dollars for euros and learn that the new exchange rate is 0.76 euro per U.S. dollar. How many euros can you purchase with the $10,000 at the new exchange rate?

3.   How many fewer euros can you purchase due to the weakness in the dollar in Problem (2) versus (1)?

■ Answers to Chapter 1

Exercise 1

1. b	6. c	11. l
2. a	7. f	12. m
3. e	8. d	13. n
4. h	9. j	14. k
5. g	10. i	

Exercise 2

1. For money to be put to its best use in helping to generate new production and the associated new jobs, money must get from the hands of those who don't currently need it (savers) to those who can best use it (borrowers). Well-functioning financial markets facilitate this transfer of money.

2. Rising interest rates generally cause a slowdown in the rate of economic growth. Higher interest rates increase the cost of capital for businesses, thereby reducing the number of profitable projects in which firms invest. Higher interest rates force financial institutions to raise the interest rates they pay depositors.

Exercise 3

1. B	6. F
2. S	7. B
3. S	8. S
4. F	9. B
5. S	

Self-Test

Part A

1. Inflation	7. October 19, 1987	13. stock
2. highest	8. save	14. stronger
3. business profits goods/services	9. financial intermediation	15. expensive
4. goods/services	10. Financial	16. e-finance
5. more/lower	11. exchange rates	17. Federal Reserve System
6. interest rates	12. interest	18. Black Monday

Part B

1. T	6. F	11. F	16. T
2. T	7. T	12. T	17. F
3. F	8. T	13. T	18. F
4. T	9. T	14. F	19. F
5. T	10. F	15. T	

Part C

1. d	6. b	11. a	16. c
2. e	7. c	12. a	17. d
3. c	8. b	13. c	18. d
4. a	9. b	14. c	
5. b	10. d	15. d	

Part D

1. Every time an individual, business, or government lends or borrows money there is interest paid or received. This interest represents the income or cost to the lender or borrower. Any change in the interest rate will influence the amount of lending that occurs in the economy and thus has a major influence on the economy.

2. Black Monday occurred on October 19, 1987. On this day the stock market in the United States experienced its worst single-day drop in value in its history. The decline was by 508 points, which was a 22% decline. The magnitude and suddenness of this fall generated significant wealth declines for many investors and also highlighted a number of flaws in the operation of the financial markets in the United States.

3. Interest rates and the stock market have both intensified in volatility in recent years. For example, between 1981 and 1996 the interest rate on Treasury bonds ranged from 6% to 15%. However, during the period 1936 to 1966 this security's rate ranged only between 2% and 5%. This increased uncertainty raises the risk to economic units and highlights the need for more risk management.

4. Financial intermediaries help to bring borrowers and lenders together by creating loan packages and savings vehicles that are of denominations acceptable to both parties.

5. Interest rates can affect personal consumers by raising the costs associated with buying large ticket items such as homes and automobiles. Rising interest rates can increase the cost of borrowing for companies, possibly making them less profitable.

6. Financial markets contribute to the economy by rationing capital to companies that will invest it the most successfully over the long run.

Part E

1. $10,000 × 0.95 euro/$ = 9,500 euros

2. $10,000 × 0.76 euro/$ = 7,600 euros

3. 9,500 – 7,600 = 1,900 fewer euros

Chapter 2
Overview of the Financial System

■ **Chapter Learning Goals**

By the end of this chapter, you should

1. Recognize why financial intermediaries and financial markets are necessary for efficient operation of the economy and that both savers and borrowers benefit from this efficiency.

2. Distinguish between direct and indirect financing.

3. Distinguish between primary markets and secondary markets, capital markets and money markets, and debt and equity markets.

4. Understand adverse selection and moral hazard.

5. Know the differences between depository institutions, contractual savings institutions, and investment intermediaries.

■ **Chapter Summary**

This chapter provides an overview of the structure and operation of the financial markets. This background is necessary for understanding the rest of the text. The most important message found in this chapter is that financial markets and financial intermediaries are crucial to a well-functioning economy because they channel funds from those who do not have a productive use to those who do.

Why Have Financial Markets?

Funds can be moved from those with an excess to those with a shortage either directly or indirectly. In direct financing, borrowers obtain funds directly from savers by issuing financial instruments or **securities,** which represent claims on the borrower's assets or future income. These claims represent **liabilities** or IOUs to borrowers but assets to the lenders or savers. More frequently an intermediary brings the two parties together and reduces transaction costs by taking advantage of **economies of scale.** Economies of scale result from the reduction of transaction costs per dollar of transaction as the size (scale) of transactions increase. For example, it is cheaper per loan for a bank to make 100 loans than it is for 100 lenders to contract separately with 100 borrowers. A **financial intermediary** is a business that has as one of its main purposes the matching of those with money to save and those who need additional funds. This use of an intermediary is called **indirect** financing. Because of economies of scale and the ability of intermediaries to reduce search costs, both savers and spenders can often earn more than when using direct financing. **Search costs** refer to the cost of a saver-lender locating an acceptable borrower-spender. In addition to lowering transaction costs, financial institutions also help investors to share risk. Financial intermediaries further promote risk sharing by providing **diversification** opportunities to investors. The presence of intermediaries and financial markets enables funds to move easily and efficiently from savers to spenders in a manner that puts the funds to work where they should provide the greatest return.

Types of Markets

A firm can obtain funds in financial markets in two ways. The most common method is to issue debt; the other is to issue equity. Firms sell **bonds** on the **debt markets,** and this represents lending by a saver to a firm. The saver normally receives a contractually set interest payment from the borrower for use of the loaned funds. Bonds have finite lives with specific expiration dates in the future, referred to as the **maturity** date. If the maturity date is less than one year then the bond is classified as being a **short-term** bond. Bonds with maturity dates greater than a year but less than 10 years are called **intermediate-term** bonds, while bonds with maturity dates greater than 10 years are named **long-term** bonds. Firms sell common stock in the **equity markets,** and this represents the transfer of a partial ownership interest in a firm. Stock owners are not assured of any contractual payments but are entitled to any residual funds remaining after all other claims are paid. Often common stock will make periodic or quarterly payments, called **dividends,** to shareholders.

We can further describe the debt and equity markets as either primary or secondary markets. In the **primary market**, the corporation or government agency that will ultimately use the funds sells new issues of a security. An **investment banker** is commonly used to assist in the process of a single borrower obtaining funds from many securities. The investment banker assists by underwriting the debt or equity issue. **Underwriting** means that the investment banker first provides the money to the borrower and will then proceed to obtain the money from lenders by issuing the stock or bond. In the **secondary market**, previously issued securities are resold. The New York Stock Exchange is the best known of the secondary markets. Other important secondary markets include the **over-the-counter** market, the American Stock Exchange, and the Chicago Board of Trade. One valuable service provided by the secondary market is to make securities more **liquid** by establishing a ready market for the security when the holder wishes to sell. This makes the security much more desirable. **Brokers** and **dealers** assist in the secondary markets by matching buyers and sellers of the security.

Every securities market is classified as either an **exchange** or an **over-the-counter (OTC) market.** An exchange is a market that typically has a centralized location where buyers and sellers physically meet to trade securities. Conversely, OTC markets have no centralized location or meeting place and are simply systems of networked computers in which dealers and individual investors post prices and trade with anyone willing to accept those prices or negotiate and agree on new prices. The largest and best known OTC market is the Nasdaq. Many people do not recognize the difference between a dealer and a broker. A **broker** provides the service of handling the details of a security buy or sell order given by an investor. The broker brings together the buyer and seller. An investor must use a broker to trade securities in the secondary market. A **dealer** actually takes ownership of a security and will always buy from a seller and sell to a buyer. Securities traded in the OTC market are always handled through dealers.

A final way that we can distinguish between markets is on the basis of the maturity of the securities traded in that market. The **money market** is for securities that have an initial maturity of less than one year. **Capital markets** are for securities with an initial maturity that exceeds one year. For example, stock will trade on the capital markets because it has no maturity. Treasury bills will trade in the money market because they mature in less than a year.

Increasingly, U.S. investors and businesses seek and issue securities in foreign markets. The most common securities issued in international bond markets are bonds that are denominated in a foreign currency and are listed on an exchange or market of the home country from which that currency is issued. Bonds such as these are called **foreign bonds.** For example, bonds issued by Ford in Great Britain that are denominated in British pounds are foreign bonds. However, bonds issued by Ford in Great Britain that are denominated in U.S. dollars are called **Eurobonds.** In general, Eurobonds are bonds that are issued in a foreign country but are denominated in a currency other than that foreign country's currency. Similar to Eurobonds, **Eurocurrencies** are foreign currencies that are deposited in banks outside of the home country. For example, U.S. dollars deposited in foreign branches of U.S. banks or in foreign banks outside the

United States are Eurodollars. Don't confuse the **euro** currency with the use of the term Eurobonds, Eurodollars, and Eurocurrencies. The euro is the name of the currency (like our U.S. dollars) that is used in the European Union, which is under the European Monetary System. The terms Eurodollar, Eurobond, and Eurocurrencies were used long before the European Union was ever created.

Foreign equity markets are increasing in importance. Europe and Asia have both taken a chunk out of stock trades, primarily IPOs, that normally would have been done almost exclusively in the U.S. markets. There are many possible explanations for this transition. Some suggested causes include the existence of Sarbanes-Oxley Act of 2002, tighter immigration standards in the U.S. markets, increasing wealth and thus funds for investing in other countries, and improved technology innovation in foreign markets. The true cause or causes are entirely an area open for debate at this time.

Intermediaries Help Remove Informational Asymmetries and Reduce Risk

In addition to reducing transaction costs through **economies of scale**, intermediaries can mitigate the cost associated with **asymmetric information.** Asymmetric information occurs when the borrower and the lender have different information about a transaction. For example, managers may know that the future of the firm is very shaky, but lenders continue lending to the firm because they do not have this information. There are two types of asymmetric information costs: adverse selection and moral hazard. **Adverse selection** occurs when those firms most likely to default actively seek loans. This occurs because the market interest rate is most attractive to high-risk firms. **Moral hazard** refers to the risk that a borrower may pursue projects that have greater risk of failure than the projects the borrower previously undertook and which the lender expected the borrower to invest. One way we distinguish between adverse selection and moral hazard is to recognize that adverse selection is a problem before the transaction, while moral hazard is a problem after the transaction has occurred. **Conflicts of interest** where one party to a contract has incentives to act in its own interest rather than the interest of the second party often arise from the moral hazard problem. Intermediaries help to reduce this risk due to having more resources and skill to evaluate these firms than would an individual lender.

Financial institutions can reduce the risk for many investors. Savers can deposit their funds in an institution for and encounter very little risk. The institution then loans out those funds to borrowers who are much riskier than the risk carried by the saver. The result is that the saver is making a risky loan but does not face the risk of that borrower. This risk-reduction process is referred to as **asset transformation.** Risk is also reduced by financial institutions through the process of diversification. A saver's money becomes the source of funds for the financial institution to lend to a large number of borrowers. Diversification reduces the risk of the overall portfolio.

Types of Financial Intermediaries

Financial economists categorize financial intermediaries as (1) **depository institutions,** (2) **contractual savings institutions,** and (3) **investment intermediaries.** Depository institutions make loans and accept deposits from individuals and institutions. Depository institutions include commercial banks, savings and loan associations, mutual savings banks, and credit unions. Commercial banks are by far the largest in terms of assets of the depository institutions. Contractual savings institutions acquire funds at periodic intervals on a contractual basis. Life insurance companies, fire and casualty insurance companies, and pension funds are examples of contractual savings institutions. The largest of the contractual savings institutions are life insurance companies and private pension funds. Investment intermediaries invest funds on behalf of others. This category includes finance companies, mutual funds, and money market mutual funds. The dominant investment intermediary is mutual funds, with about $7 trillion in assets as of 2009.

Regulation of the Financial System

Due to the importance of financial markets, state and federal governments have created volumes of regulations to ensure that these markets operate as efficiently and fairly as possible. Regulations are intended to assist in three areas. The first is to increase the information available to investors. Two of the most important regulatory steps taken by the federal government to increase information availability were the passage of the **Securities Act of 1933** and the creation of the **Securities and Exchange Commission (SEC).** The SEC is given primary regulatory authority over the different types of markets discussed previously. The second area of regulation is intended to ensure the soundness of the financial system. Soundness is accomplished through control of who can establish financial intermediaries, limits on competitive activities such as opening additional locations, restrictions on interest rates, stringent reporting requirements, control of certain assets that the intermediary can own, and creation of deposit insurance through agencies such as the **Federal Deposit Insurance Corporation**, the **Savings Association Insurance Fund** (for savings and loans) and the **National Credit Union Share Insurance Fund.** Until 1986, the Federal Reserve System used **Regulation Q** to limit competition by placing caps, or maximum interest rates, on savings deposits held in commercial banks. In general, regulation of financial intermediaries is needed to help prevent **financial panic** or a widespread collapse of financial intermediaries. The third area of regulation is to improve control of monetary policy. To accomplish this task the Federal Reserve establishes **reserve requirements**, which are minimum net deposits that financial intermediaries must have on deposit with the Federal Reserve System.

Regulation of the financial markets in other countries has some similarities with and some differences from the U.S. markets. The more industrialized countries such as Japan, Canada, and the nations of Western Europe have regulations most similar to, though not with as much control, as the United States. Looking at the less developed economies such as China, Thailand, and Mexico will show significant deviation and much looser regulation than in the United States.

■   Exercises

Exercise 1: Direct versus Indirect Finance

For each of the following financial transactions indicate whether it involves direct finance or indirect finance by writing in the space provided a D for direct finance or an I for indirect finance.

_____   1.   You take out a car loan from a finance company.

_____   2.   You buy a U.S. savings bond.

_____   3.   You buy a share of GM stock.

_____   4.   You buy a share of a mutual fund.

_____   5.   You borrow $1,000 from your father.

_____   6.   You obtain a $50,000 mortgage from your local S&L.

_____   7.   You buy a life insurance policy.

_____   8.   GM sells a share of its stock to IBM.

_____   9.   Chase Manhattan Bank issues commercial paper to AT&T.

_____   10. AT&T issues commercial paper to Mobil Oil Corp.

_____   11. You deposit money into a credit union, which is then lent as a car loan.

_____   12. You buy a Certificate of Deposit at a local bank.

_____   13. You loan $100,000 to a start-up company.

Exercise 2: Primary versus Secondary Markets

For each of the following financial transactions or terms indicate whether it relates to the primary market or the secondary market by writing in the space provided a P for primary market or a S for secondary markets.

_____   1.   A corporation receives cash from selling a new issue of stock.

_____   2.   Merrill Lynch underwrites an issue of stock.

_____   3.   You buy a share of Amazon.com stock.

_____   4.   You buy some Microsoft stock that is traded over the counter.

_____   5.   You instruct your broker to sell 10 General Motors bonds that you currently own.

_____   6.   Wal-Mart plans to raise additional money by selling bonds to the public.

_____   7.   The over-the-counter market trades U.S. government bonds.

_____   8.   Shares are traded on the New York Stock Exchange.

_____   9.   You loan $50,000 to a software start-up company.

_____   10. You buy 100 shares of Google from the investment banker helping to bring the company public.

_____   11. Mutual Fund A purchases 10,000 shares of IBM from Mutual Fund B.

Exercise 3: Regulatory Agency Responsibilities

Match the following regulatory agency in the right-hand column with the area it regulates in the left-hand column. Place the letter of the term in the blank provided next to the appropriate definition. Each agency will be used only once.

_____ 1.   Federally chartered credit unions

_____ 2.   All depository institutions

_____ 3.   Savings and loan associations

_____ 4.   Federally chartered commercial banks

_____ 5.   Futures-market exchanges

_____ 6.   Organized exchanges and financial markets

_____ 7.   Commercial banks, mutual savings banks, and loan associations

_____ 8.   State-chartered depository institutions

a.   Securities and Exchange Commission

b.   Commodity Futures Trading Commission

c.   Office of the Comptroller of the Currency

d.   National Credit Union Administration

e.   Federal Deposit Insurance Corporation

f.   Federal Reserve System

g.   State banking and insurance savings commission

h.   Office of Thrift Supervision

Exercise 4: Identification of Financial Intermediaries

For each of the following financial transactions or terms, indicate whether it is a depository institution, a contractual savings institution, or an investment intermediary by writing in the space provided a DI for depository institutions, CS for contractual savings, or II for investment intermediaries.

_____ 1.   Commercial bank

_____ 2.   Pension funds

_____ 3.   Fire and casualty insurance companies

_____ 4.   Mutual funds

_____ 5.   Credit unions

_____ 6.   Finance companies

_____ 7.   Life insurance companies

_____ 8.   Savings and loan associations

_____ 9.   Money market mutual funds

_____ 10. Mutual savings banks

_____ 11. State and local government retirement funds

■ Self-Test

Part A: Fill in the Blanks

1. Financial markets perform the essential function of channeling funds from savers who have excess funds to _____ who have insufficient funds.

2. In _____ finance, borrowers obtain funds directly from lenders in financial markets through the sale of securities.

3. In _____ finance, funds move from lenders to borrowers with the help of middlemen called intermediaries.

4. Financial markets directly improve the well-being of _____ by allowing them to make their purchases when they desire them most.

5. Financial markets can be classified as debt or _____ markets.

6. Financial markets can be classified as primary or _____ markets.

7. Financial markets can be classified as either money or _____ markets.

8. A(n) _____ instrument is a contractual agreement by the borrower to pay the holder of the instrument fixed dollar amounts at regular intervals.

9. A(n) _____ is a claim to share in the net income and the assets of a business firm.

10. A(n) _____ market is a financial market in which new issues of a security are sold to initial buyers by the corporation or government agency borrowing the funds.

11. The _____ market is a financial market in which only short-term debt instruments are traded, while the capital market is the market in which longer-term debt and equity instruments are traded.

12. Financial intermediaries are financial institutions that acquire funds from lenders-savers by issuing _____ and then in turn use the funds to make loans to borrowers-spenders.

13. The principal financial intermediaries fall into three categories: depository institutions (banks), _____, and investment intermediaries.

14. _____ are financial intermediaries that accept deposits from individuals and institutions and use the acquired funds to make loans.

15. Money market instruments are debt instruments with maturities of less than _____.

16. A financial intermediary that does business by underwriting security issues is called a(n) _____.

17. _____ are bonds denominated in a currency other than that of the country in which they are sold.

18. Financial intermediaries can substantially reduce transaction cost because their large size allows them to take advantage of _____.

19. When one party to a contract has incentives to act in its own interest rather than the interest of the other party, then a(n) _____ exists.

20. _____ is achieved by financial intermediaries through the transformation of financial assets into alternative assets that have risk characteristics that conform to investors' needs.

21. _____ is a widespread collapse of financial intermediaries.

Part B: True-False Questions

Circle whether the following statements are true (T) or false (F).

T F   1. The primary function of financial markets is to channel funds from those who have surplus funds, because they spend less than their income, to those who have a shortage of funds, because they wish to spend more than their income.

T F   2. When financial markets enable a consumer to buy a refrigerator before she has saved up enough funds to buy it, they are helping to increase economic welfare.

T F   3. Direct finance does not involve the activities of financial intermediaries.

T F   4. The difference between a primary market and a secondary market is that in a primary market new issues of a security are sold, while in a secondary market previously issued securities are sold.

T F   5. An over-the-counter market has the characteristic that dealers in securities conduct their trades in one central location.

T F   6. Capital markets mainly trade in short-term securities.

T F   7. Financial intermediaries are involved in the process of direct finance.

T F   8. Financial intermediaries only exist because there are substantial information and transactions costs in the economy.

T F   9. Liquidity of assets is as important a consideration for contractual savings institutions as it is for depository institutions.

T F 10. Money market mutual funds to some extent function as depository institutions.

T F 11. Foreign bonds are bonds that are sold in a foreign country and are denominated in the currency of the foreign country.

T F 12. Eurodollars are U.S. dollars deposited in banks outside of the United States that are frequently borrowed by American banks.

T F 13. The volume of new corporate bonds issued in the United States is substantially greater than the volume of new stock issues.

T F 14. Moral hazard occurs under asymmetric information and refers to a borrower using funds in a manner that reduces the likelihood of repayment.

T   F   15.   The primary role of the Securities and Exchange Commission is to make sure that investors can obtain adequate and accurate information.

T   F   16.   When one party to a contract has incentives to act in its own interest rather than the interest of the other party, then a conflict of interest exists.

T   F   17.   Risk sharing is achieved by financial intermediaries through the transformation of assets.

T   F   18.   Mutual savings banks and savings and loan associations obtain funds mainly through checkable and savings deposits and time deposits.

T   F   19.   The financial markets of most countries are similar in terms of intense regulation to U.S. financial markets.

Part C: Multiple-Choice Questions

Circle the appropriate answer.

1.   Which of the following cannot be described as indirect finance?
(a)   You take out a mortgage from your local bank.
(b)   An insurance company lends money to General Motors Corporation.
(c)   You borrow $1,000 from your best friend.
(d)   You buy shares in a mutual fund.
(e)   None of the above

2.   Which of the following is a short-term financial instrument?
(a)   U.S. Treasury bill
(b)   Share of IBM stock
(c)   New York City bond with a maturity of two years
(d)   Residential mortgage

3.   Which of the following statements about the characteristics of debt and equity is true?
(a)   They can both be short-term financial instruments.
(b)   Bond holders are residual claimants.
(c)   The income from bonds is typically more variable than that from equities.
(d)   Bonds pay dividends.
(e)   None of the above

4.   Which of the following markets in the United States is never set up as an organized exchange?
(a)   Stock market
(b)   Corporate bond market
(c)   U.S. government bond market
(d)   Futures market

5. Which of the following is an example of the adverse selection problem?
    (a) The owner of an on-line gambling company rushes to the bank to take advantage of a low interest rate.
    (b) A company president spends money borrowed for new equipment on a training program for employees.
    (c) Money intended for a low-risk project is spent on a higher-risk project offering a higher return.
    (d) The bank refuses to make a loan to a company because the loan application specifies the money is for "general use."
    (e) None of the above

6. Which of the following is a depository institution?
    (a) Life insurance company
    (b) Credit union
    (c) Pension fund
    (d) Finance company

7. The primary assets of a mutual savings bank are
    (a) money market instruments.
    (b) corporate bonds and stock.
    (c) consumer and business loans.
    (d) mortgages.

8. The primary liabilities of a savings and loan are
    (a) bonds.
    (b) mortgages.
    (c) deposits.
    (d) commercial paper.

9. Savings and loan associations are regulated by the
    (a) Office of the Comptroller of the Currency.
    (b) Federal Home Loan Bank System and FSLIC.
    (c) Securities and Exchange Commission (SEC).
    (d) Office of Thrift Supervision.

10. A bond denominated in a currency other than that of the country in which it is sold is called a(n)
    (a) foreign bond.
    (b) Eurobond.
    (c) equity bond.
    (d) currency bond.

11. Which of the following can be described as involving direct finance?
    (a) A corporation issues new shares of stock.
    (b) People buy shares in mutual funds.
    (c) A pension fund manager buys commercial paper in the secondary market.
    (d) An insurance company buys shares of common stock in the over-the-counter markets.

12. Which of the following is a long-term financial instrument?
    (a) A negotiable certificate of deposit
    (b) A banker's acceptance
    (c) A six-month loan
    (d) A U.S. Treasury bill

(e) None of the above

13. Which of the following is primarily an investment intermediary?
    (a) Life insurance company
    (b) Credit union
    (c) Pension fund
    (d) Mutual fund
    (e) None of the above

14. In prior decades, these institutions primarily originated residential housing mortgages.
    (a) Savings and loan associations
    (b) Life insurance companies
    (c) Consumer loan companies
    (d) Both (a) and (c)

15. Which of the following is *not* a reason that the government regulates financial markets?
    (a) To increase information available to investors
    (b) To ensure the soundness of the financial system
    (c) To guarantee consumers that financial institutions will not put customers' money in unsafe investments
    (d) To improve control of monetary policy
    (e) All of the above are reasons the government regulates financial markets

16. Regulation Q did which of the following?
    (a) Eliminated the interest rate ceilings that banks could pay on savings deposits.
    (b) Capped the interest rates offered on Treasury securities.
    (c) Set maximum interest rates that banks could pay on savings deposits.
    (d) Established the Securities and Exchange Commission.

17. How do financial institutions help reduce the exposure of investors to risk?
    (a) They lower transactions costs.
    (b) They create assets with difference risk characteristics.
    (c) They insure investors' assets that are invested into equities.
    (d) Both (a) and (c)
    (e) Both (a) and (b)

18. When does diversification reduce investors' exposure to risk?
    (a) When all of the securities in the portfolio move the same
    (b) When the securities in the portfolio do not move together exactly the same
    (c) When the number of securities in the portfolio increases
    (d) When the number of securities in the portfolio decreases

Part D: Short Answer Questions

1. What does the term "default" mean when it refers to a financial security?

   _____

   _____

2. What is the difference between a foreign bond and a Eurobond?

   _____

_____

3. What is the major advantage of equity security ownership, and what is the major disadvantage?

_____

_____

4. What differences exist between the major industrialized countries in regard to their use of financial intermediaries and in their reliance on bonds versus stocks?

_____

_____

5. What is the benefit of diversification to an investor's portfolio?

_____

_____

6. What is asset transformation?

_____

_____

7. Why is adverse selection a problem for investors?

_____

_____

■ Answers to Chapter 2

Exercise 1

1.	I	6.	I	11.	I
2.	D	7.	I	12.	I
3.	D	8.	D	13.	D
4.	I	9.	D		
5.	D	10.	D		

Exercise 2

1.	P	7.	S
2.	P	8.	S
3.	S	9.	P
4.	S	10.	P
5.	S	11.	S
6.	P		

Exercise 3

1.	d	5.	b
2.	f	6.	a
3.	h	7.	e
4.	c	8.	g

Exercise 4

1.	DI	6.	II	11.	CS
2.	CS	7.	CS		
3.	CS	8.	DI		
4.	II	9.	II		
5.	DI	10.	DI		

Self-Test

Part A

1.	spenders	8.	debt	15.	one year
2.	direct	9.	equity	16.	investment banker
3.	indirect	10.	primary	17.	Eurobonds
4.	consumers	11.	money	18.	economies of scale
5.	equity	12.	liabilities	19.	conflict of interest
6.	secondary	13.	contractual savings institutions	20.	Risk sharing
7.	capital	14.	Depository institutions	21.	Financial panic

Part B

1.	T	6.	F	11.	T	16.	T
2.	T	7.	F	12.	T	17.	T
3.	T	8.	F	13.	T	18.	T
4.	T	9.	F	14.	T	19.	F
5.	F	10.	T	15.	T		

Part C

1. c	6. b	11. a	16. c
2. a	7. d	12. e	17. e
3. e	8. c	13. d	18. b
4. c	9. d	14. a	
5. a	10. b	15. c	

Part D

1. Default is when a borrower is unable to make the interest or payments of principal at the time they are due.

2. When a bond is sold in a foreign country and the funds are raised in the foreign country's currency, it is called a foreign bond. A Eurobond is when the bond sold in a foreign country is sold in the currency of the issuing firm's country.

3. The major advantage is that the equity owners share in any increases in profitability or asset value. Debt holders do not enjoy this benefit. The disadvantage is that the equity holders only have a claim on the residual value of the firm. Debt holders get paid before the equity holders receive any portion of their claim.

4. Major developed countries usually obtain their funds indirectly through financial intermediaries and rely less on direct financing. The relative importance of bonds versus stocks varies widely across countries.

5. The benefit of diversification is that portfolio volatility is reduced when assets that do not move together perfectly are combined in a portfolio.

6. Asset transformation is where financial intermediaries design assets with different risk characteristics to meet the heterogeneous needs of borrowers and lenders.

7. Adverse selection is a problem for investors because asymmetric information that exists prior to a transaction can be used by the informed trader at the expense of the uninformed trader.

Chapter 3
What Do Interest Rates Mean and What Is Their Role in Valuation?

■ **Chapter Learning Goals**

By the end of this chapter, you should

1. Be able to distinguish between the terms interest rate, yield to maturity, current yield, and return.
2. Know how to compute the current market price of a bond given the market interest rate and the bond's coupon rate, face amount, and time to maturity.
3. Recognize the inverse relationship between bond prices and market interest rates.
4. Compute current yield and yield on a discounted basis. You should also know that changes in these rates move in the same direction as yield to maturity.
5. Know what duration measures and the factors that influence the duration value.
6. Know the difference between real and nominal interest rates.

■ **Chapter Summary**

The goal of this chapter is to help you fully develop an understanding of interest rates and their role in valuation. This chapter distinguishes between interest rates, yield to maturity, current yield, and return. This chapter also introduces the concept of duration as a method to measure interest-rate risk.

Present Value

We value bonds using the concept of **present value** or **present discounted value.** Present value is conceptually based on the fact that if rational individuals were given the choice between a sum of money today (say $10) and the same sum of money (the same $10) one year from now, they would prefer the $10 today. This preference is based on the fact that the investors can take the $10 now and invest it and earn interest. If they could earn 10 percent, they would have $11 one year from now (the initial $10 + $1 interest). Based on this example, if individuals had a choice between $10 today or $11 one year from now, they would be indifferent between the two amounts. Present value uses this same indifference concept but reverses the calculation. For example, if individuals could receive $10 one year from now, what amount would they take today in order to be indifferent between money today or the $10 one year from now?

Using the 10 percent interest rate the amount would be $9.091; that is, $\left\{ \dfrac{1}{(1+0.1)} 10 = 9.091 \right\}$.

Formally, the present value of a cash payment, or **cash flow,** or a series of cash flows is equal to the sum of the discounted future cash flow(s):

$$PV = \sum_{t=1}^{n} \frac{CF_t}{(1+i)^t},$$

where PV is the present value of the cash flow, CF is the cash flow that occurs in the future, i is the annual interest rate, and t is the number of periods in the future that the cash flow occurs.

To compute the current market value of a bond, find the present value of the interest payments and add the present value of the final principal payment. This calculation is shown in the following equation:

$$\text{Bond Value} = \sum_{t=1}^{n} \frac{\text{Interest Payment}}{(1+i)^t} + \frac{\text{Principal Payment}}{(1+i)^n}$$

You can modify this method to compute the **yield to maturity** for a bond. The yield to maturity is the interest rate that equates the current market value of the bond to the present value of the payments received. For simple interest loans, the yield to maturity is equal to the simple interest rate, but for bonds, the yield to maturity can be very different from the **coupon interest rate.** The coupon interest rate is printed on the bond and never changes. Every year, the issuing firm pays the bondholder an amount equal to the coupon rate times the face amount. For a bond with a given coupon rate, as the market price of the bond falls, the yield to maturity increases. This inverse relationship also holds when the bond price increases. Only when the coupon bond is priced by the market at its face amount will the coupon rate be equal to the yield to maturity.

Assume a bond that matures in 10 years and pays an 8% coupon is currently selling for $850. The equation for finding the yield to maturity is:

$$850 = \sum_{t=1}^{10} \frac{80}{(1+i)^t} + \frac{1000}{(1+i)^{10}}.$$

To find this yield to maturity, find the value of "I" that makes this equality hold. This calculation can be done only by trial and error or by using a financial calculator. Using a financial calculator, the answer is 10.49%. Notice that the yield to maturity is greater than the coupon rate. When a bond is selling for less than its principal value, as is the case here, the yield to maturity will be greater than the coupon rate. When the bond is selling for more that the principal amount, the yield to maturity will be less than the coupon rate. The coupon rate and yield to maturity are equal only when the bond is selling for par value.

Types of Credit Instruments

There are four types of credit instruments: (1) the **simple loan,** (2) the **fixed payment** or **fully amortized loan,** (3) **coupon bonds,** and (4) **discount bonds.** The terms of simple interest loans call for interest and principal to be repaid at maturity. The fixed payment loan has the principal being repaid along with accrued interest in regular monthly payments. This fixed payment loan is what most consumers are familiar with because this approach is the type of loan offered for most car and mortgage loans. The coupon bond makes periodic interest payments followed by payment of the entire par, or face value, at maturity. Finally, the discount bond has reduced or zero-interest payments until the face value is paid at maturity. The lender earns interest through the fact that the discount bond is sold for a low dollar amount, say $300, but the payment the lender receives at the maturity date is the face value, usually $1,000, and so the interest earned is the difference between the price paid and the principal repayment.

Yields on Bonds

Even though the yield to maturity is the best measure of the interest rate on a debt instrument, other measures are in general use because of the difficulty of computing yield to maturity. One popular approximation is the **current yield.** The current yield is defined as the yearly coupon payments divided by the current market price of the security. Formally, the current yield is:

$$i_c = \frac{C}{P},$$

where C is the yearly payment and P is the price of a bond or perpetuity. For bonds that have no maturity date, called perpetuities or consols, the current yield is the same as the yield to maturity. The current yield on a perpetuity bond is close to the yield to maturity on a coupon bond when the term to maturity is long and when the bond's price is near the bond's face value. Regardless of whether the current yield is a good approximation of the yield to maturity, a change in the current yield always signals a change in the same direction as the yield to maturity.

The yield calculation, known as the yield, on a discount bond for a one-year discount bond is:

$$i = \frac{F - P}{P},$$

where F is the face value of the discount bond and P is the current price of the discount bond. Again, a change in the yield on a discount bond always signals a change in the same direction as the yield to maturity.

The Distinction between Real and Nominal Interest Rates

We must distinguish between **real** and **nominal** interest rates. The real rate is the nominal rate adjusted for inflation. If current market rates are 9% but inflation is 5%, the real rate is 4% (9%–5%). The Fisher equation set the nominal rate equal to the real rate plus inflation. The real rate and the nominal rate have not moved together over time. The Fisher equation is:

$$i = i_r + \pi^e,$$

where the real rate of interest is i_r and π^e is the expected rate of inflation. Prior to 1997, real interest rates were not observable in the United States. The use of the term "not observable" is based on the feature of the Fisher equation that the inflation element in the equation is <u>expected</u> inflation, not historical inflation. The problem is in observing expectations. However, in January 1997, the U.S. Treasury started issuing bonds whose interest and principal payments vary with changes in the price level and are called **indexed bonds.** Because the actual return on indexed bonds will include actual levels of inflation, the interest rate paid on these bonds will be just the real rate. Subtracting this observed real rate from the observed nominal rate on non-indexed bonds provides insight into the expected level of inflation.

The Distinction between Interest Rates and the Rate of Return

You should make a distinction between the **interest rate** and the **rate of return** (or just return). The **rate of return,** which is often simply referred to as the **return (R),** for an asset is equal to the value of all the regular cash payments (C) plus the difference between the prices at which the asset was bought (P_t) and sold (P_{t+1}), all divided by the amount paid to purchase the asset. This equation is:

$$R = \frac{C + (P_{t+1} - P_t)}{P_t}.$$

The return on a bond will not necessarily equal the interest rate on that bond. This is because the price of the bond will go up or down based on the movement of interest rates in the market. As a result, the holder of a bond may take a loss on the price of the bond even though the holder is getting interest payments. Because the change in the price of the bond can be substantial, it is possible for the holder of a bond to actually have a negative return even when the bond is paying as agreed and even when the yield to maturity is positive.

The connection between bond values and interest rates is often difficult to understand at first. Look back at the bond valuation equation above under the Present Value section. Notice that for any given coupon payment and par value, an increase in *i* will result in a decrease in the present value of the coupon payments and the value of the principal payment. A decrease in *i* will have the opposite effect. This inverse relationship between interest rates and bond values is an important principal of valuation and thus bond returns. The fact that bond prices can go up or down leads to the impression that a lender can have a negative return on a bond even if the coupon payments are made as provided in the bond agreement.

Interest Rate and Reinvestment Risk

The inverse relationship between bond values and interest rates leads to what is called **interest-rate risk.** As interest rates rise the value of the bond declines and the owner of the bond will face a lower return. This decline in value is a capital loss. The prices and returns for long-term bonds are more volatile due to this interest-rate risk than those for shorter-term bonds. Another kind of risk associated with investment in bonds is called **reinvestment risk.** This is the risk that when the investor wishes to reinvest the proceeds from the coupon payments or from the maturity value of a bond, the interest rates available on similar bonds to those originally purchased will have declined. For example, if a lender was receiving 8% on a coupon bond and when the $80 of coupon payments were received, they could only reinvest these dollars at a return of 6%, the lender has experienced reinvestment risk. A major assumption of the yield to maturity calculation is that coupon payments are always invested at the same rate that the bond is earning, and when interest rates decline, this reinvestment assumption does not hold, and actual returns are lower than expected.

Duration

Of concern to lenders is how much interest rate risk they face when they purchase a bond. **Duration** is a method for calculating the effective maturity on any debt security and will help to answer this risk question. Duration can be defined as the weighted-average of the maturities of the cash payments. Consider a zero coupon bond and a 10% coupon bond. An owner of the 10% coupon bond receives $100 interest payments per year. However, the owner of the zero coupon bond receives no cash flows until the bond is either sold or matures. The duration formula computes the average maturity for a bond on a present value basis. Duration views maturity from the perspective of the timing of cash flows from both the coupon payment and the maturity value. All else equal, the longer the time to maturity of a bond, the longer is duration. Also, all else equal, when interest rates rise, the duration of a coupon bond falls. A third factor is that, all else equal, the greater the coupon rate, the shorter the duration of the bond. The greater is the duration of a security, the greater is the percentage change in the market value of the security for a given change in interest rates. Therefore, the greater is the duration, the greater is the interest-rate risk.

■ Exercises

Exercise 1: Present Discounted Value

Calculate the present discounted value for the following payments:

1. $500 two years from now when the interest rate is 5%. _____

2. $500 two years from now when the interest rate is 10%. _____

3. $500 four years from now when the interest rate is 10%. _____

4. $250 at the end of one-year and $250 two years from now with interest staying at 10%. _____

5. $150 at the end of each year for three years followed by $50 at the end of the fourth year with interest staying at 10%. _____

6. Using your computations in 2, 3, 4, and 5, which series of cash flows has the highest present value even though each series receives a total of $500 through time? Describe why that cash flow series has the highest present value.

7. What do the preceding calculations indicate about the present value of a payment as the interest rate rises?

    _____

8. What do the preceding calculations indicate about the present value of a payment as it is paid further in the future?

    _____

Exercise 2: Yield to Maturity

A. Suppose you are offered a $1,000 fixed-payment car loan that requires you to make payments of $600 a year for the next two years.

    1. Write down the equation that can be solved for the yield to maturity on this loan; that is, the equation that equates the present value of the payments on the loan to the amount of the loan.

        _____

    2. Calculate the present value of the loan payments when the interest rate is 10%.

        _____

    3. Must the yield to maturity be above or below 10%? _____

    4. Calculate the present value of the loan payments when the interest rate is 15%.

        _____

    5. Must the yield to maturity be above or below 15%? _____

    Verify that the present value of the loan payments is approximately $1,000 when the interest rate is 13%, indicating that this is the yield to maturity.

    6. What would the yield to maturity have to be if the payments stay at $600 per year but the loan amount is only $900?

B.   Suppose you are thinking of buying a $1,000 face-value coupon bond with a coupon rate of 10%, a maturity of three years, and a price of $1,079.

1.   Is the yield to maturity going to be above or below 10%? _____ Why?

_____

2.   Write down the equation that can be solved for the yield to maturity of this bond; that is, the equation that equates the present value of the bond payments to the price of the bond.

_____

3.   Calculate the present value of the bond when the interest rate is 8%.

_____

4.   Must the yield to maturity be above or below 8%? _____

5.   Calculate the present value of the bond when the interest rate is 15%.

_____

6.   Must the yield to maturity be above or below 5%? _____

Verify that the present value of the loan payments is approximately $1,079 when the interest rate is 7%, indicating that this is the yield to maturity.

C.   For once in your life, lightning strikes, and you win the lottery. The lottery commission has offered you two payout options: Either you can take a lump sum payout of $100,000,000 today, or you can take $7,500,000 per year for the next 20 years.

1.   Which option would you choose if your discount rate is 5%?

2.   Which option would you choose if your discount rate were only 3%?

3.   At what discount rate are you indifferent between the two payout options?

Exercise 3: Yield to Maturity and Yield on a Discount Bond

For discount bonds with a face value of $1,000, fill in the yield to maturity (annual rate) in the following table.

Price of the Discount Bond	Maturity	Yield to Maturity
$900	1 year (365 days)	
$950	6 months (182 days)	
$975	3 months (91 days)	

Note: For bonds with a maturity of six months, the annual yield to maturity equals $(1 + i_{six})^2$, where i_{six} is the return over six months; for bonds with a maturity of three months, the yield to maturity at an annual rate equals $(1 + i_{three})^4$, where i_{three} is the return over three months.

In the preceeding table, which bond would understate the yield to maturity the least according to the yield on a discount bond?

_____

_____

Exercise 4: Current Yield

For the five U.S. Treasury bonds on June 6, 2013, fill in the value of the current yield in the following table:

Coupon Rate	Maturity Date	Price	Yield to Maturity	Current Yield
4	Jan 2025	97 12/32	5.76%	
7 1/2	Jan 2025	102 22/32	5.61%	
5 1/8	June 2026	95 9/32	6.48%	
9 3/8	Feb 2034	117 27/32	7.10%	
7 1/2	Nov 2044	100 28/32	7.42%	

1. For which of these bonds is the current yield a good measure of the interest rate? Why?

2. Which bond should be the least sensitive to changes in interest rates? Why?

3. Which bond should be the most sensitive to changes in interest rates? Why?

Exercise 5: The Rate of Return

1. For a consol with a yearly payment of $100, calculate the return for the year if its yield to maturity at the beginning of the year is 10% and at the end of the year is 5%. (Hint: Calculate the initial price and end-of-year price first; then calculate the return.)

2. For a 10% coupon bond selling at par with two years to maturity, calculate the return for the first year if its yield to maturity at the beginning of the year is 10% and at the end of the year is 5%. (Hint: Calculate the initial price and end-of-year price first, then calculate the return.)

3. Which of the bonds is a better investment? _____

4. Why do you think your answer to Question 3 had the better return?

Exercise 6: Real Interest Rates

Calculate the real interest rate in the following situations:

1. The interest rate is 3%, and the expected inflation rate is –3%. _____

2. The interest rate is 10%, and the expected inflation rate is 20%. _____

3. The interest rate is 6%, and the expected inflation rate is 3%. _____

4. The interest rate is 15%, and the expected inflation rate is 15%. _____

5. In which of these situations would you (everything else equal) be a lender?

6.   In which of these situations would you (everything else equal) be a borrower?

_____

Exercise 7: Duration

1.   Calculate the duration of each of the following bonds:

Bond Number	Coupon Rate	Years to Maturity	Interest Rate	Duration
1	8%	10	8%	
2	8%	5	8%	
3	10%	5	8%	
4	0%	5	8%	

2.   Which bond, 1 or 2, has the shorter duration, and why does that relationship exist?

_____

3.   Bond 3 is the same as bond 2 except for the coupon rate. Which one of these two bonds has the shorter duration and why?

_____

4.   Which bond is the most sensitive to changes in interest rates?

_____

■ Self-Test

Part A: Fill in the Blank

1. A simple loan provides the borrower with an amount of funds that must be repaid at the _____ along with an interest payment.

2. A(n) _____ loan requires the borrower to make the same payment every period until the maturity date.

3. A coupon bond pays the owner a fixed coupon payment every year until the maturity date, when the _____ value is repaid.

4. Its _____ equals the coupon payment expressed as a percentage of the face value of the bond.

5. A(n) _____ bond is bought at a price below its face value, but the face value is repaid at the maturity date.

6. The concept of _____ tells us that a dollar in the future is not as valuable as a dollar today; that is, a dollar received n years from now is worth $1/(1 + i)^n$ today.

7. The _____ is the economist's preferred measure of the interest rate.

8. Bond prices and interest rates are _____ related.

9. The current yield equals the _____ payment divided by the price of the coupon bond.

10. Relative to yield to maturity, the yield on a discount bond _____ interest rates.

11. How well you have done by holding a security over a period of time is measured by the security's
_____ —the payments to the owners plus the changes in its value, expressed as a percentage
of the purchase price.

12. For bonds with maturities greater than the holding period, capital gains and losses can be substantial
when _____ change.

13. The real interest rate is defined as the nominal interest rate minus _____.

14. Duration is a measure of the amount of _____ risk a bond has.

15. All else being equal, the longer the duration of a bond the _____ the interest-rate risk.

16. The higher the coupon rate for a bond, the _____ the duration of that bond.

17. For all zero coupon bonds, the duration of that bond is the same as its _____.

18. Fixed payment loans are also called _____ loans.

Part B: True-False Questions

Circle whether the following statements are true (T) or false (F).

T F   1.   A bond that pays the bondholder the face value at the maturity date and makes no interest
payments is called a discount bond.

T F   2.   The yield to maturity of a coupon bond that is selling for less than its face value is less than
the coupon rate.

T F   3.   A dollar tomorrow is worth more to you today if the interest rate is 10% than if it is 5%.

T F   4.   The present value of a security that pays you $55 next year and $133 three years from now is
$150 if the interest rate is 10%.

T F   5.   You would prefer to own a security that pays you $1,000 at the end of 10 years than a security
that pays you $100 every year for 10 years.

T F   6.   The yield to maturity on a $20,000 face value discount bond that matures in one year's time
and currently sells for $15,000 is 33 1/3%.

T F   7.   The yield to maturity on a coupon bond can always be calculated as long as the coupon rate
and the price of the bond are known.

T F   8.   The current yield is the most accurate measure of interest rates, and it is what economists
mean when they use the term interest rates.

T F   9.   The yield on a discount bond understates the yield to maturity, and the longer the maturity of
the discount bond the greater is the understatement.

T F 10.   The current yield is a more accurate approximation of the yield to maturity, the nearer the
bond's price is to the par value and the shorter the maturity of the bond.

T F 11.   You would prefer to hold a one-year Treasury bond with a yield on a discount bond of
10% to a one-year Treasury bond with a yield to maturity of 9.9%.

T F 12. A five-year $1,000 coupon bond selling for $1,008 with a 9% current yield has a higher yield to maturity than one-year discount bond with a yield on a discount bond of 8.9%.

T F 13. When interest rates rise from 4% to 5%, current bondholders are made better off.

T F 14. If interest rates on all bonds fall from 8% to 6% over the course of the year, you would rather have been holding a long-term bond than a short-term bond.

T F 15. Business firms are more likely to borrow when the interest rate is 2% and the price level is stable than when the interest rate is 15% and the expected inflation rate is 14%.

T F 16. The price of a bond will equal its par value only when its yield to maturity is the same as the current market rate for similar bonds.

T F 17. An investor expecting interest rates to fall and attempting to trade the bonds for a capital gain in the future should buy a high coupon bond.

T F 18. A short-term corporate bond is exposed to more interest-rate risk than a long-term zero-coupon Treasury.

Part C: Multiple-Choice Questions

Circle the appropriate answer.

1. A discount bond
    (a) pays the bondholder the same amount every period until the maturity date.
    (b) at the maturity date pays the bondholder the face value of the bond plus an interest payment.
    (c) pays the bondholder a fixed interest payment every period and repays the face value at the maturity date.
    (d) pays the bondholder the face value at the maturity date.

2. A $5,000 coupon bond with a coupon rate of 5% has a coupon payment every year of
    (a) $50.
    (b) $500.
    (c) $250.
    (d) $100.

3. With an interest rate of 5%, the present value of a security that pays $52.50 next year and $110.25 two years from now is
    (a) $162.50.
    (b) $50.00.
    (c) $100.00.
    (d) $150.00.

4. If a security pays you $105 next year and $110.25 the year after that, what is its yield to maturity if it sells for $200?
    (a) 4%
    (b) 5%
    (c) 6%
    (d) 7%

5. Which of the following $1,000 face value securities has the lowest yield to maturity?
   (a) 5% coupon bond selling for $1,000
   (b) 5% coupon bond selling for $1,200
   (c) 5% coupon bond selling for $900
   (d) 10% coupon bond selling for $1,000
   (e) 10% coupon bond selling for $900

6. If a $5,000 face value discount bond maturing in one year is selling for $4,000, then its yield to maturity is
   (a) 5%.
   (b) 10%.
   (c) 25%.
   (d) 50%.
   (e) none of the above.

7. The current yield on a $5,000 10% coupon bond selling for $4,000 is
   (a) 5%.
   (b) 10%.
   (c) 12.5%.
   (d) 15%.

8. The yield on a discount bond for a one-year $1,000 Treasury bill selling for $975 is
   (a) 2.5%.
   (b) 5.0%.
   (c) 7.5%.
   (d) 10%.
   (e) 12.5%.

9. What is the return on a 15% coupon bond that initially sells for $1,000 and sells for $700 next year?
   (a) 15%
   (b) 10%
   (c) 5%
   (d) 15%

10. In which of the following situations would you rather be borrowing?
    (a) The interest rate is 20%, and expected inflation rate is 15%.
    (b) The interest rate is 4%, and expected inflation rate is 1%.
    (c) The interest rate is 13%, and expected inflation rate is 15%.
    (d) The interest rate is 10%, and expected inflation rate is 15%.

11. A credit market instrument that provides the borrower with an amount of funds that must be repaid at the maturity date along with an interest payment is known as a
    (a) simple loan.
    (b) fixed-payment loan.
    (c) coupon bond.
    (d) discount bond.

12. A _____ pays the owner a fixed coupon payment every year until the maturity date, when the _____ value is repaid.
   (a) coupon bond; discount
   (b) discount bond; discount
   (c) coupon bond; face
   (d) discount bond; face

13. Which of the following statements is true about the duration value?
   (a) The longer the time to maturity, the shorter is the duration.
   (b) The higher the coupon rate, the longer is the duration.
   (c) The duration of a portfolio of securities is the weighted average of the duration of the individual securities in the portfolio.
   (d) The lower the duration, the greater is the interest-rate risk.

14. Which of the following statements is true about the yield to maturity (YTM) on a bond?
   (a) The YTM is greater than the coupon rate when the bond is selling below face value.
   (b) The YTM is greater than the coupon rate when the bond is selling above face value.
   (c) A zero coupon bond has a YTM equal to the coupon rate on the bond.
   (d) The YTM on a consol bond is the same as the YTM on a similar coupon bond.

15. How much are you willing to pay for a $1,000 face-value zero-coupon bond that has 20 years to maturity with a discount rate of 7%?
   (a) $516.84
   (b) $123.92
   (c) $258.42
   (d) $745.92

16. How much would you pay for that same zero-coupon bond in 10 years holding the discount rate at 7%?
   (a) $508.35
   (b) $612.91
   (c) $485.24
   (d) $945.32

17. Suppose that you are a bond portfolio manager who has become concerned that rising crude prices will lead to higher inflation over the next 24 months. Which portfolio adjustment strategy seems most consistent with your forecast?
   (a) Buy longer-term government bonds.
   (b) Buy longer-term corporate bonds.
   (c) Buy short-term bonds.
   (d) None of the above

Part D: Short Answer Questions

1. How can a bond with a coupon rate of 10% and being sold at par offer the same return to the investor as a bond paying interest of 6% per year and selling below par, assuming that both are held until maturity?

    _____

    _____

2. The bonds from Question 1 can have the same percentage return, but they do not have the same level of interest-rate risk. Explain how we know this statement is correct.

    _____

    _____

3. What is meant by the term "reinvestment rate risk," and why is it of concern to purchasers of bonds?

    _____

    _____

4. Explain how corporate bonds can have less interest-rate risk than government bonds of similar term to maturity.

    _____

    _____

5. Explain why some investors may prefer bonds that pay low coupon rates compared to high coupon rates.

    _____

    _____

6. Explain why real interest rates can be negative.

    _____

    _____

Part E: Examples and Practice Problems Using Excel

The following examples, which are correlated to your textbook, make use of Microsoft® Excel's built-in functions to do financial calculations. After you review these examples, you will be prompted to solve several problems on your own.

Example 3.1 PV (present value) of one future payment (p. 38 in text)

1. Open Excel and click on Insert. Click on f_x *(the function wizard)* and then click on financial. (You will need to repeat this step for all calculations.)

2. Click on PV calculations and a box will pop up. Fill in

   Rate: 0.15

   Nper: 2

   Pmt: 0

   FV: −250

The correct answer of $189.0359168 will appear.

Use this method to calculate the prices (present value) of zero coupon bonds.

Example 3.3 Fixed payment loan (p. 41 in text)

1. Repeat Step 1 in Example 1.

2. Click on PMT and a box will pop up. Fill in:

   Rate: 0.07

   Nper: 20

   PV: −100,000

The correct answer of $9439.292574 will appear.

Example 3.4 Price of a bond when the yield to maturity is known (p. 43 in text)

1. Repeat Step 1 in Example 1.

To calculate the price of a bond when the yield to maturity or interest rate is known:
Using the previous example, rephrase the question as "what is the price of a bond that has a 10% coupon and a yield to maturity of 12.25?"

This problem has a two-part solution.

First calculate the PV of the coupons.

1. Repeat Step 1 from Example 1.

2. Click on PV calculations and a box will pop up. Fill in:

Rate: 0.1225

Nper: 8

Pmt: 100

FV: 1,000

The answer of $889.20 will appear.

Yield to maturity of a coupon bond when the price is known. There is no example in the text for this calculation but it serves as a useful exercise in using the Excel function wizard to calculate the yield to maturity.

1. List the price of the bond in a cell as a positive number and then in the cells below it, the coupon payments as a negative number for each year. The last number should be the last coupon payment and the face value of the bond.

2. Repeat Step 1 in Example 1.

3. Click on IRR and a box will pop up. Highlight the cells you have filled in and the answer will appear. The cells should look like this:

889.2

−100

−100

−100

−100

−100

−100

−100

−1100

Table 3.3 Calculating duration on a $1,000, ten-years, 10% coupon bond when its interest rate is 10%. This example uses the information from Table 3 in the text to illustrate the calculation of duration using the Excel financial function.

1. Repeat Step 1 from Example 1.

2. Click on Duration calculations and a box will pop up. Fill in

Settlement:	September 25, 2013	(the date the bond is bought)
Maturity:	September 25, 2023	(the date the bond matures)
Coupon:	10%	(the coupon rate)
Yld:	10%	(the current yield)
Frequency:	1	(the number of coupon payments per year)

The answer of 6.7590 will appear. (The difference from text answer of 6.7585 is due to rounding.)

With the help of Excel's f_x *(the function wizard)* solve the following problems.

1. What will your **monthly** mortgage payment for a 30-year $100,000 loan be if the interest rate is 7%?

2.   Your loan-shark friend is willing to lend you $3,000 today, if you pay him back $3,850 in two years. What is the annual interest rate that he is charging you?

3.   How much will your loan-shark friend lend you if he wants $3,850 from you in two years, and he charges you an 8.25% interest rate?

4.   Your friend is offering to sell you a bond issued by a company you have never heard of and don't have time to investigate. His asking price is $1,025, and he told you that the bond has five years left until maturity and a 6% coupon. He also told you that the bond is investment grade. To buy the bond, you have to withdraw money from your savings account. If your savings account pays 4% interest, should you buy this bond?

5.   Your dog chewed your copy of *The Wall Street Journal*, so you cannot not see the price of a bond that you are interested in. You know that the bond has six years left to maturity, a 4.5% coupon rate, and a yield to maturity of 5.1%. What bond price was printed in the paper?

■ Answers to Chapter 3

Exercise 1

1. $453.51 = $500/(1 + 0.05)^2$

2. $413.22 = $500/(1 + 0.10)^2$

3. $341.51 = $500/(1 + 0.10)^4$

4. $433.88 = $250/(1 + 0.1)^1 + 250/(1 + 0.1)^2$

5. $407.18 = $150/(1 + 0.1)^1 + 150/(1 + 0.1)^2 + 150/(1 + 0.1)^3 + 50/(1 + 0.1)^4$

6. The cash flows in Answer 4 above have the highest present value because they are received sooner than in the cash flows in 2, 3, or 4.

7. As the interest rate increases, the present value falls.

8. As the time to receipt of the cash flow increases, the present value falls.

Exercise 2

Part A

1. $1,000 = $600/(1 + i) + $600/(1 + i)^2$
2. $1,041.32
3. above

4. $975.43
5. below
6. 13.06% using financial calculator

Part B

1. below, because the price of the bond is above the par value.

2. $1,079 = $100/(1 + i) + $100/(1 + i)^2 + $1,100/(1 + i)^3$

3. $1,051.54

4. below (because the PV is less than the current price of $1,079)

5. $1,136.16

6. above (because the PV is greater than the current price of $1,079)

Part C

1. The present value of an annuity of $7,500,000 per year for 20 years discounted at 5% is $93,466,577.77 (financial calculator). Thus, you should choose the lump-sum payout of $100,000,000.

2. When the discount rate drops to 3%, the present value of the annual annuity of $7,500,000 increases to $111,581,062. Now you would choose the annuity.

3. Setting the $100,000,000 equal to the discounted annuity payments results in a discount rate of 4.22%, the rate at which you would be indifferent between the two payout options.

Exercise 3

Price of the Discount Bond	Maturity	Yield to Maturity
$900	1 year (365 days)	11.11%
$950	6 months (182 days)	10.80%
$975	3 months (91 days)	10.65%

The three-month bond understates the YTM by the smallest amount.

Exercise 4

Coupon Rate	Maturity Date	Price	Yield to Maturity	Current Yield
4	Jan 2025	97 12/32	5.76%	4.11%
7 1/2	Jan 2025	102 22/32	5.61%	7.30%
5 1/8	June 2026	95 9/32	6.48%	5.38%
9 3/8	Feb 2034	117 27/32	7.10%	7.96%
7 1/2	Nov 2044	100 28/32	7.42%	7.43%

1. The 11/ 2044, 7 1/2% is the bond where current yield is a good measure of yield to maturity. This is because as the term increases and as price approaches par, the two interest rates converge.

2. The 1/2025, 7 1/2% coupon should be the least sensitive to changes in interest rates because it has the higher coupon rate of the two bonds maturing 1/2012.

3. The 11/2044, 7 1/2% coupon bond should be the most sensitive to changes in interest rates because its maturity is 10 years longer than the next closest bond and also has the lower coupon rate of the two bonds.

Exercise 5

1. 110%, which is calculated as follows: The initial price of the consol is $1,000 = $100/0.10 while next year the price is $2,000 = $100/0.05. The return is therefore 110% = 1.10 = ($2,000 − $1,000 + $100)/$1,000.

2. 14.76%, which is calculated as follows: The initial price of the coupon bond is $1,000 because the interest rate equals the coupon rate when the bond is at par. Next year, when the bond has one year to maturity, the price is $1,047.62 = $100/(1 + 0.05) + $1,000/(1 + 0.05). The return is therefore 14.76% = 0.1476 = ($1,047.62 − $1,000 + $100)/$1,000.

3. The consol is a better investment.

4. The interest rate on two bonds has the same decline; the bond with the longer maturity—the consol—has a larger increase in its price.

Exercise 6

1. 6%

2. −10%

3. 3%

4. 0%

5.   You would rather be a lender in situation 1 because the real interest rate is the highest.

6.   You would rather be a borrower in situation 2 because the real interest rate is lowest.

Exercise 7

1.   Bond 1 = 7.25   Bond 2 = 4.31   Bond 3 = 4.20   Bond 4 = 5.00   (using spreadsheet)

2.   Bond 2 has the shorter duration because if all else is equal, a shorter-term bond will have a shorter duration than a longer-term bond.

3.   Bond 3 has the shorter duration because if all else is equal, the higher a coupon rate the shorter the duration.

4.   Bond 1 is the most sensitive to changes in interest rates because it has the longest duration.

Self-Test

Part A

1.   maturity date
2.   fixed payment
3.   face
4.   coupon rate
5.   discount
6.   present value
7.   yield to maturity
8.   inversely
9.   annual coupon
10.   underestimates
11.   return
12.   interest rates
13.   expected inflation
14.   interest-rate
15.   greater
16.   lower
17.   term to maturity
18.   fully amortized

Part B

1.   T
2.   F
3.   F
4.   T
5.   F
6.   T
7.   F
8.   F
9.   T
10.   F
11.   T
12.   F
13.   F
14.   T
15.   F
16.   T
17.   F
18.   F

Part C

1.   d
2.   c
3.   d
4.   b
5.   b
6.   c
7.   c
8.   a
9.   d
10.   d
11.   a
12.   c
13.   c
14.   a
15.   c
16.   a
17.   c

Part D

1. The total return on a bond consists of both interest income and changes in the value of the bond. The investor holding the 10% bond will receive only the coupon payments. However, the investor in the discount bond will receive the 6% in coupon payments and will also have the value of the bond increase up to par value at maturity.

2. The 10% coupon bond has a lower duration than the 6% discount bond. The lower duration results from the fact that the cash flows are received sooner for the 10% bond. The lower the duration, the lower is the amount of interest-rate risk.

3. Reinvestment rate risk refers to the fact that as investors receive interest and principal payments on their bonds, they may have to reinvest these receipts at a rate lower than they currently receive on the existing bond.

4. The higher coupon rates of corporate bonds cause them to have lower durations than government bonds of similar term to maturity.

5. Some investors prefer low-coupon-rate bonds to better take advantage of swings in interest rates when pursuing capital gains.

6. Recall: Nominal rate = real rate + expected inflation. Thus if expected inflation is higher than nominal rates, the real rate of return will be negative.

Part E

1. $665.30 (rate: 0.07/12, nper: 360, pv: –100,000)

2. 13.28%

3. $3,285.53

4. 5.42% is the yield to maturity, so if you trust your friend, you should buy the bond.

5. $969.65

Chapter 4
Why Do Interest Rates Change?

■ Chapter Learning Goals

By the end of this chapter, you should

1. Know that the four factors that influence asset choice are wealth, expected return, risk, and liquidity, and how changes in these factors impact the quantity demanded for assets.

2. Know the factors that affect the demand and supply for bonds and how each of these factors shifts the demand and supply curves.

3. Know the factors that affect the demand and supply for money and how each of these factors shifts the demand and supply curves.

4. Understand the loanable funds theory of interest rate determination.

5. Determine the direction of the change in interest rates that results from a change in economic variables.

6. Know what the income and wealth effects are and understand how they tend to offset each other.

■ Chapter Summary

This chapter starts with a discussion of the primary factors that influence people's decisions to hold assets. The chapter continues with its main purpose, which is to provide a framework for understanding the change in interest rates that result from changes in economic variables. For example, if inflation expectations fall, interest rates will fall, and bond prices will rise. The models presented here help explain why this happens.

Determinants of Asset Demand

The following four factors determine how much of a particular asset investors will hold: (1) investor wealth, (2) the relative expected return, (3) the relative degree of risk associated with the return, and (4) asset liquidity. Each of these factors will influence the quantity demanded of assets in a predictable manner. Increases in investor wealth, expected return, and liquidity will cause corresponding increases in the quantity demanded of assets. Increases in risk will reduce the quantity demanded.

Investor Wealth

When an **investor's wealth** increases, the investor is more likely to purchase more, and thus the quantity demanded of assets increases. This increased wealth can arise from events such as a pay raise, an increase in the value of common stock owned, or an increase in the value of a personal residence or other real estate owned.

Expected Returns

The **expected return** on any asset is simply the sum of the probability-weighted possible outcomes. Formally,

$$R^e = p_1 \times R^1 + p_2 \times R_2 + \cdots + p_n \times R_n$$

where

> R^e = expected return
> n = number of possible outcomes
> R_i = return on the ith state of nature
> p_i = probability of occurrence of the return R_i

The higher an asset's expected return relative to other assets, the quantity demanded of the asset with a higher expected return will rise.

Risk

The **standard deviation** of an asset's returns is a measure of risk that essentially measures the dispersion of an asset's returns around its mean.

$$\sigma = \sqrt{p_1 *(R_1 - R^e)^2 + p_2 *(R_2 - R^e)^2 + \cdots + p_n *(R_n - R^e)^2}$$

where

> p_1 = probability of occurrence of outcome or return 1
> n = number of possible outcomes or states
> R_1 = return in state 1
> R_2 = return in state 2
> R^e = expected return
> p_i = probability of occurrence on the return R_i

The quantity of assets with higher risk, measured by standard deviation of returns, should see their demand fall over time.

Liquidity

Liquidity attempts to measure how quickly an asset can be converted to cash at low cost. The principle of low cost includes the loss of value that may be incurred in order to convert an asset to cash. For example, an automobile is not a highly liquid asset. The car can be converted to cash by selling it, but in order to sell it quickly, we would have to lower the price below a fair market value, and part of the cost of selling that automobile would be its loss in value. High liquidity is a positive attribute for a stock and will help to increase the quantity demanded.

■ Supply and Demand in the Bond Market

Demand Curve

Demand curves demonstrate the relationship between the quantity demanded of the asset and the price when all other variables are held constant.

In this framework, we must first determine the expected return on a bond to ultimately determine the supply and demand for that bond. The expected return on a bond can be expressed as below:

$$i = R^e = \frac{F - P}{P}$$

where

i = interest rate or yield to maturity
R^e = expected return
F = face or value of the coupon bond
P = purchase price of the discount bond

The demand curve illustrates the quantity of bonds demanded to be inversely related to bond prices. That is, the quantity of bonds demanded increases as interest rates increasesbecause bond prices decrease as interest rates increase.

Supply Curve

The supply curve illustrates the relationship between the quantity of bonds supplied and the respective bond prices holding all other economic variables constant. The quantity of bonds supplied increases as interest rates decrease.

Market Equilibrium

In the bond market, a **market equilibrium** occurs when the quantity of bonds demanded equals the quantity of bonds supplied: $B^d = B^s$. The market-clearing price is obtained at this equilibrium. This equilibrium is illustrated in the graph below to be at the intersection point 1.

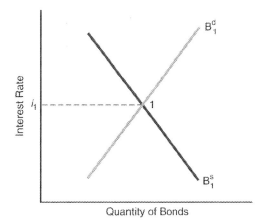

When the quantity of bonds supplied is greater than the quantity of bonds demanded, the area of the left of the intersection above, there is said to be an **excess supply** of bonds. Conversely, when the quantity of bonds supplied (the area to the right of the intersection point) is less than the quantity of bonds demanded, there is **excess demand** for bonds.

Supply and Demand Analysis

In the supply and demand analysis framework, or **asset market approach,** to modeling asset prices, interest rates are determined by stocks (amounts) of assets rather than flows.

When we receive news that there is a change in any of the variables discussed above, you can find the resulting interest rate by shifting the demand and supply curves accordingly.

The **loanable funds theory** of interest rates is based on equilibrium between the demand and supply of bonds. If bond prices are listed on the vertical axis and the quantity of bonds is listed on the horizontal axis, the demand curve for bonds will be downward sloping (see the graph on the previous page). (Note that a way for remembering that demand curves slope down is that the words demand and down start with the letter D.) As the price of bonds rises, the quantity demanded falls. Similarly, we can plot the supply of bonds as an upward-sloping curve. This indicates that as the price of bonds increases, firms will make more available for sale. The intersection of the demand and supply curves represents the market-clearing equilibrium and shows what the price of bonds will be and what quantity firms will sell.

Graphing the Loanable Funds Theory

Bond prices and interest rates always move in opposite directions. The interest rate that corresponds to each bond price can be put on the right-hand vertical axis so that market-clearing interest rates can be read directly off the graph. Often, all that is of concern is the interest rate, so this could be put on the left axis. However, this leaves an unusual-looking graph because the interest rates go down as you move higher on the vertical axis. To solve this problem, the interest rates can be listed from lower to higher, but then the graph will still be unusual because the demand curve will be upward sloping. We can solve this problem by renaming the curves. The upward-sloping demand for bonds curve becomes the supply of loanable funds curve, and the downward-sloping supply curve becomes the demand for loanable funds curve. This is why financial economists call the model the loanable funds theory.

Using the Loanable Funds Theory

The loanable funds framework helps determine what new interest rate results from changes in economic variables. The demand for bonds is increased by increased wealth, increased expected return, increased liquidity, and lower expected future interest rates. An increased demand for bonds is reflected by a shift in the entire demand curve to the right.

The supply of bonds is increased by increased expected profitability of investments, expected inflation, and greater government deficits. An increase in the supply of bonds is reflected by a shift in the entire supply curve to the right.

■ Changes in Equilibrium Interest Rates

Shifts in supply or demand curves differ from movements along supply or demand curves. Movement along the supply or demand curves results from changes in bond prices (i.e., interest rates). Shifts in supply or demand curves result when the quantity of bonds supplied or demanded changes at each given price level as a result of some factor other than changes in bond prices or interest rates.

Shifts in the Demand for Bonds

The textbook introduces four factors that cause the demand curve for bonds to shift: (1) wealth, (2) expected returns on bonds relative to alternative assets, (3) risk of bonds relative to alternative assets, and (4) liquidity of bonds relative to other assets.

The authors conclude that wealth increases during business cycle expansions, causing the demand for bonds to increase and the demand curve for bonds to shift to the right. However, recessions, which generally lead to a decrease in wealth, cause the demand for bonds to drop and the demand curve for bonds to shift to the left.

Future expected increases in expected returns or interest rates drive down bond prices, causing the demand curve for bonds to shift to the left. Conversely, lower expected future interest rates result in higher bond prices and cause the demand curve to shift to the right. Expected increases (decreases) in inflation result in similar shifts in the demand curve as expected increases (decreases) in expected returns or interest rates.

As the riskiness of bonds relative to other assets rises, the demand for bonds drops, and the demand curve shifts to the left. Of course, the opposite occurs when the riskiness of bonds drops relative to other assets.

Liquidity is a desirable characteristic for financial assets. Consequently, increases in liquidity cause the demand for bonds to increase and the demand curve for bonds to shift to the right.

Shifts in the Supply of Bonds

Three factors are introduced that can affect the supply of bonds: (1) expected profitability of investment opportunities, (2) expected inflation, and (3) government activities.

During business cycle expansions, the number of possible profitable investment opportunities increases. Consequently the expected profitability of investment opportunities increases, enticing corporations to seek additional investment capital and resulting in a shift to the right in the supply of bonds.

Increases in expected inflation are expected to result in lower real interest rates, holding all else constant. Corporations recognize lower real interest rates to be a cheaper source of funds. Thus, higher expected inflation causes the supply of bonds to rise and the supply curve for bonds to shift to the right.

Government activities are often financed through the issuance of government bonds when government expenditures are higher than government revenues. Thus, budget deficits result in an increase in the supply of bonds and a shift to the right in the supply curve.

Changes in Expected Inflation: The Fisher Effect

Irving Fisher recognized that increases in expected inflation are associated with rising interest rates (the **Fisher effect**). Formally, nominal interest rates are equal to the real interest rate plus the expected rate of inflation. This Fisher effect is the same one we first covered in this text in Chapter 3 when we introduced nominal versus real interest rates.

Business Cycle Expansion

Historically, business cycle expansions combined with a rise in personal income or wealth result in higher interest rates. However, interest rates fall during business cycle contractions or recessions.

■ The Practicing Manager

Profiting from Interest-Rate Forecasts

Two general models used to produce interest-rate forecast are offered. Both models are based on the supply and demand for bonds. The first model is characterized by analysts' attempts to predict what will happen to factors that affect the supply and demand for bonds. In other words, this model requires forecasters to predict the strength of the economy, the profitability of investment opportunities, the expected inflation rate, and the size of government deficits. Using a similar framework, the Federal Reserve attempts to forecast interest rates by analyzing the Flow of Funds Accounts and their impacts on the supply and demand for credit. Sometimes this forecasting is done based on a feel for where these variables are headed. Some forecasters formalize their prediction models and use what are called **econometric models** that include multiple complex equations intended to model economic relationships and to estimate mathematically statistical relationships between numerous variables and interest rates.

■ Exercises

Exercise 1: Expected Returns

1. If an ACME Corporation bond has a return of 15% one-third of the time, 10% one-third of the time, and 5% the other third of the time, then its expected return is _____%.

2. If an XYZ Corporation bond has an 18% return 25% of the time, a 16% return 50% of the time, and a 6% return the other 25% of the time, then its expected return is _____%.

3. If the ABC Corporation stock has a 12% return half of the time and a 10% return the other half of the time, then its expected return is _____%.

4. If the McHoops Corporation stock has a 12% return 75% of the time and a 4% return the remainder of the time, then its expected return is _____%.

5. If the Teddy Bear Corporation stock has an 8% return 50% of the time and 6% return 50% of the time, then its expected return is _____%.

Exercise 2: Theory of Asset Demand

In the second column of the following table indicate whether the quantity demanded of the asset will increase (+) or decrease (−):

Variable	Change in Variable	Change in Quantity Demanded
Wealth	−	_____
Liquidity of asset	+	_____
Riskiness of asset	+	_____
Expected return of asset	−	_____
Riskiness of other assets	−	_____
Liquidity of other assets	+	_____
Expected return of other assets	−	_____

Exercise 3: Risk Reduction and Diversification

Suppose that you already own common stock in Solar Energy, Ltd., which has a return of –10% when energy prices are low and +20% when energy prices are high. If, in addition, you buy an equal amount of the following securities, write down your total expected return in the two states of the world: low energy prices and high energy prices.

	Low Energy Prices	High Energy Prices
1. Stock in Mobil Oil Co., which has a return of –10% when energy prices are low and +20% when energy prices are high		
2. Treasury bonds, which are just as likely to have a return of 10% or 20% when energy prices are high or low	_____	_____
3. Stock in Energy Intensive Products, Inc., which has a return of +20% when energy prices are low and –10% when energy prices are high	_____	_____

Exercise 4: Supply and Demand Analysis of the Bond Market

The quantity of bonds demanded and supplied at different interest rates is listed in the following table.

Point	Interest Rate	Quantity Demanded	Point	Interest Rate	Quantity Supplied
A	20%	40	E	20%	0
B	15%	30	F	15%	10
C	10%	20	G	10%	20
D	5%	10	H	5%	30

1. Draw the demand and supply curves for bonds in Figure 4A.

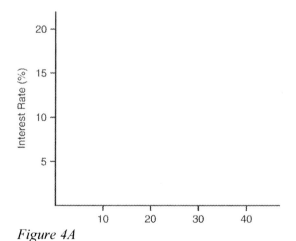

Figure 4A

2. What is the equilibrium interest rate? _____

3. When the interest rate is 20%, then there is a condition of excess _____ in the bond market, the price of bonds will _____, and the interest rate will _____.

Exercise 5: Factors That Shift Supply and Demand Curves for Bonds

For each of the following situations (holding everything else constant), indicate in the space provided how the supply and demand curves for bonds shift: D → for demand curve to the right, ← D for demand curve to the left, S → for supply curve to the right, and ← S for supply curve to the left.

_____   1.   A decline in brokerage commission on bonds.

_____   2.   Expected inflation rises.

_____   3.   There is a new tax on purchases and sales of gold.

_____   4.   There is a large federal budget deficit.

_____   5.   Businesspeople become more optimistic about the success of their investments in new plant and equipment.

_____   6.   Bond prices become more volatile.

_____   7.   The economy booms, and wealth rises.

_____   8.   Stock prices become more volatile.

_____   9.   People suddenly expect a bear market (a decline in prices) for stocks.

_____   10. People suddenly expect interest rates to rise.

Exercise 6: Analyzing a Change in the Equilibrium Interest Rate

Suppose the supply and the demand for long-term bonds are as marked in Figure 4B and market equilibrium is at point 1. Suppose that, as occurred in the early 1980s, the federal government begins to run a large budget deficit and at the same time the volatility of interest rates increases. Draw in the new supply and demand curves in Figure 4B.

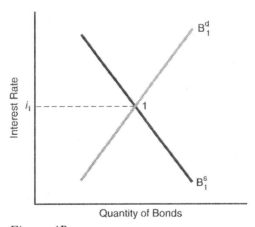

Figure 4B

What happens to the interest rate? _____

_____

Exercise 7: Supply and Demand Analysis of the Money Market

Suppose the supply and the demand for money are as drawn in Figure 4C. Now the Federal Reserve decreases the money supply, and as a result income falls. Draw the new supply and demand curves in Figure 4C.

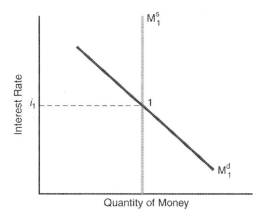

Figure 4C

What happens to the interest rate? _____

_____

Exercise 8: Expected Returns and Standard Deviation

Use the following data to answer Questions 1, 2, and 3.

Record nominal crude oil prices are causing analysts to change their forecasts for stock returns of U.S. Regular Conventional Retail Gasoline producers. Three equally likely scenarios are being forecast for the returns of gasoline producer stocks over the next year.

Scenario	Annual Return Forecast
Worst Case	−17.0%
Average Case	1.5%
Best Case	20.0%

1. Compute the expected return for gasoline producer stocks over the next year.

2. Compute the expected standard deviation of annual return forecasts for gasoline producers.

3. Suppose that analysts revise their forecasts such that they now predict there is a 50% chance that the average case scenario will occur, but only a 25% chance for either the best- or worst-case scenarios. Find the new expected return and standard deviation of returns for gasoline producer stocks.

Exercise 9: Expected Returns on Bonds

1. If a one-year discount bond with a face value of $1,000 is trading at $925, what is the expected return for the bond?

2. How much should an investor pay for a one-year discount bond with a face value of $1,000 if her required rate of return is 15%?

Exercise 10: The Fisher Effect

1. According to the Fisher effect, if the current annualized nominal rate of return on a 13-week Treasury Bill is 1.4% and the expected rate of inflation is 3.0%, then what is the expected real rate of return for the next year?

2. Suppose that the expected rate of inflation drops to 2% and the real rate of return increases to 3%. If the 13-week T-Bill is the measure for nominal rate, then what is the expected return for the T-Bill?

Exercise 11: Keynes' Liquidity Preference (this principle is noted in footnote 5, which provides a website location where this model is discussed)

1. Suppose that the demand for money is $1,500 million, while the supply of money and bonds are $1,250 million and $1,000 million, respectively. According to Keynes' liquidity preference framework, if the market rate of interest is in equilibrium, then the demand for bonds is_____?

■ Self-Test

Part A: Fill in the Blanks

1. A(n) _____ is a piece of property that is a store of value.

2. Faced with the decision of whether to buy one asset or another, an investor must consider the following four factors: _____, _____, _____, and _____.

3. The quantity demanded of an asset is usually _____ related to wealth.

4. The quantity demanded of an asset is _____ related to its expected return (relative to alternative assets).

5. The quantity demanded of an asset is _____ related to the risk of its return relative to alternative assets.

6. The quantity demanded of an asset is _____ related to its liquidity relative to alternative assets.

7. The supply and demand analysis for bonds, known as the _____ framework, provides one theory of how interest rates are determined.

8. The bond price is _____ related to the interest rate when all other economic variables are held constant.

9. The _____ for bonds, the relationship between the quantity supplied and the interest rate, is downward sloping when the interest rate is plotted.

10. The market interest rate is the _____, which occurs when the quantity of bonds demanded equals the quantity supplied; that is, at the intersection of the supply and the demand curves.

11. The demand curve shifts to the right when wealth _____.

12. The supply curve shifts to the right when businesses have a(n) _____ amount of attractive investment opportunities as in a business cycle boom.

13. The supply curve shifts to the right when expected inflation _____.

14. The lower the price of a bond, *ceteris paribus*, the _____ the demand for bonds.

15. An alternative theory of how interest rates are determined is provided by the _____ framework, which analyzes the supply and demand for money.

16. The supply and demand analysis of the money market indicates that interest rates _____ when income or the price levels rise.

17. The liquidity effect indicates that higher money supply growth leads to a(n) _____ in interest rates.

18. If interest rates are expected to increase, then lenders will prefer to lend _____ term.

Part B: True-False Questions

Circle whether the following statements are true (T) or false (F).

T   F   1.   The quantity demanded of an asset is positively related to its expected return relative to alternative assets.

T   F   2.   Everything else equal, when the expected return on an asset falls, the quantity demanded rises.

T   F   3.   Holding everything else constant, when the liquidity of an asset falls, the quantity demanded falls.

T   F   4.   Holding everything else constant, when an asset becomes riskier, the quantity demanded rises.

T   F   5.   Of the four determinants of asset demand only liquidity has a direct relationship with quantity demanded; the other three have inverse relationships.

T   F   6.   If equal amounts of money were invested in two assets with one asset having an expected return of 12% and the second an expected return of 20%, the expected return on the portfolio is 32%.

T   F   7.   The demand curve for bonds slopes downward because at a lower bond price, the expected return on the bonds is higher and the quantity demanded is higher.

T   F   8.   The term "loanable funds" comes from labeling the demand curve for bonds as one for demanding a loan and the supply curve for bonds as the supply of loanable funds.

T   F   9.   A rise in the price of a bond shifts the demand curve for bonds to the left.

T   F   10.   When businesspeople become optimistic about the future health of the economy, the supply curve for bonds shifts to the left.

T   F   11.   A rise in the expected future price of long-term bonds shifts the demand curve for long-term bonds to the right.

T   F   12.   A federal budget surplus will shift the supply curve for bonds to the right.

T   F   13.   The Fisher effect suggests that periods of high interest rates will also tend to be periods of high inflation.

T   F   14.   In Keynes' view of the world in which there are only two assets, an excess demand in the money market implies that there is an excess demand in the bond market.

T F 15. If the stock market becomes riskier, the demand curve for money shifts to the right.

T F 16. The reason Milton Friedman was unwilling to accept the view that lower interest rates will result from higher money growth is that he disagreed with Keynes' liquidity preference analysis.

T F 17. The government should increase the money supply to obtain lower interest rates.

T F 18. Using the loanable funds framework is a common method for financial institutions to form expectations of interest rate changes.

T F 19. The demand for loanable funds is dependent upon factors such as the strength of the economy and the profitability of investment opportunities.

T F 20. An interest rate forecast technique similar to the loanable funds theory is the economic model technique.

T F 21. If interest rates are expected to rise, the manager will prefer to borrow long-term now.

Part C: Multiple-Choice Questions

Circle the appropriate answer.

1. The quantity demanded of rare coins falls when (holding everything else constant)
    (a) bond values increase.
    (b) wealth rises.
    (c) interest rates decline.
    (d) the volatility of stock prices increase.
    (e) None of the above is true.

2. You would be more willing to buy gold (holding everything else constant) if
    (a) the price of gold became more volatile.
    (b) you realized that your house was worth more than you thought; that is, your wealth rose.
    (c) bonds became easier to sell.
    (d) all of the above occurred.
    (e) Both (a) and (c) of the above occurred.

3. When the interest rate is below the equilibrium interest rate, there is an excess _____ for (of) bonds and the interest rate will _____.
    (a) supply; fall
    (b) supply; rise
    (c) demand; rise
    (d) demand; fall

4. When brokerage commissions in the housing market are raised from 6% to 7% of the sales price, the _____ curve for bonds shifts to the _____.
    (a) demand; right
    (b) demand; left
    (c) supply; left
    (d) supply; right

5. When rare coin prices become less volatile, the _____ curve for bonds shifts to the _____.
    (a) demand; right
    (b) demand; left
    (c) supply; left
    (d) supply; right

6. When the expected inflation rate decreases, the demand for bonds shifts to the _____, the supply of bonds shifts to the _____, and the interest rate _____.
    (a) right; right; rises
    (b) right; left; falls
    (c) left; left; falls
    (d) left; right; rises

7. When people revise their expectations of next year's short-term interest rate downward, the demand for long-term bonds shifts to the _____ and their interest rate _____.
    (a) right; rises
    (b) right; falls
    (c) left; falls
    (d) left; rises

8. In a recession, normally, the demand for bonds shifts to the _____, the supply of bonds shifts to the _____, and the interest rate _____.
    (a) right; right; rises
    (b) right; left; falls
    (c) left; left; falls
    (d) left; right; rises

9. In the money market, when the interest rate is below the equilibrium interest rate, there is an excess _____ for (of) money, people will try to sell bonds, and the interest rate will _____.
    (a) demand; rise
    (b) demand; fall
    (c) supply; fall
    (d) supply; rise

10. If the price level falls, the demand curve for money will shift to the _____ and the interest rate will _____.
    (a) right; rise
    (b) right; fall
    (c) left; rise
    (d) left; fall

11. When stock prices become more volatile, the _____ curve for bonds shifts to the _____.
    (a) demand; right
    (b) demand; left
    (c) supply; left
    (d) supply; right

12. Holding everything else equal, an increase in the money supply causes
    (a) interest rates to decline initially.
    (b) interest rates to increase initially.
    (c) bond prices to increase initially.
    (d) Both (a) and (c) above

13. The equilibrium interest rate is obtained when
    (a) the demand for money equals the supply of money.
    (b) the demand for bonds equals the supply of bonds.
    (c) the amount of bonds investors want to purchase equals the amount of bonds borrowers want to supply.
    (d) All of the above are equilibrium conditions.

14. Under which of the following conditions will managers want to borrow short term?
    (a) Long-term rates are expected to decline in the near future.
    (b) Short-term rates are currently lower than long-term rates.
    (c) Short-term rates are currently higher than long-term rates but are expected to fall soon.
    (d) Long-term rates are at their lowest level in more than 10 years.
    (e) Long-term rates are expected to increase in the near future.

15. Which of the following causes the supply curve for bonds to shift to the left?
    (a) The economy is in the rapid-growth phase of the business cycle.
    (b) The expected level of inflation is decreased.
    (c) The government is successful at reducing the size of the budget deficit.
    (d) The real rate of interest increases for business borrowing.
    (e) All of the above will cause the supply curve for bonds to shift to the left.

Part D: Short Answer Questions

1. Distinguishing between changes in demand (supply) for bonds and changes in quantity demanded (quantity supplied) for bonds is important for understanding the influence of various economic factors on the demand and supply of bonds and thus the interest rate. What distinguishes changes in demand (supply) from changes in quantity demanded (quantity supplied)?

    _____

    _____

    _____

2. What factors cause the demand and supply curve for bonds to shift?

    _____

    _____

3. How does the low level of savings in the United States contribute to the existence of higher interest rates?

    _____

    _____

■ Answers to Chapter 4

Exercise 1

1.   10%
2.   14%
3.   11%
4.   10%
5.   7%

Exercise 2

Variable	Change in Variable	Change in Asset Demand
Wealth	−	−
Liquidity of asset	+	+
Riskiness of asset	+	−
Expected return of asset	−	−
Riskiness of other assets	−	−
Liquidity of other assets	+	−
Expected return of other assets	−	+

Exercise 3

	Low Energy Prices	High Energy Prices
1.	−10.0%	20.0%
2.	2.5%	17.5%
3.	5.0%	5.0%

Exercise 4

1.

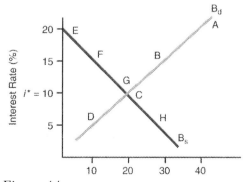

Figure 4A

2.   The equilibrium interest rate is 10% where the quantity demanded equals the quantity supplied.

3.   When the interest rate is 20%, then there is a condition of excess demand, the price of bonds will rise, and the interest rate will fall.

Exercise 5

1.	D →	6.	← D
2.	← D, S→	7.	D →, S →
3.	D →	8.	D →
4.	S →	9.	D →
5.	S →	10.	← D

Exercise 6

The new supply and demand curves are $B^s{}_2$ and $B^d{}_2$, and the market equilibrium moves from point 1 to point 2. As can be seen in Figure 4B, the interest rate rises to i_2.

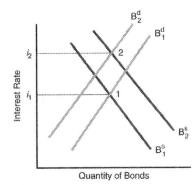

Figure 4B

Exercise 7

The new supply and demand curves are $M^s{}_2$ and $M^d{}_2$, and the market equilibrium moves from point 1 to point 2. As the figure is drawn, the interest rate rises, but if the shift of the demand curve is greater, then the interest rate could fall instead of rise. What we are seeing here is a combination of the liquidity effect and the income effect of a money supply decrease. Because they have opposite effects, the overall impact on the interest rate is ambiguous.

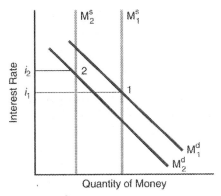

Figure 4C

Exercise 8

1. $E(R) = [(1/3) \times (-17) + (1/3) \times (1.5) + (1/3) \times (20)] = 1.5\%$

2. Standard Deviation: $\sigma = [(1/3) \times (-17 - 1.5)^2 + (1/3) \times (1.5 - 1.5)^2 + (1/3) \times (20 - 1.5)^2]^{(1/2)}$
    $= 15.10\%$

3. $E(R) = [(0.25) \times (-17) + (0.5) \times (1.5) + (0.25) \times (20)] = 1.5\%$

$\sigma = [(0.25) \times (-17 - 1.5)^2 + (0.5) \times (1.5 - 1.5)^2 + (0.25) \times (20 - 1.5)^2]^{(1/2)}$

$= 13.08\%$

Exercise 9

1. $E(R) = (1,000 - 925)/925 = 0.0811$ or 8.11%

2. Price $= 1,000/(1.15) = 869.57$

Exercise 10

1. Nominal $=$ Real $+ E(I)$

$1.4 =$ Real $+ 3.0$

Real $= -1.6$

2. T-Bill $= 2 + 3 = 5\%$

Exercise 11

1. $B^s + M^s = B^d + M^d$

$1,000 + 1,250 = B^d + 1,500$

$B^d = 750$

Self-Test

Part A

1. asset
2. wealth, expected return, liquidity, risk
3. positively
4. positively
5. negatively
6. positively
7. loanable funds
8. inversely
9. supply curve
10. market equilibrium
11. increases
12. greater
13. rises
14. higher
15. liquidity preference
16. rise
17. decrease
18. long

Part B

1. T
2. F
3. T
4. F
5. F
6. F
7. T
8. F
9. F
10. F
11. T
12. F
13. T
14. F
15. T
16. F
17. F
18. T
19. T
20. F
21. T

Part C

1. e
2. b
3. b
4. a
5. b
6. b
7. b
8. c
9. a
10. d
11. a
12. d
13. d
14. a
15. c

Part D

1. Changes in the demand (supply) for bonds are shown as shifts in the demand (supply) curve. These changes cause the amount demanded (supplied) to be higher or lower at every interest rate. Movements along the respective curves are called changes in quantity demanded or supplied.

2. Changes in the demand for bonds are associated with changes in wealth, relative expected returns, relative risk, and relative liquidity. Changes in supply are caused by changes in profitable investment opportunities, expected inflation, and government activities.

3. Low levels of savings imply that individual wealth is lower than it would be if consumers had saved and invested their existing wealth in productive assets. This lower wealth shifts the demand curve for bonds to the left, resulting in a higher rate of interest.

Chapter 5
How Do Risk and Term Structure Affect Interest Rates?

■ Chapter Learning Goals

By the end of this chapter, you should

1. Know what is meant by "term structure of interest rates" and "risk structure of interest rates."

2. Understand how each of the following factors affects interest rates: (a) default risk, (b) liquidity, (c) taxes, (d) maturity.

3. Know the three facts about the shape and movement of the yield curve over time.

4. Understand the three theories cited to explain the yield curve and how successful each is in explaining its shape and movement.

■ Chapter Summary

In the last chapter, we analyzed one interest rate. In this chapter, we examine interest rates among securities that differ in risk and maturity.

The Risk Structure of Interest Rates

Securities with the same maturity will often have different yields. We call the relationship among these interest rates the **risk structure of interest rates,** although default risk, liquidity, and income taxes all affect the risk structure. The difference between interest rates on bonds with default risk and default-free bonds is called the **risk premium.** The risk of **default** is the chance that the issuers of the security will fail to pay the interest or principal as promised. Bonds with no risk of default are called **default-free bonds.** Treasury securities are default risk free because the government can always print money and increase taxes to raise funds when needed. As the probability of default increases, the interest rate spread between default free securities and risky securities increases. Several companies publish bond ratings that provide an indication of bonds' default risk. These **credit-rating agencies** are investment advisory firms that estimate the probability of default for corporate and municipal bonds in addition to evaluating the quality of the bonds. The higher the rating, the lower is the default risk. The highest rating is AAA (the rating used by Standard & Poor's). Bonds rated as BBB or better are collectively called **investment grade,** while those rated below BBB, such as BB, are referred to collectively as **junk bonds** (also sometimes referred to as high-yield bonds.)

The **liquidity** of a security refers to how easily investors can sell it quickly without a significant loss of value. As liquidity falls, the interest rate must increase to compensate for difficulty in selling the security.

Finally, **income taxes** affect interest rates. Investors should be concerned about the after-tax returns they receive. As a result, tax-free municipal bonds have lower rates than taxable corporate bonds because municipal bonds are exempt from federal income taxes. For example, if you earn an 8% return on a taxable bond and have to pay 25% in taxes, you get to keep only 6% of the total. However, if the bond is tax free you would get to keep the full 8%.

The Term Structure of Interest Rates

The **term structure of interest rates** relates the interest rate spreads on securities similar in every respect except time to maturity. The yield curve illustrates the term structure of interest rates for bonds that have different terms to maturity but have the same liquidity, default risk, and tax treatment. The most common security used to create a yield curve is Treasury bonds because all Treasury bonds have zero default risk and no liquidity risk. Yield curves are commonly referred to by their shapes and are generally classified as either normal upward-sloping, flat, or downward-sloping. Upward-sloping yield curves are referred to as **normal yield curves** and downward-sloping yield curves are often called **inverted yield curves.**

The Shape of the Yield Curve

Economists have observed three empirical findings regarding yield curves:

1. Interest rates on different maturity bonds move together over time.

2. Yield curves are more likely to be upward sloping when short-term rates are low and downward sloped when short-term rates are high.

3. Yield curves are usually upward sloping.

Plausible theories of the term structure of interest rates attempt to explain these three empirical findings.

Theories of the Term Structure of Interest Rates

We have three theories to explain why interest rates differ with maturity.

1. The **expectations theory** states that the interest rate on a long-term security will equal the average of short-term rates expected over the life of the long-term bond. In other words, buying a single bond with five years to maturity and receiving a 7% return would be no different than buying a series of one year bonds over a five-year period.

   The *shortcoming* of this theory is that it does not explain the upward slope of yield curves. The reason for this shortcoming is that the because the most frequently observed shape of the yield curve is upward sloping, this theory implies that future short-term rates are always expected to be higher. There is no reason that assumption should be true in that future rates can be expected to rise or fall, not just rise.

2. The **market segmentation theory** sees the markets for different maturity bonds as completely separate and segmented. Each maturity has its own demand-and-supply function that establishes the interest rate. As the demand for bonds of different maturities shifts over time, the return on long-term and short-term bonds will shift accordingly.

   The *shortcoming* of this theory is that because the segments of the yield curve are assumed to be segmented (independent), it cannot explain why interest rates tend to move together or why the slope of the yield curve is positive when short-term rates are low (or inverted when short-term rates are high).

3. The **liquidity premium theory** combines the first two theories to suggest that the long-term interest rate will equal an average of short-term rates plus a term premium that responds to supply-and-demand conditions. The liquidity premium theory is the only theory consistent with all three of the empirical observations.

Evidence on the Term Structure

Studies from the 1980s suggest that the spread between short-term and long-term interest rates helps predict future short-term rates only part of the time. Further studies in the late 1980s and early 1990s find that the term structure contains information about future very short-term rates (the next several months) and long-term rates (over several years) but fail to provide much information about intermediate-term rates.

Using the Term Structure to Forecast Interest Rates

The shape of the yield curve enables financial managers to infer market expectations of future interest rates. For example, an upward-sloping yield curve suggests that future short-term interest rates, which are also known as **forward rates,** are going to be higher than **spot rates** or current short-term interest rates. Because the expectations theory is inadequate by itself to explain interest rates, consideration of the liquidity premium must also be included in the estimate of forward rates to give an accurate forecast of future rates.

■ Exercises

Exercise 1: Default Risk and Liquidity Effects on the Risk Structure

Figure 5A plots the supply and demand curves in the corporate bond market and the Treasury bond market. If the health of the economy improves so that the probability of bankruptcy decreases, draw the new supply and demand curves in Figure 5A.

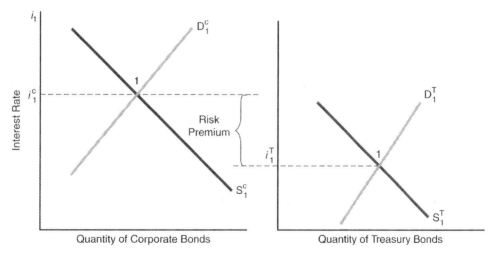

Figure 5A

1. What happens to the interest rate on corporate bonds? _____

2. What happens to the interest rate on treasury bonds? _____

3. What happens to the size of the risk premium? _____

Exercise 2: Tax Effects on the Risk Structure

Suppose your income tax bracket is 25%.

1. What is your after-tax return from holding a one-year tax-exempt municipal bond with an 8% yield to maturity?

    _____

2. What is your after-tax return from holding a one-year corporate bond with a 10% yield to maturity?

    _____

3. If both these securities have the same amount of risk and liquidity, then which one of them would you prefer to own?

    _____

4. What does this example suggest about the relationship found in the bond market between interest rates on tax-exempt municipal bonds and those on other securities?

    _____

Exercise 3: Expectations Hypothesis of the Term Structure

An investor is presented with the following two alternative investment strategies: Purchase a three-year bond with an interest rate of 6% and hold it until maturity, or purchase a one-year bond with an interest rate of 7% and when it matures, purchase another one-year bond with an expected interest rate of 6% and when it matures, purchase another one-year bond with an interest rate of 5%.

1. What is the expected return over the three years for the first strategy?

    _____

2. What is the expected return over the three years for the second strategy?

    _____

3. What is the relationship between the expected returns of the two strategies?

    _____

4. Why does our analysis of the expectations hypothesis indicate that this is exactly what you should expect to find?

    _____

    _____

    _____

Exercise 4: Deriving a Yield Curve

Given that the expectations hypothesis of the term structure is correct, plot in Figure 5B the yield curve when the expected path of one-year interest rates over the next 10 years is the following: 1%, 2%, 3%, 4%, 5%, 5%, 4%, 3%, 2%, 1%.

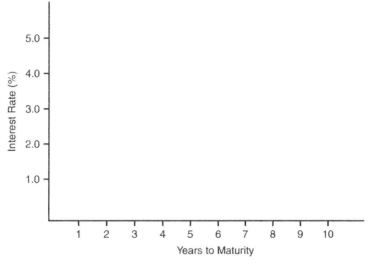

Figure 5B

Exercise 5: Inferring Market Predictions of Future Interest Rates

1. In 1980, short-term interest rates were very high, and the yield curve looked like the one in Figure 5C. What was the market predicting about future short-term interest rates?

    _____

    _____

    _____

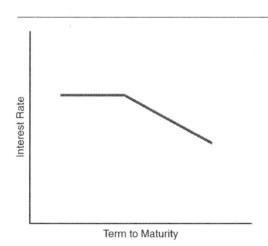

Figure 5C

Exercise 6: Inferring the Liquidity Premium

Suppose that the expected one-year interest rates over the next five years are 5%, 6%, 7%, 8%, and 9%. Comparatively, the interest rate on a five-year bond is 8.5%.

1. According to the expectations hypothesis, what should the expecting return on the five-year bond to be equivalent to the series of one-year interest rates?

2. Assume that the difference between the expected return calculated in part 1 and the five-year rates is due to the liquidity premium. What is the liquidity premium for the five-year bond?

Exercise 7: Shapes of the Yield Curve

1. Which shape of the yield curve suggests that short-term rates will decrease in the future?

2. Which shape of the yield curve suggests that short-term rates will rise in the future?

Exercise 8: Credit-Rating Agencies

1. What are credit-rating agencies?

2. What credit rating would a credit-rating agency give to a U.S. Treasury bond?

3. What are the highest credit ratings a credit-rating agency gives to an investment grade bond and to a junk bond?

■ Self-Test

Part A: Fill in the Blanks

1. The relationship among interest rates on different securities with the same term to maturity is called the _____ of interest rates.

2. One attribute of a bond that influences its interest rate is its _____, the chance that the issuer of the bond will default; that is, be unable to make interest payments or pay off the face value when the bond matures.

3. As default risk increases, the _____ (the spread between the bond's interest rate and the interest rate on a default-free bond) rises.

4. Another attribute of a bond that influences its interest rate is its _____; that is, how quickly and cheaply it can be converted into cash if the need arises.

5. The less liquid a bond is, the _____ its interest rate will be relative to more liquid securities.

6. Income tax rules also have an impact on the risk structure of interest rates. The tax exemption of municipal bonds _____ their market interest rate relative to Treasury securities.

7. The risk structure of interest rates is explained by three factors: default risk, liquidity, and the _____ treatment of the bond.

8. The relationship among interest rates on bonds with different terms to maturity is called the _____ interest rates.

9. It is graphed as the _____, a plot of the yields on default-free government bonds with differing terms to maturity.

10. Although the expectations theory can explain the empirical fact that interest rates on bonds of different maturities tend to move together over time, it is unable to explain the fact that yield curves are usually _____ sloping.

11. The _____ theory of the term structure sees markets as completely separated or segmented. It assumes that bonds of different maturities are not substitutes at all.

12. The _____ of the term structure states the following: The interest rate on a long-term bond will equal an average of short-term interest rates expected to occur over the life of the long-term bond plus a risk premium that responds to supply-and-demand conditions for that bond.

13. This theory takes the view that bonds of different maturities are _____, so that the expected return on a bond of one maturity does influence the expected return of a bond with a different maturity, but it also allows investors to prefer one bond maturity over another.

14. A rise in short-term interest rates indicates that short-term interest rates will, on average, be _____ in the future and long-term interest rates will rise along with them.

15. Yield curves are usually upward sloping, suggesting that the risk premium is _____ because of people's preference for short-term bonds.

16. When short-term interest rates are low, yield curves are more likely to have a steep _____ slope; when short-term interest rates are high, yield curves are more likely to slope downward.

17. U.S. Treasury bonds are generally considered the only type of bond to be _____.

18. _____ are firms that evaluate the quality of municipal and corporate bonds and their likelihoods of default.

19. Bonds with ratings lower than Baa (or BBB) are often called _____ bonds.

Part B: True-False Questions

Circle whether the following statements are true (T) or false (F).

T   F   1.   The term structure of interest rates is the relationship among interest rates of bonds with the same maturity.

T   F   2.   The greater is a bond's default risk, the higher is its interest rate.

T   F   3.   Because municipal bonds bear substantial default risk, their interest rates tend to be higher than interest rates on default-free U.S. Treasury bonds.

T   F   4.   Negotiable certificates of deposit tend to have lower interest rates than Treasury bills.

T F 5. The risk premium on a bond only reflects the amount of risk this bond has relative to a default-free bond.

T F 6. When income tax rates fall, the interest rate spread between tax-exempt municipal bonds increases relative to the interest rate on corporate bonds.

T F 7. A yield curve reports the yield on bonds that will be for sale at different times in the future.

T F 8. The risk structure of interest rates is explained by three factors: default risk, liquidity, and the income tax treatment of the security.

T F 9. A plot of the interest rates on default-free government bonds with different terms to maturity is called a term structure curve.

T F 10. The difference between the expectations theory of the term structure and the liquidity premium theory is that the liquidity premium theory allows for a liquidity premium, while the expectations hypothesis does not.

T F 11. The expectations hypothesis of the term structure assumes that bonds of different maturities are perfect substitutes.

T F 12. The market segmentation theory of the term structure is unable to explain why yield curves usually slope upward.

T F 13. The liquidity premium theory combines elements of both the market segmentation theory and the expectations theory.

T F 14. The liquidity premium theory assumes that bonds of different maturities are not substitutes.

T F 15. The expectations theory is unable to explain why interest rates on bonds of different maturities tend to move together over time.

T F 16. Investment grade bonds never default.

T F 17. Enron's bankruptcy caused the spread between the highest quality bonds and lower quality bonds to narrow.

T F 18. The spread between long- and short-term rates always helps to predict future short-term interest rates.

Part C: Multiple-Choice Questions

Circle the appropriate answer.

1. Which one of the following long-term bonds tends to have the highest interest rate?
    (a) Corporate Baa bonds
    (b) U.S. Treasury bonds
    (c) Corporate Caa bonds
    (d) Municipal bonds

2. When the default risk on corporate bonds increases, other things equal, the demand for corporate bonds _____ and the demand for Treasury bonds _____.
    (a) rises; falls
    (b) rises; rises
    (c) falls; rises
    (d) falls; falls

3. When the corporate bond market becomes less liquid, other things equal, the demand for corporate bonds _____, and the demand for Treasury bonds _____.
    (a) rises; falls
    (b) rises; rises
    (c) falls; rises
    (d) falls; falls

4. The risk premium on corporate bonds falls when
    (a) brokerage commissions fall in the corporate bond market.
    (b) a flurry of major corporate bankruptcies occurs.
    (c) the Treasury bond market becomes more liquid.
    (d) both (b) and (c) of the above occur.

5. The interest rate on municipal bonds rises relative to the interest rate on corporate bonds when
    (a) there is a major default in the municipal bond market.
    (b) income tax rates are raised.
    (c) Treasury securities become more widely traded.
    (d) corporate bonds become riskier.

6. If income taxes were substantially increased to cover the costs of a new national health care program, the interest rate spread between tax-exempt municipal bonds and corporate bonds would
    (a) increase.
    (b) decrease.
    (c) be unchanged.
    (d) More information is needed.

7. Which of the following theories of the term structure is able to explain the fact that when short-term interest rates are low, yield curves are more likely to slope upward?
    (a) Expectations theory
    (b) Market segmentation theory
    (c) Liquidity premium theory
    (d) Both (b) and (c) of the above
    (e) Both (a) and (c) of the above

8. If the expected path of one-year interest rates over the next three years is 4%, 1%, and 1%, then the expectations theory predicts that today's interest rate on the three-year bond is
    (a) 1%.
    (b) 2%.
    (c) 3%.
    (d) 4%.

9. If the expected path of one-year interest rates over the next five years is 2%, 2%, 4%, 3% and 1%, the expectations theory predicts that the bond with the highest interest rate today is the one with a maturity of
    (a) one year.
    (b) two years.
    (c) three years.
    (d) four years.
    (e) five years.

10. If the yield curve slopes upward mildly for short maturities and then slopes sharply upward for longer maturities, the liquidity premium theory (assuming a mild preference for short-term bonds) indicates that the market is predicting
    (a) a rise in short-term interest rates in the near future and a decline further out in the future.
    (b) constant short-term interest rates in the near future and a rise further out in the future.
    (c) a decline in short-term interest rates in the near future and a rise further out in the future.
    (d) a decline in short-term interest rates in the near future, which levels off, and an increase out in the future.

11. When the Treasury bond market becomes more liquid, other things equal, the demand curve for corporate bonds shifts to the _____, and the demand curve for Treasury bonds shifts to the _____.
    (a) right; right
    (b) right; left
    (c) left; left
    (d) left; right

12. A plot of the interest rates on default-free government bonds with different terms to maturity is called
    (a) a risk-structure curve.
    (b) a term-structure curve.
    (c) a yield curve.
    (d) an interest-rate curve.

13. The one-year interest rate that is expected to exist three years from now is called a _____ rate.
    (a) spot
    (b) forward
    (c) nominal
    (d) real

14. During the stock market crash of October 19, 1987 (Black Monday), the bond market was also impacted. Which of the following statements is true about what happened to bonds?
    (a) All bond prices fell because both the bond and stock markets were perceived as riskier.
    (b) U.S. Treasury bonds fell less than junk bonds because Treasuries have zero default risk.
    (c) Junk and Treasury bonds both rose in price due to investors preferring bonds over the now riskier stocks thus increasing demand for both types of bonds.
    (d) Junk bonds fell in price due to their perceived increase in risk while Treasury bonds increased in price due to their relative decrease in risk.

15. Which bond is least likely to default?
    (a) A
    (b) BBB
    (c) AA
    (d) AA-

16. According to Moody's and Standard & Poor's, which ratings are considered speculative?
    (a) Baa and BBB, respectively
    (b) Ba and BB, respectively
    (c) B and B, respectively
    (d) Caa and CCC, respectively

17. Interest rates that are observed today are called
    (a) one-year forward rates.
    (b) forward spot rates.
    (c) spot rates.
    (d) two-year forward rates.

Part D: Short Answer Questions

1. What is meant by the risk structure of interest rates?

   _____

   _____

2. What is meant by the term structure of interest rates?

   _____

   _____

3.   What influence do changes in personal income tax rates have on the level of interest rates?

_____

_____

4.   What is the primary difference between the pure-expectation hypothesis and the liquidity premium hypothesis?

_____

_____

5.   Empirically, what is likely to happen to short-term interest rates if they are high? In particular, if the yield curve is steeply inverted?

_____

_____

6.   Explain the effects of liquidity on interest rates.

_____

_____

■ Answers to Chapter 5

Exercise 1

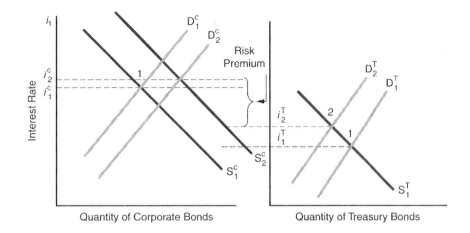

1. The interest rate on corporate bonds would probably rise. Both the demand and supply curves shift to the right. If the supply curve shifts out more than the demand curve, the interest rate rises.

2. The interest rate on Treasury bonds rises.

3. The risk premium depends on the size of the interest rate increase on corporate bonds relative to that on Treasury bonds. The analysis in the chapter suggests that the risk premium would probably fall.

Exercise 2

1. 8%

2. $7.5\% = 10\% \times (1 - 0.25)$

3. You would prefer to hold the tax-exempt municipal bond because it has a higher after-tax return.

4. Because you would prefer the municipal bond with the lower before-tax interest rate, this example indicates that municipal bonds will have lower market interest rates than they otherwise would because of their tax advantages.

Exercise 3

1. $6\% = 0.06 = [0.06 + 0.06 + 0.06]/3$

2. $6\% = 0.06 = [0.07 + 0.06 + 0.05]/3$

3. The expected returns are identical.

4. Our analysis of the expectations hypothesis indicates that when the three-year interest rate equals the average of the expected future one-year rates over the life of the three-year bond, the expected returns on strategies 1 and 2 are equal. In our example here, the three-year interest rate of 6% is the average

of the one-year rates over the life of the three-year bond (6% = [7% + 6% + 5%]/3), so the expected return from the two strategies must be the same.

Exercise 4

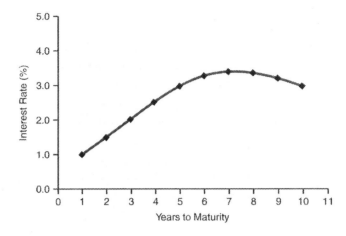

Exercise 5

1. The market is predicting that there will be a mild decline in short-term interest rates in the near future and an even steeper decline further out in the future.

Exercise 6

1. 7% = (5% + 6% + 7% + 8% + 9%)/5

2. 1.5% = 8.5% − 7%

Exercise 7

1. An inverted yield curve

2. A normal, upward-sloping yield curve

Exercise 8

1. Credit-rating agencies are investment advisory firms that rate the quality of municipal and corporate bonds and estimate the probability of default.

2. Because U.S. Treasury bonds are free of default risk, they would not be rated by credit-rating agencies.

3. The highest rating for investment grade bonds is AAA by Standard & Poor's and Aaa by Moody's. The highest rating for junk bonds is BB by Standard & Poor's and Ba by Moody's.

Self-Test

Part A

1. risk structure
2. default risk
3. risk premium
4. liquidity
5. higher
6. lowers
7. income tax

8. term structure
9. yield curve
10. upward
11. market segmentation
12. liquidity premium theory
13. substitutes

14. higher
15. positive
16. upward
17. default free
18. Credit-rating agencies
19. junk

Part B

1.	F	7.	F	13.	T
2.	T	8.	T	14.	F
3.	F	9.	F	15.	F
4.	F	10.	T	16.	F
5.	T	11.	T	17.	F
6.	F	12.	F	18.	F

Part C

1.	c	7.	d	13.	b
2.	c	8.	b	14.	d
3.	c	9.	d	15.	c
4.	a	10.	b	16.	c
5.	a	11.	d	17.	c
6.	a	12.	c		

Part D

1. The risk structure of interest rates refers to the fact that bonds of equal maturity have varying interest rates. This variation is due to differences in default risk, liquidity, and taxes across different issues of bonds.

2. The term structure of interest rates refers to the fact that bonds with the same default risk, liquidity, and tax characteristics will have different interest rates due to their different times to maturity. These differences arise from expectations of future short-term rates, demand and supply differences for bonds of different maturities, and supply and demand differences due to liquidity premiums, which vary by maturity.

3. Increases in taxes make the after-tax rate of return on municipal bonds more attractive to investors relative to taxable corporate bonds. This changes results in a lower demand for corporate bonds, which will cause their price to decline and rates to rise. The higher after-tax return will have the same impact on Treasury bonds, which will also raise their rates.

4. The main difference between the pure-expectations hypothesis and the liquidity-premium hypothesis is that the liquidity-premium hypothesis recognizes that investor's expect a risk premium for holding bonds over longer periods because they prefer shorter-term securities, thus explaining the upward-sloping yield curve.

5.   When short-term rates are high and long-term rates are low, future changes in rates should be a decline in short-term rates eventually leading to an upward-sloping yield curve.

6.   Liquidity can be defined as the ability to quickly convert an asset into cash without causing abnormal price variation. Because investors appear to prefer shorter-term instruments, short-term instruments are more frequently traded and thus liquid. However, longer-term instruments may trade infrequently. Thus any trade could cause the price of a particular bond issue to change abruptly. The comparative lack of liquidity in long-term bonds causes investors to require a liquidity premium, which may increase the longer the term to maturity.

Chapter 6
Are Financial Markets Efficient?

■ Chapter Learning Goals

By the end of the chapter you should

1. Understand the reasoning behind the efficient markets hypothesis.
2. Understand how expectations are formed.
3. Understand how securities prices move over time.

■ Chapter Summary

Efficient Market Hypothesis

The **efficient market hypothesis,** or **theory of efficient capital markets,** states that all available information is reflected in securities' prices. Expected returns are assumed to equal the optimal forecasts of returns. In other words, the best or optimal forecast of a security's return using all available information is the same as the security's equilibrium return in an efficient market.

The return for a security comes from income (dividends) and capital gains. Formally,

$$R = \frac{P_{t+1} - P_t + C}{P_t},$$

where R is the percentage return earned over the holding period, P_{t+1} is the price of the security at the end of the holding period, P_t is the price of the security at the beginning of the holding period, and C is the dividend or income earned over the holding period. Using this basic return formula, we can use the efficient market hypothesis to forecast future security prices.

Suppose that you have the following information about the High Tech Company of America; the consensus market estimate of the expected return of the company's stock (R) is 20%, the current share price of the stock (P_t) is $25, and the expected dividend (C) is $1 per share. According the hypothesis, the price of the stock at the end of the period will be:

$$0.20 = \frac{P_{t+1} - 25.00 + 1.00}{25.00}$$

Solving for the stock price at the end of the period,

$$P_{t+1} = 29.00.$$

Rationale Behind the Hypothesis

When optimal forecasts of a security's returns are above the equilibrium return for that security, then an **unexploited profit opportunity** exists. Knowing this, you would then buy the stock until the unexploited profit opportunity is eliminated. Similarly, if the optimal forecasts for a security are below the equilibrium return for that security, then you would sell the security until the unexploited profit opportunity no longer exists. Thus in an efficient market a sufficient number of investors will recognize the unexploited profit opportunity and will buy or sell enough shares to eliminate the opportunity. This increased buying of undervalued securities and selling of overvalued securities is what is referred to as **arbitrage.** Unexploited market opportunities are arbitraged away in an efficient market.

Stronger Version of the Efficient Market Hypothesis

The strong form of the efficient market hypothesis states that an efficient market not only requires that expectations are optimal forecasts using all publicly available information but also requires security prices to reflect the intrinsic or true value of the corporation, which also incorporates non-public information. The intrinsic value of the corporation considers items known as **market fundamentals** that have a direct impact on future income streams of securities. Evidence exists that investors can exploit inside information and earn excess returns. Although such returns can be earned, this result does not go against markets being efficient because inside information is not publically available. There are insider trading laws that control this type of potential exploitation.

■ Evidence on the Efficient Market Hypothesis

Evidence in Favor of Market Efficiency

Performance of Investment Analysts and Mutual Funds

Historically, neither investment advisers nor mutual funds have outperformed various measures of the market. Hence, having performed well in the past does not indicate than an investment advisor or a mutual fund will perform well in the future.

Do Stock Prices Reflect Publicly Available Information?

Older empirical evidence suggests that when a company announces positive earnings and stock splits, this information does not cause stock prices to rise. This behavior is consistent with an efficient market in which security prices already have this expected information included in the stock price.

Random-Walk Behavior of Stock Prices

A **random-walk** describes the movements of stock prices as being unpredictable, with just as much chance that the price of a stock will go down as compared to up. If stock prices do follow a random-walk, then the market is efficient.

Technical Analysis

Technical analysis is the study of historical asset prices with the goal of finding patterns in the movement of those asset prices.

Although older studies of technical analysis suggest that predictable patterns do not exist, more recent research suggests that some price patterns may be predictable.

Evidence Against Market Efficiency

The following are anomalies or trading rules that are repetitive and have been predictable.

Small-Firm Effect

The small-firm effect refers to the abnormally high returns that small company stocks have earned over the long-term relative to large company stocks. This high return is even after accounting for the higher risk.

January Effect

The January effect is the tendency of stock prices to increase at abnormally high rates from about the end of December through January. It is believed to be caused by tax-loss selling in December, followed by the search and purchase of what are believed to be oversold stocks in January.

Market Overreaction

Some research suggests that when new unexpected positive or negative information about a company is released, investors have a tendency to rush to buy or sell the stock, causing the company's stock price to go above or below its equilibrium price. Identifying such overreactions can allow investors to earn excess returns as the price gradually works back to it fair value.

Excessive Volatility

Some studies suggest that stock prices move up and down much more than they should relative to variation in the underlying fundamentals of companies. This phenomenon is closely related to market overreaction with the difference being that excess volatility is not dependent upon the announcement of any single news issue.

Mean Reversion

Mean reversion states that stocks have long-term equilibrium returns to which they will gravitate over time. Thus, a period of below-average stock returns will be followed by a period of above-average stock returns, and vice versa.

New Information Is Not Always Immediately Incorporated into Stock Prices

Recent data suggests that stock prices do not instantaneously fully reflect new information. Consequently, stock prices will continue to rise for a period of time following positive news and will drop for a period of time following negative news.

How Valuable Are Published Reports by Investment Advisers?

The data suggest that investment advisers underperform the broad market over the long term.

Should You Be Skeptical of Hot Tips?

Absolutely! Hot tips only pay off if you are one of the first persons to receive new information regarding a company.

Do Stock Prices Always Rise When There Is Good News?

No. Stock prices are more likely to rise on good news when the good news exceeds the market's expectations.

Efficient Markets Prescription for the Investor

If markets are efficient, then investors cannot outperform the market over the long run. Because commissions and fees reduce the actual returns an investor earns, investors should seek low-cost strategies geared toward tracking the performance of the market. Low-cost strategies include investing in mutual funds that are managed to track the performance of the market, or buying and holding individual stocks for a long period of time.

Behavioral Finance

Behavioral finance is the use of psychological, sociological, and anthropological concepts to study stock price movement. Behavior finance has gained more attention in recent years and is leading to breakthroughs in understanding security price behavior.

Recall that the efficient market hypothesis states that abnormal profit opportunities are quickly bid away through investors buying undervalued stocks or selling overvalued stocks. The process of selling shares that an investor does not own is called short selling. To effectuate a **short sale,** an investor borrows shares from his broker and sells them in the open market. The investor hopes to buy the shares back at a lower price at a later date. The potential loss from a short sale is infinite because stock prices have no bounded maximum value. Thus, investors must be willing to accept the chance of infinite losses to short-sale a stock to push its overvalued price down to the equilibrium value. However, psychologists' research suggests that individuals are averse to losses; that is, losing money hurts relatively more than making money. Consequently, short selling does not occur to the extent necessary to push overvalued stock prices down to equilibrium levels.

■ Exercises

Exercise 1: Definitions and Terminology

Match the following terms in the right-hand column with the definition or description in the left-hand column. Place the letter of the term in the blank provided next to the appropriate definition.

_____ 1. The use of psychological, sociological, and anthropological concepts to study stock price movement

_____ 2. The gravitation of stock returns to long-term equilibrium returns through time

_____ 3. The selling of shares that one does not own

_____ 4. A(n) _____ is based on the theory that prices reflect all available information.

_____ 5. A(n) _____ is a situation where the price of an asset shifts from its fundamental value in reaction to some market news.

_____ 6. Economic events that have a direct impact on future income streams of securities are called _____.

_____ 7. A study of past stock prices and patterns used to predict future stock prices is called _____.

_____ 8. The theory that day-to-day stock price changes are accidental or haphazard is called _____.

_____ 9. The tendency of stock prices to increase at abnormally high rates following a period of tax loss selling

_____ 10. The _____ is the tendency of small firms to outperform the stock market.

_____ 11. Security prices moving wildly above their true values is a(n) _____.

_____ 12. _____ is a situation in which someone can earn a higher than normal return.

_____ 13. Past performance is no guarantee of _____.

_____ 14. Evidence that stock prices move up and down much more than they should relative to variation in company fundamentals

a. unexploited profit opportunity

b. small-firm effect

c. bubble

d. short sale

e. January effect

f. excessive volatility

g. mean reversion

h. efficient market hypothesis

i. market overreaction

j. technical analysis

k. random walk

l. market fundamentals

m. behavioral finance

n. future results

Exercise 2: Implications of Efficient Markets Theory

A.   Information is assimilated rapidly in the stock market. If you read in the *Wall Street Journal* that Montana Power Company has just been granted a utility rate increase, can you profit from this knowledge by rushing out to purchase this stock?

_____

_____

_____

B.   How would your answer to Part A change if you had happened to get advance word on the Public Service Commission's decision from your brother-in-law?

_____

_____

C.   When there is a pronounced price change in a stock, the SEC will carefully study the buy and sell orders and who has been involved in them to determine if anyone traded on the basis of insider information. Does such activity by the SEC indicate that the stock market is not informationally efficient?

_____

_____

_____

D.   As a financial advisor, it is your responsibility to recommend the most suitable investments to meet your clients' needs. If a client believes that markets are efficient, which would be more suitable—an actively managed large capitalization equity growth mutual fund or a passively managed stock index mutual fund, such as an index fund that tracks the S&P 500 index?

_____

_____

_____

E.   Which stock portfolio investment strategy should be employed if markets are efficient—a short-term day trading strategy or a long-term buy-and-hold strategy?

_____

_____

F.   How much should investors pay for equity analysis newsletters?

_____

_____

■ Self-Test

Part A: Fill in the Blanks

1. Predictions known as _____ will be correct on average, although they will not always be perfectly accurate.

2. Individuals will make mistakes, but they will not be _____ wrong in any one direction.

3. The theory of _____ is the application of rational expectations to the pricing of securities in financial markets.

4. Efficient markets theory suggests that security _____ reflect all available information at that time.

5. Efficient markets theory suggests that individuals ought to be skeptical of stockbrokers' _____.

6. Acting on stock analysis' recommendations will not yield abnormally high returns on average because market _____ already reflect this information.

7. Even when economists select analysts who have done well in the past, the evidence indicates that financial analysis do not consistently _____ the overall market.

8. The _____ hypothesis contends that future changes in stock prices should for all practical purposes be unpredictable.

9. A stock's price sometimes falls when good news about the stock is announced because announced earnings fall short of those _____ by market participants.

10. The efficient markets theory suggests that relying on the published reports of financial analysts and the hot tips given to you by your broker is probably an inferior strategy when compared to the _____ and _____ strategy.

11. One piece of evidence that goes against market efficiency is the _____ effect that some financial economists attribute to tax issues.

12. When new unexpected information becomes available about a stock, market participants often _____, and the price reaction temporarily puts the price out of equilibrium.

13. Some financial economists use the theory of rational _____ to help explain why asset prices deviate from their fundamental market value for longer periods of time.

14. _____ uses concepts from psychological and other sociological ideas to study the movement of stock prices.

15. When an investor sells stock which she does not own, she has executed a(n) _____.

Part B: True-False Questions

Circle whether the following statements are true (T) or false (F).

T F 1. Expectations that are formed solely on the basis of past information are known as rational expectations.

T F 2. If the optimal forecast of a return on a financial asset exceeds its equilibrium return, the situation is called an unexploited profit opportunity.

T F 3. In an efficient market, all unexploited profit opportunities will be eliminated.

T F 4. Everyone in a financial market must be well informed about a security if the market is to be considered efficient.

T F 5. The efficient markets theory suggests that published reports of financial analysts can guarantee that individuals who use this information will outperform the market.

T F 6. The overwhelming majority of statistical studies indicate that financial analysts do indeed pick financial portfolios that outperform the market average.

T F 7. According to the efficient markets hypothesis, picking stocks by throwing darts at the financial page is an inferior strategy compared to employing the advice of financial analysts.

T F 8. Mutual funds that outperform the market in one period are highly likely to consistently outperform the market in subsequent periods due to their superior investment strategies.

T F 9. Efficient markets theory indicates that one should be skeptical of hot tips.

T F 10. Stock prices always rise when favorable earnings reports are released.

T F 11. If the efficient markets theory is true, no investor will consistently "beat the market."

T F 12. Technical analysis uses ideas from psychology and sociology to study the movement of stock prices.

T F 13. If an investor believes that a company's stock price is going to rise, then she will execute a short sale.

T F 14. The study of historical stock prices to identify predictable trends is known as behavioral finance.

T F 15. When a company's stock price moves up and down more than the changes in the company's fundamentals, then the stock is experiencing excessive volatility.

Part C: Multiple-Choice Questions

Circle the appropriate answer.

1. Suppose you read a story in the financial section of the local newspaper that announces the proposed merger of Apple Computer, Inc. and Microsoft Corporation. The announcement is expected to greatly increase the profitability of Apple. If you should not decide to invest in Apple stock, you can expect to earn

   (a) above-average returns because you will get to share in the higher profits.
   (b) above-average returns because your stock will definitely appreciate as the profits are earned.
   (c) a normal return because stock prices adjust to reflect changed profit expectations almost immediately.
   (d) none of the above.

2. Assume that you own a ranch and lease land from the Bureau of Land Management (BLM), which allows you to graze cattle on the government land at a price that is below the market equilibrium price. If the government should raise the price for grazing cattle on BLM land, you can expect the value to the ranch to

   (a) fall because ranching is no longer as profitable.
   (b) be unaffected. (The value of the ranch is not dependent on the price of grazing rights.)
   (c) rise because the value of the BLM land rises.
   (d) rise because the value of the BLM land falls.

3. Efficient markets theory suggests that purchasing the published reports of financial analysts

   (a) is likely to increase one's returns by an average of 10%.
   (b) is likely to increase one's returns by an average of about 3% to 5%.
   (c) is not likely to be effective strategy for increasing financial returns.
   (d) is likely to increase one's returns by an average of about 2% to 3%.

4. After the announcement of higher quarterly profits, the price of a stock falls. Such an occurrence is

   (a) clearly inconsistent with efficient markets theory.
   (b) possible if market participants expected lower profits.
   (c) consistent with efficient markets theory.
   (d) not possible.

5. Since a change in regulations permitting their existence in the mid-1970s, discount brokers have grown rapidly. Efficient markets theory would seem to suggest that people who use discount brokers

   (a) will likely earn lower returns than those who use full-service brokers.
   (b) will likely earn about the same as those who use full-service brokers but will net more after brokerage commissions.
   (c) are going against evidence that suggests that the financial analysis provided by full-service brokers can help one outperform the overall market.
   (d) are likely to be poor.

6. Efficient markets theory suggests that stock prices tend to follow a "random walk." Thus the best strategy for investing in stock is
    (a) a "churning strategy" of buying and selling often to catch the market swings.
    (b) turning over your stock portfolio each month after selecting stocks by throwing darts at the stock page.
    (c) a "buy-and-hold strategy" of holding onto stocks to avoid brokerage commissions.
    (d) to do none of the above.

7. Unexploited opportunities are quickly eliminated in financial markets through
    (a) changes in asset prices.
    (b) changes in dividend payments.
    (c) accounting conventions.
    (d) exchange-rate translations.

8. Stockbrokers have at times paid newspaper reporters for information about articles to be published in future editions. This suggests that
    (a) your stockbroker's hot tips will help you outperform the overall market.
    (b) financial analysts' reports contain information that will help you earn a return that exceeds the market average.
    (c) insider information may help ensure returns that exceed the market average.
    (d) Each of the above is true.

9. Efficient capital markets theory suggests that if an unexploited profit opportunity arises in an efficient market,
    (a) it will tend to go unnoticed for some time.
    (b) it will be quickly eliminated.
    (c) financial analysts are your best source of this information.
    (d) prices will reflect the unexploited profit opportunity.

10. Research has provided some support for the markets being inefficient based on any of the following reasons, except
    (a) excessive volatility.
    (b) January effect.
    (c) small-firm effect.
    (d) some investors are able to consistently "beat the market."

11. Which of the following is a fundamental factor that will probably impact the price of common stock of Nike Corporation?
    (a) The past prices of Nike stock
    (b) The number of people who participate in sports is expected to decrease
    (c) An increase in the cost of chemicals used to make paper
    (d) All three factors are fundamental and will influence the price of Nike's stock.

12. Which of the following has been used to earn a return on assets that is consistently greater than the equilibrium return?

    (a) Forecasts of returns by analysts
    (b) Investing in the mutual fund that performed the best during the most recent year
    (c) Throwing darts at a list of stocks and investing in those the darts land on
    (d) Just being consistently lucky

13. If a company's stock price is above its equilibrium price and an investor wants to attempt to earn abnormal profits or minimize losses, then he can

    (a) buy half the number of shares he normally would purchase.
    (b) sell the shares he currently owns.
    (c) short-sale the stock and buy it back at a lower price later.
    (d) Both (b) and (c)

14. According to which pricing anomaly would you purchase shares in late December and sell them in late January?

    (a) The small-firm effect
    (b) The Christmas effect
    (c) The January effect
    (d) Mean reversion

15. If a period of abnormally high stock returns is followed by a period of abnormally low stock returns, then stock returns are have said to have

    (a) experienced excessive volatility.
    (b) entered into a trend.
    (c) followed a random walk.
    (d) mean revered.

Part D: Short Answer Questions

1. How is the random-walk model of stock pricing similar to the efficient market model of stock prices?

    _____

    _____

2. In the United States, it is illegal for investors to trade securities based on information that is not publicly available to everyone. What impact do you think this legal restraint has on market efficiency?

    _____

    _____

3. What information do analysts and other investors use to determine the price they are willing to pay for a security?

    _____

    _____

4.   What does a "rational bubble" have to say about security prices and efficient markets?

_____

_____

5.   What is believed to cause the January effect?

_____

_____

6.   What is behavioral finance?

_____

_____

7.   Why is past performance no guarantee of future results?

_____

_____

Part E: Problems

1.   Suppose the FPL group pays an annual dividend of $2.72 and the stock price is expected to rise from its current price of $73.34 to $81.75 over the next year. What is the expected return for FPL group over the next year?

2.   Analysts estimate the required rate of return for Intel to be 15% per annum over the next five years. Intel currently pays a yearly dividend of $0.32 per share. The stock's price is currently $22.88. What is the stock price expected to be in one year?

3.   What is the expected growth rate in the price of the stock using the information in Problem 2?

4.   If Intel's stock price continues to increase at the rate computed in Problem 3, what should the stock price be at the end of five years?

■ Answers to Chapter 6

Exercise 1

1.	m	6.	l	11.	c
2.	g	7.	j	12.	a
3.	d	8.	k	13.	n
4.	h	9.	e	14.	f
5.	i	10.	b		

Exercise 2

A. No, by the time you purchase Montana Power Company stock, its price will already reflect the increase in expected profits, and therefore you should not expect to earn an above-normal profit from this purchase.

B. The information you receive from your brother-in-law is known as insider or advance information if he is associated with the Public Service Commission. Insider information can allow you to earn a higher than normal rate of return, though you risk going to jail if you and your brother-in-law get caught.

C. No, the stock market is still informationally efficient if people can profit from insider information as long as an investor in that market cannot make an above-normal return by gathering information available to the public. Apart from inside information, financial economists generally believe that the stock market comes close to the ideal of an informationally efficient market.

D. A passively managed stock index fund would be more suitable because an implication of the efficient markets hypothesis is that money managers will not outperform the market over the long run. Furthermore, the lower transaction costs of index funds will enhance investor returns.

E. A long-term buy-and-hold strategy should be employed to minimize transaction costs associated with buying and selling shares.

F. Because the efficient markets hypothesis implies that analysts cannot outperform the market in the long run, investors should not buy investor newsletters. Therefore, they should pay nothing.

Self-Test

Part A

1. optimal forecasts	5. stock tips	9. expected	13. bubbles
2. consistently	6. prices	10. buy, hold	14. Behavioral finance
3. efficient capital markets	7. outperform	11. January	15. short sale
4. prices	8. random-walk	12. overreact	

Part B

1.	F	6.	F	11.	T
2.	T	7.	F	12.	F
3.	T	8.	F	13.	F
4.	F	9.	T	14.	F
5.	F	10.	F	15.	T

Part C

1.	c	6.	c	11.	b
2.	a	7.	a	12.	d
3.	c	8.	c	13.	d
4.	c	9.	b	14.	c
5.	b	10.	d	15.	d

Part D

1. These two models of stock prices are the same. They both conclude that all known relevant information is already included in the price and that analysts cannot consistently predict the future direction of the stock price.

2. The markets are a little less efficient because of this law. For example, if an officer in a company has information about the firm that, if known, would cause the price to fall, then not being able to sell the stock and drive the price down to the new equilibrium would cause the stock to be mispriced. Insider trading laws are based on the potential for the unethical nature of the transaction, not on market efficiency.

3. Analysts and investors will of course observe the past financial and operating behavior of firms to learn about the decisions of management. However, the most important information is based on what they expect to happen. Today's price is set to reflect the expected benefits that will accrue to the security owner over the time he owns the security.

4. In a rational bubble, investors are aware that the prices are above their fundamental levels. However, they continue to hold these assets because of the belief that someone else may buy the asset for a higher price in the future. Investors are aware that the bubble may burst, but that event is unpredictable. So, there are no unexploited profit opportunities—investors may suffer large losses and know it.

5. Year-end tax-loss selling is believed to cause the January effect.

6. Behavioral finance is the use of psychological, sociological, and anthropological concepts to study stock price movement.

7. Past performance is no guarantee of future results because studies suggest that investment advisers and money managers who outperform the market over one time period are not any more likely to outperform the market over the next time period.

Part E

1. Expected return = $[(81.75 - 73.34) + 2.72]/73.34 = 15.2\%$

2. Expected return = $[(P_{t+1} - 22.88) + 0.32]/22.88 = 15.0\%$

    Solving for P_{t+1}, next year's price is 25.99.

3. Stock price growth rate = $(25.99 - 22.88)/22.88 = 13.6\%$

4. $P_{t+5} = (1 + 0.136)^5 \times 22.88 = \$43.29$

Chapter 7
Why Do Financial Institutions Exist?

■ Chapter Learning Goals

By the end of this chapter, you should

1. Be familiar with the basic aggregate financial structure favored by businesses.
2. Define and explain moral hazard and adverse selection.
3. Apply the concepts of moral hazard and adverse selection to explain eight puzzles of financial markets.
4. Understand conflicts of interest.
5. Know where conflicts of interest occur.

■ Chapter Summary

This chapter deals primarily with obstacles that exist that reduce the smooth functioning of direct financing financial markets and lead to the benefits of financial intermediaries. After introducing the observed capital structure employed by business firms, this chapter leads into two of the most important concepts encountered in financial markets: **moral hazard** and **adverse selection.** These two concepts can be used to analyze why firms utilize the capital structures observed in the economy. The analysis demonstrates that because agents run firms, **agency costs** are prevalent. Financial markets have developed methods to minimize these costs.

Observed Financial Structure

It is an observed fact that the majority of funds used by businesses come from debt obligations. Equity financing represents only a small percentage of the total capital structure of business firms. In the United States, the largest component of debt comes from nonbank financial intermediaries. Two primary reasons for the use of intermediaries are that they can significantly reduce transaction costs due to economies of scale and their lending expertise.

The chapter presents eight basic facts about the financial system: (1) stocks are not the most important source of external financing; (2) issuing debt and equity securities is not the primary way in which businesses finance operations; (3) indirect finance, which involves financial intermediaries, is much more important than direct finance; (4) financial intermediaries—in particular, banks—are the most important source of external funds used to finance businesses; (5) the financial system is one of the most heavily regulated sectors; (6) only large, well-established corporations have easy access to securities markets; (7) collateral is an important feature of debt contracts for both households and businesses; and (8) debt contracts are complicated legal documents that place significant restrictions on the actions of the borrower.

Transaction Costs

High transaction costs can reduce the number of investment opportunities available to the public. Financial intermediaries help to reduce transaction costs, enabling small savers and borrowers to gain from financial markets. One way to reduce transaction costs is to bundle the funds from many investors together so that the investments can achieve economies of scale. Financial intermediaries can also reduce transaction costs by developing expertise in areas such as computer technology.

■ Asymmetric Information: Adverse Selection and Moral Hazard

The role of information in the financial markets is a significant one. **Asymmetric information** occurs when one party has more information than the other party to the transaction. Adverse selection and moral hazard are two types of information asymmetry. **Adverse selection** is when one party has more information than the other party before a transaction occurs. **Moral hazard** is information asymmetry that arises after a transaction has occurred. For example, a company uses the proceeds from a bond issue for purposes that raise the company's credit risk and the probability that the company will default on all outstanding credit. Asymmetric information can cause conflicts of interest between owners of a company and the agents that manage the company on their behalf. **Agency theory** attempts to explain how the conflicts arise and the resultant behavior of owners and managers.

The Lemons Problem

A famous example of adverse selection is known as the **lemons problem** because it was developed using the used car market as an example. Suppose that you have a car for sale that you know is a cherry in every way. Because buyers cannot determine the car's true value, you will only be offered a price that reflects the value of the average used car. Because the car is worth more than this, you refuse to sell. Everyone with an above-average car will also refuse to sell, and as a result, the average value of the cars left will fall. This will cause those with cars that are above this new average to withdraw from the market. Eventually, only bad cars will be left, and the market for used cars essentially fails.

Extending the Lemons Problem to Capital Markets

A similar situation exists in the stock and bond markets. The only securities that may be offered for sale are ones at or below average quality. Skeptical investors will refuse to pay the true value of good securities because they cannot know which are good and which are bad. This explains two of the puzzles noted regarding security markets. That is, stock represents only 11% of external financing, and bonds represent only 32%. This implies that despite all the publicity regarding stocks and bonds, marketable securities are not the primary method for financing firm activities. The majority of financing comes from private lending through loan agreements of which banks are the major lender.

Solutions to the Adverse Selection Problem

One solution to the adverse selection problem is for firms that are experts at collecting and evaluating information to rate securities. The problem with this is that investors will **free ride** on the collection efforts and not pay for the information. A solution to the free ridership problem is for intermediaries to engage in **private financing** so that the information is never made public. The free rider problem explains puzzles 3 and 4, which note that indirect financing and banks are the most important sources of external funds.

The fifth puzzle is that the financial system is among the most heavily regulated sectors of the economy. This is because government regulation encourages firms to reveal honest information for investors, and this is needed to reduce the adverse selection problem. Governments do not provide free information about firms to avoid the necessity of disclosing bad news about specific firms when it arises.

However, the government does regulate securities markets, thereby encouraging firms to reveal information about them. For example, the Securities and Exchange Commission requires publicly traded companies to have independent **audits** to certify that firms are adhering to standard accounting principles and practices.

Adverse selection only interferes with the functioning of financial debt markets if a lender suffers a loss when a borrower is unable to make loan payments and thereby defaults. This explains the sixth and seventh puzzles. Large, well-established firms are the primary issuers of marketable securities because they have a larger net worth, which serves the same function as collateral, and have much to lose if they borrow too much. In addition, many loans are collateralized by physical assets to reduce the likelihood that the lender will suffer losses. The belief that the larger companies are more likely to be the primary issuers of marketable securities is known as the **pecking order hypothesis.**

The Moral Hazard Problem

The moral hazard problem explains the final puzzle, which is that debt contracts are typically extremely complicated legal documents that place substantial restrictions on the behavior of the borrower.

Moral hazard is the asymmetric information problem that occurs after a transaction has taken place. After a transaction, there are incentives for the issuer of securities to pursue actions that may harm the purchaser of the securities. This problem affects the ability of firms to issue debt and equity.

The moral hazard associated with equities is known as the **principal-agent problem.** The principal-agent problem arises from differing objectives of managers, the agents, who own very little of the firm, and the majority owners of the firm, the principals. The principals are concerned more about maximizing shareholder wealth than the managers are because the managers can extract wealth or other non-pecuniary benefits from the company before the owners of the firm receive the residual income.

Owners can attempt to solve the principal-agent problem by monitoring the activities of managers. However, monitoring, or **costly state verification,** can be expensive and a drag on firm profitability. Government regulation produces some information but does not solve the moral hazard problem. Venture capital firms, which are firms that provide funding to new businesses in exchange for partial ownership of the firm, are a type of financial intermediary that also help to reduce the moral hazard problem.

Solutions to the Moral Hazard Problem

Debt covenants accompany virtually every debt contract. These covenants attempt to restrict the activities of the borrower in such a way as to limit the amount of risk that they can take with the borrowed funds. These covenants also require any collateral be kept in good condition and require the borrower to provide periodic information about his activities. There are four types of restrictive covenants. (1) Covenants to discourage undesirable behavior, such as restricting the uses of the money. (2) Covenants to encourage desirable behavior, such as requiring a minimum level of some of current assets relative to current liabilities. (3) Covenants to keep collateral valuable, such as requiring a specific level of upkeep for a specific assets. (4) Covenant to provide information. There is more on this fourth restriction in the next paragraph.

Although restrictive covenants help reduce the moral hazard problem, they do not eliminate the problem completely because it is almost impossible to write covenants that rule out every risk-taking activity. In addition, for covenants to be valuable they must be **monitored** and **enforced.** Little monitoring and enforcement will occur if every security holder relies on other security holders to perform these activities. Financial intermediaries solve this problem by making private loans. The intermediary making private loans receives the benefits of monitoring and enforcement and will work to shrink the moral hazard problem inherent in debt financing contracts.

Factors That Increase Adverse Selection and Moral Hazard Problems

Financial economists have found five economic factors to increase the adverse selection and moral hazard problems. (1) Increases in interest rates increase the adverse selection problem because the better borrowers will refuse to borrow at the higher rates. (2) Falling prices cause a loss of collateral value and of borrower net worth, so the adverse selection and moral hazard problems increase. (3) A decline in the stock market also causes a loss of firm value and will increase both the moral hazard and adverse selection problems. (4) An increase in risk will make it harder for intermediaries to screen the bad from the good borrowers and will lead to fewer loans being made. (5) Bank panics may cause banks to go out of business and reduce the number of loans available. Most **financial crises** have had at least some of these elements present.

Financial crises are significant economic events that are often characterized by an unusually high failure of financial and non-financial firms and sharp drops in the value of financial assets. Four factors that can help to cause financial crises are increases in interest rates, increases in uncertainty, asset markets effects on balance sheets and bank panics, and government fiscal imbalances.

Higher interest rates can drive away borrowers with good credit quality, leaving higher proportions of poor credit quality borrowers for lenders to serve. Higher interest rates can also lead to higher interest costs for corporations, driving down profitability and **cash flows,** the difference between cash expenditures and receipts. Thus, higher interest rates result is an increase in adverse selection via two factors.

Bank panics occur because depositors believe that banks are withholding information about their financial health, leading them to rush to withdraw money from financial institutions. The contraction in deposits causes banks to reduce the amount of loans or credit to borrowers. Consequently, many firms become insolvent, causing **debt deflation** or a substantial decline in the prices of debt. The increased cost of debt leads to further indebtedness, adverse selection, and moral hazard.

Government fiscal imbalances result from weakening economic conditions within the country, which raises doubts about the ability of the country to meet its debt obligations. Due to this weakness, the public may be reluctant to purchase the debt and the banks take over more of this lending need. Declining debt values lead to less secure bank balance sheets, and lending will contract. Foreign investors may also find it less attractive to invest in the troubled country, and the domestic currency will fall in value, causing significant problems for firms that have debt denominated in foreign currencies.

What Are Conflicts of Interest and Why Do We Care?

Financial institutions can lower the cost of information production by taking one information resource and spreading it over many different services. That is, they can achieve **economies of scope.** However, by financial institutions providing multiple services to customers, the competing interests of these services can result in misleading information or concealment of information to customers. Any increase in conflicts of interest can reduce information production in the financial markets resulting in more asymmetric information, causing the markets to become less efficient. Conflicts of interest can lead to incentives that can result in unethical behavior.

Types of Conflicts of Interest

There are four areas of financial services that produce the greatest potential for conflicts of interest: (1) underwriting and research in investment banking, (2) auditing and consulting in accounting firms, (3) credit assessment and consulting in credit-rating agencies, and (4) universal banking. Investment banks typically produce research for the benefit of their customers and underwrite securities of these same companies by selling them to the public. If underwriting fees exceed commissions generated by research for customers, then there is an incentive for the investment banks to issue biased research to the benefit of their underwriting clients. Investment banks sometimes also offer underpriced initial public offerings

(IPOs), shares of companies going public, to managers of other companies in the hopes of earning those companies' future underwriting business. This practice is known as **spinning** and is a form of kickback. This can result in higher underwriting costs for those companies, raising their cost of capital, thereby reducing market efficiency.

Accounting firms sometimes provide both auditing services and non-auditing consulting services, known as management advisory services, to a client. This arrangement can result in two potential sources of conflicts of interest: (1) pressure on auditors to state what their clients wish them to state in order to keep high-fee management advisory services, and (2) reluctance of auditors to criticize advice or systems implemented by their non-audit colleagues. Conflicts of interest may also rise from an auditor providing a favorable audit in order to retain audit business.

Credit Assessment and Consulting in Credit-Rating Agencies

Conflicts of interest can arise from the fact that credit-rating agencies are paid by the issuers of securities to have their securities rated. In addition, some credit-rating agencies have begun to provide consulting services that may conflict with their rating services.

Universal Banking

Various types of conflicts of interest can arise from universal banking. They include: (1) the sale of securities from the underwriting department to bank customers wanting unbiased advice, (2) the placement of underwritings in the bank's managed trust accounts because of lack of customer demand, (3) the use of the underwriting department to earn fees from companies that have loans with the bank to subsidize the increased credit risk of those companies since the loans were originally issued, (4) overly favorable loan terms to companies in order to earn underwriting business, and (5) coercive tactics to sell insurance products to bank customers.

When Are Conflicts of Interest a Serious Problem?

In general, conflicts of interest are a serious problem when they result in a decline in information, making it harder for investors to eliminate the moral hazard and adverse selection problems, resulting in less capital available for investment causing fewer investment opportunities. If incentives to exploit conflicts of interest are not sufficient to offset the decrease in a firm's reputation over the long run, then conflicts of interest may not result in the reduction of the flow of reliable information in the marketplace. However, in the short run, it may be possible for managers of a corporation to exploit a firm's reputational rents before the marketplace can adjust for the conflicts of interest.

What Has Been Done to Remedy Conflicts of Interest?

The Sarbanes-Oxley Act of 2002 and the Global Legal Settlement of 2002 have been implemented to help reduce conflicts of interest. The Public Accounting Return and Investor Protection Act, better known as the Sarbanes-Oxley Act, has four major components: (1) It created the Public Company Accounting Oversight Board (PCAOB) to register public accounting firms and institute accounting and quality control rules to oversee accounting firms, ensuring independent audits. The SEC oversees the PCAOB, which can also investigate, discipline, and impose sanctions on accounting firms. (2) It reduces potential conflicts of interest by making it unlawful for registered public accounting firms to simultaneously provide auditing and non-auditing services to a firm, with the possible exception of services constituting less than 5% of the total amount of revenues paid by a client to an auditor. (3) It increased charges for white-collar crimes and obstruction of investigations. (4) It has measures to improve the quality of information by mandating that an accounting firm's audit committee be independent of the firm and that the CEO and CFO of the company certify the company's financial statements.

The Global Settlement of 2002 was brought about by then New York Attorney General Elliott Spitzer along with the SEC, NASD, NASAA, and NYSE against the 10 largest investment banks in the United States. The five primary terms are that (1) it separates research and investment banking activities; (2) it bans spinning; (3) it requires the publication of analysts' recommendations, ratings, and price targets; (4) it requires the investment banks to provide independent research for customers from at least three firms for the next five years with oversight from an independent monitor; and (5) it fined the investment banks more than $1.4 billion to fund investor education and independent research.

■ Exercises

Exercise 1: Financial Structure Definitions and Terminology

Match the terms on the right with the definition or description on the left. Place the letter of the term in the blank provided next to the appropriate definition or description.

_____ 1.	Problem of too little information gathering and monitoring activity because the person undertaking the activity cannot prevent others from benefiting from the information and monitoring	a. adverse selection
		b. moral hazard
		c. collateralized debt
_____ 2.	Another term for equity capital, the difference between a firm's assets and its liabilities	d. restrictive covenants
		e. collateral
_____ 3.	Problem that results when the manager behaves contrary to the wishes of stockholders due to the separation of ownership and control	f. financial crises
		g. incentive compatible
_____ 4.	Term describing the solution that high net worth provides to the moral hazard problem in debt contracts by aligning the incentives of the borrower to that of the lender	h. principal-agent problem
		i. net worth
		j. free-rider problem
_____ 5.	Major disruptions in financial markets characterized by sharp declines in asset prices and the failure of many financial and non-financial firms	k. venture capital
		l. pecking order hypothesis
_____ 6.	Property that is pledged to the lender if a borrower cannot make his or her debt payments	m. debt deflation
		n. cash flows
_____ 7.	Clauses in bond and loan contracts that either proscribe certain activities that borrowers may have incentive to undertake, or require certain activities that borrowers may not have incentive to undertake	o. agency theory
		p. credit-rating agencies
_____ 8.	The predominant form of household debt contracts, accounting for about 85% of household debt	
_____ 9.	The problem in which borrowers have incentives to use funds obtained from external sources to finance riskier projects than originally envisioned by the lender	
_____ 10.	The lemons problem	
_____ 11.	Firms that receive equity share from new businesses in exchange for their funds	

_____ 12.   Attempts to explain how goals conflict between the owners
       and managers of a firm

_____ 13.   The difference between a firm's cash receipts and cash
       expenditures

_____ 14.   A substantial decline in the price of debt

_____ 15.   The belief that larger companies are more likely to issue
       marketable securities

_____ 16.   Organizations that assess the quality of securities

Exercise 2: Adverse Selection and Moral Hazard

The eight basic puzzles of financial markets in the United States are listed below. For each of the following puzzles, indicate whether it can be explained by adverse selection (A), moral hazard (M), or both (B).

_____ 1.   Stocks are not an important source of finance for American businesses.

_____ 2.   Issuing marketable securities is not the primary way businesses finance their operations.

_____ 3.   Indirect finance, which involves the activities of financial intermediaries, is many times more important than direct finance, in which businesses raise funds directly from lenders in financial markets.

_____ 4.   Banks are the most important source of external funds to finance businesses.

_____ 5.   The financial system is among the most heavily regulated sectors of the economy.

_____ 6.   Only large, well-established corporations have access to securities markets to finance their activities.

_____ 7.   Collateral is a prevalent feature of debt contracts for both households and businesses.

_____ 8.   Debt contracts are typically extremely complicated legal documents that place substantial restrictions on the behavior of the borrower.

_____ 9.   When applying for a car loan, banks require borrowers to complete a detailed application form to calculate the customer's credit score.

■ Self-Test

Part A: Fill in the Blanks

1.   Economic analysis of the eight puzzles indicates that our financial structure is best understood as a response to the problems of adverse selection and _____.

2.   Since 1984, American corporations have repurchased such large numbers of shares that stock market financing has been _____.

3. In the United States, _____ are a far more important source of capital market financing than are stocks.

4. Indirect finance, which involves the activities of _____, is many times more important than direct finance.

5. Banks are the most important source of _____ funds to finance businesses.

6. The financial system is among the most heavily _____ sectors of the economy.

7. Only large, _____ corporations have access to securities markets to finance their activities.

8. _____ are a prevalent feature of debt contracts for both households and businesses.

9. Because borrowers have more and better information about the potential returns and associated risks of their investment alternatives than do lenders, financial markets are characterized by _____.

10. _____ is the problem created by asymmetric information before the transaction occurs.

11. _____ is the problem created by asymmetric information after the deal has been made.

12. _____ in financial markets occurs when bad credit risks are the ones who most actively seek financing and are thus the ones mostly likely to be financed.

13. _____ in financial markets occurs when borrowers have incentives to engage in activities that are undesirable (i.e., immoral) from the lender's point of view.

14. Because financial intermediaries such as banks hold mostly non-traded bank loans, they are better able to avoid the _____ problem that would otherwise reduce their willingness to incur the costs to produce information concerning a borrower's creditworthiness.

15. _____ that force firms to adhere to standard accounting principles and debt contracts are examples of financial market mechanisms that reduce principal-agent problems.

16. Although means have been devised for reducing adverse selection and moral hazard problems, _____ remind us that financial markets are not immune to the disruptions.

17. The reduction in transaction cost per dollar of investment as the size of transactions increase is known as _____.

18. _____ are services that make it easier for customers to conduct transactions.

19. _____ is the difference between assets and liabilities.

20. The _____ Act mandates than an accounting firm's audit committee be independent.

21. _____ are paid by issuers of securities to rate their securities.

Part B: True-False Questions

Circle whether the following statements are true (T) or false (F).

T   F   1.   Stocks are the most important source of external finance for American businesses.

T   F   2.   In the United States, bonds are a more important source of external finance for business than are stocks.

T   F   3.   Most other countries have a larger share of external financing supplied by marketable securities.

T   F   4.   Financial intermediaries benefit savers by reducing transaction costs.

T   F   5.   The "lemons problem" is a term used to describe moral hazard.

T   F   6.   The free-rider problem helps to explain why adverse selection cannot be eliminated solely by the private production and sale of information.

T   F   7.   Banks avoid the free-rider problem by primarily making private loans rather than purchasing securities that are traded in financial markets.

T   F   8.   Collateral, which is property promised to the lender if the borrower defaults, reduces the consequences of adverse selection because it reduces the lender's losses in the case of default.

T   F   9.   Firms with higher net worth are the ones most likely to default.

T   F   10.   Equity contracts are subject to a particular example of moral hazard called the principal-agent problem.

T   F   11.   Moral hazard helps to explain why firms find it easier to raise funds with equity rather than debt contracts.

T   F   12.   Venture capitalists, unlike banks, are able to reduce moral hazard problems by placing individuals on the board of directors of the firm receiving the loan.

T   F   13.   One way of describing the solution that high net worth provides to the moral hazard problem is to say that it makes the debt contract incentive compatible.

T   F   14.   The requirement that the borrower keep her collateral in good condition as one of the conditions to receiving a loan is called a restrictive covenant.

T   F   15.   Debt-deflation occurs when the price level rises, reducing the value of business firms' net worth.

T   F   16.   Costly state verification is the fee charged by the SEC for selling its annual reports to firms.

T   F   17.   Collateral is usually only required by banks for the purpose of financing home purchases.

T   F   18.   Everyone has easy access to the securities markets for financing activities.

T   F   19.   The federal government is the most important source of external funds for businesses.

T   F   20.   The Global Legal Settlement Act of 2002 separates research and investment banking activities.

T   F   21.   Moral hazard and adverse selection problems may result in less capital available for investment.

Part C: Multiple-Choice Questions

Circle the appropriate answer.

1. Which of the following is *not* a problem for individual investors due to transaction costs?
   (a) The cost per share is high for the small quantity of shares individuals normally purchase.
   (b) Many bonds only sell in amounts of $1,000 or more, making transaction costs per bond high because most investors can afford only a small quantity of bonds.
   (c) The smaller dollar amount invested makes it difficult for an investor to adequately diversify, thus increasing transaction costs to do so.
   (d) All three of the above are problems.

2. Which of the following statements concerning external sources of financing for non-financial businesses in the United States is true?
   (a) Since the mid-1980s, American corporations in the aggregate have had a net decline in shares of stock as a source of external financing.
   (b) Issuing marketable securities is not the primary way businesses finance their operations.
   (c) Direct finance is many times more important than indirect finance as a source of external funds.
   (d) All of the above are true.
   (e) Only (a) and (b) of the above are true.

3. Poor people have difficulty getting loans because
   (a) they typically have little collateral.
   (b) they are less likely to benefit from access to financial markets.
   (c) Both (a) and (b) of the above are true.
   (d) Neither (a) nor (b) of the above is true.

4. Financial intermediaries provide their customers with
   (a) reduced transaction costs.
   (b) increased diversification.
   (c) reduced risk.
   (d) all of the above.

5. Because of the adverse selection problem,
   (a) lenders are reluctant to make loans that are not secured by collateral.
   (b) lenders may choose to lend only to those who do not need the money.
   (c) lenders may refuse loans to individuals with high net worth.
   (d) Only (a) and (b) of the above are true.

6. The fact that most used cars are sold by intermediaries (i.e., used car dealers) provides evidence that these intermediaries
   (a) help solve the adverse selection problem in this market.
   (b) profit by becoming experts in determining whether an automobile is of good quality or a lemon.
   (c) are unable to prevent purchasers from free-riding off the information they provide.
   (d) do all of the above.
   (e) do only (a) and (b) of the above.

7. Mishkin and Eakin's analysis of adverse selection indicates that financial intermediaries in general, and banks in particular, because they hold a large fraction of non-traded loans,
    (a) play a greater role in moving funds to corporations than do securities markets as a result of their ability to overcome the free-rider problem.
    (b) provide better-known and larger corporations a higher percentage of their external funds than they do to newer and smaller corporations, which tend to rely on the new issues market for funds.
    (c) Both (a) and (b) of the above
    (d) Neither (a) nor (b) of the above

8. The principal-agent problem arises because
    (a) principals find it difficult and costly to monitor agents' activities.
    (b) agents' incentives are not always compatible with those of the principals.
    (c) principals have incentives to free-ride off the monitoring expenditures of other principals.
    (d) All of the above
    (e) Only (a) and (b) of the above

9. Equity contracts
    (a) are agreements by the borrowers to pay the lenders fixed dollar amounts at periodic intervals.
    (b) have the advantage over debt contracts of a lower cost of state verification.
    (c) are used much more frequently to raise capital than are debt contracts.
    (d) are none of the above.

10. Factors that lead to worsening conditions in financial markets include
    (a) declining interest rates.
    (b) declining stock prices.
    (c) unanticipated increases in the price level.
    (d) only (a) and (c) of the above.
    (e) only (b) and (c) of the above.

11. Of the sources of external funds for non-financial businesses in the United States, loans from financial intermediaries account for approximately _____ of the total.
    (a) 6%
    (b) 30%
    (c) 50%
    (d) 60%

12. High net worth helps to diminish the moral hazard problem of bonds by
    (a) requiring the state to verify the debt contract.
    (b) collateralizing the debt contract.
    (c) making the debt contract incentive compatible.
    (d) giving the debt contract characteristics of equity contracts.

13. Which of the following is a good approach to reducing the "lemons" problem in financial markets?
    (a) Reduce government regulation of security markets to allow business firms to more freely produce and publish information about the company.
    (b) Keep private firms from selling information at a high price, which earns them profits.
    (c) Encourage the growth of financial intermediaries, so they are better able to make loans to business firms of all sizes.
    (d) Have the government outlaw asymmetric information.

14. Which of the following firms is more likely to use security markets to raise funds?
    (a) A small firm that is new in an industry and thus not well known by most bankers
    (b) A large firm that is owned primarily by a small number of investors
    (c) A firm that is privately owned and does not have any common stock publicly traded
    (d) A large firm that has a large number of stockholders

15. Buying bonds in a firm that has a high net worth is beneficial to the investor because
    (a) it eliminates the adverse selection problem.
    (b) the firm is less likely to take on additional debt.
    (c) if the firm defaults the investors can take title to the net worth, sell it off, and use the proceeds to recoup some of the loan losses.
    (d) the net worth represents cash the company has which can be used to make payment on the bonds.

16. Which country experienced an 80% decline in the value of its currency, resulting in insolvency for firms holding substantial amounts of debt denominated in foreign currencies?
    (a) Mexico
    (b) Thailand
    (c) South Korea
    (d) Indonesia

17. Which of the following economic events did *not* occur during the Mexican and East Asian financial crises?
    (a) Loans to companies in these countries by U.S. lenders increased due to the decline in the value of the foreign currency.
    (b) The net worth of banks decreased, leading to a reduction in lending.
    (c) The net worth of borrowers decreased due to stock market declines, leading to increased loan defaults.
    (d) The decline in currency values lead to an increase in inflation and high interest rates.

18. Governments regulate financial systems because
    (a) they need to ensure stability and protect consumers.
    (b) taxes help finance other important functions of government.
    (c) Both (a) and (b)
    (d) None of the above

19. The development of financial intermediaries is largely due to practice of the concept known as
    (a) asymmetric information.
    (b) economies of scale.
    (c) moral hazard.
    (d) None of the above

20. A substantial decline in the price of debt is known as
    (a) bank crises.
    (b) recession.
    (c) debt deflation.
    (d) financial contagion.

21. Monitoring is also known as
    (a) costly state verification.
    (b) information asymmetry.
    (c) moral hazard.
    (d) adverse selection.

22. When are conflicts of interest a serious problem?
    (a) When incentives to exploit conflicts of interest are not sufficient to offset the decrease in a firm's reputation
    (b) When incentives to exploit conflicts of interest are sufficient to offset the decrease in a firm's reputation
    (c) When conflicts of interest cause a decrease in information production
    (d) When conflicts of interest cause an increase in information production
    (e) Both (b) and (c)

23. Why type(s) of conflicts of interest can arise from universal banking?
    (a) Auditing and consulting
    (b) The use of underwriting fees to subsidize loan terms
    (c) The placement of low-demand underwritings in managed accounts
    (d) Credit assessment and consulting
    (e) Both (b) and (c)

24. If an accounting firm offers auditing and management advisory services, what potential conflicts may result?
    (a) Reluctance of auditors to criticize advice given by the management advisory employees
    (b) Spinning
    (c) Overly favorably loan terms
    (d) Overstated credit quality

25. Which of the following is not a component of the Sarbanes-Oxley Act?
    (a) The creation of PCAOB
    (b) The banning of spinning
    (c) The requirement for reporting material off-balance sheet activities
    (d) The increase of charges for white collar crimes

Part D: Short Answer Questions

1. Few American households directly own any securities. What are the two main factors that effectively prohibit households from direct participation in the securities markets?

    _____

    _____

2. How have financial intermediaries helped individual investors participate in investing in the financial markets?

    _____

    _____

3. What is a venture capital firm?

    _____

    _____

4. What influence does the legal system in a country have on the effective use of restrictive covenants and collateral as ways to reduce moral hazard and adverse selection?

    _____

    _____

5. Why does the U.S. government choose to regulate financial markets to reduce the asymmetric information problem rather than provide the information to all citizens?

    _____

    _____

6. Describe one way that financial intermediaries reduce transaction costs.

    _____

    _____

7. How do transaction costs influence small investors?

    _____

    _____

8. Why are conflicts of interest important?

    _____

    _____

■ Answers to Chapter 7

Exercise 1

1.	j	6.	e	11.	k	16.	p
2.	i	7.	d	12.	o		
3.	h	8.	c	13.	n		
4.	g	9.	b	14.	m		
5.	f	10.	a	15.	l		

Exercise 2

1.	B	6.	B
2.	B	7.	B
3.	B	8.	M
4.	B	9.	A
5.	B		

Self-Test

Part A

1.	moral hazard	8.	Covenants	15.	Government regulations
2.	declining	9.	asymmetric information	16.	financial crises
3.	bonds	10.	Adverse selection	17.	economies of scale
4.	intermediaries	11.	Moral hazard	18.	Liquidity services
5.	external	12.	Adverse selection	19.	Net worth of equity capital
6.	regulated	13.	Moral hazard	20.	Sarbanes-Oxley
7.	well-established	14.	free-rider	21.	Credit-rating agencies

Part B

1.	F	8.	T	15.	F
2.	T	9.	F	16.	F
3.	F	10.	T	17.	F
4.	T	11.	F	18.	F
5.	F	12.	T	19.	F
6.	T	13.	T	20.	T
7.	T	14.	T	21.	T

Part C

1.	a	8.	d	15.	c	22.	e
2.	e	9.	d	16.	d	23.	e
3.	a	10.	b	17.	a	24.	a
4.	d	11.	d	18.	a	25.	b
5.	d	12.	c	19.	b		
6.	e	13.	c	20.	c		
7.	a	14.	d	21.	a		

Part D

1. Households generally have only a small number of dollars to invest. This leads to two factors. One, transaction costs are high as a percentage of the total purchase, making the security unprofitable after costs. The second factor is the lack of diversification because they are not able to purchase a large portfolio of assets.

2. Through economies of scale, financial intermediaries reduce the cost of investing small dollar amounts so that households can now afford to make these investments. For example, mutual funds handle massive volumes of small investor accounts and combine their funds to purchase large blocks of securities at lower per-unit costs than the individual would have to pay.

3. A venture capital firm is a partnership that uses its funds to invest in small entrepreneurial firms. These firms would have difficulty raising funds in the public markets due to moral hazard. Venture capitalists own most of the firm and participate in management. Participation reduces both moral hazard and the free-rider problem.

4. In order for covenants to be enforced and collateral to be taken and sold, the creditors must go through the legal system. If the system does not allow absolute compliance with these two tools then there is little incentive for borrowers to comply with covenants or be concerned about the taking of collateral. Many of the less-developed countries are held back in their economic growth due to the legal system's weak adherence to these tools.

5. If the government provided information about firms to the public, they would have to provide factual information, whether good or bad. Providing bad information would be politically unpopular, and thus elected government officials do not wish to be put in this position. Requiring private sector firms to provide certain standard reports forces important information to be fairly disclosed.

6. One way financial intermediaries reduce costs is through economies of scale. In particular, financial intermediaries bundle services or funds together to reduce the transaction cost per dollar of investment.

7. High transaction costs can affect small investors in various ways. They can cause investments to be too costly, forcing investors to not participate in the financial markets. In addition, high transaction costs can cause small investors to be less diversified.

8. Conflicts of interest are important because they can lead managers to keep information from customers and investors thereby increasing information asymmetry. On average, if information asymmetry increases then markets become less efficient.

Chapter 8
Why Do Financial Crises Occur and Why Are They So Damaging to the Economy?

■ Chapter Learning Goals

By the end of this chapter, you should

1. Be familiar with the causes of financial crises.
2. Define and explain the stages of a financial crisis.
3. Know relation between financial crises and economic activity.

■ Chapter Summary

This chapter describes the causes and dynamics of financial crises. Building on the framework established in Chapter 7, the analysis of how asymmetric information can generate adverse selection and moral hazard, called **agency theory,** provides the basis for defining a **financial crisis**—a disruption in the financial system that prevents the efficient transfer of funds from savers to households and firms with productive investment opportunities. This chapter applies the analysis to explain the course of events in a number of past financial crises including the recent subprime crisis and European sovereign debt crisis.

Dynamics of Financial Crises in Advanced Economies

In advanced economies such as in the United States, financial crises typically have two or three stages.

Stage One: Initiation of Financial Crisis

The first stage of a financial crisis can be triggered several ways. One such way is **financial liberalization,** the elimination of restrictions on financial institutions and market. Likewise, the introduction of novel financial products can cause destabilization. Although these changes can be beneficial in the long run, in the short run they can often cause a **credit boom,** while they can reduce screening, as understanding of the new environment often lags behind the surge in the demand for credit. Without proper monitoring, risk taking grows unchecked, and eventually the risk taking causes loss to mount and loss of asset value to lenders. With less capital, financial institutions **deleverage,** i.e., cut back on their lending in response to a weaker balance sheet. As a result of this deleveraging, loans become scarce and firms are no longer able to fund attractive investment opportunities, leading to a drop in overall economic activity.

An irrational increase of asset prices can also trigger a financial crisis. As experienced in the late 1990s with technology stocks, the price of an asset can be driven significantly above its fundamental value by irrational exuberance. This is called an **asset-price bubble.** When the bubble collapses and prices realign with fundamental values, borrowers who used inflated assets as collateral become less creditworthy.

Owing to the potential for adverse selection, a spike in interest rates can also trigger a financial crisis. As rates increase, only progressively riskier borrowers are willing to pay the high borrowing costs. As a result, lenders will no longer want to make loans. Increased rates can also contribute to a crisis through its action on cash flows. As businesses are heavily internally financed, a sharp increase in rates will cause the firm to seek more external funding as interest payments deplete internal cash supplies. In addition, a general increase in uncertainty can exacerbate information asymmetry problems, as seen in the Panic of 1907 or the failure of Lehman Brothers.

Stage Two: Banking Crisis

Faced with deteriorating balance sheets and unable to pay off creditors, some banks will fail. If many banks fail, this leads to a **banking crisis.** Bank runs occur as depositors operate on a first-come first-served basis. Uncertainty regarding the health of even a small fraction of banks can cause a panic, which can lead to a "fire sale" of assets by all banks to meet redemption requests. These fire sales can cause weaker banks that would have survived under normal circumstances to fail. Eventually, insolvent firms are sold off or liquidated. This reduces the uncertainty, and financial markets are able to function well again.

Stage Three: Debt Deflation

In some cases, the recovery can be short-circuited by **debt deflation,** a significant unanticipated decline in asset values accompanied by increased indebtedness and lower net worth. In most advanced economies, fixed debt contracts are typically long maturity and in nominal (not real) terms. Therefore, an unanticipated decline in the price level raises the real value of borrowing firms' liabilities without raising the real value of firms' assets, causing a loss of real net worth. The Great Depression is the most notable example of debt deflation in U.S. history.

The 2007–2009 Financial Crisis

The financial crisis of 2007–2009 is evidence that the danger for severe financial crises is still present even for advanced economies. Financial innovation in mortgage markets, agency problems in mortgage markets, and asymmetric information in the credit rating process combined to produce the conditions necessary for a financial crisis. Innovations such as securitization expanded the mortgage market, making it profitable to offer mortgages to subprime borrowers with less than stellar credit. Financial engineering made this possible by creating new ways to share risk with products such as mortgage-backed securities and collateralized debt obligations (CDOs). However, the new risk-sharing arrangements created agency problems between the originators of loans and the bearers of the default risk. These issues were further exacerbated by conflicts of interest at credit rating agencies, which often severely understated the riskiness of the newly created securities.

The residential housing boom was a key factor in creating the profitability for mortgage originators and lenders. As housing prices peaked in 2006, the instability of the system became evident. Default rates soon skyrocketed as homeowners often walked away from underwater mortgages. This caused a collapse in the value of mortgage-backed assets, which weakened financial institutions with exposure to these assets, and a deleveraging soon followed. High-profile firms such as Bear Sterns, Merrill Lynch, and Lehman Brothers were forced to find buyers or face bankruptcy.

■ Exercises

Exercise 1: Definitions and Terminology

Match the terms on the right with the definition or description on the left. Place the letter of the term in the blank provided next to the appropriate definition.

_____ 1. Reduction in lending in response to lenders' weaker balance sheets

_____ 2. Disruption in the financial system that prevents the efficient transfer of funds

_____ 3. The elimination of restrictions on financial markets and institutions

_____ 4. Standardized security created by bundled mortgages

_____ 5. The bundling together of small loans into standard debt securities

_____ 6. Structure credit product that paid out cash flows into a number of tranches of unequal risk

_____ 7. Mortgages made to borrowers with less than stellar credit

_____ 8. Economies that are in the early stage of market development

_____ 9. Massive short-sales of a currency intended to cause a decline in the currency's value

_____ 10. Significant unanticipated decline in asset values accompanied by increased indebtedness

a. debt deflation

b. subprime mortgage

c. collateralized debt obligations (CDOs)

d. speculative attack

e. deleveraging

f. mortgage-backed security

g. emerging market economies

h. securitization

i. financial liberalization

j. financial crisis

Exercise 2: Dynamics of Financial Crisis

List the three stages of a financial crisis in an advanced economy.

1. _____

2. _____

3. _____

■ Self-Test

Part A: Fill in the Blanks

1. When emerging market economies face large _____ that they cannot finance, they often force banks to purchase government debt.

2. The process of liberalizing restrictions on financial institutions and markets while opening up to flows of capital and financial firms from other nations is called _____.

3. _____ made it possible for borrowers with less than stellar credit to obtain mortgages.

4. The development of new, sophisticated financial instruments and products called _____ included innovations like structured credit products.

5. During a(n) _____, prices of assets may be driven far above their fundamental values.

6. A(n) _____ is characterized by multiple banks failing simultaneously.

7. Although financial liberalization promotes financial development in the long run, in the short run, it can lead to a(n) _____.

8. As precursor to the financial crisis of 2007–2009, _____ saw a massive price boom in due to the development of the subprime mortgage market.

9. During the financial crisis of 2007–2009, credit rating agencies had severe _____ that led them to wildly inflate the ratings of clients that also gave them advising business.

10. The East Asian crisis of 1997 was initiated by the mismanagement of _____.

11. The Great Depression saw the most significant _____, as the decline in price levels led to increased indebtedness and loss of net worth.

12. The _____ is comprised of hedge funds, investment banks, and other nondepository financial firms.

13. The _____ spread from Greece to Ireland, Portugal, Spain, and Italy as their governments were forced to embrace austerity measures to shore up their public finances and interest rates climbed to double-digit levels.

Part B: True-False Questions

Circle whether the following statements are true (T) or false (F).

T F 1. Financial crises have largely been eliminated due to advances in financial innovation.

T F 2. The stages of a financial crisis are identical in advanced and emerging economies.

T F 3. Although usually beneficial in the long run, in the short run, financial liberalization can cause credit booms.

T F 4. Asset-price bubbles occur when prices rise far above fundamental values.

T F 5. The most significant instance of debt deflation in the United States occurred during the Great Depression.

T F 6. Agency problems occurred in the mortgage market because originators of loans always hold the loan.

T F 7. The shadow banking system was largely immune from the financial crisis of 2007–2009.

T F 8. International markets were insulated from the financial crisis of 2007–2009 in the United States.

T F 9. The bankruptcy of Lehman Brothers reduced uncertainty in financial markets.

T F 10. In emerging markets, financial liberalization and severe fiscal imbalances are the primary triggers for crises.

T F 11. The 1998 crisis in Russia was an example of fiscal imbalances causing a crisis in an emerging market.

T F 12. "Twin crises" happen when a currency crisis and a financial crisis occur simultaneously.

Part C: Multiple-Choice Questions

Circle the appropriate answer.

1. Which of the following is not a stage of financial crisis in an advanced economy?
    (a) Initiation of the financial crisis
    (b) Currency crisis
    (c) Banking crisis
    (d) Debt deflation

2. The financial crisis of 2007–2009 was impacted by which of the following key areas?
    (a) Residential housing price collapse
    (b) Run on the shadow banking system
    (c) Failure of high profile firms
    (d) All of the above

3. The following all can initiate a financial crisis in emerging market economies except
    (a) financial liberalization.
    (b) financial globalization.
    (c) stronger lender balance sheets.
    (d) severe fiscal imbalances.
    (e) All of the above

4.   Which of the following is not a stage of financial crisis in an emerging market economy?

(a)   Initiation of the financial crisis

(b)   Currency crisis

(c)   Full-fledged financial crisis

(d)   Debt deflation

5.   The following all can initiate a financial crisis in advanced economies except

(a)   financial liberalization.

(b)   financial innovation.

(c)   spikes in interest rates.

(d)   large budget surpluses.

6.   The originate-to-distribute model was exposed to

(a)   agency problems.

(b)   currency devaluation.

(c)   speculative attacks.

(d)   debt deflation.

7.   The shadow banking system consists of

(a)   hedge funds.

(b)   investment banks.

(c)   other nondepository financial firms.

(d)   all of the above.

8.   Which of the following is an example of globalization causing an emerging market financial crisis?

(a)   The Great Depression in the United States

(b)   Mexico in 1994

(c)   East Asia in 1997

(d)   All of the above

(e)   Both (b) and (c) above

Part D: Short Answer Questions

1.   What were the stages of the Great Depression?

_____

_____

2.   What triggered the financial crisis of 2007–2009?

_____

_____

■ Answers to Chapter 8

Exercise 1

1.	e	6.	c
2.	j	7.	b
3.	i	8.	g
4.	f	9.	d
5.	h	10.	a

Exercise 2

1.   Initiation of the crisis

2.   Banking crisis

3.   Debt deflation

Self-Test

Part A

1.	fiscal imbalances	9.	conflict of interest
2.	financial globalization	10.	financial globalization
3.	Subprime mortgages	11.	debt deflation
4.	financial engineering	12.	shadow banking system
5.	asset-price boom	13.	European sovereign debt crisis
6.	bank panic		
7.	credit boom		
8.	residential housing prices		

Part B

1.	F	6.	F	11.	T
2.	F	7.	F	12.	T
3.	T	8.	F		
4.	T	9.	F		
5.	T	10.	T		

Part C

1.	b	6.	a
2.	d	7.	d
3.	c	8.	e
4.	d		
5.	d		

Part D

1. The Great Depression began with a stock market crash (bursting of an asset-price bubble). Later, a run on banks caused a bank panic. These conditions caused a worsening of asymmetric information problems and finally a debt deflation.

2. The financial crisis of 2007–2009 was triggered by the mismanagement of financial innovations, most notably subprime lending and associated structured products. Increase in housing prices (asset-price bubble) fueled by the available of credit eventually burst as prices hit unsustainable levels. The growth of credit was fueled by a lack of understanding of the complex new instruments that were created by financial engineers, such as mortgage-backed securities and collateralized debt obligations (CDOs).

Chapter 9
Central Banks and the Federal Reserve System

■ Chapter Learning Goals

By the end of this chapter, you should

1. Be able to discuss the formal organizational structure of the Federal Reserve System.

2. Understand the actual balance of power in the Federal Reserve System.

3. Be able to discuss why the Fed enjoys an unparalleled level of independence and what factors contribute to this independence.

4. Understand the main similarities and differences among the central banks of other major countries and the Federal Reserve System.

■ Chapter Summary

This chapter describes the unique structure of the Federal Reserve System and its evolution since 1913. Although Congress granted the Federal Reserve a high degree of independence, a clearer understanding of its decisions requires that we acknowledge the political and bureaucratic forces influencing its behavior.

The Organization of the Fed

The formal structure of the Federal Reserve System reflects Americans' distrust of the concentration of power in banking. Although many feared the creation of a central bank, the banking panic of 1907 convinced many others that a banking system without a **lender of last resort** could be prone to failures, panics, and payment problems. Thus, the formal structure of the Federal Reserve reflects a compromise among these concerns.

Although the Federal Reserve formally shares responsibility across separate, cooperating entities, it is fundamentally a hierarchical organization. At the top is the **Board of Governors**—a group of seven members appointed to 14-year terms by the president of the United States and confirmed by the Senate. The president appoints one member as chair, currently Janet Yellen, who serves a four-year term and may be reappointed. The chairman of the Board of Governors wields great power in Washington, D.C., as evidenced by the chair's frequent trips to Capitol Hill to testify on economic policy matters.

The 12-member **Federal Open Market Committee** or **FOMC** determines monetary policy decisions by a majority vote. Open market operations are the most important policy tool that the Fed has for controlling the money supply. The committee consists of the seven members of the Board of Governors, the president of the Federal Reserve Bank of New York, and presidents from other Federal Reserve banks. The chairman of the Board of Governors also serves as the Chairman of the FOMC. Presidents from the other

Federal Reserve banks also attend FOMC meetings, and their input is important although they have no formal vote. It is, however, the Board of Governors that dictates the future course of monetary policy (though the FOMC goes to some lengths to achieve consensus). Although there are 12 members of the FOMC, the chair of the Federal Reserve is the true controlling voice on this committee.

The Green, Blue, and Beige Books

In the media it is common to hear commentators speak of the beige book. The FOMC has three color bound books containing information valuable to them in their decision making. The green book contains the results of many statistical economic studies. The blue book contains values on current and projected monetary aggregates. The well-known beige book provides information on survey and talks with key business and financial institutions regarding the state of the economy. This beige book is the only one released to the public.

How Independent Is the Fed?

On the surface, the Federal Reserve is a highly independent government agency. Probably no other federal government institution enjoys greater formal independence. There are two types of central bank independence: **instrument independence** and **goal independence**. Goal independence is the ability of a central bank to establish monetary policy goals. Instrument independence is the ability of a central bank to set monetary policy instruments. Three factors contribute to the Federal Reserve's independence. First, the Fed is not directly dependent on congressional appropriations to finance its operations. The interest earned on the Federal Reserve's massive holdings of United States Treasury securities finances the bulk of the Fed's budget. These earnings are so significant that in recent years the Fed has had net earnings of about $20 billion. Thus, the Fed has a degree of discretionary budgetary authority not granted to other agencies.

Second, the president of the United States appoints the seven members of the Board of Governors of the Federal Reserve System to 14-year terms on a staggered biannual basis. Therefore, when appointees serve their entire term, any individual president can at most appoint four members to the board in an eight-year period. Under this constraint, even a reelected president would be unable to appoint a majority of the board until the end of his second term in office. The 14-year term affords greater autonomy to board members than is found almost anywhere else in government.

Third, the chairman of the Board of Governors presently serves a four-year term that is not necessarily concurrent with the presidential term. For example, Ronald Reagan did not have the opportunity to appoint a Fed chairman until the summer of 1983, almost three full years into the president's term. Stuck with another president's appointee for the first three years of his term, an incoming president is likely to feel strong pressure from the financial and banking community to retain the present chairman. The present chairman is a known quantity, and financial market participants often favor the known quantity to someone who may substantially change existing arrangement.

Although the Fed retains a relatively high degree of independence, it is not free from political pressure. The Governors know that what Congress gives, Congress can also take away. In the middle to late 1970s, Congress passed legislation that made the Fed more accountable to Congress for its actions. Politicians need favorable economic conditions to help them win reelection, lenders and the housing industry want low interest rates, and still other groups, such as retirees on fixed incomes, want low inflation. Given these pressures, the theory of bureaucratic behavior suggests that the Federal Reserve will do best for itself by avoiding conflict with these groups.

In addition, the Fed's desire to hold as much power as possible explains why it lobbies to gain greater regulatory control over banks. Often the Fed needs the support of the president to get certain items it deems appropriate through Congress. This need for an ally can have a bearing on the Fed's decisions. In the past, the Fed has been able to mobilize effectively the banking lobby to kill legislation that would have limited the Fed's power.

Structure and Independence of Foreign Central Banks

The European Central Bank (ECB) started operations in January 1999 and was established by the Maasricht Treaty. It controls monetary policy for the 12 euro countries that are currently members of the European Union, and its goal and instrument independence is consistent with the goal of maintaining price stability. It is considered the most independent of all central banks. In monetary policy decisions, no vote is taken and decisions are made based upon a consensus of the Governing Council, which is equivalent to the FOMC in the United States.

The degree of independence of central banks in other countries varies. The Bundesbank, the Central Bank in Germany, has the greatest degree of independence. The Bundesbank makes monetary policy, does not have to report to any part of the federal government, and has price stability as its sole stated primary function. The Bank of England is at the other extreme and is under the stated statutory authority of the government. Interest rates were set by the Chancellor of the Exchequer until May 1997, when the Bank of England was given responsibility for establishing interest rates. However, the Chancellor of the Exchequer sets the inflation target for the Bank of England. The government maintains the right to overrule the Bank "in extreme economic circumstances." Between these two extremes are the Bank of Japan and the Bank of Canada.

Beginning April 1998, the new Bank of Japan Law provided the Bank of Japan with increased goal and instrument independence with the monetary policy goal of price stability. However, the Ministry of Finance still maintains veto power over the budget for the bank. The stated objective of the Bank of Japan is to attain price stability.

Comparatively, the Bank of Canada jointly sets the inflation target for monetary policy with the government. Otherwise the Bank of Canada does effectively control monetary policy.

Should the Fed Be Independent?

Good arguments have been made both for retaining the Fed's independence and for restricting it. The strongest argument to be made for an independent Federal Reserve rests on the belief that subjecting the Fed to more political pressure would impart an **inflationary bias** to monetary policy. Recent research supports this argument by suggesting that economies of countries with more independent central banks tend to have lower rates of inflation without slowing down growth. The argument also exists that political independence is necessary to isolate economic decisions from the political goals of the reelection cycles.

However, critics of an independent central bank contend that it is undemocratic to have monetary policy controlled by a group that is not directly responsive to the electorate. Critics also argue that the fiscal policy of the legislative and executive branches could be better coordinated with monetary policy with a political accountability link.

■ Exercises

Exercise 1: Definitions and Terminology

Match the terms on the right with the definition or description on the left. Place the letter of the term in the blank provided next to the appropriate definition.

_____ 1. Reserves held at the discretion of the bank

_____ 2. Mandatory that all banks have these deposits at the Federal Reserve Bank

_____ 3. The buying and selling of bonds by the Fed for the purpose of monetary policy

_____ 4. Are required to be members of the Federal Reserve

_____ 5. A commercial banker from each Fed district serves on it

_____ 6. Its members are the seven Board of Governors and presidents of five Federal Reserve banks

_____ 7. The percentage of total bank deposits that must be held at the Fed or in vault cash

_____ 8. All members are appointed for 14-years terms by the president of the United States

_____ 9. The interest rate charged by the Fed to borrow from it

_____ 10. Tends to cause inflation just before an election to slower unemployment and interest rates

a.   discount rate

b.   excess reserves

c.   Federal Open Market Committee

d.   Federal Advisory Council

e.   open market operations

f.   political business cycle

g.   required reserve ratio

h.   required reserves

i.   national banks

j.   Board of Governor

k.   discount window

Exercise 2: Structure of the Federal Reserve System

The authors of the Federal Reserve Act of 1913 designed a decentralized central banking system that reflected their fears of centralized financial power. Today, this decentralization is still evident in the allocation of responsibilities and duties among the various Federal Reserve entities. Match the Federal Reserve entity to its responsibilities and duties given on the left by placing the appropriate letter in the space provided.

	Responsibilities and Duties	Federal Reserve Entity
_____ 1.	Clears checks	a. Board of Governors
_____ 2.	"Establishes" discount rate	b. Federal Open Market Committee
_____ 3.	Reviews discount rate	c. District Federal Reserve Banks
_____ 4.	Appointed by the president of the United States	
_____ 5.	Serve 14-year terms	
_____ 6.	Decides discount rate	
_____ 7.	Decides monetary policy	
_____ 8.	Evaluates bank merger applications	
_____ 9.	Determines margin requirements	
_____ 10.	Sets discount rate in practice	

Exercise 3: The Independence of the Federal Reserve

The Senate, on July 27, 1983, confirmed the nomination of Paul A. Volcker to a second four-year term as chairman of the Federal Reserve. The 84 to 16 vote was generally regarded as a strong vote of confidence in Volcker's efforts to bring inflation under control. Volcker, however, was not without his detractors. For example, Senator DeConcini (D-Ariz.) complained that the Fed chairman had "almost single-handedly caused one of the worst economic crises" in U.S. history by not checking the rise in interest rates. "We should be telling Mr. Volcker that in a democracy, we do not combat inflation by placing 12 million citizens on the rolls of the unemployed," DeConcini added.

Although congressional criticism of Fed policies, such as the remarks made by Senator DeConcini, is often intended for the representative's constituents, it does not go unnoticed at the Federal Reserve. After all, the independence of the Federal Reserve was created by congressional legislation, not Constitutional guarantee. Members of Congress have, at times, shown their displeasure of Fed policies by introducing bills threatening the removal of independence. Observers complain that members of the Federal Open Market Committee are so mindful of these threats that political pressures affect monetary policy decisions by constricting the set of feasible policy options considered by the FOMC.

A. How do statements such as those made by Senator DeConcini constrain Federal Reserve policy making?

_____

_____

_____

_____

B. Many proposals for reforming the Fed have been motivated by concerns that it has not been independent enough and has accommodated too much inflation. Defenders of Federal Reserve independence note that inflation in Germany, Switzerland, and the United States was lower than that in France, Italy, and Great Britain over the period 1960–1984. Speculate as to which countries have the relatively more independent central banks.[1]

_____

_____

Exercise 4: Should the Fed Be Independent?

A. List three arguments made by those who support a Federal Reserve that is independent of direct control from either the executive or legislative branches of government.

1. _____

2. _____

3. _____

---

[1] See King Banaian et al., Central Bank Independence: An International Comparison, Federal Reserve Bank of Dallas *Economic Review*, March 1983, 1–13.

B. List four arguments that favor a Federal Reserve that is brought under the control of Congress or the president.

1. _____

2. _____

3. _____

4. _____

■ Self-Test

Part A: Fill in the Blanks

1. The major reason that the Untied Stated did not have a central bank for so many years was because Americans feared _____.

2. The _____ resulted in such widespread losses to depositors that the pubic finally was convinced that a central bank was needed.

3. Each of the _____ Federal Reserve districts has one main Federal Reserve Bank.

4. The president of the _____ Federal Reserve is always a member of the FOMC.

5. The most frequently used method to enact monetary policy is with _____.

6. All _____ are required to be members of the Federal Reserve System.

7. Monetary policy is established by the _____.

8. In addition to control over open market operations and the discount rate, the Fed controls monetary policy with its control of _____.

9. Probably the most independent Central Bank in the industrialized world is in _____.

10. The strongest argument for Fed independence is to avoid excess influence from the _____.

11. Banks do not like to maintain reserves because these deposits do not _____.

12. Security purchases and sales directed by the FOMC are actually carried out at the trading desk of the Federal Reserve _____.

13. The most important factor that provides the Fed independence is a separate source of _____.

14. _____, in addition to independent funding, contributes to the Fed's independence.

15. Some argue that it is _____ for the Fed to be so independent.

Part B: True-False Questions

Circle whether the following statements are true (T) or false (F).

T   F   1.   The Federal Reserve Act, which created a central banking system with regional banks, reflected a compromise between traditional distrust of monied interests and a concern for eliminating bank panics.

T   F   2.   The three largest Federal Reserve banks in terms of assets—New York, Chicago, and San Francisco—hold approximately 50% of the assets in the Federal Reserve System.

T   F   3.   In practice, each of the 12 Federal Reserve banks sets the discount rate.

T   F   4.   Membership in the Federal Reserve has continued to rise since a low in 1947.

T   F   5.   Rising interest rates in the 1970s made Fed membership more costly, accelerating the withdrawal of banks from the systems.

T   F   6.   The Monetary Control Act of 1980 has reduced the distinction between member and nonmember banks.

T   F   7.   District Federal Reserve Banks essentially have no input regarding monetary policy decisions because the Board of Governors has sole responsibility for monetary policy.

T   F   8.   Open-market operations, believe it or not, were not envisioned as a monetary policy tool when the Federal Reserve was created.

T   F   9.   Past chairmen of the Board of Governors have typically had strong personalities and have tended to dominate policy decisions of the board and the FOMC.

T   F   10. The theory of bureaucratic behavior may explain why the Fed seems to be so preoccupied with the level of short-term interest rates.

T   F   11. The Fed continues to defend its current discount policy, although economic theory suggests that alternatives would improve monetary control. This apparent paradox is possibly explained by the theory of bureaucratic behavior.

T   F   12. The Fed's policy of delaying release of the FOMC directives is consistent with the theory of bureaucratic behavior.

T   F   13. The theory of bureaucratic behavior suggests that monetary policy reflects only political and bureaucratic concerns.

T   F   14. Placing the Fed under the control of the executive branch may lead to a monetary policy that is more responsive to political pressures.

T   F   15. Supporters of placing the Fed under control of the executive branch believe that the electorate should have more control over monetary policy.

Part C: Multiple-Choice Questions

Circle the appropriate answer.

1. The primary motivation behind the creation of the Federal Reserve System was the desire to

    (a) lessen the occurrence of bank panics.
    (b) stabilize short-term interest rates.
    (c) eliminate state regulated banks.
    (d) finance World War I.

2. The theory of bureaucratic behavior indicates that

    (a) government agencies attempt to increase their power and prestige.
    (b) government agencies attempt to avoid conflicts with the legislative and executive branch of government.
    (c) both (a) and (b) of the above are true.
    (d) neither (a) nor (b) of the above is true.

3. The regional Federal Reserve banks

    (a) "establish" the discount rate.
    (b) ration discount loans to banks.
    (c) clear checks.
    (d) do all of the above.
    (e) do only (a) and (b) of the above.

4. Although the regional Federal Reserve banks "establish" the discount rate, in truth, the discount rate is determined by

    (a) Congress.
    (b) the president of the United States
    (c) the Board of Governors.
    (d) the Federal Reserve Advisory Council.

5. A majority of the Federal Open Market Committee is comprised of

    (a) the 12 Federal Reserve bank presidents.
    (b) the five voting Federal Reserve bank presidents.
    (c) the seven members of the Board of Governors.
    (d) none of the above.

6. Monetary policy is determined by

    (a) the Board of Governors.
    (b) the Federal Reserve banks from each district.
    (c) the Federal Open Market Committee.
    (d) the Federal Reserve Advisory Council.

7. Power within the Federal Reserve is divided between
    (a) banking, agriculture, labor, industry, and public interests.
    (b) geographic regions.
    (c) the public and private sectors.
    (d) all of the above.

8. Although the Fed enjoys a relatively high degree of independence for a government agency, it feels political pressure from the president and Congress because
    (a) Fed members desire reappointment every three years.
    (b) the Fed must go to Congress each year for operating revenues.
    (c) Congress could limit Fed power through legislation.
    (d) of all of the above.
    (e) of only (b) and (c) of the above.

9. The theory of bureaucratic behavior may help explain why the Fed
    (a) remains concerned about short-term interest rates.
    (b) reports more than one monetary aggregate.
    (c) lobbied for the Monetary Control Act of 1980.
    (d) does all of the above.

10. Supporters of keeping the Federal Reserve independent from both the executive and legislative branch of government believe that a less independent Fed would
    (a) pursue overly expansionary monetary policies.
    (b) be more likely to pursue policies consistent with the political business cycle.
    (c) ignore short-run problems in favor of longer-run concerns.
    (d) do only (a) and (b) of the above.

11. Which of the following are entities of the Federal Reserve System?
    (a) Federal Reserve Banks
    (b) The FDIC
    (c) The Board of Advisors
    (d) All of the above are Federal Reserve entities.
    (e) Only (a) and (b) of the above are Federal Reserve entities.

12. According to the textbook, the Fed is
    (a) remarkably free of the political pressures that influence other government agencies.
    (b) more responsive to the political pressures that influence other government agencies.
    (c) severely constrained in its policy making by the congressional threat to reduce Fed independence.
    (d) both (a) and (c) of the above.

13. Each Federal Reserve district bank is owned by
    (a) the citizens of that district.
    (b) the Federal Reserve Board.
    (c) the banks from that district that are members of the Federal Reserve.
    (d) the U.S. government.

14. Each Federal Reserve Bank owner
     (a) receives a fixed dividend of 6% on its shares each year.
     (b) has a claim on the earnings of the Federal Reserve Bank.
     (c) has a vote on major decisions of the Federal Reserve Bank.
     (d) has only (a) and (b) of the above.

15. One reason the New York Federal Reserve Bank plays a special role in the Federal Reserve System is because
     (a) the president of the bank is a permanent member of the FOMC.
     (b) it is close to the major security exchanges and can thus make trades quicker.
     (c) there are more banks in this district than in all the other districts combined.
     (d) most chairmen of the Board of Governors were at one time employed by this bank.

Part D: Short Answer Questions

1. What legislative changes by Congress have made the Fed more accountable to the political system?

     _____

     _____

2. What is the primary relationship between central bank independence throughout the world and its control of monetary policy goals?

     _____

     _____

3. The directors of Federal Reserve district banks are classified as either A, B, or C. What requirements exist for being in each of these three classes? What are the differences?

     _____

     _____

■ Answers to Chapter 9

Exercise 1

1.	b	6.	c
2.	h	7.	g
3.	e	8.	j
4.	i	9.	a
5.	d	10.	f

Exercise 2

1.	c	6.	b
2.	c	7.	b
3.	a	8.	a, c
4.	a	9.	a
5.	a	10.	a

Exercise 3

A. Such statements put the Fed on notice that if its policies become too unpopular with the electorate, the Fed risks losing its coveted independence.

B. Germany, Switzerland, and the United States have central banks that are relatively more independent than their counterparts in France, Italy, and Great Britain. This finding is consistent with the view that political pressure imparts an inflationary bias to monetary policy.

Exercise 4

Part A

1. Greater focus on long-run objectives

2. Less pressure to finance deficits and less pressure to pursue inflationary policies

3. More likely to pursue policies in the public interest even if politically unpopular

Part B

1. Greater accountability. If the Fed makes mistakes there is no way of voting them out, thus the system is undemocratic.

2. Coordination of fiscal and monetary policy would be easier.

3. President is ultimately held responsible for economic policy, yet he does not have control over monetary policy, an important element determining economic health.

4. Lack of evidence indicating that an independent Fed performs well.

Self-Test

Part A

1. centralized power
2. 1907 bank panic
3. 12
4. New York
5. open market operations
6. national banks
7. Federal Open Market Committee
8. reserve requirements
9. European Central Banks
10. Political re-election cycle
11. earn interest
12. Bank of New York
13. income
14. long appointments to office
15. undemocratic

Part B

1.	T	6.	T	11.	T
2.	T	7.	F	12.	T
3.	F	8.	T	13.	F
4.	F	9.	T	14.	T
5.	T	10.	T	15.	T

Part C

1.	a	6.	c	11.	a
2.	c	7.	d	12.	a
3.	d	8.	c	13.	c
4.	c	9.	d	14.	a
5.	c	10.	d	15.	a

Part D

1. In 1975, Congress passed legislation that the Fed must announce its objective for the growth rates of the monetary aggregates. In 1978, Congress started requiring the Fed to explain how these objectives are consistent with the economic plans of the president of the United States. In 1994, it began to reveal the FOMC directive immediately after each FOMC meeting. In November 2007, Chairman Bernanke announced major enhancements to Fed communication regarding the frequency and horizon of forecasts. There have been recent pressures for the Fed to be less secretive in its deliberations on monetary policy and to put them under the budgetary control of Congress.

2. The more independent the central bank, then generally the lower is the level of inflation. The price stability is not done at the expense of economic performance. Countries with independent central banks are no more likely to have high unemployment or greater output fluctuations than less independent central banks.

3. Class A directors are professional bankers. Class B directors are prominent leaders from industry, labor, agriculture, or the consumer sector. Class C directors are appointed by the Board of Governors and cannot be officers, employees, or stockholders of banks. Up until 2010, all nine directors appointed the president of the bank, but the Dodd-Frank legislation in July 2010 excluded the three class A directors from involvement in choosing the president of the bank

Chapter 10
Conduct of Monetary Policy:
Tools, Goals, Strategy, and Tactics

■ Chapter Learning Goals

By the end of this chapter, you should

1. Understand the Federal Reserve's Balance Sheet.
2. Know the three tools the Federal Reserve uses to conduct monetary policy.
3. Understand how changes in the three tools of monetary policy impact the money supply and interest rates.
4. Know the goals of the Federal Reserve in conducting monetary policy.
5. Know the history of the Fed's monetary policy procedures.

■ Chapter Summary

This chapter begins by presenting the basic balance sheet of the Federal Reserve and the tools that the Fed uses to implement monetary policy. Following presentation of the monetary policy tools, the chapter presents the important goals that the Federal Reserve attempts to achieve through its conduct of monetary policy and regulatory duties. The general operating strategy employed by the Federal Reserve to achieve these goals is presented in the second part of the chapter. The third section ties together the first two sections by examining the Fed's past policy procedures. This historical perspective provides important insights when it comes to assessing current and future monetary policy actions. Concluding this chapter is a brief section that discusses the Fed's ability to control the money supply.

The Federal Reserve's Balance Sheet

Monetary policy actions by the Federal Reserve affect its balance sheet. The text presents a simplified balance sheet that is comprised of assets and liabilities. The liabilities on the balance sheet are (1) **currency in circulation**, which is currency outside of banks, and (2) **reserves**, currency held at banks plus deposits held at the Federal Reserve. These liabilities are also called monetary liabilities of the Federal Reserve. Increases in these liabilities cause an increase in the money supply. Reserves are classified as either reserves that the Fed requires banks to hold, **required reserves**, or reserves held in excess of required amount, **excess reserves**. Since 2008, the Fed has paid interest on reserves at a level that set a fixed amount below federal funds target rate. The percentage of all deposits that banks are required to hold in reserve is called the **required reserve ratio** and is currently 10%.

The liabilities of the Federal Reserve plus the monetary liabilities of the U.S. Treasury, Treasury currency, and coins in circulation, make up the monetary base.

The assets of the Federal Reserve are (1) government securities and (2) discount loans. The Fed holds government securities issued by the U.S. Treasury. A purchase of Treasury securities increases the Fed holdings and increases the money supply. Discount loans are made by the Federal Reserve to the banking system. Increases in the amount of discount loans provided by the Fed results in an increase in the money supply. The **discount rate** is the interest rate charged on discount loans.

The Market for Reserves and the Federal Funds Rate

Changes in reserves affect another important interest rate, the **federal funds rate**. The federal funds rate is the interest rate charged on overnight loans made between banks. The Fed sets a target federal funds rate to conduct its monetary policy. As with the supply and demand for bonds covered in Chapter 4, there is a supply and demand function for reserves. The federal funds rate is determined by the intersection point of the supply and demand curves. Demand is based on the quantity of reserves that banks must hold through these required reserves plus any excess reserves they choose to hold. The supply for reserves is determined by the Fed. As the Fed makes changes in the supply of reserves they can move along the demand curve and change the total amount of reserves in the system. The tools used by the Fed to shift the supply and demand curves are discussed in the following section.

Tools of Monetary Policy and How These Tools Affect the Federal Funds Rate

The Fed has three basic tools that are available to conduct monetary policy and affect the Fed funds rate. The most important is **open market operations**. These operations involve the buying and selling of bonds to control the amount of reserves in the system. Purchasing bonds increases the amount of reserves and leads to an expansion of the monetary base and the money supply. Selling bonds has the opposite effect. The bonds used in open market operations are those issued by the U.S. Treasury and government agencies. This tool has the following advantages: (1) They are under the control of the Fed; (2) implementation is flexible and precise; (3) wrong decisions can be easily reversed; and (4) they can be implemented quickly with no administrative delays.

Open market operations fall into two categories: (1) dynamic open market operations, which attempt to change the amount of reserves, and (2) defensive open market operations, which are used to balance changes in other factors that impact reserves.

Open market operations are performed by the Federal Reserve Bank of New York. Traders at the bank communicate and trade with the primary dealers of government securities. Temporary and permanent transactions occur between the bank and the dealers. Two types of temporary transactions are used: (1) repurchase agreements or repos and (2) matched sale-purchase transactions or reverse repos. A repo is a transaction where the Fed purchases securities with the condition that the seller will buy the securities back in 1 to 15 days. A reverse repo is a transaction in which the Fed sells securities with the condition that the buyer will sell them back to the Fed in a short period of time.

A second tool is the discount policy, which is the process of banks obtaining loans from the Fed to meet their reserve requirements or to deal with a temporary liquidity problem. The loans are usually classified into one of three categories; (1) primary credit, (2) secondary credit, or (3) seasonal credit. Primary credit is discount lending offered to banks at the discount rate, which is about a percent higher than the federal funds rate. It is a source of liquidity for banks and is also known as a standing lending facility because healthy banks can borrow whatever is needed. Secondary credit represents loanable funds offered to banks experiencing financial difficulties. The interest rate charged for secondary credit is one-half percent higher than the discount rate. Seasonal credit is lending to banks operating in agricultural and vacation areas that experience seasonal fluctuations in customer deposits.

Discount lending was originally established under the Federal Reserve System to provide liquidity as a **lender of last resort** to prevent financial panics. The lender of last resort function provided by the Federal Reserve System creates a moral hazard problem by limiting financial institutions' risk of failure from liquidity issues even in the presence of increased risk exposure by institutions. Consequently, the Fed must consider the costs of moral hazard against the benefit of reduced chances of financial panic in deciding how frequently to act as a lender of last resort.

The third tool is to change the reserve requirements. Increasing the percentage of deposits that make up required reserves reduces banks' excess reserves and the money supply. The opposite occurs with a decrease in reserve requirements. This tool is rarely used because it has the potential for creating major liquidity problems for banks that do not have large excess reserves. Reserve requirements on all checkable deposits plus automatic transfer savings (ATS), NOW and super-NOW accounts, and non-interest bearing checking accounts were set at 3% of the first $45.4 million and 10% for all checking deposits over this amount as of late 2003. Under normal circumstances the reserve requirement can be adjusted from 8% to 14%.

The importance of these tools and the ability of the Fed to use these tools to meet economic goals cannot be overemphasized. Without the intervention of the Fed after the stock market crash on October 19, 1987, and after the destruction of the World Trade Center on September 11, 2001, the U.S. financial system could have led our country into an economic disaster.

The Goals of Monetary Policy

The chapter presents six basic goals that are most often mentioned as objectives of monetary policy: (1) high employment, (2) economic growth, (3) price stability, (4) interest-rate stability, (5) financial-market stability, and (6) foreign exchange market stability.

Price Stability

Of these goals, **price stability** has received more attention in recent years and has risen to the point where many consider it the most important goal of monetary policy. Higher rates of inflation since the mid-1960s have focused greater attention on the costs of price volatility. An inflationary environment makes planning for the future difficult and may strain a country's social fabric due to its effect on the distribution of wealth. Inflation makes it harder for businesses to plan for the future. It creates social conflict due to the inequality of real earnings as different groups compete for wage increase. Extreme price instability is called hyperinflation. A commonly used approach to monetary policy is to use an inflation or money supply measure as a **nominal anchor**. A nominal anchor is a variable value that the Fed tries to maintain through the use of its money supply tools. Attempting to retain that anchor value assists to give the Fed direction in its decision making and keeps the Fed from accidently straying from the price stability objective.

High Employment

The Employment Act of 1946 and the Humphrey-Hawkins Act of 1978 commit the government to promoting high employment. By high employment, economists mean a level of unemployment consistent with labor market equilibrium. This level of unemployment is the **natural rate of unemployment.** Economists often estimate the natural rate of unemployment to between 5% and 6%, although there are many who disagree. This natural rate is acceptable because some unemployment will always exist from **frictional** and **structural** factors. Frictional unemployment arises from matching the right person to the right job, and structural unemployment is due to a mismatch of job skills with jobs available.

Economic Growth

This goal is to increase the level of productivity in the economy. The approach is to get firms to invest and consumers to save. Increased investment will create more jobs and increase the standard of living. Saving makes more funds available for firms to borrow and invest.

Interest Rate Stability

The problems created by frequently changing interest rates are similar to those with inflation. Uncertainty increases about future costs, and both firms and consumers are reluctant to make long-term commitments. Productivity will decline increasing unemployment and aggregate earnings.

Stability of Financial Markets

Financial crises can interfere with the ability of financial markets to channel funds to people with productive investment opportunities. This result causes production to be lower than what could be achieved with optimal allocation of resources.

Dollar Stabilization

In the mid-1980s, inflation having declined to an acceptable level, the Fed began to pay more attention to stabilizing the value of the dollar. Exchange rate fluctuations have a relatively large impact on the domestic economy now that international financial and goods markets have become more integrated. The Federal Reserve no longer treats the United States as a closed economy. When deciding the course of monetary policy, the Fed pays careful attention to the expected change in the value of the dollar.

Conflicts Among Goals

Although achieving all the above-mentioned goals would be highly desirable, conflicts arise between goals in the short run. Higher employment, or interest rate stability, may mean higher inflation in the short run. Because expansionary monetary policies initially tend to stimulate aggregate output and employment and lower interest rates, such policies appear attractive at first. However, an expansionary monetary policy will lead to inflationary pressures if continued for long. Thus, the Federal Reserve faces difficult trade-offs and must weigh the benefits and costs of each action if it is to promote economic well-being.

Fed Targets

Because the Fed's control over policy goals is imprecise, the Fed employs an **intermediate targeting strategy** to guide monetary policy. The Fed judges its actions by observing the behavior of an intermediate target, such as a monetary aggregate. The intermediate target provides a readily available proxy for the Fed's goals that it manipulates through variations in its **instrument** or **operating targets**. In turn, the Fed changes its operating target, say, reserve aggregates such as the monetary base, through use of its policy tools, primarily open-market operations.

The Fed has a choice between targeting a monetary aggregate or an interest rate, such as the federal funds interest rate. Here again, the Federal Reserve faces a trade-off. If it targets a monetary aggregate, interest rate volatility is likely to increase, and if it targets the federal funds rate, it loses control over the money supply.

Inflation Targeting

Given the uncertain relationship between monetary targets and goal variables, countries such as New Zealand, Canada, the United Kingdom, Sweden, and Finland have recently adopted inflation targeting as their policy strategy. There are several advantages to using inflation as the target variable. One advantage is that authorities have more flexibility in the variables they use because they are not targeting a single measure. Another benefit is that the public understands the inflation variable and authorities can easily communicate with the public. The single variable of inflation also provides reasonable accountability of the central bank to achieving their long-term goal of price stability.

Inflation targeting also has its critics. There are four disadvantages attached to the inflation target model: (1) the delay in receiving the inflation information, (2) too much rigidity, (3) potential for increased output fluctuation, and (4) low economic growth.

Central Banks' Response to Asset-Price Bubbles: Lessons from the 2007–2009 Financial Crisis

History has shown that economies are routinely subjected to asset-price bubbles. There are two main drivers of asset-price bubbles: credit and irrational exuberance. For credit driven bubbles, easy credit is used to purchase particular assets and thereby raises asset prices. The increase in prices encourages further lending for these assets because it increases the value of the collateral or raises the value of assets at financial institutions. This feedback loop can generate a bubble in which asset prices rise well above their fundamental value, as the recent 2007–2009 financial crisis demonstrated. When the bubble bursts, the effects are severe. The subsequent decline in credit (deleveraging) and fall in business and household spending endangers the operation of the financial system as a whole. In comparison, bubbles caused by irrational exuberance pose less risk to the overall financial system, as the tech stock bubble of the late 1990s demonstrated.

There are conflicting opinions on whether a central bank should respond to bubbles. Because asset bubbles are nearly impossible to identify, those against intervention (including the Fed under Alan Greenspan) argue that it is unlikely that a central bank can better identify a bubble than other (and typically better compensated) market participants. This argument applies strongly to irrational-exuberance-caused bubbles and less so to credit-driven bubbles. Monetary policy should not be used to prick bubbles due to potential harmful effects of such actions. **Macroprudential regulation**, regulatory policy to affect what is happening in credit markets, may be a useful tool for credit-driven bubbles.

Choosing the Policy Instrument

Once the monetary target has been determined, whether it be a monetary aggregate or inflation, the central bank must establish a working policy as to how to control the variable and achieve long-run price stability and the economic balance desired for the economy. The first thing the bank must establish is the **policy instrument** (also called an **operating instrument**) that responds to the central bank's tools. This policy instrument is may be reserve aggregates, or it could be interest rates. The next step is to identify the **intermediate target** that is a variable that the policy instrument responds to. Frequently a measure of the money supply such as M2 could be used for this purpose. Changes in M2 could be directly linked to an expected change in nonborrowed reserves. The specific policy instrument chosen by the central bank must meet four criteria. It must be (1) observable and measurable, (2) controllable, and (3) have a predictable effect on the goals.

Nonconventional Monetary Policy Tools and Quantitative Easing

Although in normal times conventional monetary policy tools, which expand the money supply and lower interest rates, are enough to stabilize the economy, when the economy experiences a full-scale financial crisis like the one we have recently experienced, conventional monetary policy tools cannot do the job for two reasons. First, the financial system seizes up to such an extent that it becomes unable to allocate capital to productive uses, and so investment spending and the economy collapse along the lines we discussed in Chapter 8. Second, the negative shock to the economy can lead to the **zero-lower-bound problem**, in which the central bank is unable to lower the policy interest rate further because it has hit a floor of zero, as occurred at the end of 2008. The zero-lower-bound problem occurs because people can always earn more from holding bonds than holding cash, and therefore nominal interest rates cannot be negative. For both these reasons, central banks need non-interest-rate tools, known as **nonconventional monetary policy tools** to stimulate the economy. These nonconventional monetary policy tools take three forms: (1) liquidity provision, (2) asset purchases, and (3) commitment to future monetary policy actions.

■ Exercises

Exercise 1: Definitions and Terminology

Match the terms on the right with the definition or description on the left. Place the letter of the term in the blank provided next to the appropriate definition.

_____ 1.	Private firms that are used by the Fed to carry out open market operations	a. defensive open market operations
_____ 2.	Open market sale of bonds that will be reversed normally within 15 days	b. dynamic open market operations
_____ 3.	Purchases that lead to an expansion of the Fed's balance sheet and the monetary base	c. free reserves
_____ 4	The buying and selling of bonds by the Fed to cause changes in the money supply.	d. federal funds rate
_____ 5.	Excess reserves minus discount-window loans	e. quantitative easing (QE)
_____ 6.	The level of unemployment considered to be full employment	f. natural rate of unemployment
_____ 7.	An extreme condition of price instability	g. open market operations
_____ 8.	Variables the Fed tries to change that have a direct impact on prices and employment	h. primary dealers
_____ 9.	Variables the Fed tries to change directly through use of its tools of monetary policy	i. real bills doctrine
_____ 10.	Open market operations intended to change the level of reserves	j. reserves
_____ 11.	Open market operations intended to offset other factors that influence reserves	k. hyperinflation
_____ 12.	A principle that says making discount loans for "productive" purposes will not be inflationary	l. policy instrument
_____ 13.	A major liability of the Federal Reserve	m. repurchase agreement
_____ 14.	The cost to a bank or borrowing free reserves	n. intermediate target
_____ 15.	The sum of reserves and currency in circulation	o. monetary base
_____ 16.	Currency held outside of banks	p. required reserve ratio
_____ 17.	Reserves held in excess of required levels	q. excess reserves
_____ 18.	The percentage of all deposits that banks are required to hold in reserve	r. currency in circulation
		s. asset-price bubble
		t. zero-lower-bound problem

_____ 19. Pronounced increased of asset prices away from fundamental
values

_____ 20. Inability to lower the policy interest rate further because it
has hit a floor of zero

Exercise 2: Goals of Monetary Policy

A. Although the Federal Reserve System tends to be intentionally vague about the exact policy goals it may
be pursuing at any one time, Federal Reserve personnel stress six basic goals more often than any
others. These goals include:

1. _____

2. _____

3. _____

4. _____

5. _____

6. _____

B. What do economists mean by "full" employment? Do they mean zero unemployment?

_____

_____

C. What is the natural rate of unemployment?

_____

_____

Exercise 3: Intermediate and Operating Targets

Although there is some ambiguity as to whether a particular variable is better categorized as an
intermediate target or a policy instrument, list below those variables generally thought to be in each
category.

A. Intermediate targets

1. _____

2. _____

B.Policy instrument

   1. _____

   2. _____

Exercise 4: Criteria for Choosing Intermediate Targets

Selecting an intermediate target requires careful thought by members of the Federal Open Market Committee. The wrong choice can mean adverse consequences for the economy. Debate has tended to center around the choice between targeting a monetary aggregate or an interest rate. List the three criteria for choosing one variable as an intermediate target over another.

1. _____

2. _____

3. _____

Exercise 5: Discount Policy

What are the three categories of discount loans?

_____

_____

_____

Exercise 6: Nonconventional Monetary Policy

What are the three nonconventional monetary policy tools?

_____

_____

_____

■ Self-Test

Part A: Fill in the Blanks

1. The Employment Act of 1946 and the Humphrey-Hawkin's Act commit the U.S. government to promoting _____.

2. Current estimates place the natural rate of unemployment at around _____.

3. The goal of _____ often conflicts with the goal of high employment.

4. Variables that have a direct effect on employment and the price level are often called _____.

5. There are two different types of targets, interest rates and _____.

6. A good intermediate target must be measurable, _____ by the Fed, and it must have a predictable effect on the goal.

7. When the Fed provides loans to banks when no one else will, the bank is called the _____.

8. When the Fed was created, changing the _____ was the primary tool of monetary policy.

9. The two types of asset-price bubbles are _____ and _____.

10. In July of 1993, the Fed abandoned using any _____.

11. Rules for use of the discount window are frequently referred to as _____.

12. If the Fed buys bonds to lower interest rates, the money supply _____ and the money supply curve shifts to the _____.

13. One problem with measurement of the interest rate is that the Fed is most concerned with the _____ rate of interest, which is difficult to measure because of not knowing the _____ rate of inflation.

14. The Plaza Agreement and the Louvre Accord were intended to _____ the exchange rate between the major industrialized countries currencies.

15. Some businesses hire _____ for the purpose of monitoring Fed activities and trying to project the Fed's long- and short-run goals.

16. The liabilities held on the Federal Reserve's balance sheet are _____ and _____.

17. The assets held on the Federal Reserve's balance sheet are _____ and _____.

18. The percentage of all deposits that banks are required to hold in reserve is called the _____.

Part B: True-False Questions

Circle whether the following statements are true (T) or false (F).

T F 1. The Federal Reserve desires interest rate stability because it reduces the uncertainty of planning for the future.

T F 2. The Federal Reserve attempts to get the unemployment rate to zero because any unemployment is wasteful and inefficient.

T F 3. The natural rate of unemployment is zero.

T F 4. The discount rate is the Fed's preferred policy instrument.

T F 5. An advantage of an intermediate targeting strategy is that it provides the Fed with more timely information regarding the effect of monetary policy.

T F 6. If the Fed targets a monetary aggregate, it is likely to lose control over the interest rate because of fluctuations in the money demand function.

T F   7. A monetary policy is the best tool for dealing with asset-price bubbles.

T F   8. The most important characteristic a variable must have to be useful as an intermediate target is that it must have a predictable impact on a goal.

T F   9. The Fed may lend to individual and corporation under "unusual and exigent circumstance" to ensure the health of the financial system.

T F   10. Open market operations did not play an important policy role in the Federal Reserve System until about the 1960s.

T F   11. The passage of the Banking Act of 1935 limited the Fed's ability to alter reserve requirements by requiring it to secure presidential approval.

T F   12. Treasury influence over the Fed was reduced when the Fed and Treasury came to an agreement known as the "Accord."

T F   13. The difference between excess reserves and discount loans is known as free reserves.

T F   14. The Fed's use of free reserves as a guide to monetary policy in the 1960s proved a failure because it led to procyclical monetary growth.

T F   15. Although the Fed professed an interest in stabilizing interest rates, its actions during the 1960s and 1970s indicates that the Fed seemed to be preoccupied with stabilizing money growth.

T F   16. The discount rate is the rate charged on overnight loans between banks.

T F   17. A repo is a transaction in which the Fed sells securities with the condition that the buyer will sell them back to the Fed in a short period of time.

T F   18. Secondary credit represents loanable funds offered to banks experiencing financial difficulties.

Part C: Multiple-Choice Questions

Circle the appropriate answer.

1. Even if the Fed could completely control the money supply, not everyone would be happy with monetary policy because
    (a) the Fed is asked to achieve many goals, some of which are incompatible with one another.
    (b) the goals that are stressed by the Fed do not include high employment, making labor unions a vocal critic of Fed policies.
    (c) the Fed places primary emphasis on exchange rate stability, often to the detriment of domestic conditions.
    (d) its mandate requires it to keep Treasury security prices high.

2. Because timely information on the price level and economic growth is frequently unavailable, the Fed has adopted a strategy of
    (a) targeting the exchange rate because the Fed has the ability to control this variable.
    (b) targeting the price of gold because it is closely related to economic activity.
    (c) using an intermediate target such as a monetary aggregate.
    (d) stabilizing the CPI because the Fed has a high degree of control over the CPI.

3. Which of the following are potential operating instruments?
    (a) Monetary base
    (b) Nonborrowed reserves
    (c) Federal funds interest rate
    (d) Nonborrowed monetary base
    (e) All of the above

4. Fluctuations in money demand will cause the Fed to lose control over a monetary aggregate if the Fed emphasizes
    (a) a monetary aggregate target.
    (b) an interest-rate target.
    (c) a nominal GNP target.
    (d) all of the above.

5. Although the Fed professed to target monetary aggregates in the 1970s, its behavior indicates that it actually targeted
    (a) exchange rates.
    (b) nominal GNP.
    (c) nominal interest rates.
    (d) the monetary base.

6. Most economists question the desirability of targeting real interest rates by pointing out that
    (a) the Fed does not have direct control over real interest rates.
    (b) changes in real interest rates have little effect on economic activity.
    (c) real interest rates are extremely difficult to measure.
    (d) All of the above are correct.
    (e) Only (a) and (c) of the above are correct.

7. The Fed's policy of keeping interest rates low to help the Treasury finance World War I by rediscounting eligible paper caused
    (a) inflation to accelerate.
    (b) aggregate output to decline sharply.
    (c) the Fed to rethink the efficacy of the real bills doctrine.
    (d) both (a) and (b) of the above.
    (e) both (a) and (c) of the above.

8. The Fed added to the problems it helped create in the early 1930s by
    (a) raising the discount rate in 1936–1937.
    (b) raising reserve requirements in 1936–1937.
    (c) contracting the monetary base in 1936–1937.
    (d) expanding the monetary base in 1936–1937.

9. Which of the following is the "right tool" for reigning in credit bubbles?
    (a) irrational exuberance
    (b) monetary policy
    (c) macroprudential regulation
    (d) central bank intervention

10. The Fed's policy of "leaning against the wind" through targeting free reserves and the federal funds interest rate actually proved to be
    (a) anticipated.
    (b) procyclical.
    (c) neutral.
    (d) stabilizing.

11. Upward movements in interest rates
    (a) create hostility toward the Fed and lead to demands that the Fed's power be curtailed.
    (b) make it more difficult for construction firms to plan how many houses to build.
    (c) increase consumers' willingness to purchase houses.
    (d) do all of the above.
    (e) do only (a) and (b) of the above.

12. Chairman Bernanke's writings suggest that
    (a) inflation targeting should only be used in extreme circumstances.
    (b) transparency of central bank objectives is important.
    (c) asset-price bubbles are a thing of the past.
    (d) Only (a) and (b) of the above are true.

13. If the Fed was interested in conducting defensive open market operations, they would
    (a) sell bonds in the open market.
    (b) buy bonds in the open market.
    (c) engage in a match sale-purchase transaction.
    (d) enter into a repurchase agreement.

14. The Fed can affect the volume of loans at the discount window by controlling
    (a) the free reserves.
    (b) the discount rate.
    (c) the quantity of loans given.
    (d) all of the above.
    (e) only (b) and (c).

15. The European System of Central Banks, which exist under the European Union, sets as its primary objective
    (a) high levels of employment.
    (b) stabilization of exchange rates.
    (c) price stability.
    (d) a balance among employment, exchange rate stabilization, and price stability.

16. Defensive open market operations are used to
    (a) change the amount of reserves.
    (b) balance changes in other factors that impact reserves.
    (c) raise interest rates.
    (d) lower interest rates.

17. Primary credit
    (a) is discount lending offered to banks at the discount rate.
    (b) represents loanable funds offered to banks experiencing financial difficulties.
    (c) is lending to banks operating in agricultural and vacation areas that experience seasonal fluctuations in customer deposits.
    (d) None of the above

18. The lender of last resort function provided by the Federal Reserve System creates a(n) _____ problem by limiting financial institutions' risk of failure from liquidity issues even in the presence of increased risk exposure by institutions.
    (a) monetary policy
    (b) credit
    (c) reserves
    (d) moral hazard

Part D: Short Answer Questions

1. List and define the assets and liabilities included on the Federal Reserve's balance sheet.

    _____

    _____

    _____

2. The existence of the FDIC appears to make the lender-of-last-resort function of the Fed not necessary. This assumption does not hold true. What are the two reasons for the continued need for the lender-of-last-resort function?

    A. _____

    B. _____

3. Why is the tool of changing reserve requirement rarely used by the Fed?

    _____

    _____

4. Explain how the money supply is increased through the process of the Fed purchasing bonds in the open market.

_____

_____

_____

_____

5. What are the types of temporary transactions that the Federal Reserve uses in coordination with dealers in performing open market operations?

_____

_____

6. Why was discount lending created by the Federal Reserve?

_____

_____

■ Answers to Chapter 10

Exercise 1

1.	h	7.	k	13.	j	19.	s
2.	m	8.	n	14.	d	20.	t
3.	e	9.	l	15.	o		
4.	g	10.	b	16.	r		
5.	c	11.	a	17.	q		
6.	f	12.	i	18.	p		

Exercise 2

Part A

1. high employment

2. economic growth

3. price stability

4. interest rate stability

5. stability in financial markets

6. stability in foreign exchange markets

Part B

Economists do not believe that it would be desirable to lower the unemployment rate to zero. By "full" unemployment, economists mean the natural rate of unemployment—the level of unemployment consistent with labor market equilibrium.

Part C

The natural rate of unemployment is an unemployment level greater than zero that is consistent with full employment where the supply of labor equals the demand for labor.

Exercise 3

Part A

1. monetary aggregates such as M1, M2, or M3

2. short- or long-term interest rates

Part B

1. reserve aggregates such as reserves, nonborrowed reserves, or the monetary base

2. interest rates such as the federal funds rate or the T-bill rate

Exercise 4

1. measurability

2. controllability

3. the ability to predictably affect goals

Exercise 5

1. primary credit

2. secondary credit

3. seasonal credit

Exercise 6

1. liquidity provision

2. asset purchases

3. commitment to future monetary policy actions

Self-Test

Part A

1. high employment
2. 5 to 6%
3. price stability
4. intermediate targets
5. monetary aggregates
6. controllable
7. lender of last resort
8. discount rate
9. credit & irrational exuberance
10. monetary aggregates
11. moral suasion
12. increases, right
13. real, expected
14. stabilize
15. Fed watchers
16. currency in circulation, reserves
17. government securities, discount loans
18. required reserve ratio

Part B

1.	T	7.	F	13.	T
2.	F	8.	T	14.	T
3.	F	9.	T	15.	F
4.	F	10.	F	16.	F
5.	T	11.	F	17.	F
6.	T	12.	T	18.	T

Part C

1.	a	7.	e	13.	d
2.	c	8.	b	14.	e
3.	e	9.	c	15.	c
4.	b	10.	b	16.	b
5.	c	11.	e	17.	a
6.	e	12.	b	18.	d

Part D

1. The liabilities on the balance sheet are (1) currency in circulation, which is currency outside of banks, and (2) reserves, currency held at banks plus deposits held at the Federal Reserve.

    The assets of the Federal Reserve are (1) government securities and (2) discount loans.

2. A. The FDIC does not have adequate funds to cover the needs if a large number of banks fail.

    B. Because of the deposits above $100,000 are not covered by FDIC insurance, there are more than $300 billion of deposits that are not covered by the FDIC.

3. Raising the reserve requirement can create immediate liquidity problems for banks that do not have any or many excess reserves. The Fed would partially defeat its purpose because of the need that would arise for additional discount loans to help banks with their liquidity problem. Changing reserves would also create uncertainty for banks and increase the difficulty of managing their liquidity.

4. When the Fed purchases bonds, the seller of the bonds deposits the money in their account at the bank thus increasing the bank's liabilities. This deposit also increases the reserves of the bank. This placing of deposits and reserves in the system through the Fed purchase results in an increase in-the-money supply.

5. Two types of temporary transactions are used: (1) repurchase agreements or repos and (2) matched sale-purchase transactions or reverse repos. A repo is a transaction where the Fed purchases securities with the condition that the seller will buy the securities back in 1 to 15 days. A reverse repo is a transaction in which the Fed sells securities with the condition that the buyer will sell them back to the Fed in a short period of time.

6. Discount lending was originally established under the Federal Reserve System to provide liquidity as a lender of last resort to prevent financial panics.

Chapter 11
The Money Markets

■ Chapter Learning Goals

By the end of this chapter, you should

1. Know why the money markets exist.

2. Identify the major participants in the money markets and why they are active in this market.

3. Be able to list the major securities that are traded in the money market.

4. Know the different features of the various money market securities.

■ Chapter Summary

This chapter provides facts about the operation of the money markets, the participants in that market, and the type of securities sold in this market. The money market is an extremely active market and is important to businesses, the government, and individuals.

The Money Markets

The term **money markets** is used to refer to the markets where large denomination, low risk, short-term financial securities are traded. The trading of these securities is done through electronic communication (phone and computer) among those wishing to buy or sell these securities. Money market transactions are usually in very large amounts (in excess of $1 million) and very few individual investors participate directly in this market; thus it is also referred to a **wholesale market**. Although banks are able to lend large amounts for short periods of time, they are unable to replace the public money market due to the fact that banks face greater regulation and the associated costs that the participants in the money market confront. Because most participants in the money market face very little asymmetric information the intermediation of banks is not beneficial or needed.

The Purpose of the Money Markets

The need for money markets arises primarily from the fact that individuals, businesses, and government often face a short-term **timing difference** between when they receive money and when money needs to be spent. If those with temporary surplus funds kept the money in a checking account their return would be very low and perhaps zero (actually the real return could be negative after taking inflation into consideration). The money in the account would be incurring an **opportunity cost** of lost interest. Those with a shortage of funds would face not paying their payments on time or having to borrow from a longer-term and more expensive source of external funds. These suppliers and demanders of short-term funds will sell and buy money market securities to overcome this timing problem. Partly due to the short-term nature of these securities, both the interest rate and the risk are low.

Who Participates in the Money Markets?

There are six primary money market participant groups: (1) **U.S. Treasury**—the only participant that is always a demander of funds, never a supplier. The borrowing helps to fill the gap between spending and when tax revenues are received. (2) **Federal Reserve System**—the Fed buys and sells these securities in order to help control the money supply in the economy. The details of controlling the money supply are presented in Chapters 9 and 10). (3) **Commercial banks**—primarily involved in-the-money market to balance out their needs for funds that the Fed requires them to have on reserve. The banks with excess reserves lend to those with reserve shortages. (4) **Businesses**—usually larger corporations that have a short-term surplus or shortage of cash that they would like to invest or lend. (5) **Investment and security firms**—investment companies serve primarily as dealers in these securities and add to the liquidity of the market. Finance companies, insurance companies, and pension funds need to have quick access to liquid funds in order to meet the cash demands of their businesses. Finance companies need to lend whenever a qualified borrower requests the money, insurance companies must meet the recurring claims requests, and pension funds have to have funds available primarily to meet their obligations to the retirees. (6) **Individuals**—usually place idle funds in money market mutual funds to overcome the often lower interest rate available on accounts at financial institutions, such as banks and credit unions.

The Money Market Instruments

The major money market instruments are:

1. **Treasury Bills**—Issued by the U.S. Treasury and are sold with maturities of 4, 13, and 26 weeks from the time of issuance. Treasury-bills had a minimum denomination of $10,000 until 1998 at which time the minimum denomination was reduced to $1,000. T-bills are issued at a discount and can be redeemed at their par or face value. This practice is referred to as discounting.

    The annualized yield on a Treasury-bill can be computed as:

    $$i_{yt} = \frac{F - P}{P} \times \frac{365}{n},$$

    where i_{yt} is the annualized yield on the investment, F is the face value, P is the purchase price, and n is the number of days until maturity or until the security is sold. Suppose that you purchase a T-bill that matures in 91-days for $989. The annualized rate is

    $$i_{yt} = \frac{1,000 - 989}{989} \times \frac{365}{91} = 0.0446 = 4.46\%.$$

    T-bills have both a **deep market**, which means having many different buyers and sellers, and a **liquid market**, meaning they can be easily bought and sold without loss of value. New issues are sold every Tuesday. They are sold at auction through **competitive bidding** with the highest bidder getting the first purchase, the second highest bidder the second purchase, etc. Some buyers may participate on a **noncompetitive** basis, and they are issued T-bills at the weighted average rate earned by all competitive bidders. In 1976, the Treasury switched to book entry securities, which are only documented in the Fed's computer.

2. **Federal Funds**—Overnight borrowing and lending among commercial banks for the purpose of meeting the Fed's reserve requirements. The interest rate is very competitively determined and is extremely sensitive to changes in economic conditions.

3. **Repurchase Agreements**—These securities are often called **repos.** They operate by having one firm with a need for funds sell Treasury securities they have to another firm with the commitment that the demander will repurchase the Treasury securities at maturity. Most have a 3- to 14-day maturity. The use of the Treasury security makes repos essentially a short-term collateralized loan. Thus, repos have low interest rates.

4. **Negotiable Certificates of Deposit—Term Securities**, which have a specified maturity date and are issued by banks in denominations of $100,000 or more with few CDs denominated less than $1 million. Because CDs have maturity dates, CDs are called term securities instead of demand deposit. They are **bearer instruments,** and maturities normally range from one to four months. The actual interest rate paid on the CD is negotiated between the bank and the customer.

5. **Commercial Paper**—These are **unsecured promissory notes** issued by corporations that mature in less than 270 days. They are sold only by the largest, most secure business firms. The interest rate varies based on the level of risk of the company. The majority of commercial paper is sold directly to the buyer without the use of a dealer. This process is known as a **direct placement.** The paper is usually backed by a line of credit the issuer has available at a commercial bank.

6. **Banker's Acceptances**—Banker's Acceptances are crucial for the smooth flow of international trade. This security is created out of a **time draft.** To illustrate what happens, assume that a German shoe manufacturer wants to export shoes to a U.S. buyer who owns and operates retail shoe stores. The German seller wants to be sure to get paid before shipping the shoes, and the U.S. buyer wants assurance of getting the shoes before paying the money. The buyer's bank agrees to guarantee the payment and sends a **letter of credit** documenting this agreement to the seller in Germany. The seller takes the letter to his or her bank, and the bank creates a **time draft**, which allows the German bank to get the money from the U.S. bank after the shoes are shipped. The U.S. bank receives the draft and stamps it "accepted," which creates the Banker's Acceptance. The acceptance is now a marketable money market security. The bank ultimately makes the payment to the owner of the acceptance at maturity and gets the money from the buyer of the shoes.

7. **Eurodollars**—These are deposits in banks in England that are denominated in U.S. dollars. These funds are often used to make loans to firms in other countries that desire to borrow dollars rather than the domestic currency of their country. Another popular use of Eurodollars is as a substitute for Federal Funds. If the interest rate is lower on Eurodollars, U.S. banks will borrow Eurodollars overnight to meet their reserve requirements. The rate foreign banks pay on Eurodollars is the **London interbank bid rate** and the rate at which these funds are lent is called the **London interbank offer rate (LIBOR).** LIBOR is similar to the interest rate on federal funds in the United States.

The interest rates on all of the money market securities move closely together. This correlation is due to the fact that they are all short term and of low risk. Two significant differences that distinguish one security from another are default risk and liquidity.

How Money Market Securities Are Valued

The price or present value (*PV*) of a money market instrument can be computed by discounting the future value (*FV*) of the security as follows:

$$PV = \frac{FV}{(1+i)^n}$$

Treasury-bills have a par value or future value of $1,000. For example, the price of a Treasury-bill with a yield of 3% and one-year to maturity is

$$PV = \frac{1000}{(1 + 0.03)^1} = \$970.87.$$

■ Exercises

Exercise 1: Definitions and Terminology

Match the following terms in the right-hand column with the definition or description in the left-hand column. Place the letter of the term in the blank provided next to the appropriate definition.

____ 1. They deal in the secondary money market for their customers.

____ 2. The funds in these accounts can be accessed at any time if cash is needed.

____ 3. Made up of short-term, low-risk, and highly banks liquid securities

____ 4. Indirectly controlled by the Fed in implementing companies' monetary policy.

____ 5. Sometimes used to help meet Fed reserve requirements.

____ 6. The form of record keeping for all Treasury marketable securities since 1976

____ 7. Where most transactions are large, which thus precludes significant individual participation

____ 8. The amount paid on Eurodollar deposits

____ 9. Primary function in-the-money markets is to "make a market" for these securities

____ 10. The technique for initially selling Treasury Bills

____ 11. Funds can be accessed by the investor only after the maturity date.

____ 12. Maturity is always less than 270 days to avoid bid rate registration with the SEC.

____ 13. An order to pay a specified sum to the bearer at a future date

____ 14. Investor pays less for a security than it will be worth when it matures.

____ 15. Environment where securities can be bought and sold quickly with low transaction cost

____ 16. Issuers bypass the dealer and sell directly to the end investor.

a. wholesale markets

b. money markets

c. money center banks

d. T-bills

e. competitive bid

f. book-entry

g. federal funds rate

h. demand deposits

i. term security

j. banker's acceptance

k. Eurodollars

l. London interbank offer rate

m. commercial paper

n. direct placement

o. discounting

p. liquid market

Exercise 2: The Need for Money Markets

1. The money markets have been active since the early 1800s but have dramatically increased in importance and size since the 1970s. Why has the U.S. economy experienced a significant increase in money market activity?

2. What types of advantages do money markets provide over banks?

3. Describe the key characteristics of money markets and the markets in which they are traded.

Exercise 3: Returns on Treasury Bills

For each of the three Treasury Bills shown below, calculate the annualized yields.

T-Bill	Maturity Value	Current Market Value	Days to Maturity	Annualized Yields
1	$10,000	$9,900	90	
2	$10,000	$9,550	360	
3	$1,000,000	$940,500	270	

Exercise 4: Banker's Acceptances

1. Banker's Acceptances are used primarily for conducting international trade transactions. Due to increased international trade the use of Banker's Acceptances has increased significantly since the 1960s. What are the three advantages for exporters that make these securities so popular?

    a.

    b.

    c.

2. What are the five steps for using banker's acceptances?

    a.

    b.

    c.

    d.

    e.

3. Describe the secondary market for banker's acceptances.

   _____

   _____

   _____

4. Explain the level of risk associated with banker's acceptances.

   _____

   _____

   _____

■ Self-Test

Part A: Fill in the Blanks

1. The largest money market borrower is the _____.

2. Individuals with small amounts of money that they want to invest short-term can invest these funds in money market securities by buying _____.

3. Treasury bills are sold at a(n) _____ from the par value.

4. The market for Treasury bills is _____ due to the many buyers and sellers, and it is also considered liquid because they can be bought and sold _____ with _____ transaction costs.

5. Fed funds are _____ investments done on a daily basis.

6. Repurchase agreements are much like Fed funds except that _____ can participate.

7. Negotiable CDs are _____ instruments, and whoever holds them receives the payments at maturity. They are sold in minimum amounts of _____ dollars.

8. A(n) _____ is created when the buyers bank stamps the _____ "accepted."

9. Dollar deposits in bank accounts in England are known as _____.

10. Borrowers in the Eurodollar market pay the _____ rate.

11. Money market mutual funds are a(n) _____ investment fund.

12. Most Treasury Bills are sold at _____ where the highest bidder gets the first T-bills sold.

13. The security that banks use to lend and borrow overnight is called _____, and they are used to help meet _____ imposed by the Federal Reserve.

14. A popular form of money market security issued by large corporations is _____, and it matures in less than _____ days.

15. _____ is when an intermediary provides the role of creating liquidity where it did not previously exist.

16. Treasury bills are offered weekly with prices set by a procedure known as _____.

17. Term used for an account that can be drawn on at anytime is known as a(n) _____.

18. U.S. dollar-denominated deposit held in British banks are known as _____.

Part B: True-False Questions

Circle whether the following statements are true (T) or false (F).

T F 1. The Federal Reserve can influence the Fed funds interest rate by buying and selling securities.

T F 2. Because repurchase agreements are essentially short-term loans collateralized by Treasury securities, the risk of default is zero.

T F 3. To be a money market security, the security must mature in one year or less from the time it was originally issued.

T F 4. With the exception of money market mutual funds, money market securities are traded in a wholesale market.

T F 5. Business firms do not like to participate in the money market because they tie up cash that they may need to pay unexpected bills.

T F 6. The majority of the funds invested by money market mutual funds are placed in Treasury Bills.

T F 7. Banks are issuers of negotiable CDs, banker's acceptances, federal funds, and repurchase agreements.

T F 8. In the past 10 years, the real rate of interest on T-bills has mostly been positive because inflation has been lower then the nominal rate on this security.

T F 9. Money market mutual funds became very popular in the 1980s due to the decline in interest rates on non-money-market marketable securities.

T F 10. The Federal Reserve uses only Treasury Bills to change the money supply when they conduct monetary policy.

T F 11. Due to the similarities among money market securities the returns on these securities move very closely together.

T F 12. Eurodollars are the only type of foreign currency deposited at banks in England.

T F 13. Like Treasury Bills, commercial paper has a deep and liquid secondary market.

T   F   14.   A common use of funds raised by issuing commercial paper is to finance loans that finance companies make to their customers.

T   F   15.   If an importer defaults on payment to the bank for the banker's acceptance when it is due, the bank will still make the payment to the exporter.

T   F   16.   Money market securities have a moderate default risk.

T   F   17.   Money market securities can have long-term maturity dates, up to 10 years.

Part C: Multiple-Choice Questions

Circle the appropriate answer.

1.   In which of the following cases would direct use of the money markets be appropriate?
   (a)   A firm has surplus cash on hand that it will not need for approximately six months.
   (b)   The federal government needs $5 million to build a new bridge.
   (c)   Melissa the investor has an extra $5,000 she would like to invest for 30 days.
   (d)   A commercial bank has an immediate need for additional cash to make a loan.
   (e)   Both (a) and (d) of the above are correct.

2.   Which of the following is **not** a money market source of required reserves for banks?
   (a)   Repurchase agreements
   (b)   Treasury bonds
   (c)   Federal funds
   (d)   Eurodollars
   (e)   All of the above are sources.

3.   Which of the following money market securities has zero default risk?
   (a)   Federal funds
   (b)   Eurodollars
   (c)   Banker's acceptances
   (d)   Treasury Bills
   (e)   Both (a) and (d) are default free.

4.   Which of the following is the most common money market security owned by money market mutual funds?
   (a)   Commercial paper
   (b)   Treasury bills
   (c)   Repurchase agreements
   (d)   Eurodollars
   (e)   Negotiable CDs

5. Which of the following applies to money market mutual funds?
    (a) They are term deposits.
    (b) Like most money market securities, a large amount of money is needed to economically invest in them.
    (c) They have the same amount of risk as bank deposits because they are insured by the federal government.
    (d) You can write checks against the money in the fund.
    (e) Both (c) and (d) are correct.

6. Which of the following is correct about Eurodollars?
    (a) This market has grown rapidly primarily due to depositors receiving a higher rate of return than in the domestic market.
    (b) Eurodollars are demand deposits and can be accessed at any time by the depositor.
    (c) More variable rate securities are having their interest rate tied to the Eurodollar rate.
    (d) Because Eurodollar deposits are in U.S. dollars, the United States is the only depositor in this market.
    (e) Both (a) and (c) are correct.

7. Which one of the following combinations generally has the lowest and highest interest rates, respectively?
    (a) Federal funds, commercial paper
    (b) T-bills, prime rate
    (c) T-bills, commercial paper
    (d) Certificates of deposit, commercial paper
    (e) Federal funds, certificates of deposit

8. Which of the following money market rates is not listed daily in the *Wall Street Journal*?
    (a) Federal funds rate
    (b) London interbank bid rate
    (c) Banker's acceptance rate
    (d) Treasury bills rate
    (e) All of the above are listed daily.

9. Which of the following financial institutions holds the largest percentage of U.S. government securities?
    (a) Credit unions
    (b) Savings and loans
    (c) Commercial banks
    (d) Finance companies

10. Which of the following statements about participants in the money markets is correct?
    (a) The U.S. Treasury is the largest supplier and demander of money market funds.
    (b) The Federal Reserve is responsible for issuing Treasury securities and federal funds.
    (c) Banks are the major issuer of negotiable CDs, banker's acceptances, federal funds, and repurchase agreements.
    (d) Both large and small businesses are active in the money market.

11.   The maximum percent of a new issue of T-Bill that any one dealer is allowed to purchase is
   (a) 35%.
   (b) 50%.
   (c) 65%.
   (d) 100%.

12.   Which of the following statements is correct about federal funds?
   (a) Most federal funds borrowings are secured loans.
   (b) Banks attempt to loan federal funds when they are below the reserve requirement.
   (c) Federal funds loans are usually formal written agreements between commercial banks.
   (d) The term to maturity of federal funds loans is overnight.

13.   Which of the following statements is correct about repurchase agreements?
   (a) Borrowers often sell Treasury securities in repurchase agreements.
   (b) The most common maturity for repos is from three to six months.
   (c) The Federal Reserve does not use repos to help conduct monetary policy.
   (d) The repo market has never had a default and is thus considered virtually default risk free.

14.   Second to only Treasury bills, _____ is the most popular money market security.
   (a) banker's acceptances
   (b) negotiable CDs
   (c) Eurodollars
   (d) commercial paper

15.   Which of the following sequence of events is the order of document creation in creating a banker's acceptance?
   (a) letter of credit, shipping documents, bank time draft, banker's acceptance
   (b) shipping documents, letter of credit, bank time draft, banker's acceptance
   (c) letter of credit, bank time draft, shopping documents, banker's acceptance
   (d) time draft, letter of credit, shipping documents, banker's acceptance
   (e) time draft, shipping documents, letter of credit, banker's acceptance

16.   Investors who put funds in money market are usually
   (a) trying to avoid taxes.
   (b) holding on to funds while earning higher rate than bank offers.
   (c) attempting to earn high returns while lowering risk.
   (d) None of the above

17.   The U.S. Treasury Dept is unique because it
   (a) is always a demander of money market funds.
   (b) is always a supplier of money market funds.
   (c) directly controls the money supply.
   (d) Only (a) and (c) above

18. Commercial banks
    (a) hold a large percentage of U.S. Government securities.
    (b) are a major issuer of negotiable CDs.
    (c) can trade on behalf of their customers.
    (d) All of the above

Part D: Short Answer Questions

1. What factor was instrumental in banks not being able to meet the short-term financing need that was filled by the creation and growth of the money markets?

2. What are the main features that distinguish all money market securities from other securities?

3. Why do insurance companies, both life and property and casualty, invest large amounts in money market securities?

4. Why are money market mutual funds so popular with individuals?

5. Why is it important for money markets to be deep and liquid?

6. What is the purpose of federal funds?

7. How do money markets benefit individual investors?

■ Answers to Chapter 11

Exercise 1

1. c	5. k	8. l	11. i	14. o
2. h	6. f	9. d	12. m	15. p
3. b	7. a	10. e	13. j	16. n
4. g				

Exercise 2

1. Most short-term lending was originally accomplished by banks. However, starting in the 1970s, interest rates began to rise to above normal levels. Due to regulatory constraints on banks' ability to pay prevailing rates on deposits, there was a net outflow of funds from banks. Increase trading in the money markets resulted in order to obtain current rates on invested funds.

2. Money markets have lower costs in situations where asymmetric information problems are not a problem. Because banks cannot loan out 100% of the deposits they receive, they must reduce the interest rates they pay to depositors. Thus, money market instruments can pay higher interest rates than banks.

3. Money market instruments have three basic characteristics: They are sold in large denominations, they have low default risk, and they have maturities of one year or less. Because money market instruments are offered in large denominations, the money markets are called wholesale markets.

Exercise 3

T-Bill	Maturity Value	Current Market Value	Days to Maturity	Annualized Yield
1	$10,000	$9,900	90	4.1%
2	$10,000	$9,550	360	4.8%
3	$1,000,000	$940,500	270	8.6%

Exercise 4

1. (a) The exporter is paid immediately.

    (b) The exporter is shielded from foreign exchange risk because his local banks pays him in domestic funds.

    (c) The exporter does not have to assess the credit worthiness of the importer because the importer's bank guarantees payment.

2. The five steps for using banker's acceptances are

    (a) The importer's banks sends an irrevocable letter of credit to the exporter.

    (b) Upon receipt of the letter, the exporter ships the goods and delivers the letter to its bank with proof of shipment of the goods.

    (c) The exporter's bank creates a time draft on the letter of credit and sends the proof of shipment and time draft to the importer's bank.

    (d) The importer's bank stamps the time draft and returns it to the exporter's bank.

    (e) The importer deposits funds at its bank to cover the banker's acceptance when it matures.

3. Banker's acceptances can be traded until maturity because they are payable to the bearer. Bank's acceptances are sold on a discounted basis like T-bills.

4. Banker's acceptances are considered low risk because of the low risk of default due to the participation of only large money center banks in the banker's acceptances market.

Self Test

Part A

1. U.S. Treasury	8. banker's acceptance, time draft	14. commercial paper, 270
2. money market mutual funds	9. Eurodollars	15. liquidity intervention
3. discount	10. London interbank offer	16. competitive bidding
4. deep, quickly, low	11. open-end	17. demand deposit
5. overnight	12. competitive bids	18. Eurodollars
6. nonbanks	13. federal funds, reserve requirements	
7. bearer, 100,000		

Part B

1. T	6. F	11. T	16. F
2. F	7. T	12. F	17. F
3. T	8. T	13. F	
4. T	9. F	14. T	
5. F	10. F	15. T	

Part C

1. e	6. e	11. a	16. b
2. b	7. b	12. d	17. a
3. d	8. b	13. a	18. d
4. a	9. c	14. b	
5. d	10. c	15. a	

Part D

1. Banks are subject to greater regulation than the money market participants. This regulation, such as reserve requirements and interest rate ceilings, placed a cost burden on banks that put them at a cost disadvantage in meeting the short-term funding needs of money market participants.

2. All money market securities are usually sold in large denominations (approximately $1,000,000), they have very low default risk, and they mature in one year or less from the original issue date.

3. Insurance companies are a perfect example of the business need filled by the money markets. Insurance companies generate large amounts of cash that will be needed on very short notice to meet the claims of their clients. They must have highly liquid low-risk assets with the highest return available. Some money market securities are ideal for meeting this need (T-bills, commercial paper, negotiable CDs).

4. MMMFs allow individuals to participate in the competitive returns on the highly-liquid, low-risk money market securities that individuals would normally not be able to purchase due to the large dollar denomination of money market securities.

5.   It is important for money markets to be deep and liquid to minimize the risk that investors will not be able to sell their securities.

6.   The purpose of federal funds is to provide banks with immediate access to funds when they are short of their minimum reserve requirements. Fed funds provide are a source of funds that will not alert the Fed of any possible liquidity issues.

7.   Money markets benefit individual investors by providing them access to large-denomination securities even though they may only have a small amount of funds to invest.

Chapter 12
The Bond Market

■ Chapter Learning Goals

By the end of this chapter, you should

1. Understand how capital markets operate.
2. Know the different types of bonds.
3. Understand bond yield calculations.
4. Know how to compute the value of a bond.

■ Chapter Summary

This chapter discusses capital market securities, which are securities that have an original maturity greater than one year. Although bonds, mortgages, and stocks are all capital market securities, this chapter focuses on bonds.

Purpose of the Capital Market

While the money markets are for short-term securities, the capital markets are long-term securities. The main reason that firms and individuals borrow using long-term securities is to reduce the risk that interest rates rise before the debt is paid off.

Capital Market Participants

Corporations, federal, and local governments are the main issuers of capital market securities. Corporations issue capital market securities to fund investment projects for which they do not have sufficient capital or to maintain a certain level of capital in case of emergency needs. Households are the main buyers of capital market securities.

Capital Market Trading

Trading in capital securities occurs in the primary and secondary markets. Primary market transactions include **initial public offerings (IPO)**. An IPO is the first public issuance of securities by a corporation. Secondary markets are where previously issued securities trade. Over-the-counter markets and organized exchanges are two types of secondary markets. Organized exchanges typically have a centralized location where trading occurs and are governed by trading rules or protocol.

Types of Bonds

Bonds represent a debt owed to an investor by an issuer. The issuer is obligated to pay the coupon rate, which is stated as a percent of par, on specific dates. The face value or par is the amount the issuer has to pay the investor at maturity. Bond holders have some claim on the assets and earnings of the firm in the event of bankruptcy. Corporate bonds, municipal bonds, and long-term government notes and bonds are types of bonds traded in the capital market.

Treasury Bonds

The U.S. Treasury finances the government debt through the issuance of Treasury notes and bonds. Treasury notes have maturities between 1 and 10 years, while Treasury bonds have maturities greater than 10 years. (Treasury bills are money market securities that have maturities of less than one year.) Treasury note and bond prices are stated as a percent of $100 par value. Treasury notes and bonds are virtually free of default risk.

Treasury Bond Interest Rates

The interest rates on Treasury notes and bonds are low because of their low risk of default. Long-term Treasury securities typically have higher interest rates than short-term Treasury securities because of the increased interest-rate risk associated with the longer holding period.

Treasury Inflation-Indexed Securities (TIPS)

In 1997, the Treasury began issuing securities that have a constant interest rate over the life of the security, but the principal amount is indexed to inflation based on the consumer price index. At maturity, investors receive the greater of the original par value of the bonds or the inflation-adjusted principal. The benefit of inflation-indexed securities is that their value will not be eroded by inflation.

Treasury STRIPS

In 1985, the Treasury began offering **Separate Trading of Registered Interest and Principal Securities (STRIPS)**. STRIPS are offered in book entry form meaning they do not have physical certificates. STRIPS are **zero coupon bonds**; they do not pay any interest over the life of the security. You pay less than par value for a STRIP and receive face value at maturity. The Treasury creates STRIPS by separating the principal repayment from the periodic interest payments. Prior to the creation of STRIPS, Merrill Lynch separated the principal from interest payments on Treasury securities and created the Treasury Investment Growth Fund or TIGRs.

Agency Bonds

Congress has authorized several U.S. government agencies to issue bonds to raise funds for purposes that it states are in the national interest. The Government National Mortgage Association (Ginnie Mae) and the Federal National Mortgage Association (Fannie Mae) are two well-recognized issuers of agency bonds. The risk of default is low for agency bonds as it is unlikely that the federal government would like agency bonds default as evidenced by the bailout of Fannie Mae and Freddie Mac in 2008. The reduced liquidity of agency bonds contributes to the differences between Treasury and agency securities.

Municipal Bonds

State, county, and local governments issue municipal bonds. Municipal bonds are either **general obligation bonds** or **revenue bonds.** General obligation bonds are backed by the full faith and credit of the issuer, while revenue bonds are backed by the cash flows of a particular project. Municipal bonds of different issuers carry different levels of default risk. Municipal bonds that are issued for essential public projects are exempt from federal taxes. To determine a tax-free interest rate that is the equivalent of a taxable interest rate, multiply the taxable interest rate times (1 minus the investor's marginal tax rate). That is,

$$\text{Equivalent tax-free rate} = \text{taxable interest rate} \times (1 - \text{marginal tax rate}).$$

For example, if a corporate bond pays 7%, then the equivalent tax-free rate for an investor in the 28% marginal tax is

$$\text{Equivalent tax-free rate} = 0.07 \times (1 - 0.28) = 0.0504 \text{ or } 5.04\%.$$

The comparison of these numbers tells us that from a return perspective an investor would be indifferent between a taxable return of 7% and a tax-free return of 5.04%.

Corporate Bonds

Corporate bonds typically have a par value of $1,000 and pay interest semi-annually. Most corporate bonds can be called or redeemed early at the option of the issuer. The contract that states the obligations of the bond issuer and the lender's right is called the **bond indenture.** The default risks of corporate bonds vary by issuer and by issue and are reflected in bond ratings.

Bearer bonds had certificates with coupons attached that investors clipped and sent to the issuer to receive payment. Bearer bonds have been replaced with registered bonds, which do not have physical certificates.

The bond indenture specifies restrictions on management designed to protect bondholders, which are known as **restrictive covenants**. An example of a restrictive covenant is a limit on dividends a firm can pay.

Call provisions state the price and time at which the issuer can force the holder to sell the bond back. Call provisions may require the issuer to pay more than par to redeem a bond issue early. The incentive for an issuer to redeem a bond issue early is to reduce its interest payments. In a period of falling interest rates, corporations can redeem bonds early and issue new bonds at lower interest rates. Corporations include sinking fund provisions in the indenture to reduce the rate they have to pay investors. A **sinking fund** requires the issuer to pay off a portion of the issue each year. This reduces the probability of default for the issue. Call provisions provide two additional benefits to issuers: flexibility in financing that will benefit shareholders and flexibility to change the firm's capital structure as cash flows change. Because call provisions benefit bond issuers, investors require higher interest rates on callable issues.

Some bond issues are **convertible** into common stock at the option of the bondholder. Because the conversion feature is a benefit to bondholders, convertible bond issues have lower interest rates holding all else constant.

Bonds can also be classified by the collateral that secures the bond and the priority of claims in the event of bankruptcy. Bond types are (1) secured bonds, (2) unsecured bonds, and (3) junk bonds. **Secured bonds** are backed by specific collateral. Mortgage bonds and equipment trust certificates backed by non-real estate real property, such as heavy equipment are two examples of secured bonds. **Unsecured bonds** are not backed by any specific asset but rather by the general creditworthiness of the issuer. Debentures are subordinate to secured bonds on claims of assets in the event of bankruptcy. Subordinated debentures are debentures whose claims are lower in priority to debentures and secured bonds. Variable rate bonds can be secured or unsecured bonds. They differ by having a coupon payment rate that changes when some benchmark interest rate changes. **Junk bonds** carry ratings less than BBB by Standard & Poor's or Baa by Moody's. Junk bonds are considered speculative because they have higher probabilities of default than higher grade bonds. Because the secondary market for junk bonds is not very active, junk bonds often suffer from poor liquidity. Bonds rated BBB or better by Standard & Poor's or Baa by Moody's are called investment grade bonds.

Financial Guarantees for Bonds

Some bond issuers choose to purchase insurance that guarantees the payment of interest and principal or **financial guarantees** to bondholders. Issuers purchase insurance to improve the credit rating of a bond issue and reduce the interest rate they must pay investors. The creditworthiness of the insurance company then determines the credit quality of the bond issue. A new way to insure bonds is through a **credit default swap (CDS)**, a form of insurance against default in the principal and interest payments of a credit default issued by a third party. Due to the Commodity Futures Modernization Act, a party could purchase a CDS without having an insurable interest in the credit instrument.

Bond Yield Calculations

Current Yield

Current yield is an approximation of yield-to-maturity presented in Chapter 3. The current yield equals the coupon payment divided by the current price of the bond:

$$i_c = \frac{C}{P}$$

where C is yearly coupon payment and P is the price of the bond. The current yield equals the yield-to-maturity when the bond is priced at par. In general, current yield is a better approximation for long-term bonds than f or short-term bonds.

Yield on a Discount Basis

Yield on a discount basis or discount yield was created to help price bonds before computers became available. The discount yield is:

$$i_{db} = \frac{F - P}{F} \times \frac{360}{\text{days to maturity}}$$

where i_{db} is the yield on a discount basis, F is the face value of the discount bond, and P is the purchase price of the bond. Intuitively, the discount yield is the capital gain return based on the face value times the number of periods in a year depending on how long the bond is held. The use of the face value as the original purchase price and 360 days instead of 365 days in a year cause the discount yield to understate the interest rates on bonds compared to yield-to-maturity.

Suppose that you purchase a six-month Treasury bill for $965. What is the discount yield?

$$i_{db} = \frac{1000 - 965}{1000} \times \frac{360}{180} = 0.07 \text{ or } 7\%.$$

Note: a basis point is one-hundredth of a percent or 0.0001.

Finding the Value of Coupon Bonds

The value of a coupon bond is the present value of the expected coupon payments and the par or face value received at maturity. In general, the value of any asset can be determined by identifying the expected cash flows, specifying the required return for the asset, and computing the present value of the cash flows by discounting them at the required rate of return.

Finding the Price of Semi-Annual Bonds

The price of a semi-annual coupon bond is the present value of the semi-annual coupon payments and the face value to be received at maturity. Formally,

$$P_{semi} = \frac{C/_2}{(1+i)^1} + \frac{C/_2}{(1+i)^2} + \frac{C/_2}{(1+i)^3} + \cdots + \frac{C/_2}{(1+i)^n} + \frac{F}{(1+i)^n}$$

where P_{semi} is the price of the semi-annual coupon bond, C is the yearly coupon payment, F is the face value, n is the number of periods until maturity, and i is the required six-month return. For example, if market interest rates have risen to 7% semi-annually (or 14% annually), what is the price of a 6.5% coupon, two-year semi-annual bond?

$$P_{semi} = \frac{65/_2}{(1+0.07)^1} + \frac{65/_2}{(1+0.07)^2} + \frac{65/_2}{(1+0.07)^3} + \frac{65/_2}{(1+0.07)^4} + \frac{1000}{(1+0.07)^4}$$

$$= \$60.75 + \$56.77 + \$53.06 + \$49.59 + \$762.90 = \$983.06$$

Investing in Bonds

Although the cash flows associated with bonds are more certain than the cash flows associated with stocks, bonds are not without risk. The values of bonds fluctuate as interest rates go up and down. This relationship is inverse in that as rates increase, bond values decline, and values increase when rates decline. Using the example immediately above, if interests rates increased to 16% (8% semi-annually), the value of this same bond would decrease to $950.32. The price sensitivity of bonds with respect to interest rates is called **interest-rate risk**. Long-term bonds are more sensitive to changes in interest rates than short-term bonds.

■ Exercises

Exercise 1: Definitions and Terminology

_____ 1. The first public issuance of securities by a corporation

_____ 2. Treasury securities that have maturities of 1 to 10 years

_____ 3. The market in which initial public offerings occur

_____ 4. Bonds that are not issued by the Treasury but are issued to raise funds in the national interest

_____ 5. Bonds that are typically free from Federal income taxes

_____ 6. Bonds whose principal amount changes based on the consumer price index

_____ 7. Treasury securities with maturities less than one year

_____ 8. The market in which previously issued securities trade

_____ 9. Treasury securities that pay no coupon interest

_____ 10. Treasury securities with maturities greater than 10 years

_____ 11. Insurance against default in principal and interest payments of a credit instrument

a.   STRIPS

b.   primary market

c.   secondary market

d.   IPO

e.   Treasury bills

f.   Treasury notes

g.   Treasury bonds

h.   agency bonds

i.   municipal bonds

j.   Treasury inflation-indexed bonds.

k.   credit default swap (CDS)

■ Self-Test

Part A: Fill in the Blanks

1. _____ are constraints on a company's management designed to protect bondholders.

2. The contract that provides the obligations of the bond issuer is called the _____.

3. The par value of most corporate bonds is _____.

4. _____ provisions state the price and time an issuer can force the holder to sell a bond back to the issuer.

5. Bonds represent a(n) _____ owed to a lender by a borrower.

6. _____ bonds are backed by specific collateral.

7. The conversion feature of a convertible bond is a benefit to _____.

8. _____ bonds have credit ratings less than BBB by Standard & Poor's.

9. _____ is an approximation of yield-to-maturity.

10. _____ bonds are more sensitive to changes in interest rates than _____ bonds.

Part B: True-False Questions

T   F   1.   Ginnie Mae bonds are a type of agency bond.

T   F   2.   Subordinated debentures claims are senior to debentures claims against a bond issuer.

T   F   3.   Borrowers issue long-term bonds to decrease the risk associated with interest rate increases before the debt is re-paid.

T   F   4.   OTC markets and organized exchanges are types of primary markets.

T   F   5.   Mortgage bonds are a type of secured bond.

T   F   6.   Bond issuers purchase financial guarantees for bondholders to reduce the interest rate they must offer investors.

T   F   7.   A limit on the payment of dividends is an example of a restrictive covenant.

T   F   8.   A sinking fund requires an issuer to pay off a portion of a bond issue every year.

T   F   9.   Revenue bonds are backed by the full faith and credit of the issuing municipality.

T   F 10.   One benefit of municipal bonds is they are free from federal taxes.

Part C: Multiple-Choice Questions

1.   The current yield for a corporate bond that pays a 6% coupon and is priced at $950 is
    (a)   5.3%.
    (b)   6.0%.
    (c)   6.3%.
    (d)   6.5%.

2.   The discount yield for a six-month T-bill that is priced at $950 is
    (a)   5.0%.
    (b)   10.0%.
    (c)   10.5%.
    (d)   11.0%.

3.   What is the price of a 5% annual coupon, 10-year corporate bond if the market rate for similar bonds is 5%?
    (a) $950.00
    (b) $975.00
    (c) $1,000.00
    (d) $1,025.00

4. What is the price of a 7.5% semi-annual, two-year corporate bond if interest rates have risen to 9.5% since the bond was issued?
    (a) $765.00
    (b) $964.33
    (c) $1,000.00
    (d) $1,066.35

5. What is the price of a 7.5% semi-annual, two-year corporate bond if interest rates have dropped by 2% since the bond was issued?
    (a) $765.00
    (b) $815.74
    (c) $1,000.00
    (d) $1,037.39

6. What is the price of an 8% annual coupon, five-year corporate bond if the market rate of interest is 7.5%?
    (a) $1,020.23
    (b) $1,040.23
    (c) $980.23
    (d) $960.23

7. What is the equivalent tax-free rate on a corporate bond that pays 6.25% for an investor with a marginal tax rate of 33%?
    (a) 2.06%
    (b) 4.19%
    (c) 5.14%
    (d) 9.33%

8. If an investor has a marginal tax rate of 28%, which of the following bonds should he purchase?
    (a) 9% taxable bond
    (b) 9.5% taxable bond
    (c) 6.4% tax-free bond
    (d) 6.9% tax-free bond

9. What is the price of a $1,000 STRIP if it has 10 years until maturity and the market rate is currently 4.5%?
    (a) $624.33
    (b) $643.93
    (c) $721.24
    (d) $1,021.24

10. What is the price of a $1,000 STRIP if it has 10 years until maturity and the market rate is currently 7%?

    (a) $508.35
    (b) $555.21
    (c) $621.45
    (d) $765.34

Part D: Short Answer Questions

1. What is the price difference between an 8% semi-annual coupon bond with 20 years until maturity and an 8% annual coupon bond with 20 year until maturity if the market rate is 7%? What causes the price difference?

2. When would a corporation want to call a bond prior to maturity?

3. How did the Commodity Futures Modernization Act change the market for credit default swaps?

■ Answers to Chapter 12

Exercise 1: Definitions and Terminology

1.	d	6.	j	11.	k
2.	f	7.	e		
3.	b	8.	c		
4.	h	9.	a		
5.	i	10.	g		

Self-Test

Part A

1.	Restrictive covenants	6.	Secured
2.	bond indenture	7.	bondholders
3.	$1,000	8.	junk
4.	Call	9.	current yield
5.	debt	10.	Long-term, short-term

Part B

1.	T	6.	T
2.	F	7.	T
3.	T	8.	T
4.	F	9.	F
5.	T	10.	T

Part C

1.	c	6.	a
2.	b	7.	b
3.	c	8.	d
4.	b	9.	b
5.	d	10.	a

Part D

1. The price of the 8% semi-annual coupon bond with 20 years until maturity is $1,106.78. The price of the 8% annual coupon bond with 20 years until maturity is $1,105.94. Thus the price difference is $0.84. The semi-annual coupon bond has a higher price because coupon payments are received every 6 months instead of 12 months, so payments received earlier result in higher present value for those interim cash flows.

2. Corporations generally want to consider calling bond issues when interest rates are dropping. In particular, a corporation would want to call a bond prior to maturity when the costs of calling the bond issue are less than the interest savings the firm can lock in by issuing bonds with lower rates.

3. The Commodity Futures Modernization Act preempted state gaming laws allowing speculators to purchase credit default swaps on instruments without holding an insurable interest in these positions. Speculators were allowed to, in essence, legally bet on whether a firm would fail in the future.

Chapter 13
The Stock Market

■ Chapter Learning Goals

By the end of this chapter, you should

1. Know why businesses, individuals, and governments are active in securities markets.
2. Understand how stocks are traded in the capital markets.
3. Know the risk and return features of common stock and preferred stock.

■ Chapter Summary

This chapter details the trading and valuation of common stocks.

Investing in Stock

Common stockholders are the owners or residual claimants of a firm. In the event of bankruptcy, stockholders are due the assets and income that remain after all creditors and preferred stockholders.

Common Stock versus Preferred Stock

The two types of stock are common stock and preferred stock. **Common stockholders** are the owners of a firm and have voting rights. Depending on the dividend policy of a firm, common stockholders may also receive dividends. **Preferred stockholders** receive a fixed dividend making it similar to a bond. The fixed dividend makes the price of preferred stock stable as long as interest rates are not volatile. Preferred stockholders have priority in claims relative to common stockholders but do not have voting rights unless its dividends have not been paid. Dividends paid by the company to investors in common stock or preferred stocks are not tax deductible by the payer.

How Stocks Are Sold

Organized Securities Exchanges

Organized securities exchanges typically have a centralized location where trading occurs. The largest organized exchange in the United States is the New York Stock Exchange (NYSE). Traditionally, the term "exchange" has been used to refer to a physical location. Modern technology has "muddied" the use of that term because the NYSE does a significant volume of its trading using electronic networks that do not require a physical exchange location. After its mergers with electronic communication network, Archipelago and Euronext, the combined NYSE Euronext currently has about 8,500 firms that trade through the exchange and the average market value of these companies exceeds $19.6 billion. The daily volume of shares traded now top 4 billion per day. A company must apply for listing on an exchange to have its stock traded. Each exchange establishes requirements for listing. The NYSE started pricing stocks in decimals rather than eighths of a dollar on January 29, 2001.

Over-the-Counter Markets

The **over-the-counter markets** do not typically have centralized trading locations but rather are systems of computers over which trading occurs. The **National Association of Securities Dealers Automated Quotation System (NASDAQ)** is an over-the-counter market in which dealers make a market by quoting bid prices and ask prices to buy and sell securities. The over-the-counter market is important to providing liquidity intervention to increase demand for thinly traded securities.

Organized versus OTC Trading

Organized exchanges are auction markets that have specialists that are responsible for making orderly markets in several securities. Floor traders will take buy and sell orders from brokerage firms and go to the appropriate trading post on the exchange and will yell orders to the specialist. On the NYSE, each stock is assigned one specialist. Even though each stock is assigned to only one specialist, each specialist will have more than one stock for which they are responsible for providing orderly trading. The NYSE also has the SuperDOT (Super designated Order Turnaround System) that routes orders to specialists directly. About 75% of the buy and sell orders on the exchange are completed using SuperDot.

Comparatively, over-the-counter markets have multiple dealers that buy and sell each stock. Dealers or market makers earn profits through buying stock at the bid price and selling them at the ask price. The difference between the bid price and the ask price is known as the bid-ask spread. Market makers update their bid prices and ask prices regularly as orders are executed and prices move.

Although both the OTC trading firms and the NYSE are heavily regulated, they are both for-profit entities and compete for business. As with all for-profit corporations, they have a responsibility to increase the wealth of their shareholders.

Electronic Communication Networks (ECNs)

ECNs are computerized trading systems that match buy orders and sell orders on price and quantity. ECNs accept orders from both dealers and individual investors. The text identifies four advantages of ECNs over other trading system: (1) transparency—unfilled orders are seen by other traders; (2) cost reduction through reduced spreads; (3) faster execution via automated execution; and (4) after hours trading. The primary disadvantage of ECNs is that they work well for large volume professional traders and should not be used by those trading low volume stocks.

Exchange Traded Funds (ETFs)

ETFs are stocks that trade like any other common stock. The major difference is that ETFs are backed by a portfolio of stocks that was created prior to the issuance of the ETF. ETFs can best be understood with an example. Powershares put together a portfolio of stocks that is designed to mimic the performance of the 100 of the largest most innovative non-financial companies. The company then created an ETF that reflects the price performance of that 100-stock portfolio. All ETFs are created in similar fashion but are composed of other securities, such as the content of the S&P 500 Index or the Dow Jones Industrial Average. There are ETFs for domestic stock indexes, international stocks indexes, and fixed income securities.

There are several important advantages to ETFs. Investors can use the same type of orders that they can place with regular common stock, such as limit order and stop orders. These ETFs can be purchased on margin. Once the initial portfolio has been put together, the ongoing management costs are very low. And there is no minimum amount that must be initially invested, unlike mutual funds that often require a minimum amount of a couple of thousand dollars. ETFs are similar to index mutual funds except for the advantages just listed. The one major disadvantage of ETFs is that a brokerage commissions must be paid to buy or sell the shares.

Computing the Price of Common Stock

The value of any asset is the discounted value of the future cash flows expected to occur over the life of an asset. The text offers four models to value equities: the one-period valuation model, the generalized dividend valuation model, the Gordon growth model, and the price earnings valuation model.

The One-Period Valuation Model

The **one-period valuation model** states that the value or price of a stock equals the discounted value of next period's dividend plus the discounted value of the expected price of the stock at the end of next period. Formally,

$$P_0 = \frac{Div_1}{(1+k_c)} + \frac{P_1}{(1+k_c)}$$

where P_0 is the current price of the stock, Div_1 is the dividend to be paid at the end of year 1, k_c is the required rate of return on equity, and P_1 is the expected price of the stock at the end of year 1. For example, IBM is expected to be $107, and the expected dividend at the end of next year is $0.81. If the company's required return on equity is 12%, then the value of IBM's stock is

$$P_0 = \frac{\$0.81}{(1+0.12)} + \frac{107}{(1+0.12)} = 96.26.$$

The Generalized Dividend Valuation Model

The **generalized dividend valuation model** states that the price of any stock is equal to the summation of the present value of all dividends. According to this model, the only cash flows associated with a stock come from dividends. Mathematically, the model is as follows:

$$P_0 = \sum_{t=1}^{\infty} \frac{Div_t}{(1+k_c)^t}.$$

The Gordon Growth Model

The **Gordon growth or constant growth model** states that a stock that is expected to have a constant growth rate of dividends forever can be determined by dividing the next period's expected dividend by the difference between the company's required rate of return on equity and expected growth rate:

$$P_0 = \frac{D_1}{(k_c - g)}.$$

where: P_0 is the current price of the stock, Div_1 is the dividend to be paid at the end of year 1, k_c is the required rate of return on equity, and g is the expected growth rate in dividends. This model requires that the growth rate be constant and less than the company's required return on equity. Suppose that IBM's required return on equity is 12%, the expected growth rate in dividends is 11.25%, and the current dividend is $0.72. According to the constant growth model, the value of IBM is

$$P_0 = \frac{0.72 \times (1+0.01125)}{(0.12 - 0.1125)} = 106.80.$$

Note:
$$D_1 = D_0 (1 + g).$$

Price Earnings Valuation Method

The price earnings approach to stock valuation states that the price of a stock equals the price earnings ratio (P/E) times the firm's expected earnings. The **P/E ratio** tells us how much investors are willing to pay per dollar of earnings. Higher P/E ratios can mean that either a company's earnings are expected to rise quickly in the future or the company is low risk and investors are willing to pay a premium for the company's stock.

$$P_0 = \frac{P}{E} \times E$$

IBM currently has a P/E ratio of 18 and is expected to make $6.16 per share next year. What is the value of IBM?

$$18 \times 6.16 = 110.88$$

How the Market Sets Security Prices

A security's price is established by the buyer who is willing and able to pay the most. The buyer who is willing to pay the most should be able to use the asset most effectively. Uncertainty about an asset can be reduced by increasing the information available about the asset. This may result in an increase in the value of the asset.

Errors in Valuation

Errors in valuation of a stock can arise from at least three factors: (1) difficulty in estimating future growth—forecasting the future is always challenging; (2) difficulty in estimating risk—minor misstatements of the interest rate significantly distorts the present value; and (3) difficulty in forecasting dividends.

Stock Market Indexes

A stock market index is comprised of a portfolio of stocks that is expected to have characteristics similar to some other stocks or be representative of some pre-specified group of companies. The performance of the index is supposed to track the performance of those companies. The most recognized indices are the Dow Jones Industrials Average (DJIA) and the Standard and Poor's 500 Index (S&P 500). Both of these indices are supposed to reflect the performance of the broad market.

Buying Foreign Stocks

Investors can diversify their portfolios by having some international exposure. They can achieve international diversification by either purchasing foreign shares listed on a foreign exchange or by purchasing American depository receipts (ADRs). An ADR is a receipt for shares of a foreign company that a U.S. bank has purchased and placed in its vault. ADRs are traded in the United States in dollars. Furthermore, the issuing bank converts the dividends into dollars. Foreign firms with ADRs traded in the United States are not subject to SEC disclosure requirements.

Regulation of the Stock Market

To restore faith in the U.S. securities markets during the Great Depression, Congress passed the Securities Act of 1933 and the Securities and Exchange Act of 1934. The goals of these acts are (1) to require firms to truthfully disclose the status of their business and (2) to require the fair treatment of investors by brokers, dealers, and exchanges. The Securities and Exchange Commission (SEC) was created to enforce these laws.

The Securities and Exchange Commission

The SEC protects investors and maintains the integrity of the securities markets by promoting information disclosure by corporations. The SEC has five main divisions: the Division of Corporate Finance, the Division of Trading and Markets, the Division of Risk, Strategy, and Financial Innovation, the Division of Investment Management, and the Division of Enforcement. The Division of Corporate Finance collects required filings including quarterly reports, annual reports, and registration statements. The Division of Trading and Markets regulates the major market participants by issuing rules to maintain efficient and orderly markets. The Division of Risk, Strategy, and Financial Innovation provides sophisticated and data-driven economic and risk analyses to help inform the agency's policy making, rule making, enforcement, and examinations. The Division of Investment Management regulates the investment management industry by creating rules and regulations regarding investment companies such as mutual funds. The Division of Enforcement investigates possible violation of securities markets' rules and regulations. The SEC can bring civil suits against violators.

Exercise 1: Definitions and Terminology

_____ 1. The largest organized exchange in the United States

a. preferred stock

_____ 2. Shares that have voting rights

b. ECNs

_____ 3. Systems of computers over which trading occurs

c. P/E ratio

_____ 4. Regulates the major market participants

d. ADR

_____ 5. Shares that receive a fixed dividend

e. S&P 500

_____ 6. The price of a stock divided by its earnings per share

f. common stock

_____ 7. Computerized trading systems that match buy and sell orders on price and quantity

g. NYSE

h. Division of Corporate Finance

_____ 8. Collects required SEC filings

_____ 9. A receipt for shares of a foreign company that a U.S. bank purchased and placed in its vault

i. OTC markets

j. Division of Trading and Markets

_____ 10. A stock index that reflects the performance of the broad market

■ Self-Test

Part A: Fill in the Blanks

1. _____ stockholders are the owners of the firms.

2. The _____ is an OTC market in which brokers and dealers quote prices to buy and sell.

3. _____ are auction markets in which specialists are responsible for maintaining orderly markets.

4.   Both the _____ and the _____ are indices that track the performance of the broad market.

5.   The _____ protects investors by promoting information disclosure.

6.   The _____ Act of _____ requires firms to disclose the status of their business.

7.   If an investor wants to diversify her portfolio internationally, she can buy either _____ or _____ shares.

8.   Stock returns are of capital gains and _____.

9.   The P/E ratio tells how much investors are willing to pay per dollar of _____.

10. The _____ model assumes that a firm's dividends will growth at the same rate forever.

Part B: True-False Questions

T   F   1.   The value of any asset is the present value of all future cash flows.

T   F   2.   The Generalized Dividend model assumes that the growth rate of dividends for a firm will be constant.

T   F   3.   An advantage of ECNs is the reduction of trading costs through smaller spreads.

T   F   4.   The Philadelphia Stock Exchange is the largest organized securities exchange in the United States.

T   F   5.   The P/E ratio model states that the value of a stock is the P/E ratio times last year's earnings per share.

T   F   6.   ADRs are traded in the home currency of the foreign company.

T   F   7.   A security's price is set by the buyer who is willing to pay the least.

T   F   8.   The Division of Enforcement of the SEC collects required filings including registration statements.

T   F   9.   Common stockholders have priority in claims relative to common stockholders.

T   F   10. The one-period valuation model states that the value of a common stock equals the value of next period's dividend plus the discounted value of next period's expected stock price.

Part C: Multiple-Choice Questions

1.   Which of the following is not a benefit of ECNs?
     (a) Unfilled orders seen by other traders
     (b) After hours trading
     (c) Specialist intervention
     (d) Faster automated order executions

2. What is the value of the common stock of Wachovia Corporation if the dividend is currently $1.84, the expected growth rate of dividends is 10%, and the required rate of return is 14%?
   (a) $13.14
   (b) $18.40
   (c) $46.00
   (d) $50.60

3. What is the value of Wachovia Corporation's common stock if it has a P/E ratio of 13.26 and analysts expect the company to earn $4.78 per share next year?
   (a) $36.05
   (b) $63.38
   (c) $65.58
   (d) $73.38

4. The largest organized securities exchange in the United States is the
   (a) American Stock Exchange.
   (b) Philadelphia Stock Exchange.
   (c) New York Stock Exchange.
   (d) Boston Stock Exchange.

5. What type of security has no voting rights and pays a fixed dividend for the life of the security?
   (a) Common stock
   (b) Convertible preferred stock
   (c) Preferred stock
   (d) Variable-rate preferred stock

6. Which stock valuation model states that the value of any stock equals the summation of the present value of all future dividends?
   (a) Generalized dividend valuation model
   (b) Gordon growth model
   (c) One-Period valuation model
   (d) Price Earnings Valuation method

7. Which stock valuation model states that the value of common stock is the current dividend divided by the difference between the required rate of return and the company's expected growth rate of dividends?
   (a) Generalized dividend valuation model
   (b) Gordon growth model
   (c) One-period valuation model
   (d) Price Earnings Valuation method
   (e) None of the above

8. If Wachovia Corp. is expected to pay a dividend of $2.02 next year and the company's stock price is expected to be $55.66, then what is the current value of the company's shares if the required rate of return is 14%?
    (a) $50.60
    (b) $63.45
    (c) $73.45
    (d) $397.57

9. Why might a company have a high P/E ratio?
    (a) The company's earnings are expected to grow quickly in the future.
    (b) The company is considered high risk.
    (c) The company is considered low risk.
    (d) Investors are willing to pay a premium for the stock.
    (e) (a), (c), and (d)

10. Which division of the SEC is most responsible for regulating the investment management industry?
    (a) The Division of Corporate Finance
    (b) The Division of Investment Management
    (c) The Division of Enforcement
    (d) The Division of Trading and Markets

Part D: Short Answer Questions

1. What differentiates organized exchanges from over-the-counter markets?

2. What are possible causes of errors in stock valuation?

3. What are differences between common stock and preferred stock?

■ Answers

Exercise 1: Definitions and Terminology

1.	g	6.	c
2.	f	7.	b
3.	i	8.	h
4.	j	9.	d
5.	a	10.	e

Self-Test

Part A

1.	Common	6.	Securities, 1933
2.	NASDAQ	7.	ADRs, foreign
3.	organized exchanges	8.	dividends
4.	DJIA, S&P 500	9.	earnings
5.	SEC	10.	Gordon Growth

Part B

1.	T	6.	F
2.	F	7.	F
3.	T	8.	F
4.	F	9.	F
5.	F	10.	F

Part C

1.	c	6.	a
2.	d	7.	e
3.	b	8.	a
4.	c	9.	e
5.	c	10.	b

Part D

1. Differences between organized exchanges and over-the-counter markets are

   (a) Organized exchanges usually have a centralized trading location while OTC markets do not.

   (b) Organized exchanges have specialists while OTC markets have dealers or market makers.

   (c) Organized exchanges are normally auction markets while OTC markets are dealer quote driven markets.

2. Possible causes of errors in stock valuation are

   (a) Difficulty in estimating future growth.

   (b) Difficulty in estimating risk.

   (c) Difficulty in forecasting dividends.

3. Most common stock issues have voting rights but preferred stock issues only have voting rights in extenuating circumstances. Owners of common stock are the residual owners of the firms, that is, they receive what is left over after everyone else is paid. If the firm is growing, then what common holders receive should grow over time. Preferred shareholders receive the same dividend amount regardless of improved performance of the firm.

Chapter 14
The Mortgage Markets

■ Chapter Learning Goals

By the end of this chapter, you should

1. Be familiar with the history of the development of the mortgage market.

2. Know the major factors that go into creating a mortgage contract.

3. Have an understanding of the types of mortgage loans that are available and the benefits and costs of each type of contract.

4. Be able to discuss the role that government agencies have in the activities of the secondary market for mortgages.

■ Chapter Summary

Chapter 14 provides an insight into the world of mortgages. Although mortgages have been around in one form or another for many decades, only in relatively recent times has this market been refined to the point that it is a significant part of the financial markets. The chapter gives some important historical developments, presents a few of the most important variables that go into mortgage creation, and develops how the market has matured and grown through innovation.

What Is a Mortgage?

Mortgages are loans that are made for the purpose of allowing the borrower to purchase real estate. They are used to finance residential home purchases, office buildings, and even large complexes such as shopping centers. Because the majority of mortgage loans are used for purchasing residential housing, this chapter will concentrate on that segment of the mortgage market. Mortgages are long-term-collateralized loans that typically have a variety of payment options available to the home buyer.

The Major Characteristics of Residential Mortgages

For many years, the ability of the average American to obtain a mortgage loan was severely restricted. It was not until after World War I that the state and federal lending laws were changed to allow participation in the mortgage market by most citizens. The Great Depression resulted in many defaults on mortgage loans, which again led to changes in the mortgage market. Contributing to the mortgage problem was the fact that most mortgages were constructed with **balloon payments.** Balloon payment mortgages required the owner to make only interest payments for three to five years, and then the entire principal of the loan became due. The lack of loanable funds during the depression made refinancing impossible for most homeowners. The federal government stepped in and took over the financing and allowed the borrowers to pay off the mortgage over a long period of time. This action started a trend toward long-term mortgages.

In place of the balloon mortgage came the **amortized loan.** In most **conventional loans,** that is, loans that are not guaranteed by the Veterans Administration (VA) or the Federal Housing Administration (FHA), the lender requires the borrower to make a **down payment** at the time of signing the contract. The balance of the loan is paid off usually in equal dollar installments over the life of the loan. Each monthly payment includes both the interest owed and some payment toward the remaining loan balance. After the last payment, the loan balance is zero. This payment process is referred to as **fully amortizing** the loan.

A major factor to borrowers is the size of the interest payment. The final rate that is applied to the mortgage loan depends on three factors: (1) the current level of long-term interest rates, (2) the life of the mortgage, with longer-terms having a higher rate, and (3) the number of **discount points** paid at closing. Discount points are interest payments made at the beginning of the loan. They are expressed as a percentage of the value of the loan. For example, two points on a $100,000 mortgage is 2% of the $100,000 or $2,000. The higher the points, the lower the interest rate, but points increase the amount of cash that the buyer must have available at the time the loan is made.

The length of time for a residential mortgage is 15 or 30 years, although other terms are available. The longer the term, the higher the interest rate and the greater the dollar amount of total interest paid. The benefit to borrowers is that the monthly payment is lower, allowing them to afford a larger and more expensive home than would be possible with a shorter-term mortgage.

There are three main factors that are important in whether or not a potential homeowner will be able to obtain a mortgage. First is the amount of **collateral** available. The lender will take a **lien** on the house, which gives the lender the right to sell the home to pay off the remaining mortgage balance should the borrower default. The larger the down payment, the greater is the equity in the home and more protection for the lender. The higher the down payment, the smaller the loan needed and the more likely the loan will be made. The third factor is the existence of **mortgage insurance.** This insurance guarantees to make up a discrepancy between the value of the property and the loan amount should a default occur. Private mortgage insurance (PMI) is usually required on loans that have less than a 20 percent down payment. The final point is the borrower's qualifications. The borrower must meet certain guidelines established by the secondary market agencies and lending institutions before the loan can be made.

Mortgage Interest Rates

The mortgage interest rate is the single most differentiating factor for mortgage products offered by lenders. The interest rate is determined by three main factors: current long-term market rates, the length of the mortgage, and the number of discount points paid. Market rates are determined by supply and demand for long-term funds. Supply and demand for long-term funds are influenced by global, national, and regional economic conditions. Longer-term mortgages typically have higher interest rates than short-term mortgages. Conventional mortgages are usually offered in 15- or 30-year terms but can be available in other terms such as 10- or 20-year periods. Discount points are interest payments made at the beginning of a loan. For example, a loan with one discount point means the borrower pays 1% of the loan amount at closing. In exchange for points, the lender will lower the interest rate on a loan.

There is a simple calculation called the Effective Annual Rate that can be used to determine if it is beneficial to pay discount points. The Effective Annual Rate (EAR) should be computed both with and without the discount points. First, compute the monthly interest from the annualized rate. For example, a 12% loan would have a monthly interest rate of 1%. Then compute the compounded annualized rate as follows:

$$(1 + \text{Monthly Rate})^{12} - 1 = \text{Effective annual rate.}$$

Calculate the EAR with and without discount points and compare the two rates. One should also consider how long the property will be held when choosing mortgages. Paying points up front normally only makes sense if the property is held for an extended period of time. Typically, points should not be paid if the property is paid off in five years or less.

Loan Terms

Mortgages have many eligibility requirements. One requirement is collateral, the real estate being pledged to secure the loan. Typically, the property being bought is used as collateral. To use a property for collateral, the lending institution will place a lien against it. A lien is a public record that attaches to the title of a property. It gives the holder of the lien the right to sell the property should the borrower default on the loan. The lien stays on record until the property has been fully paid.

Lenders often require a down payment when obtaining a mortgage. The down payment is a portion of the purchase price paid in advance to lower the amount borrowed. The amount of down payment required depends on the type of loan and normally varies from 5% to 20%.

Lenders protect themselves by requiring that the borrower purchase Private Mortgage Insurance (PMI). PMI is an insurance policy that makes up the difference between the property value and the loan amount should a default occur. PMI is usually required when the loan-to-value ratio (LTV) is more than 80%.

Borrowers must first qualify for a mortgage before a financial institution will create the loan. Because financial institutions typically sell mortgages to federal agencies in the secondary mortgage market, there are established guidelines to follow. The rules of loan qualification are complex and change regularly. The guidelines are based on the borrower's credit worthiness and ability to repay the loan based on existing outstanding debt and monthly income.

Types of Mortgage Loans

Insured and Conventional

Some mortgages are guaranteed by either the VA or the FHA and are called **insured loans.** The loans are made by regular mortgage lending firms, but these two organizations guarantee the lender against loss in the event of default. Certain criteria must be met to qualify for one of the insured mortgage loans. Loans that are not guaranteed by the VA or FHA are called **conventional loans.**

Fixed and Adjustable Rates

In **fixed rate mortgages,** the interest rate on the loan does not vary over the life of the mortgage. This rate allows the mortgage payment to be constant over the life of the loan. Fixed rates are the preferred method of financing. Lenders prefer **adjustable rate mortgages (ARMs)** because this approach allows the interest rate to fluctuate with general interest rate movements and reduces the amount of interest-rate risk. With ARMs, the loan rate is tied to some market rate, such as the rate on Treasury Bills, and the mortgage rate moves up and down with the Treasury Bill rate. The amount of movement in any one period and over the life of the loan is usually **capped** by establishing a maximum value the rate can go up to.

Other Special Types of Mortgages

Graduated Payment Mortgages (GPM)—The loan payment is lower in the first few years, then the payment rises. This allows the homebuyer to purchase a larger home with payments that are acceptably low, and as their income rises, the payment increases. This type of mortgage is good if the borrower is confident of earnings increases.

Growing Equity Mortgage (GEM)—Here the initial payment is the same as a regular conventional mortgage but over time the payment increases, and the increased payment amount goes toward the principal. This accelerated payment of principal reduces the life of the loan. Borrowers should keep in mind that they can usually make additional payments on their principal on any conventional loan without any penalty. They do not need the Growing Equity Mortgage.

Second Mortgages—These mortgages are loans secured by the same property that is used to secure the first mortgage. Payments are made on the second mortgage just like the first mortgage payments. The second mortgage is junior (subordinate) to the first mortgage in receiving payment of principal in the event the borrower defaults. A significant advantage of the second mortgage is that the interest paid is tax deductible just like the first mortgage interest.

Reverse Annuity Mortgage (RAM)—The RAM is a financial innovation used by retired people to convert the equity in their home into a liquid asset. The lending institution makes a monthly payment to the homeowner. Each payment then increases the lender's claim against the house. In other words, the mortgage loan is increasing with each payment and the accumulation of interest. When the person dies, the house is sold, the mortgage paid off, and any remaining funds placed in the deceased's estate.

Option ARM—The Option ARM is an adjustable rate mortgages that gives the borrower the option of reducing the monthly payment. If the option is exercised instead of reducing the mortgage balance, the amount owed steadily increases.

Mortgage Lending Institutions

Whether the borrower obtains the loan from a commercial bank, a savings and loan, a mortgage company, or other lender, the lender is not likely to remain the lender for the full life of the loan. Most mortgage lenders will sell the loan to another lender. The borrower may not even be aware of the transactions. The selling of the loan does not cause any changes in the loan agreement. The only difference may be that the payments are sent to a new business address. Sometimes the original lender will continue to receive the payments and then sends them to the buyer of the mortgage loan. They function as a **servicing agent** for the firm that purchased the loan.

The Secondary Mortgage Market

One problem with mortgage loans for lenders was that they committed their money for a long period of time. This commitment reduced liquidity and subjected the lender to significant interest-rate risk. What was needed was a secondary market for mortgages. This problem has been solved by the creation of three government agencies, which have as their charge the creation and functioning of a secondary market for mortgage loans. The Federal National Mortgage Association (Fannie Mae), the Government National Mortgage Association (Ginnie Mae), and the Federal Home Loan Mortgage Association (Freddie Mac) are the three agencies.

The Securitization of Mortgages

The way the secondary market works is that an original lender will collect a portfolio of mortgages, called a **mortgage pool,** and will use these mortgages and their payments as collateral for payments on a new security call a **mortgage pass-through.** Because the mortgage loans are used as collateral for the pass-through security, the pass-through is also called a **securitized mortgage.** The pass-through is created by the appropriate government agency mentioned above. When the payments are received on the original loan the payments are "passed through" to a trustee who makes payment to the purchasing government agency.

The differences among Fannie Mae, Ginnie Mae, and Freddie Mac are primarily the specific loan markets they serve. Fannie Mae was created to provide a secondary market for mortgages held by thrift organizations. Ginnie Mae is charged with providing the secondary market for insured mortgages held by commercial banks and mortgage companies. Freddie Mac assists savings and loans with their mortgage market needs. The pass-through securities created by Freddie Mac are called **participation certificates.** Five factors distinguish Ginnie Mae (GNMA) mortgage pools from Freddie Mac (FHLMC) pools. FHLMC pools (1) contain conventional loans, (2) are not federally insured, (3) contain mortgages of different rates, (4) are larger, and (5) have a minimum denomination of $100,000 (versus $25,000 for GNMA). **Collateralized mortgage obligations (CMOs)** are securities classified by when prepayment is likely to occur allowing a more efficient risk sharing of prepayment risk. The private sector of the economy also provides some secondary market alternatives for original mortgage lenders through the creation of **private pass-through securities (PIPs).**

Subprime loans were made for those borrowers who did not qualify for conventional loans at market rates due to either a poor credit rating or insufficient income-to-loan value. The average subprime FICO score was 624 versus 742 for prime mortgage loans. Piggyback loans, NoDoc, or NINJA (no income no asset loans) encouraged borrowers to commit to these loans that may have been larger than they could realistically handle. The emergence of this easy credit increased demand leading to the real estate bubble in the 2000s.

■ Exercises

Exercise 1: Definitions and Terminology

Match the following terms in the column on the right with the definition or description in the column on the left. Place the letter of the term in the blank provided next to the appropriate definition.

_____ 1. All mortgages backed by the FHA and the VA have this protection feature.

_____ 2. A percent of the loan amount that is paid at the time the loan is made to reduce the interest rate.

_____ 3. Securities that are issued and are backed by a pool of mortgage loans.

_____ 4. The inclusion of both principal and interest in the monthly payment.

_____ 5. An account maintained by a mortgage servicer containing funds held to pay insurance and taxes.

_____ 6. Provided by private firms to protect the lender against loss in the event of mortgage default.

_____ 7. When the entire principal payment is due at one time at the end of the loan period.

_____ 8. A loan that uses real estate as collateral.

_____ 9. Mortgage loans that are not guaranteed by the FHA or VA.

_____ 10. A pass-through security having different maturity groups for payment of principal.

_____ 11. A public record identifying a property as security for a loan.

_____ 12. Portion of the purchase price paid up front.

_____ 13. Loan servicing feature established to permit the lender to make tax and insurance payments for the borrower.

_____ 14. Mortgages whose interest rates are allowed to fluctuate with general interest rate movements.

_____ 15. Loans to borrowers who did not qualify for conventional loans due to poor credit or low income

a.   lien

b.   amortization

c.   balloon loans

d.   discount points

e.   private mortgage insurance

f.   insured mortgages

g.   conventional mortgages

h.   reserve accounts

i.   mortgage pass-through

j.   collateralized-mortgage obligations

k.   mortgage

l.   down payment

m.   reserve accounts

n.   adjustable-rate mortgages

o.   subprime loan

Exercise 2: Fixed versus Adjustable Rate Mortgage Loans

Explain the advantages and disadvantages to the lender and the borrower of having a fixed rate versus an adjustable rate mortgage loan.

_____

_____

_____

Exercise 3: Loan Payment Calculations

For each of the three mortgages, calculate the monthly payment for principal and interest.

Mortgage	Amount of Loan	Length of Loan in Months	Interest Rate	Monthly Payment
1	$100,000	180	8.0%	
2	$100,000	360	8.0%	
3	$100,000	360	9.0%	

Exercise 4: Secondary Mortgage Markets

The federal government was instrumental in development of the secondary mortgage market after the Great Depression and again in the late 1960s. What were the major steps taken by the federal government to develop the secondary market?

_____

_____

_____

Exercise 5: Subprime Loans

What are two reasons that borrowers would not qualify for conventional loans?

_____

_____

■ Self-Test

Part A: Fill in the Blanks

1. When a loan is paid through a series of payments where each payment includes both interest and principal payments, the loan is being _____.

2. The mortgage defaults during the Great Depression resulted partially because most mortgage loans had _____ payments requiring the payment of the full principal sum after only three to five years.

3. _____ are interest payments made at the beginning of a mortgage loan. The higher these payments, up to a point, the _____ the interest rate.

4. To protect the mortgage lender, a(n) _____ will be placed against the property thus having the property serve as _____ for the loan.

5. Conventional mortgage loans normally require a(n) _____, which reduces the loan amount below the market value of the real estate.

6. Mortgage lenders frequently protect themselves against loss by requiring that borrowers purchase _____, which covers any difference between the loan balance and the property value upon default.

7. Insured mortgages are guaranteed by either the _____ or the Veterans Administration.

8. Mortgages that carry the same interest rate over the life of the loan are called _____ mortgages.

9. If the interest rate on a mortgage can vary over the life of the loan, it is referred to as a(n) _____ mortgage.

10. Many lenders maintain a(n) _____ account where they store the funds, paid by borrowers, that are used to pay taxes and insurance on the property.

11. Mortgage lenders group mortgage loans into mortgage _____ for the purpose of using them to back other securities, which can be sold.

12. _____ mortgages are low-risk securities that have higher yields than comparable government bonds and attract funds from around the world.

13. A type of pass-through security that has different prepayment schedules for payment of the principal over the life of the loan is called a(n) _____.

14. Lenders prefer adjustable rate mortgages because they reduce the lender's exposure to _____ risk.

15. Mortgages not insured by the VA or FHA are called _____ mortgages.

16. _____ is required on most loans with a loan to value ratio of more than 80% and protects lenders against loss in the event of default.

17. Retired persons can live off of the equity they have build up in their home with a(n) _____.

18. _____ are securities classified by when prepayment is likely to occur allowing a more efficient risk sharing of prepayment risk.

Part B: True-False Questions

Circle whether the following statements are true (T) or false (F).

T F   1. The major borrowers in the mortgage market are businesses and governments.

T F   2. Most mortgage loans in the early history of the United States were made directly between individuals.

T F 3. Mortgage interest rates tend to stay above the rate on Treasury bonds, but the two rates generally move in the same direction.

T F 4. If a borrower defaults on a mortgage loan, the lender cannot sell the property without the permission of the owner because of the need of everyone for shelter.

T F 5. A title search is done before a mortgage loan is made to insure that the property being purchased is free from liens.

T F 6. A "rule of thumb" for the amount of money a borrower can obtain for a mortgage is that the total payment (loan, insurance, taxes) cannot exceed 40% of the borrower's gross monthly income.

T F 7. Lenders that make conventional mortgage loans do not make insured mortgage loans because the VA and FHA are responsible for making those loans.

T F 8. One common way for loan originators to make money on a mortgage loan that is eventually sold is to charge a loan origination fee when they make the loan.

T F 9. The secondary market for mortgages in the United States was founded by the federal government.

T F 10. The majority of mortgage loans are for the purpose of purchasing residential homes.

T F 11. Not until after World War I did the federal government permit national commercial banks to make mortgage loans.

T F 12. The most common lifetime for a mortgage loan is 20 years.

T F 13. One disadvantage of the down payment for the lender is that it increases moral hazard.

T F 14. Before the creation of a secondary market for mortgages, a major problem for mortgage lenders was lack of diversification because most lenders issued loans over a small geographic area.

T F 15. Adjustable rate mortgages have the added risk to the borrower that the rate has no upper limit and will continue to rise as long as interest rates in general increase.

T F 16. Residential mortgages are only available to borrowers who pay a 10% down payment and meet strict income qualifications.

T F 17. It is possible for homebuyers to buy down the interest rate on their loan by paying what is known as discount points.

T F 18. A lien is taken off of a title after the borrower has paid 80% of the total loan amount.

Part C: Multiple-Choice Questions

Circle the appropriate answer.

1. As a group the largest mortgage lenders are
   (a) savings and loans.
   (b) mortgage companies.
   (c) credit unions.
   (d) commercial banks.

2. Of the following statements, which one is correct about second mortgages?
   (a) The interest payments are not tax deductible.
   (b) The second mortgage has the same priority in default as the primary mortgage.
   (c) It gives property owners an easy way to get cash from the equity in their home.
   (d) This mortgage is generally more costly to obtain than it would be to refinance.

3. Which of the following types of mortgage loans has a lower payment during the first few years of the loan and then the payments increase?
   (a) Graduated payment mortgages
   (b) Growing equity mortgages
   (c) Shared appreciation mortgages
   (d) Equity participation mortgages

4. Which of the following types of mortgage loans allow the lender to share in any increase in the market value of the property?
   (a) Graduated payment mortgages
   (b) Growing equity mortgages
   (c) Shared appreciation mortgages
   (d) Equity participation mortgages

5. Which of the following types of mortgage loans allows a third party (not the lender) to share in any increase in the market value of the property?
   (a) Graduated payment mortgages
   (b) Growing equity mortgages
   (c) Shared appreciation mortgages
   (d) Equity participation mortgages

6. Reverse annuity mortgages have all except which of the following characteristics?
   (a) The amount of the mortgage loan increases over time.
   (b) The lender makes monthly payments to the borrower.
   (c) The home does not serve as collateral because the estate of the borrower will pay the loan after their death.
   (d) The borrower is usually a retired person seeking to get money from the equity in his or her home.

7. Which of the following was a problem faced by mortgage lenders in trying to sell their mortgages in the secondary market prior to the creation of mortgage-backed securities?
   (a) The large dollar amounts of most single mortgages made finding a buyer difficult.
   (b) Mortgages were not standardized, making them harder to sell.
   (c) The lack of default risk made the returns too low resulting in too few buyers.
   (d) Due to their simple design, mortgages were easy to service, and lenders frequently charged too much for the loan resulting in too few buyers.

8. Of the following secondary market pass through securities, which one is not guaranteed by the federal agency?
    (a) GNMA (Ginnie Mae) pass-throughs
    (b) FHLMC (Freddie Mac) pass-throughs
    (c) FNMA (Fannie Mae) pass-throughs
    (d) All three of the above are guaranteed against default by the agency.

9. Which of the following agencies issues collateralized mortgage obligations?
    (a) GNMA (Ginnie Mae) pass-through securities
    (b) FHLMC (Freddie Mac) pass-through securities
    (c) FNMA (Fannie Mae) pass-through securities
    (d) All three of the issue collateralized mortgage obligations.

10. Which of the following does not influence the size of the interest rate on a mortgage loan?
    (a) The specific location of the property
    (b) The length of time the mortgage is outstanding
    (c) The number of discount points paid by the buyer at closing
    (d) The current level of interest rates in the economy

11. Of the following, which one will increase the risk to the lender?
    (a) The purchase of private mortgage insurance
    (b) A large down payment
    (c) The higher the mortgage payment relative to the monthly income of the borrower
    (d) The ability to put the loan in a mortgage pool and sell it in the secondary market

12. Which of the following is true about adjustable rate mortgages (ARMs)?
    (a) The amount of the rate movement each period and over the life of the loan is capped.
    (b) Borrowers prefer ARMs due to the interest rate being lower than fixed rate mortgages.
    (c) ARMs increase the interest-rate risk faced by lenders.
    (d) Lenders do not prefer ARMs and thus charge a higher interest rate for them.

13. FHLMC and GNMA pass-through securities are different in several ways. Which of the following is not a difference between these two securities?
    (a) FHLMC sells in minimum denominations of $100,000 versus $25,000 for GNMA.
    (b) FHLMC contains conventional mortgages, while GNMA has insured mortgages.
    (c) GNMA mortgage pools are smaller than FHLMC pools.
    (d) GNMA issues participation certificates, and FHLMC issues pass-through securities only.

14. Which of the following terms does not apply to pass-through securities?
    (a) Prepayment risk
    (b) Collateralized mortgage obligations
    (c) Private mortgage insurance
    (d) Participation certificates
    (e) Securitized mortgages

15. Applicants for FHA or VA loans have to meet certain special qualifications. All except which of the following may apply?
    (a) Having served in the military
    (b) A specific income level or lower
    (c) A limit on the size of the loan that is guaranteed
    (d) Must work for a federal or state government agency

16. What is the effective annual rate for a 5.5%, 30-year fixed rate mortgage?
    (a) 6.0%
    (b) 5.74%
    (c) 5.64%
    (d) 5.44%

17. What is the interest rate for a 30-year fixed rate mortgage with an effective annual rate of 6.168%?
    (a) 5.75%
    (b) 5.875%
    (c) 6.0%
    (d) 6.125%

18. Demand in the housing market in the early 2000s was driven by which of the following?
    (a) Subprime borrowers
    (b) Speculators
    (c) Both (a) and (b)
    (d) None of the above

Part D: Short Answer Questions

1. Loan length, points, down payment, and mortgage insurance all play a role in interest rate on a mortgage loan. What amount should borrowers desire for each of these factors if they want their interest rate as low as possible?

    _____

    _____

2. What is a mortgage-backed security?

    _____

    _____

3. How is a collateralized mortgage obligation different from a regular pass-through security?

    _____

    _____

4. What is the benefit to investors of the availability of mortgage-backed mutual funds?

_____

_____

5. What are typical requirements to qualify for a residential mortgage?

_____

_____

6. Describe the characteristics of adjustable rate mortgages (ARMs).

_____

_____

■ Answers to Chapter 14

Exercise 1

1.	f	6.	e	11.	a
2.	d	7.	c	12.	l
3.	i	8.	k	13.	m
4.	b	9.	g	14.	n
5.	h	10.	j	15.	o

Exercise 2

Lenders prefer an adjustable rate mortgage because it reduces their interest-rate risk exposure. The long-term nature of mortgages makes them very sensitive to interest rate changes. Borrowers prefer fixed rate loans to avoid interest-rate risk. However, with fixed rates, the borrower does not benefit if interest rates decline. They may be able to refinance the loan if rates decline, but this alternative is expensive. Both types of loans are generally taken because the borrower gets a much lower rate initially and the lender caps the rate amount of rate movement.

Exercise 3

Mortgage	Amount of Loan	Length of Loan in Months	Interest Rate	Monthly Payment
1	$100,000	180	8.0%	$955.65
2	$100,000	360	8.0%	$733.76
3	$100,000	360	9.0%	$804.62

Exercise 4

Following the Great Depression, Congress allowed the government to take over delinquent loans and permitted payment over a long-period of time. It also established and authorized FNMA, the FHA, and the VA to buy or guarantee mortgages. In the late 1960s, Congress created two more agencies, GNMA and FHLMC, to also purchase pooled mortgages from certain mortgage lenders and repackage them into marketable securities.

Exercise 5

Subprime loans are for borrowers who did not qualify for conventional loans at market rates due to either a poor credit rating or insufficient income-to-loan value.

Self-Test

Part A

1.	amortized	8.	fixed rate	14.	interest rate
2.	balloon	9.	adjustable rate	15.	conventional
3.	discount points, lower	10.	reserve accounts	16.	private mortgage insurance
4.	lien, collateral	11.	pools	17.	reverse annuity mortgage
5.	down payment	12.	securitized	18.	Collateralized mortgage obligations (CMOs)
6.	private mortgage		Insurance		
7.	Federal Housing Administration	13.	collateralized mortgage obligation		

Part B

1.	F	7.	F	13.	F
2.	T	8.	T	14.	T
3.	T	9.	T	15.	F
4.	F	10.	T	16.	F
5.	T	11.	T	17.	T
6.	F	12.	F	18.	F

Part C

1.	d	7.	b	13.	d
2.	c	8.	b	14.	c
3.	a	9.	b	15.	d
4.	c	10.	a	16.	c
5.	d	11.	c	17.	c
6.	c	12.	a	18.	c

Part D

1. To minimize the interest rate, the borrower would want to make the time short, pay high points, make a large down payment, and purchase mortgage insurance.

2. Mortgage-backed securities are bonds issued by (mostly) government agencies that use the bond proceeds to purchase pools of mortgages from lenders. When the mortgage payments are made, the funds are used to pay the interest and principal payments on the mortgage-backed security (bonds).

3. In a regular pass-through, each principal and interest payment is distributed among the bondholders in proportion to the amount of bonds they own. Collateralized mortgage obligations divide the bondholders into classes. Class 1 receives their share of the interest, but they receive all principal payments until this class of bonds is totally paid off and none are outstanding. From that point all principal payments go to class 2 until it is totally paid off, etc.

4. Mortgage-backed mutual funds allow investors with only small amounts to invest to participate in the mortgage market, which normally requires large sums of money to own a diversified portfolio of mortgages. Investors also obtain a high degree of liquidity not normally available in direct mortgage investment.

5. Borrowers must meet a variety of conditions and requirements for financial institutions to extend mortgage funds. First, the borrower must meet credit criteria to be determined by the lender from credit rating services. Also the borrower must have enough income to support existing obligations and the loan in questions. This is usually factored as an acceptable percentage of available income. The loan company will also require a lien be place and probably down payment of a determined percentage of the purchase price. Also, private mortgage insurance may be required for loans over a certain loan to value, usually 80%.

6. Adjustable rate mortgages are tied to market interest rates and can change over time. Typically, the lending institution will place limits on how far the interest rate can move up and down. ARMS lessen interest-rate risk because they are short term. They are usually offered at lower rates than fixed rate mortgages.

Chapter 15
The Foreign Exchange Market

■ Chapter Learning Goals

By the end of this chapter, you should

1. Understand the theory behind purchasing power parity.

2. Be able to explain how variables that affect the price of goods in one country will affect the exchange rate between it and another country.

3. Understand the theory behind interest rate parity.

4. Be able to use interest rate parity to predict short-run changes in exchange rates.

■ Chapter Summary

This chapter explores the determinants of the foreign exchange rate. Foreign exchange rates are important because the prices of foreign goods in our country and of our goods in foreign countries change when the exchange rate changes. This chapter presents models for explaining long-run and short-run changes in exchange rates.

Foreign Exchange Market

An **exchange rate** is the price of a currency in terms of another currency. Exchange rate prices are determined through the buying and selling of currencies in the **foreign exchange market.** There are two kinds of exchange rate transactions; spot transactions, which are more common, or forward transactions. Spot transactions involve the immediate exchange of bank deposits. Forward transactions involve the exchange of bank deposits at a specified future date.

When a currency increases in value relative to another country's, it has **appreciated**; when a currency falls in value it has **depreciated.** When a country's currency appreciates, foreign goods become less expensive, and domestic goods sold abroad become more expensive.

How Foreign Exchange Is Traded

There is more than $3 trillion of currency exchanged each day in the U.S. financial markets. Obviously with such high volume the markets must work quickly and efficiently. Currency is traded in the over the counter market. There are several hundred dealers who make a market in different currencies. Most of these dealers are banks because activity in the foreign exchange market does not involve the actual transfer of a domestic currency for a foreign currency but involves the buying and selling of ownership of bank deposits that are denominated in a dollars.

Exchange Rates in the Long Run

In the long run, the **law of one price** can help explain why currencies may appreciate or depreciate. The law of one price states that identical goods in different countries should cost the same. Purchasing power parity states exchange rates will adjust until this equality is satisfied. This theory suggests that if one country's prices rise relative to another, its currency should depreciate. This depreciation is necessary so that the cost of goods in each country will stay the same after adjusting for exchange rates.

Theory of Purchase Power Parity

There are four factors that affect exchange rates in the long run: (1) relative price levels, (2) trade barriers like tariffs and quotas, (3) preferences for domestic versus foreign goods, and (4) productivity. To understand how each of these factors affects the country's exchange rate, picture a store that has a counter with domestic pencils and foreign pencils for sale. The goal is to adjust the currency so that the pencils sell equally well. If domestic prices rise, the cost of the domestic pencils will rise. To make the foreign pencils sell at the same rate, their cost must also rise. The domestic currency must depreciate to make the foreign goods more expensive.

If foreign goods are subject to a tariff or quota, this will increase their cost to the importer, and their price will increase to cover the higher cost. To keep the now more expensive foreign pencils competitive with the domestic pencils, the domestic currency must appreciate because this will lower the cost of foreign goods. If customers simply prefer the foreign pencils, the domestic currency will depreciate because this will raise their cost relative to the domestic pencils, so the demand for each will stay the same. Finally, if the domestic country becomes more productive, it can produce the pencils more cheaply and lower their cost. To keep the foreign pencils competitive, the domestic currency must appreciate because this lowers the cost of foreign goods.

There are two major shortcoming of PPP for explaining exchange rates. The first shortcoming arises from the assumption that all goods and services are equal and identical. If one product is of high quality in a foreign market and the substitute product in the domestic market is of lesser quality, then a price disparity can exist, and exchange rate will not adjust to equate prices. A second issue is that some products and services are not traded across national boundaries. For example, housing and restaurant services are not sold internationally, so if these prices rise, there would be little direct effect on the exchange rate.

Factors That Affect Exchange Rates in the Long Run

In the long run, relative price levels, tariffs and quotas, preferences for domestic versus foreign goods, and productivity affect the exchange rate. These factors increase the demand for domestically produced goods that are traded relative to foreign traded goods, appreciating the value of the currency.

Factors That Affect Exchange Rates in the Short Run

In the short run, equilibrium in the market will be set based on the supply curve for domestic assets and the demand curve for domestic assets. The demand curve can be shifted by changes in the domestic interest rate, foreign interest rate, and changes in the expected future exchange rate.

Appendix

Interest Rate Parity (IRP)

Although the theory of purchasing power parity is useful for evaluating long-term changes in exchange rates, it does poorly at explaining short-run exchange-rate volatility. To explain short-run volatility, we turn to the **theory of interest rate parity**. According to IRP, investors should earn the same return regardless which country they choose to invest in. If this condition does not hold true, then, because of the easy movement of funds around the world, funds will flow to the country offering the best return.

An Example of IRP

If a U.S. investor buys a French bond the expected return will consist of the foreign interest rate plus the expected appreciation or depreciation in the euros. For example, if the foreign interest rate is 10% and investors expect the euros to appreciate 5% against the dollar, then the total return is 15%. Interest rate parity says that in equilibrium the return to the investor from investing in the United States must equal the return from investing abroad. The exchange rate will adjust to compensate for any differences in expected returns that result from differences in interest rates and expected future appreciation or depreciation of the foreign currency.

■ Exercises

Exercise 1: Foreign Exchange Rates and Goods Prices

1. Suppose the exchange rate between the Swiss franc and the dollar is $0.50 per franc. What would be the exchange rate if it were quoted as francs per dollar? _____

2. If you are contemplating buying a fancy Swiss watch that costs 1,000 francs, how much will it cost you in dollars? _____

3. If a Swiss is contemplating buying an American pocket calculator that costs $100, how much will it cost him in francs? _____

4. If the exchange rate changes to $0.25 per Swiss franc, has there been an appreciation or depreciation of the Swiss franc? _____ Of the dollar? _____

5. Now if you buy the Swiss watch that costs 1,000 francs, how much will it cost you in dollars? _____ Does the Swiss watch cost you more or less than before? _____

6. Now how much will it cost the Swiss in francs for the $100 pocket calculator? _____ Does it cost more or less than before? _____

7. What does the example here indicate about the effect on prices of foreign goods in a country and domestic goods sold abroad when the exchange rate appreciates?

   _____

   _____

8. Suppose that the US$/SwissFr exchange rate stays at $0.25 and the Swiss watch can still be purchased in Switzerland for 1,000 francs. Comparatively, you can buy the same watch in London for 450 pounds. If the SwissFr/British£ exchange rate is Fr0.50 should you purchase the watch in Switzerland or London?

   _____

   _____

9. Where should you purchase the watch if the price in Switzerland drops to 800 francs?

   _____

   _____

10. Suppose the price of the watch were still 1,000 francs in Switzerland and 450 pounds in London. If the US$/SwissFr exchange rate stays at $0.25, at what SwissFr/British£ exchange rate would the watch cost the same in dollars in both Switzerland and London?

    _____

    _____

Exercise 2: Law of One Price and Purchasing Power Parity

A. Suppose that Argentinean wheat costs 3,000 pesos per bushel and that American wheat costs $6 per bushel. In addition, assume that American wheat and Argentinean wheat are identical goods.

   1. If the exchange rate is 300 Argentinean pesos per U.S. dollar, what is the price of Argentinean wheat in dollars? _____

   2. What is the price of American wheat in pesos? _____

   3. What will be the demand for Argentinean wheat? _____
      Why? _____

      _____

   4. If the exchange rate is 600 Argentinean pesos per U.S. dollar, what is the price of Argentinean wheat in dollars? _____

   5. What is the price of American wheat in pesos? _____

   6. What will be the demand for American wheat? _____
      Why? _____

      _____

   7. What does the law of one price indicate will be the exchange rate between the Argentinean peso and the U.S. dollar? _____
      Why? _____

      _____

   8. If the price of American wheat rises to $10 per bushel, what does the law of one price suggest will be the new exchange rate? _____
      Is this an appreciation or depreciation of the U.S. dollar? _____

B. 1. If the American price level doubles while that in Argentina remains unchanged, what does the theory of purchasing power parity suggest will happen to the exchange rate, which initially is at 500 pesos to the dollar?

      _____

   2. If the American inflation rate is 5% and the Argentinean inflation rate is 7%, then what does the theory of purchasing power parity predict will happen to the value of the dollar in terms of pesos in one year's time?

      _____

3. If the U.S. dollar to Argentinean peso exchange rate is $0.002 and the respective inflation rates of America and Argentina are 5% and 7%, what should the U.S. dollar to Argentinean peso exchange rate be in one year?

4. If the U.S. dollar to Argentinean peso exchange rate is $0.002, but America inflation rate is only 2% compared to 7% for Argentina, what should the U.S. dollar to Argentinean peso exchange rate be in one year?

5. If the U.S. dollar to Argentinean peso exchange rate increases from $0.002 to $0.010 over the course of the year, what was the difference in the countries' inflation rates at the beginning of the year?

Exercise 3: Factors That Affect Exchange Rates

In the second column of the following table indicate whether the exchange rate will rise (+) or fall (−) as a result of the change in the factor. (Recall that a rise in the exchange rate is viewed as an appreciation of the domestic currency.)

Change in Factor	Response of the Exchange Rate
Domestic interest rate	_____
Foreign interest rate	_____
Expected domestic price level	_____
Expected import demand	_____
Expected export demand	_____
Expected productivity	_____

■ Self-Test

Part A: Fill in the Blanks

1. The exchange rate is the price of one country's _____ in terms of another country's.

2. Trades in the foreign exchange market typically involve the exchange of bank _____ denominated in different currencies.

3. Spot exchange rates involve the immediate exchange of bank deposits, while _____ exchange rates involve the exchange of deposits at some specified future date.

4. When a currency increases in value, it has _____.

5. Exchange rates are important because when a country's currency appreciates, its exports become _____ expensive.

6. When a country's currency depreciates foreign goods become _____ expensive.

7. If two countries produce an identical good, the price of the good should be the _____ throughout the world no matter which country produces it.

8. Applying the law of one price to countries' price levels produces the theory of _____.

9.   Purchasing power parity suggests that if one country's price level rises relative to another's, its currency should _____ .

10. The theory of asset demand indicates that the most important factor affecting the demand for both domestic (dollar) and foreign deposits is the _____ of these assets relative to one another.

11. The idea that if two countries produce an identical good, then the price should be the same in both countries is known as _____ .

12. Changes in either the foreign or domestic _____ , or a change in the expected future exchange rate will cause the exchange rate to change in the short run.

13. If the rise in the domestic interest rate is due to a rise in expected inflation, then the domestic currency _____ .

14. If the rise in the domestic interest rate is due to a rise in the real interest rate, then the domestic currency _____ , as happened to the dollar in the early 1980s.

15. The theory of asset demand model explains recent volatility in exchange rates as a consequence of changing _____ , which are also volatile, and play an important role in determining the demand for domestic assets (which, in turn, affects the value of the exchange rate).

16. The price of one currency in relation to another is known as the _____ .

17. _____ transactions involve the immediate exchange of bank deposits.

Part B: True-False Questions

Circle whether the following statements are true (T) or false (F).

T   F   1.   Most trades in the foreign exchange market involve the buying and selling of bank deposits.

T   F   2.   Forward transactions in the foreign exchange market involve exchanges of bank deposits more than two days into the future.

T   F   3.   One reason why the theory of purchasing power parity might not fully explain exchange rate movements is that monetary policy differs across countries.

T   F   4.   If the interest rate on franc-denominated assets is 5% and is 8% on dollar-denominated assets, then the expected return on dollar-denominated assets is higher than that on franc-denominated assets if the dollar is expected to depreciate at a 5% rate.

T   F   5.   When a country's currency appreciates, its goods abroad become more expensive, and foreign goods in that country become cheaper, all else constant.

T   F   6.   If the interest rate on dollar deposits is 10%, and the dollar is expected to appreciate by 7% over the coming year, then the expected return on the dollar deposit in terms of foreign currency is 3%.

T   F   7.   An expected rise in foreign productivity relative to domestic productivity (holding everything else constant) causes the domestic currency to depreciate.

T   F   8.   The forward price is the appropriate price to use if I want to exchange currency today.

T   F   9.   The model of foreign exchange rate behavior indicates that whenever the domestic interest rate rises relative to the foreign interest rate, the exchange rate appreciates.

T   F   10.   If a central bank lowers the growth rate of the money supply, then its currency will appreciate.

T   F   11.   If expected inflation in the United States rises from 5% to 8% and the interest rate rises from 7% to 9%, the dollar will appreciate.

T   F   12.   When the exchange rate for the Swiss francs changes from 9 Swiss francs to the dollar to 10 Swiss francs to the dollar, then the franc has depreciated.

T   F   13.   The phenomenon in which the exchange rate falls by more in the short run than it does in the long run when the money supply increases is called exchange rate overshooting.

T   F   14.   The high volatility of exchange rate movements indicates that participants in the foreign exchange market do not behave in a rational manner.

T   F   15.   When the exchange rate for the Swiss franc changes from $0.50 to $0.30 then, holding everything else constant, the franc has appreciated.

T   F   16.   The theory of purchasing power parity states that exchange rates will always be slightly better for American currency.

T   F   17.   In the long run, a rise in a country's price level causes its currency to appreciate.

T   F   18.   Increased demand for a country's demand causes its currency to appreciate.

Part C: Multiple-Choice Questions

Circle the appropriate answer.

1.   When the Swiss franc appreciates (holding everything else constant), then
   (a)   Swiss watches sold in the United States become more expensive.
   (b)   American computers sold in Switzerland become more expensive.
   (c)   Swiss army knives sold in the United States become cheaper.
   (d)   American toothpaste sold in Switzerland becomes cheaper.
   (e)   Both (a) and (d) of the above are true.

2.   The theory of purchasing power parity indicates that if the price level in the United States rises by 5% while the price level in India rises by 6%, then
   (a)   the dollar appreciates by 1% relative to the rupee.
   (b)   the dollar depreciates by 1% relative to the rupee.
   (c)   the exchange rate between the dollar and the rupee remains unchanged.
   (d)   the dollar appreciates by 5% relative to the rupee.
   (e)   the dollar depreciates by 5% relative to the rupee.

3. If, in retaliation for "unfair" trade practices, Congress imposes a quota on Japanese cars, but at the same time Japanese demand for American goods increases, then in the long run
   (a) the Japanese yen should appreciate relative to the dollar.
   (b) the Japanese yen should depreciate relative to the dollar.
   (c) the dollar should depreciate relative to the yen.
   (d) it is not clear whether the dollar should appreciate or depreciate relative to the yen.

4. If the interest rate on dollar-denominated assets is 10% and it is 8% on Swiss franc-denominated assets, then if the franc is expected to appreciate at a 5% rate,
   (a) dollar-denominated assets have a lower expected return than franc-denominated assets.
   (b) the expected return on dollar-denominated assets in francs is 2%.
   (c) the expected return on franc-denominated assets in dollars is 3%.
   (d) none of the above will occur.

5. Of the following factors, which will not cause the expected return schedule for foreign deposits to shift?
   (a) A change in the expected future exchange rate
   (b) A change in the foreign interest rate
   (c) A change in the current exchange rate
   (d) A change in the productivity of American workers

6. A rise in the expected future exchange rate shifts the expected return schedule on foreign deposits to the _____ and causes the exchange rate to _____.
   (a) right; appreciate
   (b) right; depreciate
   (c) left; appreciate
   (d) left; depreciate

7. A rise in the domestic interest rate is associated with a shift in the expected return schedule for
   (a) domestic deposits to the right.
   (b) domestic deposits to the left.
   (c) foreign deposits to the right.
   (d) foreign deposits to the left.

8. If the foreign interest rate rises and people expect domestic productivity to rise relative to foreign productivity, then (holding everything else constant) the expected return schedule for
   (a) domestic deposits shifts to the left and the domestic currency appreciates.
   (b) domestic deposits shifts to the right and the domestic currency appreciates.
   (c) foreign deposits shifts to the left and the domestic currency depreciates.
   (d) deposits shifts to the right and the domestic currency depreciates.
   (e) the effect on the exchange rate is uncertain.

9. When the value of the British pound changes from $1.25 to $1.50, then
    (a) the pound has appreciated and the dollar has appreciated.
    (b) the pound has depreciated and the dollar has appreciated.
    (c) the pound has appreciated and the dollar has depreciated.
    (d) the pound has depreciated and the dollar has depreciated.

10. When domestic real interest rates rise, the
    (a) expected return schedule for dollar deposits shifts to the right, and the dollar appreciates.
    (b) expected return schedule for dollar deposits shifts to the left, and the dollar appreciates.
    (c) the expected return schedule for dollar deposits shifts to the right, and the dollar depreciates.
    (d) the expected return schedule for dollar deposits shifts to the left, and the dollar depreciates.

11. According to the law of one price, if the price of Colombian coffee is 100 Colombian pesos per pound and the price of Brazilian coffee is 4,000 Brazilian reales per pound, then the exchange rate between the Colombian peso and the Brazilian reales is
    (a) 40 pesos per reales.
    (b) 100 pesos per reales.
    (c) 0.025 pesos per reales.
    (d) 0.01 pesos per reales.
    (e) none of the above.

12. In April 1991, one U.S. dollar traded on the foreign exchange market for about 20 Indian rupees. Thus, one Indian rupee would have purchased about
    (a) 0.01 U.S. dollars.
    (b) 0.05 U.S. dollars.
    (c) 0.50 U.S. dollars.
    (d) 5.00 U.S. dollars.

13. Which of the following is true about the foreign exchange market?
    (a) Foreign currency can be bought by brokers through the New York Stock Exchange.
    (b) Vacationers can get the same exchange rate as major business firms.
    (c) Foreign currency is bought in the over-the-counter market but is sold on an exchange.
    (d) Individuals can get foreign currency from their commercial bank.
    (e) None of the above is true.

14. If you were a U.S. investor in a French company's common stock, which of the following would you prefer to happen in order to earn the largest return?
    (a) Buy euros and invest directly in the stock through a French stock exchange with no change in the exchange rate.
    (b) Buy the stock using U.S. dollar and then have the euros appreciate relative to the dollar.
    (c) Buy the stock using U.S. dollar and then have the euros depreciate relative to the dollar.
    (d) Buy euros and invest directly in the stock through a French stock exchange and then have the dollar appreciate relative to the franc.

15. Forecasts of changes in exchange rates are important to financial institutions because
    (a) the value of their assets is affected by changes in exchange rates.
    (b) to help decide which foreign denominated assets to hold and which to sell.
    (c) in order to help increase their profits from trading foreign currencies.
    (d) All three of the above are important reasons.
    (e) Only (a) and (b) are important reasons.

16. Which market determines the prices of one currency in terms of another currency?
    (a) The over-the-counter market
    (b) The NYSE
    (c) The foreign exchange market
    (d) The Treasury market

17. _____ transactions involve the exchange of bank deposits at a specified future date.
    (a) Deferred
    (b) Spot
    (c) Delayed
    (d) Forward

18. _____ stipulates that the long-run effect of a one-time increase in-the-money supply is a proportional one-time increase in the price level.
    (a) The law of one price
    (b) Interest rate parity
    (c) Monetary neutrality
    (d) Capital mobility

Part D: Short Answer Questions

1. Why was there a dramatic swing in the competitiveness of U.S. firms in the international market place for goods and services from the 1980s to the 1990s?

    _____

    _____

2. Although *the law of one price* and *purchasing power parity* are similar in concept they apply to two different economic factors. What is the factor that distinguishes between them?

    _____

    _____

3. Is the *law of one price* or *purchasing power parity*, or neither, the correct model on which to build an exchange rate change model?

    _____

    _____

4. Both the *law of one price* and *purchasing power parity* are based on prices of goods and services and are determinants of long-run exchange rate changes. However, short-run exchanges rates are very volatile. What factors drives this short-run movement?

_____

_____

5. How is a country affected when demand for its exports increases?

_____

_____

6. What has happened if a country experiences currency appreciation?

_____

_____

■ Answers to Chapter 15

Exercise 1

1. 2 francs per dollar

2. $500

3. 200 francs

4. Depreciation of the franc; appreciation of the dollar

5. $250; less

6. 400 francs; more

7. When a country's currency appreciates, its goods abroad become more expensive and foreign goods in that country become cheaper (holding domestic prices constant in the two countries).

8. You can buy the watch in Switzerland for $250($0.25/Fr×1000Fr).

   Because the $/£ exchange rate is $0.125/£($0.25/Fr × 0.50Fr/£), you should buy the watch in London because in dollar terms it will only cost $125($0.125/£ × 1000Fr).

9. You can buy the watch in Switzerland for $200($0.25/Fr × 800Fr).

   With the $/£ exchange rate is $0.125/£($0.25/Fr× 0.50Fr/£), you should still buy the watch in London, because in dollar terms it will cost $100($0.125/Fr × 800Fr).

10. As before, the watch can be bought for $250($0.25/Fr × 1000Fr) in Switzerland. Thus, we need the SwissFr / British£ exchange rate that will result in the watch costing $250 in London. That exchange rate is 2.22Fr/£. (Solve for X: £450×(X)×$0.25/Fr = $250.)

Exercise 2

Part A

1. $10

2. 1,800 pesos

3. None, because Argentinean wheat is more expensive in both countries and the goods are identical.

4. $5

5. 3,600 pesos

6. None, because American wheat is more expensive in both countries and the goods are identical.

7. 500 pesos per dollar because only at this exchange rate will both American and Argentinean wheat be purchased.

8. 300 pesos per dollar; a depreciation of the dollar

Part B

1. The value of the dollar will fall to 250 pesos per dollar.

2. The dollar will appreciate by 2%.

3. The dollar will appreciate 2% relative to the peso (i.e., fewer dollars to buy one peso). The new exchange rate will be $0.00196/peso ($0.002 × 0.98).

4. The dollar will appreciate 5% relative to the peso to $0.0019.

5. $400\% = (0.01 - 0.002)/0.002$

Exercise 3

Change in Factor		Response of the Exchange Rate
Domestic interest rate	−	−
Foreign interest rate	−	+
Expected domestic price level	−	+
Expected import demand	−	+
Expected export demand	−	−
Expected productivity	−	−

Self-Test

Part A

1. currency
2. deposits
3. forward
4. appreciated
5. more
6. more
7. same
8. purchasing power parity
9. depreciate
10. expected return
11. the law of one price
12. interest rate
13. depreciates
14. appreciates
15. expectations
16. exchange rate
17. spot transaction

Part B

1. T
2. T
3. F
4. F
5. T
6. F
7. T
8. F
9. F
10. T
11. F
12. T
13. T
14. F
15. F
16. F
17. F
18. T

Part C

1. e	7. a	13. d
2. a	8. e	14. b
3. b	9. c	15. d
4. a	10. a	16. c
5. c	11. c	17. d
6. c	12. b	18. c

Part D

1. The value of the dollar appreciated strongly in the 1980s, making U.S. goods and services more expensive to foreign countries. The higher prices reduced the demand for U.S. products and made sales to foreigners more difficult. In the 1990s, the dollar weakened against most foreign currencies and reversed this situation.

2. The *law of one price* states that the price of an identical good produced in different countries would sell for the same price in both countries. *Purchasing power parity* extends beyond the price of individual goods and states that the exchange rate is based on the relative level of prices between countries. In other words, if one country had higher inflation than another, the low inflation country's currency would appreciate to keep the relative prices the same, even though the price of every product did not increase at the rate of inflation.

3. Neither theory is totally correct for two reasons. One is that the assumption that goods are equal between countries in many cases does not hold. There are both real and perceived differences. Second, not all goods that are included in the inflation measure are sold in different countries and thus should not have an impact on the exchange rate.

4. Remember that the exchange of currencies between countries is really the exchange of bank deposits denominated in the different currencies. The willingness of banks to hold deposits in another country's currency is the main short-run factor that influences exchange rates. This deposit preference changes the supply of one currency relative to its demand and will increase or decrease the cost (exchange rate) of the relative currencies.

5. Increased demand for a country's exports causes its currency to appreciate in the long run

6. The country has become more productive relative to other countries

Chapter 16
The International Financial System

■ Chapter Learning Goals

By the end of this chapter, you should

1. Learn how fixed and managed exchange rate systems operate.

2. Understand why international finance transactions have important implications for the conduct of monetary policy.

3. Know the evolution of the international financial system and how the Bretton Woods fixed exchange rate system worked.

4. Understand the trade-offs in the policy trilemma.

5. Understand the recent monetary crises like the breakdown of the European Monetary System in September of 1992, the Mexican Peso Crisis in 1994, and the East Asian Currency Crisis in 1997.

6. Understand the role of the IMF and the controversies that surround it.

■ Chapter Summary

The growing interdependence of the United States with other economies of the world means that our monetary policy is influenced by international financial transactions. This chapter examines the international financial system and explores how it affects the way we conduct our monetary policy.

Intervention in Foreign Exchange Market

Three international considerations affect the conduct of monetary policy: (1) direct effects of the foreign exchange market on the money supply, (2) balance of payments considerations, and (3) exchange rate considerations. If a central bank intervenes in the foreign exchange market to keep its strong currency from appreciating, as the German central bank did in the early 1970s, it will gain **international reserves**, which are Fed assets denominated in a foreign currency, and the monetary base and the money supply will rise. Interventions designed to influence a currency's value or exchange rate by a central bank are called **foreign exchange interventions**. To prevent this, the central bank might engage in **sterilization**, which involves offsetting any increase in international reserves with equal open-market sales of domestic securities in order to prevent the monetary base from rising. In order to prevent balance of payments deficits, a country's central bank (such as the Bank of England in the 1960s) might pursue contractionary monetary policy. Monetary policy is also affected by exchange rate considerations. Because an appreciation of the currency causes domestic businesses to suffer from increased foreign competition, a central bank might increase the rate of money growth in order to lower the exchange rate. Similarly, because a depreciation of the currency hurts consumers and stimulates inflation, a central bank might slow the rate of money growth in order to prop up the exchange rate.

The Fed can also use international reserve sales to boost the monetary base through **unsterilized intervention**. For example, the Fed may sell international reserves to increase the value of the domestic currency. In doing this, the Fed lowers the monetary base and is using the foreign exchange market to conduct monetary policy.

The Balance of Payments

The **balance of payments** is a bookkeeping system for recording all payments that have a direct bearing on the movement of funds between countries. All payments from foreigners are entered as credits, while all payments to foreigners are entered as debits. The current account shows international transactions that involve currently produced of goods and services. The difference between merchandise exports and imports is called the **trade balance**. The capital account describes the flow of capital between the United States and other countries.

The government uses international reserves to ensure that the balance of payments stays in balance. In particular, the net change in government international reserves equals the current account plus the capital account. Thus, current account shortfalls or deficits will cause the government to either sell international reserves or seek offsetting increases in the capital account.

A change in a country's holdings of international reserves leads to an equal change in its monetary base, which, in turn, affects the money supply. A currency like the U.S. dollar, which other countries use to denominate the assets they hold as international reserves, is called a **reserve currency**.

Exchange Rate Regimes in the International Financial System

The two types of exchange rate regimes in the international financial system are fixed rate regimes and floating rate regimes. Fixed exchange-rate regimes are characterized by the pegging of one currency relative to another currency called the **anchor currency**. Currencies' relative values are allowed to fluctuate in floating exchange rate regimes. If a country buys and sells currencies attempting to affect its currency's value, then it is said to have a **managed float regime** or a **dirty float**.

Fixed Exchange Rate Systems

Before World War I, the world economy operated under a **gold standard**, under which the currencies of most countries were convertible directly into gold, thereby fixing exchange rates between countries. After World War II, the **Bretton Woods system** was established in order to promote a fixed exchange rate system in which the U.S. dollar was convertible into gold. The Bretton Woods agreement created the **International Monetary Fund (IMF)**, which was given the task of promoting the growth of world trade by setting rules for the maintenance of fixed exchange rates and by making loans to countries that were experiencing balance of payments difficulties. The Bretton Woods agreement also set up the **World Bank** in order to provide long-term loans to assist developing countries to build dams, roads, and other physical capital. Furthermore, the Bretton Woods agreement established the General Agreement on Tariffs and Trade (GATT) to evaluate the rules of the conduct of trade between countries including tariffs and quotas. GATT later became **The World Trade Organization** (WTO).

In a fixed exchange rate regime, the central bank must purchase its domestic currency when the currency is overvalued, which causes a loss of international reserves. When the currency is undervalued, the central bank must sell domestic currency to maintain the fixed exchange rate. When a central bank's international reserves are depleted and its currency is overvalued, the bank must **devalue** the currency by lowering the par exchange rate. If the currency is undervalued and the central bank does not want to acquire international reserves, then it will **revalue** the currency by increasing the par exchange rate. When a central bank makes large changes in international reserves during a foreign exchange crises, the official reserve asset items in the balance of payments are affected. This situation is known as a **balance-of-payments crises**.

Fixing an exchange rate is beneficial to many smaller countries because it instills discipline into their economy by forcing them to make changes in their exchange rate when the anchor currency changes value. The drawback is that they also lose some control over their monetary base when they are forced to make these balancing purchase and sale of their international reserves.

A variant of a fixed exchange rate regime is a **monetary union** (or currency union) in which a group of countries decide to adopt a common currency. The most recent monetary union is the European Monetary Union (EMU), in which 11 initial countries adopted a new currency, the euro, in January 1999. The key economic advantage of a monetary union is that it makes trade across borders easier because goods and services in all the member countries are now priced in the same currency. A currency union means that individual countries no longer have their own independent monetary policy to deal with shortfalls of aggregate demand. This disadvantage of a currency union has raised questions about whether the euro zone will break apart.

The Evolution of the Managed Float System

The Bretton Woods system, because it did not allow for smooth and gradual adjustments in exchange rates when they became necessary, was often characterized by destabilizing international financial crises, in which adjustment occurred through a speculative attack on a currency, that is, a massive sale of a weak currency (or purchases of a strong currency) that would hasten the change in exchange rates. After a series of such attacks culminated in a massive intervention in the foreign exchange market by the German central bank in the first half of 1971, the Bretton Woods system finally collapsed. The international financial system then evolved into the current managed float regime, in which central banks intervene in the foreign exchange market, but exchange rates fluctuate from day to day.

Causes of the Recent Financial Crises

The European Monetary System

In 1979, eight members of the **European Community** established the **European Monetary System (EMS)** in which they agreed to fix their exchange rate against each other and to float jointly against the U.S. dollar. When the exchange rate between countries in the agreement moved outside an acceptable range, the central banks of both countries were to intervene. In the aftermath of the German reunification the German central bank was following a contractionary monetary policy to prevent inflation. At this time, other EC countries were in the midst of the most serious recession since World War II. Unfortunately, the EMS broke down in September of 1992, when the other EC countries were unwilling to contract their money supplies in order to maintain the required exchange rates.

The Mexican Peso Crisis of December 1994

In 1987, the Mexican government imposed limits on the fluctuation of the peso against the dollar. In March 1994, one of the Mexican presidential candidates was assassinated, and investors feared the devaluation of the peso was imminent. This caused a large transfer of funds to dollar-denominated accounts. To prevent the rapid loss of value, the central bank intervened and sold international reserves. The Chiapas uprising and the assassination of another ruling party candidate in the summer initiated another round of flight from the peso. Mexico's large current account deficit and the fear of the banking system collapsing only increased the flight. The new government that took office in December had no choice but to devalue the peso.

The East Asian Currency Crisis, 1997

The crisis began in Thailand. Speculators expected the Thai government to be forced to devalue the currency as the country had a large current account deficit and a weak financial system. When, initially, speculators withdraw large sums, the Thai Central Bank intervened successfully. The failure of a major financial company pushed foreign creditors to withdraw additional funds, and the central bank could no longer intervene, and the Baht was devalued. Concerns that similar problems might arise in other East Asian countries caused speculative attacks against other currencies. The weaker currencies of Indonesia, Malaysia, S. Korea, and the Philippines were devalued.

Argentina's Currency Board

To combat the historic monetary instability, a currency board was set up in 1991, at a 1 peso = 1 US$ exchange rate. The Mexican peso crisis caused Argentineans to withdraw funds from the banks, reducing money supply and increasing interest rates. The inadequate money supply pushed Argentina into a recession in 1995. A new recession began in three years later, leading to civilian unrest, a banking crisis, and the government defaulting on its debt. As the central bank had neither control over money supply nor could act as a lender of last resort, the economy collapsed. The currency board was abolished in 2002.

China's Accumulation of International Reserves

China's policy of pegging its exchange rate to the U.S. dollar at the fixed rate of 8.28 yuan caused a massive accumulation of international reserves as the long-run value of the yuan increased due to China's growing productivity and low inflation relative to the United States. This accumulation has caused several problems for China: the Chinese hold many low yielding U.S. assets (e.g., Treasury securities), threaten to set up trade barriers, and have a potential for high domestic inflation.

Capital Controls

One issue that countries face is the inflow and outflow of capital that occurs through the natural decisions of people and businesses throughout the world. Unless countries place restrictions on this inflow or outflow, their international reserves will become short or excessive and their exchange rate will fluctuate too much. Controls are often not successful and create other problems for a county so another alternative had to be put in place.

The Role of the IMF

The IMF was organized under the Bretton Woods system to help countries deal with balance of payments problems in order to maintain the fixed exchange rate system. With the collapse of the fixed exchange regime in 1971, the IMF has taken on a new role of international lender. Arguments for the IMF to become an international lender of last resort are as follows:

1. In emerging market countries, the credibility of the central bank as an inflation fighter is often doubted.
2. In case of a financial crisi,s only the IMF can prevent contagion.

Arguments against the IMF becoming an international lender of last resort are as follows:

1. Domestic financial institutions take on increasingly risk projects because they expect to be bailed out.
2. The IMF imposes identical austerity policies on all troubled nations.

■ Exercises

Exercise 1: Definitions and Terminology

Match the following terms on the right with the definition or description on the left. Place the letter of the term in the blank provided next to the appropriate definition.

_____ 1. A bookkeeping system for recording all payments that has a direct bearing on the movement of funds between a country and foreign countries

_____ 2. When central banks engage in international financial transactions

_____ 3. Merchandise exports less imports

_____ 4. When there is a desire to set an exchange rate at a higher level

_____ 5. Massive sales of a weak currency or purchases of a strong currency that hasten a change in the exchange rate

_____ 6. Asset held by central banks that is denominated in a foreign currency

_____ 7. A situation in which the par value of a currency is reset at a lower level

_____ 8. A currency (like the U.S. dollar) that is used by other countries to denominate the assets they hold as international reserves.

_____ 9. When the central bank allows the purchase or sale of domestic currency to have an effect on the monetary base and money supply

_____ 10. The international monetary system in use from 1945 to 1971 in which exchange rates were fixed and the U.S. dollar was freely convertible into gold (by foreign government and central banks only)

_____ 11. The current account balance plus items in the capital account

_____ 12. Account that describes the flow of capital between the United States and other countries

_____ 13. When foreign exchange intervention is offset by open market transactions that leave the monetary base unchanged

_____ 14. A regime under which the currency of most countries is directly convertible into gold

_____ 15. Account that shows international transactions that involve currently produced goods and services

_____ 16. Provides long-term loans to help developing countries build dams, roads, and other physical capital that would contribute to their economic development

_____ 17. An organization set up to monitor rules for the conduct of trade between countries

_____ 18. The currency to which another currency is pegged in a fixed rate regime

_____ 19. Inability to jointly pursue free capital mobility, fixed exchange rate, and independent monetary policy

_____ 20. A fixed rate regime in which a group of countries decide to adopt a common currency

a. speculative attack

b. sterilized foreign exchange intervention

c. gold standard

d. unsterilized foreign exchange intervention

e. current account

f. revaluation

g. capital account

h. Bretton Woods

i. trade balance

j. official reserve transactions balance

k. reserve currency

l. international reserves

m. foreign exchange intervention

n. devaluation

o. balance of payments

p. World Trade Organization

q. World Bank

r. anchor currency

s. monetary union

t. policy trilemma

Exercise 2: The Balance of Payments

Suppose that the U.S. economy in 2013 has generated the following data (in billions of dollars) for items in the balance of payments:

Merchandise exports	500	Capital outflows	50
Merchandise imports	600	Capital inflows	100
Net investment income	–40	Increase in U.S. official reserve assets	5
Net services	20	Increase in foreign official assets	25
Net unilateral transfers	–15		

Fill in the figures for all the numbered items in the balance of payments table below. (Hint: The Statistical Discrepancy item is deduced from the fact that the balance of payments must balance.)

U.S. Balance of Payments in 2013 (billions of dollars)

	Receipts (+)	Payments (−)	Balance
Current account:			
1. Merchandise exports	_____	_____	_____
2. Merchandise imports	_____	_____	_____
3. Trade balance	_____	_____	_____
4. Net investment income	_____	_____	_____
5. Net services	_____	_____	_____
6. Net unilateral transfers	_____	_____	_____
7. Current account balance	_____	_____	_____
Capital account:			
8. Capital outflows	_____	_____	_____
9. Capital inflows	_____	_____	_____
10. Statistical discrepancy	_____	_____	_____
11. Official reserves transactions balance	_____	_____	_____
Method of financing:			
12. Increase in U.S. official reserve assets	_____	_____	_____
13. Increase in foreign official assets	_____	_____	_____
14. Total financing of surplus	_____	_____	_____

Exercise 3: How a Fixed Exchange Rate Regime Works

The most important feature of the Bretton Woods system was that it established a fixed exchange rate regime. Figure 1 describes a situation in which the domestic currency is initially overvalued: The expected return on the foreign deposits schedule (Ret_1^f) intersects the expected return on domestic deposits schedule (Ret_1^d) at an exchange rate that is below the fixed par rate, E_{par}.

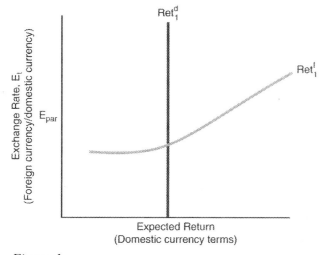

Figure 1

A. Complete the following statements:

1. In order to return the exchange rate to equilibrium at E_{par}, the central bank must intervene in the foreign exchange market to _____ the domestic currency by _____ foreign assets.

2. The central bank's purchase of domestic currency has the effect of _____ the money supply, causes the interest rate on domestic deposits to _____, and shifts the expected return schedule on domestic deposits to the _____.

B. Illustrate the effect of a central bank's purchase of domestic currency in Figure 1 by shifting the Ret_2^d

■ Self-Test

Part A: Fill in the Blanks

1. Our current international financial arrangement, called a(n) _____, is one in which exchange rates fluctuate from day to day, but central banks attempt to influence their country's exchange rates.

2. A central bank's purchase of domestic currency and corresponding sale of foreign assets in the foreign exchange market leads to a(n) _____ decline in its international reserves and its monetary base.

3. Intervention in which a central bank allows the purchase or sale of domestic currency to have an effect on the monetary base is called a(n) _____.

4. Sterilized intervention has no effect on the _____.

5. The _____ is a bookkeeping system for recording all payments that have a direct bearing on the movement of funds between a nation and foreign countries.

6. The difference between merchandise exports and imports is called the _____.

7. The _____ describes the flow of capital between the United States and other countries.

8. Before World War I, the world economy operated under a(n) _____.

9. The _____ of the pound leads to a British gain of international reserves (gold) and an equal U.S. loss.

10. The Bretton Woods agreement created the _____.

11. In addition to the International Monetary Fund, the Bretton Woods agreement created the _____.

12. On September 16, 1992, the British were forced to pull out of the _____ indefinitely.

13. The main cause of the collapse of the Exchange Rate System was that _____ wished to follow a contractionary monetary policy while _____ needed to follow an expansionary monetary policy.

14. Another term frequently used as a substitute for managed float regime is _____.

15. When Americans spend money by purchasing foreign goods, the transaction is recorded in the balance of payments account in the _____ column with a(n) _____ sign reflecting in the flow of funds to other countries.

16. In a(n) _____ the value of currencies are kept pegged relative to one currency (anchor currency) so that exchange rates are fixed.

17. In a(n) _____ the value of currencies are allowed to fluctuate against one another.

18. When the domestic currency is _____, the central bank must sell domestic currency to keep the exchange rate fixed, but as a result, it gains international reserves.

19. China accumulated large international reserves by _____ the yuan to the U.S. dollar.

Part B: True-False Questions

Circle whether the following statements are true (T) or false (F).

T F 1. The capital account balance indicates whether the country is increasing or decreasing its claims on foreign wealth.

T F 2. The official reserves transactions balance equals the current account balance plus the items in the capital account.

T F 3. The current account balance equals the difference between exports and imports.

T F   4. Under the Bretton Woods system, the dollar was overvalued if the equilibrium exchange rate (expressed as units of foreign currency per dollar) was below the par (fixed) value of the exchange rate.

T F   5. When the domestic currency is undervalued in a fixed exchange rate regime, the country's central bank must intervene in the foreign exchange market to purchase the domestic currency by selling foreign assets.

T F   6. The gold standard of the late nineteenth century always prevented inflation from developing.

T F   7. A particular problem with a fixed exchange rate system (or regime) is that it is periodically subject to speculative attacks on currencies.

T F   8. Special drawing rights (SDRs) are IMF loans to member countries.

T F   9. The Bretton Woods international financial system was toppled by a series of international financial crises.

T F 10. The World Bank makes loans to countries suffering balance of payments difficulties.

T F 11. The current international financial system is perhaps best described as a hybrid of fixed and flexible exchange rate systems.

T F 12. The ECU was a paper currency issued by the European Common Market.

T F 13. Critics of a return to the gold standard claim that it would probably not produce the price stability desired by gold standard proponents.

T F 14. A central bank that wants to strengthen its currency is likely to adopt a more contractionary policy.

T F 15. Monetary policy in a reserve currency country is less influenced by balance of payments deficits because they will be financed by other countries' interventions in the foreign exchange market.

T F 16. Central banks of nations with currency boards have better control of their money supply than those without such boards.

T F 17. When the domestic currency is overvalued, the central bank must sell domestic currency to keep the exchange rate fixed.

T F 18. If a country's central bank runs out of reserves, it cannot keep its currency from depreciating, and must devalue its currency.

T F 19. When a domestic currency is overvalued, the actions by the central bank will cause a loss of international reserves.

Part C: Multiple-Choice Questions

1. Which of the following appear as debits in the U.S. balance of payments?
   (a) French purchases of American jeans
   (b) Purchases by Japanese tourists in the United States
   (c) American exports of Apple computers
   (d) Income earned by Coca-Cola from its factories abroad
   (e) None of the above

2. Which of the following appears in the current account part of the balance of payments?
   (a) An Italian's purchase of IBM stock
   (b) Income earned by Barclay's Bank of London, England, from subsidiaries in the United States
   (c) A loan by a Swiss bank to an American corporation
   (d) A purchase by the Federal Reserve System of an English Treasury bond
   (e) None of the above

3. If Americans are buying $1 billion more English goods and assets than the English are willing to buy from the United States, and so the Bank of England sells $1 billion worth of pounds in the foreign exchange market, then
   (a) England gains $1 billion of international reserves and its monetary base rises by $1 billion.
   (b) England loses $1 billion of international reserves and its monetary base falls by $1 billion.
   (c) England gains $1 billion of international reserves and its monetary base falls by $1 billion.
   (d) England loses $1 billion of international reserves and its monetary base rises by $1 billion.
   (e) England's level of international reserves and monetary base remains unchanged.

4. An important advantage for a reserve currency country is that
   (a) its balance of payments deficits are financed by other countries' interventions in the foreign exchange market.
   (b) it has more control over its monetary policy than nonreserve currency countries.
   (c) it has more control over its exchange rate than nonreserve currency countries.
   (d) Both (a) and (b) of the above are true.

5. Under a gold standard in which one dollar could be turned into the U.S. Treasury and exchanged for 1/20 of an ounce of gold and one Swiss franc could be exchanged for 1/60 of an ounce of gold,
   (a) at an exchange rate of 4 francs per dollar, gold would flow from the United States to Switzerland and the Swiss monetary base would fall.
   (b) at an exchange rate of 4 francs per dollar, gold would flow from Switzerland to the United States and the Swiss monetary base would rise.
   (c) at an exchange rate of 2 francs per dollar, gold would flow from the United States to Switzerland and the U.S. monetary base would fall.
   (d) at an exchange rate of 2 francs per dollar, gold would flow from Switzerland to the United States and the U.S. monetary base would rise.

6. In a speculative attack against a weak currency under a fixed exchange rate system, the central bank for this country must shift the expected return schedule for domestic deposits further to the _____ through the _____ of international reserves.
   (a) left; purchase
   (b) right; sale
   (c) left; sale
   (d) right; purchase

7. Countries with deficits in their balance of payments often do not want to see their currencies depreciate because this would
   (a) hurt consumers in their country by making foreign goods more expensive.
   (b) stimulate inflation.
   (c) hurt domestic businesses by making foreign goods cheaper in their country.
   (d) hurt domestic businesses by making their goods more expensive abroad.
   (e) do both (a) and (b) of the above.

8. The International Monetary Fund is an international organization that
   (a) promotes the growth of trade by setting rules for how tariffs and quotas are set by countries.
   (b) makes loans to countries to finance projects such as dams and roads.
   (c) oversees the international financial system and makes loans to countries with balance of payments difficulties.
   (d) does each of the above.

9. When a central bank buys its currency in the foreign exchange market,
   (a) it acquires international reserves.
   (b) it loses international reserves.
   (c) the money supply will increase.
   (d) both (a) and (b) of the above occur.
   (e) both (b) and (c) of the above occur.

10. Which of the following is included in the current account balance?
    (a) U.S. official reserve assets.
    (b) unilateral transfers.
    (c) liquid private capital.
    (d) foreign purchases of American assets.

11. A central bank _____ of domestic currency and corresponding _____ of foreign assets in the foreign exchange market leads to an equal increase in its international reserves and the monetary base.
    (a) sale, purchase
    (b) sale, sale
    (c) purchase, sale
    (d) purchase, purchase

12. Under the Exchange Rate Mechanism of the European Monetary System, when the British pound depreciates below its lower limit against the German mark, the Bank of England must buy _____ and sell _____, thereby _____ international reserves.
    (a) pounds; marks; losing
    (b) pounds; marks; gaining
    (c) marks; pounds; gaining
    (d) marks; pounds; losing

13. If a domestic currency is overvalued relative to a foreign currency the central bank **must** do which of the following to keep the exchange rate fixed at the preferred value?
    (a) Sell domestic currency and purchase foreign assets.
    (b) Purchase domestic currency by selling foreign assets.
    (c) They will need to increase foreign reserves.
    (d) They do not have to take action because, under the floating exchange rate regime now being used, equilibrium will automatically result from regular market participation.
    (e) Both (a) and (c) are correct actions.

14. Under the Bretton Woods system of fixed exchange rates, if a country is running a balance-of-payments deficit and losing international reserves, the International Monetary Fund can do all of the following to increase their international reserves except
    (a) lend the deficit country international reserves contributed by other members.
    (b) encourage the deficit country to pursue contractionary monetary policies that would strengthen their currency.
    (c) encourage the deficit country to pursue contractionary monetary policies that would eliminate their balance-of-payments deficit.
    (d) purchase large volumes of the deficit country's currency to force devaluation and eliminate the deficit.

15. The International Monetary Fund (IMF) does all of the following except
    (a) attempt to encourage fixed exchange rates.
    (b) serve as a lender of funds to countries with international financial crises.
    (c) collect data on international trade.
    (d) create SDRs when there is a need for international reserves.

16. All of the following played a role in causing the East Asia financial crisis except
    (a) large current account deficit
    (b) weak financial system
    (c) strong central bank
    (d) failure of a major financial institution

17. When a currency is overvalued in a fixed exchange regime, a central bank must do what to its currency?
    (a) Revaluation
    (b) Establish a new anchor currency
    (c) Devaluation
    (d) Sell its domestic currency

18. A(n) _____ regime is characterized by a central bank that buys and sells currencies attempting to influence its domestic currency value.
    (a) fixed rate
    (b) floating rate
    (c) managed float
    (d) variable rate

19. When the current account runs a deficit, the government can do which of the following to rebalance the balance-of-payments?
    (a) Buy international reserves
    (b) Sell international reserves
    (c) Offset the deficit through the capital account
    (d) Both (b) and (c)

20. Which of the following is an organization set up to monitor rules for the conduct of trade between countries?
    (a) GAAP
    (b) WTO
    (c) World Bank
    (d) IMF

Part D: Short Answer Questions

1. What is the current emphasis of the international financial system concerning the maintenance of exchange rates?

   _____

   _____

2. How did the basic mechanism of the European Monetary System created by the European Economic Community work?

   _____

   _____

3. What does the central bank do when it engages in sterilized intervention in the foreign exchange market?

   _____

   _____

4. Describe dollarization. Give its advantages and a one example of a country whose currency has been dollarized.

   _____

   _____

5. Describe the effect of the sale of dollars and a purchase of foreign assets on the monetary supply and exchange rates.

   _____

   _____

■ Answers to Chapter 16

Exercise 1

1.	o	6.	l	11.	j	16.	q
2.	m	7.	n	12.	g	17.	p
3.	i	8.	k	13.	b	18.	r
4.	f	9.	d	14.	c	19.	t
5.	a	10.	h	15.	e	20.	s

Exercise 2

U.S. Balance of Payments in 2013 (billion of dollars)

	Receipts (+)	Payments (−)	Balance
Current account:			
1. Merchandise exports	+500		
2. Merchandise imports		−600	
3. Trade balance			−100
4. Net investment income		−40	
5. Net services	+20		
6. Net unilateral transfers		−15	
7. Current Account Balance			−135
Capital account:			
8. Capital outflows		−50	
9. Capital inflows	+100		
10. Statistical discrepancy	+60		
11. Official reserves transactions balance			+110
Method of financing:			
12. Increase in U.S. official reserve assets		−5	
13. Increase in foreign official assets	+25		
14. Total financing of surplus			+25

Exercise 3

A. 1. buy, selling

   2. reducing, rise, to the right

B.

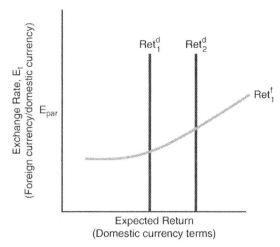

Figure 1

Self-Test

Part A

1. managed float regime
2. equal
3. unsterilized foreign exchange intervention
4. exchange rate
5. balance of payments
6. trade balance
7. capital account
8. gold standard
9. appreciation
10. International Monetary Fund
11. World Bank
12. Exchange Rate Mechanism
13. Germany, Britain
14. dirty float
15. payments, negative
16. fixed rate regime
17. floating rate regime
18. undervalued
19. pegging

Part B

1. F
2. T
3. F
4. F
5. T
6. F
7. T
8. F
9. F
10. F
11. T
12. F
13. T
14. T
15. T
16. F
17. F
18. T
19. T

Part C

1. c
2. b
3. a
4. d
5. d
6. c
7. e
8. c
9. c
10. b
11. a
12. a
13. b
14. d
15. a
16. c
17. c
18. c
19. d
20. b

Part D

1. The current international system is a hybrid of a fixed and a flexible exchange rate system. Rates fluctuate in response to market forces, but central banks and the IMF will intervene in limited select circumstances to manage exchange rates.

2. The exchange rate between every pair of currencies of the participating countries cannot fluctuate outside of limits around a fixed exchange rate. When movements occur outside of this range, both countries are required to intervene by buying or selling international reserves to bring the exchange range within the limits.

3. In sterilized intervention, the central bank may sell the domestic currency and purchase foreign assets leading to an increase in-the-money supply. To sterilize this transaction, they simultaneously sell bonds through open market operations to reduce the money supply and offset the increase from foreign exchange intervention.

4. Dollarization is the adoption of another country's currency. Advantages are that it prevents the central bank from creating inflation and it avoids the possibility of a speculative attack on the domestic currency because there is none. Panama, Ecuador, and El Salvador have all adopted dollarization.

5. A sale of dollars and the consequent open market purchase of foreign assets increase the monetary base. The resulting rise in the money supply leads to a higher domestic price level in the long run, which leads to a lower expected future exchange rate. The resulting decline in the expected appreciation of the dollar raises the expected return on foreign deposits.

Chapter 17
Banking and the Management of Financial Institutions

■ Chapter Learning Goals

By the end of this chapter, you should

1. Be able to separate bank assets from bank liabilities.
2. Distinguish between required reserves and excess reserves.
3. Know how a bank could increase its reserves.
4. Know how a bank must manage its assets and liabilities to maximize profits.

■ Chapter Summary

This chapter provides an overview of a bank's balance sheet and summarizes the main principles of bank management. We examine how banks raise funds and how they use these funds to earn a profit. The focus of this chapter is on commercial banks because they hold more than two-thirds of the assets in the banking system.

The bank balance sheet sets the banks assets equal to total liabilities plus capital. The balance sheet lists sources of bank funds (liabilities) and uses to which they are put (assets). The bank liabilities are mainly composed of **checkable deposits** and other **non-transaction deposits**. Checkable deposits are payable on demand to the depositor. They represent an asset for the depositor but a liability to the bank because these funds must be paid back. Currently, interest paid on deposits (checking and time) account for around 45% of total bank operating expenses.

Non-transaction deposits are the primary source of bank funds. They are composed of savings accounts, time deposits, and large-denomination time deposits. Because these deposits are less liquid for the bank customer, they earn a little higher rate than transaction deposits.

Banks also obtain funds by borrowing from other banks, the Federal Reserve, and corporations. Funds obtained from the Fed are called **discount loans,** and banks pay an interest rate called the **discount rate** to use these funds. The market where banks buy and sell funds among themselves is called the **Fed funds market,** and the interest rate charged in this market is the **Fed funds** rate.

A look at the following general balance sheet for a bank will be a good reference point for much of the discussion that follows.

Assets		Liabilities	
Required reserves	$ 4 million	Deposits	$40 million
Excess reserves	$ 1 million	Borrowings from Fed	$ 2 million
Loans	$50 million	Other borrowings	$ 8 million
Securities	$ 5 million	Bank capital	$10 million

Assets: (owned by bank, owed to bank) A bank must hold a portion of its assets in the form of **reserves**. Reserves are non-earning assets on deposit at the Federal Reserve or in vault cash at the bank. The purpose of reserves is to assure that the bank has sufficient funds on hand to meet the needs of its depositors for cash. **Required reserves** are the amounts required to be held by the Fed. Any reserves held above this amount are called **excess reserves**.

A bank's securities account is an important income-earning asset. A bank's securities are classified into three categories: (1) U.S. government, (2) state and local government, and (3) other securities. Banks hold only debt securities because regulations prevent them from holding stock. U.S. Government and agency securities are the most liquid and are commonly called secondary reserves.

The principal source of profits to banks is from loans. The largest category of loans for commercial banks is commercial loans made to businesses and real estate loans. The major difference between the various depository institutions is in the type of loan in which they specialize.

Bank Capital: Banks raise capital by selling stock or retaining earnings just like any other firm. The average bank holds capital equal to 8% of its assets. An important component of bank capital is the **loan loss reserve account**. When a loan fails to pay, it is charged against the loan loss account. This account is periodically replenished when earnings are available.

Bank Operations

Banks earn profits from a process called **asset transformation**. The bank sells liabilities with one set of characteristics and uses the proceeds to buy assets with a different set of characteristics. To be successful, it must make a profit in the process.

Reserve Requirements: Bank regulations establish required reserves. Before investing any deposit, the bank must set aside a portion of the deposit as a reserve. When a depositor makes a withdrawal, bank reserves are reduced by a like amount. If the bank loses too many reserves, it has four options for replacing them. (1) It can borrow from another bank in the Fed funds market at the Fed funds rate. (2) It can sell some of its securities to meet the deposit outflow. The bank will likely incur brokerage expenses and other transaction costs when it sells these securities. (3) It can acquire reserves by borrowing from the Fed at the discount rate. This is called **discount window borrowing,** and the Fed discourages it. (4) Finally, the bank could meet its reserve requirement by selling off its loans. This is probably the costliest solution because the buyers of the loans will not be familiar with the borrowers so they will pay less than face value for the loans. Holding excess reserves is insurance that none of the above actions will be required to meet reserve losses due to deposit outflows.

General Principles of Bank Management

Bank managers must make decisions regarding the firm's assets and liabilities that permit the firm to earn a profit for the bank's owners. The managers must consider and balance four primary concerns: (1) to maintain adequate **liquidity,** (2) to earn an acceptable return through **asset management** while maintaining an acceptable level of risk, (3) to raise enough funds at a low cost through **liability management** so the bank's customers' demands can be met, and (4) to engage in **capital adequacy management**.

Liquidity: Many bank liabilities are demand deposits that the customer can withdraw at any time. Plus the bank regularly has time deposits coming due that must be paid to the customer. To meet these continuing needs for funds, the bank manager must see that adequate reserves are available to make the requested payouts. These funds must come from excess reserves because required reserves are not legally available to meet outflow demands. Should payout requests exceed the available excess reserves, the bank can pursue one of the four costly options mentioned in the previous Reserve Requirements section to make up the inadequacy.

Asset Management: To maximize profits, banks must seek a diversified portfolio of the best loans and securities, minimize risk, and maintain liquidity. To find the best loans, loan officers solicit loans from firms that will make interest and principal payments on time.

Liability Management: Currently banks attempt to balance a mixture of low cost checkable deposits and the more expensive time deposits to raise the amount needed to fund their loan demand and reserve requirements. Although these time deposits are more expensive for the bank, they provide a basis of stability because depositors cannot easily withdraw these funds on demand. Banks have come to prosper with the increased issuance of negotiable CDs and other borrowings and the reduced emphasis on checkable deposits as a source of funds. These time deposits have increased the flexibility and reduced the response time of banks in meeting loan demand. The portion of assets in loans has increased resulting in higher profits. The large banks in key financial cities such as New York, called **money center banks,** have made the most effective use of these time deposits.

Capital Adequacy Management: There are three reasons a bank must give close attention to the amount of equity capital it maintains on its balance sheet. The first reason is that bank regulators establish a minimum amount of capital the bank must maintain to stay in business. Second, the capital provides a cushion for its depositors in the event that the bank has large defaults on loans. The depositors and owners are provided some protection against bank failure from the capital maintained. A final reason is the return to the owners is magnified, as measured by **Return on Equity (ROE),** the smaller the amount of capital maintained by the bank. However, this magnification of returns is offset somewhat by the reduced protection for the owners from bankruptcy when hard economic times arise. The bank manager must successfully manage these opposing forces.

Off-Balance-Sheet Activities

Increasingly, banks are becoming involved in **off-balance-sheet activities.** These activities primarily involve three types of transactions. First is that banks will implement a **loan sale,** sometimes also called a **secondary loan participation,** where they sell to another lender a security that has a claim on the payments the bank would receive from a loan they made. This action removes the loan from the bank's balance sheet because another party now has a claim against the borrower for the loan. Banks also provide backup **lines of credit** or **standby letters of credit** for which they charge a fee. These loans are made only when and if the borrower has a need for the funds. The third area is from the many miscellaneous services that banks provide to their customers, such as servicing mortgage-backed securities, trading foreign currencies, and writing letters of acceptance. Banks have also increased their generation of fee income by providing other services, such as foreign exchange trades, servicing off-balance-sheet securities like mortgage-backed bonds, and providing standby letters of credit.

Trading and Risk Management

Due to the volatile nature of interest rates and the extensive role rates play in the success of a bank's operations, banks commonly engage in risk management techniques using interest-rate swaps and derivative securities. Although the goal is risk management, most of the techniques used have the potential to be profitable transactions. This profit potential can lead to conflicts of interest as managers use these instruments to engage in speculation and less in risk reduction. Due to this potential for principal-agent conflict, it is important that banks maintain a "wall" between the trading department and the department responsible for recording and documenting these trades.

Measuring Bank Performance

How effective the bank managers are at organizing the assets, liabilities, liquidity, and capital of the firm can be measured through analysis of the bank's income statement. The **operating income** generated primarily from interest payments on its assets must be greater than the **operating expenses** incurred, which results primarily from the interest paid to their depositors. Another major component of operating expenses is the provision for loans that are expected to default, called the provision for loan losses. The **net interest margin** is the spread between the interest rate earned on assets and the interest rate paid on liabilities. The larger the net margin, the greater the operating profits of the bank. The adequacy of the profits is commonly measured by the **Return on Assets (ROA),** which is calculated by dividing the net income by total assets. The owners of the bank also look closely at the ROE, which is the net income divided by the bank's equity capital.

■ Exercises

Exercise 1: Definitions and Terminology

Match the terms on the right with the definition or description on the left. Place the letter of the term in the blank provided next to the appropriate definition.

_____ 1. Bank funds held on deposit at the Fed

_____ 2. The rate charged banks when borrowing from the Fed

_____ 3. The market where banks borrow and lend deposits among themselves

_____ 4. Trading financial instruments and the generation of fee income, for example

_____ 5. Commercial banks' sources of funds

_____ 6. Commercial banks' uses of funds

_____ 7. The primary source of bank funds

_____ 8. A simplified balance sheet that lists the changes that occur in balance sheet items

_____ 9. The acquisition of sufficiently liquid assets to meet the obligations of the bank to depositors

_____ 10. Financial instruments developed in 1961 that enabled money center banks to acquire funds quickly

_____ 11. The spread between a bank's borrowing rate and the rate it charges the customers to whom it lends

_____ 12. Risk associated with coupon paying bonds that was eliminated with the introduction of zero coupon bonds

a. equity multiplier

b. bank liabilities

c. non-transaction deposits

d. discount rate

e. capital adequacy management

f. off balance sheet activities

g. bank assets

h. financial innovation

i. net interest margin

j. required reserves

k. interest-rate risk

l. liquidity

m. negotiable CDs

n. Fed funds

o. T-account

p. deposit outflows

q. discount loans

_____ 13. Management decisions that determine the amount of "cushion" the owners have against bankruptcy

_____ 14. The lower the capital of the bank the greater the impact of this variable on the bank's ROE

_____ 15. A term used to define the approach banks have taken toward the innovation of new products and services

_____ 16. Borrowings from the Fed

_____ 17. Deposits that leave the bank because depositors make withdrawals or demand payment

Exercise 2: The Bank Balance Sheet

A. Rank each of the following asset categories in the balance sheet of commercial banks, from the least liquid to the most liquid.

physical assets _____

real estate loans _____

U.S. government securities_____

municipal securities _____

consumer loans _____

excess reserves _____

B. Rank each of the following liabilities on the balance sheet of commercial banks, from the smallest as a percentage of total liabilities to the largest.

checkable deposits _____

small denomination time deposits _____

large denomination time deposits _____

borrowings from Fed and other banks _____

Exercise 3: Bank Response to Deposit Outflows and Liquidity Management

Suppose that the First National Bank has the following balance-sheet position and that the required reserve ratio on deposits is 20 percent.

Assets		Liabilities	
Reserves	$25 million	Deposits	$100 million
Loans	$75 million	Bank capital	$10 million
Securities	$10 million		

A. If the bank suffers a deposit outflow of $6 million, what will its balance sheet now look like? Show this by filling in the amounts in the following balance sheet.

Assets		Liabilities	
Reserves	_____	Deposits	_____
Loans	_____	Bank capital	_____
Securities	_____		

Must the bank make any adjustment in its balance sheet? _____

Why? _____

B. Suppose the bank now is hit by another $4 million deposit outflow. What will its balance-sheet position look like now? Show this by filling in the amounts in the following balance sheet.

Assets		Liabilities	
Reserves	_____	Deposits	_____
Loans	_____	Bank capital	_____
Securities	_____		

Must the bank make any adjustment in its balance sheet? _____

Why? _____

C. If the bank satisfies its reserve requirements by selling off securities, how much will it have to sell?

_____

Why? _____

D. After selling off the securities to meet its reserve requirements, what will its balance sheet look like? Show this by filling in the amounts in the following balance sheet:

Assets		Liabilities	
Reserves	_____	Deposits	_____
Loans	_____	Bank capital	_____
Securities	_____		

E. If after selling off the securities, the bank is now hit by another $10 million of withdrawals of deposits, and it sells off all its securities to obtain reserves, what will its balance sheet look like? Again show this by filling in the amounts in the following balance sheet:

Assets		Liabilities	
Reserves	_____	Deposits	_____
Loans	_____	Bank capital	_____
Securities	_____		

If the bank is now unable to call in or sell any of its loans and no one is willing to lend funds to this bank, then what will happen to the bank and why?

_____

Exercise 4: Return on Equity

Using the beginning balance sheet from Exercise 3 for First National Bank, and assuming First National has a net profit after tax of $1,650,000:

A. Calculate First National Bank's Return on Assets (ROA).

_____

B. Calculate First National Bank's Equity Multiplier (EM).

_____

C. Using your answers to parts A and B above calculate First National Bank's Return on Equity (ROE).

_____

Exercise 5: Asset Management

List the four main concerns of bank asset management.

1. _____

2. _____

3. _____

4. _____

■ Self-Test

Part A: Fill in the Blank

1. The balance sheet has the characteristic that total assets equal total liabilities plus bank _____.

2. The bank's liabilities are its _____ of funds, which include checkable deposits, non-transaction deposits, borrowings, and bank equity capital.

3. The bank's assets are its _____ of funds and include reserves, cash items in process of collection, deposits at other banks, securities, loans, and other assets (mostly physical capital).

4. _____ are either bank deposits held at the Fed or currency that is physically held by banks.

5. By law a certain fraction of deposits must be held as reserves, called _____ _____.

6. Additional reserves, called _____ reserves, can be used by a bank to meet obligations to depositors.

7. The basic operation of a bank is to make profits by engaging in the process of asset _____.

8. An important consideration for a bank engaged in this process is that when it receives additional deposits, it _____ an equal amount of reserves, but when it loses deposits, it loses an equal amount of reserves.

9. Banks must ensure that they have enough ready cash to pay their depositors in the event of _____.

10. To keep enough cash on hand, the bank must engage in _____ management, the acquisition of sufficiently liquid assets to meet the obligations of the bank to depositors.

11. Excess reserves are _____ against the cost of deposit outflows.

12. Banks try to find borrowers who will pay high interest rates and are unlikely to _____ on their loans.

13. Banks try to purchase securities with _____ expected returns and low risk.

14. Banks attempt to minimize risk by _____ their holdings of both loans and securities.

15. Banks must manage the _____ of their assets so they can satisfy reserve requirements without incurring huge costs.

16. Before the 1960s, banks took their liabilities as _____ and spent their time trying to achieve an optimal mix of assets.

17. When _____ cards are used, the purchase price is immediately deducted from the cardholder's bank account.

18. The higher the cost associated with deposit outflows, the more _____ banks will want to hold.

19. Banks maintain _____ to lessen the chance that they will become insolvent.

20. Banks calculate _____ to determine how much they are earning on investments.

Part B: True-False Questions

Circle whether the following statements are true (T) or false (F).

T F 1. A bank's assets are its sources of funds.

T F 2. Bank capital equals the total assets of the bank minus the total liabilities.

T F 3. Savings accounts are the most common type of non-transaction deposit.

T F 4. Bank capital is listed as a liability in the bank balance sheet.

T F 5. State and local government securities are also called secondary reserves.

T F 6. Checkable deposits are usually the lowest cost source of bank funds.

T F   7. Checkable deposits are the primary source of bank funds.

T F   8. Interest paid on deposits makes up more than half of total bank operating expenses.

T F   9. Banks are only able to borrow reserves from the Fed.

T F 10. Collectively, reserves, cash items in process of collection, and deposits at other banks are referred to as cash items in a bank balance sheet.

T F 11. Loans provide banks with most of their revenue.

T F 12. A bank failure occurs whenever a bank is not allowed to borrow from the Fed.

T F 13. Asset management is primarily concerned with the acquisition of sufficiently liquid assets to meet the obligations of the bank to depositors.

T F 14. Off-balance-sheet activities include loans to firms located in foreign countries.

T F 15. When a bank borrows reserves from another bank, it is engaging in discount window borrowing.

T F 16. The higher the bank capital means higher returns for owners of the bank.

T F 17. Off balance sheet activities are illegal and should be reported and investigated by the Federal Reserve.

T F 18. In a loan commitment, the bank agrees to provide a loan up to a given dollar amount for a specific period of time.

Part C: Multiple-Choice Questions

Circle the appropriate answer.

1. Which of the following bank assets are the most liquid?
    (a) Consumer loans
    (b) State and local government securities
    (c) Physical capital
    (d) U.S. government securities

2. Reserves
    (a) equal the deposits banks hold at the Fed.
    (b) include bank holdings of U.S. government securities.
    (c) can be divided up into required reserves plus excess reserves.
    (d) equal both (a) and (c) of the above.

3. When a $1,000 check written on the Chase Manhattan Bank is deposited in an account at the Bank of America, then
    (a) the liabilities of Chase Manhattan Bank increase by $1,000.
    (b) the reserves of Chase Manhattan Bank increase by $1,000.
    (c) the liabilities of Bank of America fall by $1,000.
    (d) the reserves of Bank of America increase by $1,000.

4. When you deposit a $100 check in your bank account at the First National Bank of Chicago and you withdraw $50 in cash, then
   (a) the liabilities of First National Bank rise by $100.
   (b) the reserves of First National Bank rise by $100.
   (c) the assets of the First National Bank rise by $100.
   (d) the liabilities of the First National Bank rise by $50.

5. If a bank has $1 million of deposits and a required reserve ratio of 5 percent, and it holds $100,000 in reserves, then it must rearrange its balance sheet if there is a deposit outflow of
   (a) $51,000.
   (b) $20,000.
   (c) $30,000.
   (d) $41,000.
   (e) none of the above.

6. A bank will want to hold less excess reserves (everything else equal) when
   (a) it expects to have deposit inflows in the near future.
   (b) brokerage commissions on selling bonds rise.
   (c) both (a) and (b) of the above occur.
   (d) neither (a) nor (b) of the above occurs.

7. When a bank faces a reserve deficiency because of a deposit outflow, it will try to do which of the following first?
   (a) call in loans
   (b) borrow from the Fed
   (c) sell securities
   (d) borrow from other banks

8. A bank failure is more likely to occur when a bank
   (a) holds more U.S. government securities.
   (b) suffers large deposit outflows.
   (c) holds more excess reserves.
   (d) has more bank capital.

9. Which of the following statements is true?
   (a) A bank's assets are its uses of funds.
   (b) A bank's liabilities are its sources of funds.
   (c) A bank's balance sheet has the property that total assets equal the sum of total liabilities and equity capital.
   (d) All of the above are true.

10. Which of the following are reported as assets on a bank's balance sheet?
   (a) cash items in the process of collection
   (b) loans
   (c) borrowings
   (d) only (a) and (b) of the above

11. Which of the following is not a source of revenue from off-balance-sheet activities?
    (a) Loan sales
    (b) Charging interest on transaction balance
    (c) Note issuance facility
    (d) Servicing of mortgage-backed securities

12. Banks' holdings of marketable securities consist of
    (a) government securities.
    (b) corporate stock.
    (c) tax exempt municipal bonds.
    (d) corporate bonds.

13. Commercial banks are not allowed to pay interest on
    (a) demand deposits.
    (b) NOW accounts.
    (c) money market deposit accounts.
    (d) savings accounts.

14. Commercial bank innovation to avoid restrictions associated with reserve requirements resulted in the use of _____ as a source of funds.
    (a) NOW accounts
    (b) Eurodollar
    (c) overnight repos
    (d) sweep accounts

15. Required reserves are expensive for a bank to hold because of
    (a) the fees charged on them by the Fed.
    (b) the interest the bank pays on these liabilities.
    (c) the opportunity costs.
    (d) none of the above; required reserves have no costs.

16. A discount loan is a
    (a) consumer loan that has been discounted.
    (b) loan from the Fed.
    (c) loan to another bank.
    (d) none of the above.

17. A good measure of bank profitability is
    (a) ROE.
    (b) ROA.
    (c) EM.
    (d) None of the above

18. What is the interest rate called that banks pays to the Fed to use discount loans?
    (a) Fed funds rate
    (b) Repo rate
    (c) Discount rate
    (d) Prime rate

Part D: Short Answer Questions

1. What type of transaction increases the account "cash items in the process of collection?"

    _____

    _____

2. Two popular bank management tools developed in the 1960s by large money central banks are Fed funds and negotiable CDs. What is the advantage to banks of having these two financial instruments available?

    _____

    _____

3. There is a "good news–bad news" trade-off in the amount in the bank capital account. What is the "good news" and the "bad news" from the shareholder's perspective?

    _____

    _____

4. Technology is having an influence on every day life of most individuals and businesses. What three products or services have been improved or introduced in recent years by banks due to new technology?

    _____

5. Discuss the benefits and drawbacks of bank capital.

    _____

    _____

6. Describe how managers can determine how effective they are at organizing the assets, liabilities, liquidity, and capital of the firm.

    _____

    _____

■ Answers to Chapter 17

Exercise 1

1. j	7. c	13. e
2. d	8. o	14. a
3. n	9. l	15. h
4. f	10. m	16. q
5. b	11. i	17. p
6. g	12. k	

Exercise 2

Part A

1. physical assets

2. consumer loans

3. real estate loans

4. municipal securities

5. U.S. government securities

6. excess reserves

Part B

1. checkable deposits

2. large denomination time deposits

3. borrowings for Fed and other banks

4. small denomination time deposits

Exercise 3

Part A

Assets		Liabilities	
Reserves	$19 million	Deposits	$94 million
Loans	$75 million	Bank capital	$10 million
Securities	$10 million		

No. The bank does not need to make any adjustment to its balance sheet because it initially is holding $25 million of reserves when required reserves are only $20 million (20% of $100 million). Because of its initial holding of $5 million of excess reserves, when it suffers the deposit outflow of $6 million it can still satisfy its reserve requirements: Required reserves are $18.8 million (20% of $94 million), while it has $19 million of reserves.

Part B

Assets		Liabilities	
Reserves	$15 million	Deposits	$90 million
Loans	$75 million	Bank capital	$10 million
Securities	$10 million		

Yes. The bank must make an adjustment to its balance sheet because its required reserves are $18 million (20% of $90 million), but it is only holding $15 million of reserves. It has a reserve deficiency of $3 million.

Part C

$3 million. As we see In part B, the bank has a reserve shortfall of $3 million, which it can acquire by selling the $3 million of securities.

Part D

Assets		Liabilities	
Reserves	$18 million	Deposits	$90 million
Loans	$75 million	Bank capital	$10 million
Securities	$7 million		

Part E

Assets		Liabilities	
Reserves	$15 million	Deposits	$80 million
Loans	$75 million	Bank capital	$10 million
Securities	$0 million		

The bank could fail. The required reserves for the bank are $16 million (20% of $80 million), but it has $15 million of reserves. The proceeds from the distress sale of loans could result in a loss that exceeds bank capital, causing the bank to become insolvent.

Exercise 4

A. $\text{ROA} = \dfrac{\text{net profit after tax}}{\text{total assets}} = \dfrac{\$1,650,000}{\$110,000,000} = 1.5\%$

B. $\text{EM} = \dfrac{\text{total assets}}{\text{equity capital}} = \dfrac{\$110,000,000}{\$10,000,000} = 11$

C. $\text{ROE} = \text{ROA} \times \text{EM} = 1.5\% \times 11 = 16.5\%$

Exercise 5

1. Finding borrowers who will pay high interest rates yet are unlikely to default on their loans.

2. Purchasing securities with high returns and low risk.

3. Attempt to minimize risk by diversifying both holdings of loans and securities.

4. Manage the liquidity of its assets so that it can satisfy its reserve requirements without bearing huge costs.

Self-Test

Part A

1.	equity capital	8	receives	15.	liquidity
2.	sources	9.	deposit outflow	16.	fixed
3.	uses	10.	liquidity	17.	debit
4.	Reserves	11.	insurance	18.	excess reserves
5.	required reserves	12.	default	19.	capital
6.	excess	13.	high	20.	ROE
7.	transformation	14.	diversifying		

Part B

1.	F	7.	F	13.	F
2.	T	8.	T	14.	F
3.	F	9.	F	15.	F
4.	F	10.	T	16.	F
5.	F	11.	T	17.	F
6.	T	12.	F	18.	T

Part C

1.	d	7.	c	13.	a
2.	c	8.	b	14.	b
3.	d	9.	d	15.	c
4.	d	10.	d	16.	b
5.	e	11.	b	17.	b
6.	a	12.	a	18.	g

Part D

1. When a customer deposits a check written on an account at another bank, the bank does not immediately receive the money from the other bank. Until the other bank receives the check and knows that the money is being withdrawn, the deposit bank will have that check as a receivable. The receivable is recorded in this account.

2. Both are used as tools of liability management. Because reserves do not pay interest and having interest earning deposits without making loans is expensive, banks use these tools to raise funds quickly when they have a profitable opportunity and do not have excess reserves available. This allows the banks to maintain minimum reserve deposits.

3. The good news is that the smaller the amount of bank capital, the higher the return on equity to the shareholders. The bad news is that the smaller the amount of bank capital, the lower the amount of protection the shareholders have against bankruptcy losses. This is an example of the principle of a risk/return trade-off.

4. The improved availability and lower cost of computers has led banks to be major providers of credit cards. This technology is leading to the increased availability and use of debit cards and the proliferation of electronic banking facilities (i.e., ATMs).

5. Bank capital benefits the owners of a bank in that it makes their investment safe by reducing the likelihood of bankruptcy. Bank capital is also costly because the higher it is, the lower the return will be on ROE.

6. Managers can determine how effective they are at organizing the assets, liabilities, liquidity, and capital of the firm by analyzing the firm's income statement. Through effective management of the provision for loan losses, managers can reduce operating expenses. In addition, managers can seek to increase the net interest margin. Managers can compute ROA and ROE to further measure their performance.

Chapter 18
Financial Regulation

■ Chapter Learning Goals

By the end of this chapter, you should

1. Understand the history that resulted in the current set of financial regulations.

2. Know the nine categories of financial regulation and why they are needed.

3. Know the major provisions of recent regulations.

4. Be able to discuss the future of financial regulation.

■ Chapter Summary

Financial institutions have seen major changes in the last 20 years as both technological and market forces affect the industry. Regulators have been under pressure from financial firms to make changes to the regulations that will allow them to compete and to be profitable. In this chapter, we investigate what changes in regulations have occurred, their influence on the industry, and what future changes may occur.

Asymmetric Information and Bank Regulation

Banking regulations encompass a wide variety of activities of commercial banks. The concepts of asymmetric information and the resulting adverse selection and moral hazard problems are the driving forces behind the regulatory environment. Existing regulations can be classified into one of eight categories: (1) the government safety net, (2) restrictions on bank asset holdings, (3)capital requirements, (4) prompt corrective action, (5) chartering and bank examination, (6) assessment of risk management, (7) disclosure requirements, (8) consumer protection, and (9) restrictions on competition. Each of these categories is discussed in the following sections.

The Government Safety Net

Although financial institutions like banks are efficient at gathering information about the companies they lend to, the depositors in banks do not have access to this information. The result is an asymmetric information problem between the bank and it depositors. To instill confidence in banks and avoid panics, the **Federal Deposit Insurance Corporation (FDIC)** was created. In the year before FDIC insurance, more than 2,000 banks failed. Bank failures dropped to about 15 per year after Congress established the FDIC. Clearly, the insurance program satisfied its intended purpose of protecting depositors and preventing bank panics. Unfortunately, insured depositors do not monitor managerial risk taking, so moral hazard and adverse selection problems increase.

The FDIC employs two methods to handle failed banks: the payoff method and the purchase and assumption method. When the payoff method is used, the bank is allowed to fail, and the FDIC pays deposits up to the $100,000 insurance limit. Creditors are paid what is remaining after the bank is sold. In the purchase and assumption method, the FDIC reorganizes the bank and seeks a merger partner to assume all of the bank's deposits preventing any losses by depositors. This typically protects even deposits greater than the $100,000 limit.

The FDIC's **"too-big-to-fail"** policy allowed it to keep insolvent banks open if the regulators believed that major economic disruptions might result from its closure. This policy increased the moral hazard problem for big banks because even the largest shareholders would not monitor the bank's risk taking. The policy is also unfair because it gives big banks an advantage over small banks even though they pay the same FDIC insurance premiums.

Moral hazard is a concern that arises when providing a government safety net. Financial institutions may choose to take bigger risks if they are assured that the government (and ultimately the taxpayers) will bail them out if they fail. Similarly, adverse selection is also a concern that arises when providing a government safety net, as protected depositors and creditors have little reason to monitor risk taking.

The implementation of the Riegle-Neal Interstate Banking and Branching Efficiency Act of 1994 and the Gramm-Leach-Bliley Financial Services Modernization Act of 1999 led to increased consolidation in the financial services industry. The consolidation poses two problems to the government safety net: the increasing size of banks worsens the too-big-to-fail problem, and the reach of banks into other financial services may cause the government to offer the safety net to cover the new services.

Restrictions on Asset Holdings, Capital Requirements, and Prompt Corrective Action

There are two forms of bank capital requirements: (1) the leverage ratio and (2) risk-based capital requirements. The leverage ratio is a bank's capital divided by its assets and must exceed 5%. In response to concerns about the amount of risk-based assets that banks carry, especially the off-balance-sheet activities, the **Basel Accord** proposes categorizing asset by riskiness and tying capital requirements to weighted categories of the bank's assets, including off-balance-sheet assets. The Accord requires that banks as capital as least 8% of their risk-weighted assets.

To help prevent the moral hazard problem, bank regulations put restrictions on asset holdings by banks and established minimum capital standards. The **Basel Accord** set minimum capital standards for 12 industrial nations so that banks from different nations would have a level playing field on which to compete. Asset controls hold down risk through restrictions, such as not being permitted to own stock and encourage diversification by limiting the amount of loans to any one customer.

A practice known as **regulatory arbitrage** has been a negative byproduct of the Basel Accord. Regulatory arbitrage occurs when a bank replaces a relatively low risk asset on its balance sheet with a relatively high risk asset that has the same risked-based capital requirement. Consequently, the Basel Accord could lead to increased risk taking by banks. The initial Basel Accord has been modified (called **Basel 2**) in an attempt to reduce this arbitrage problem. A new accord called Basel 3 has the goal of beefing up capital standards and making them less procyclical and resistant to liquidity shocks.

Banks fail into one of five categories depending on the amount of capitalization: well capitalized, adequately capitalized, undercapitalized, significantly undercapitalized, and critically undercapitalized. As low levels of capitalization make banks more likely to fail and susceptible to moral hazard through excessive risk taking, prompt corrective action requires these banks to limit asset growth and restore capital.

Financial Supervision: Chartering and Bank Examination

Incentives are strong for people of questionable ethics to engage in bank management. Chartering is one way of reducing this adverse selection and moral hazard problem through screening of everyone wishing to obtain a bank charter. Scheduled and unannounced examinations encourage compliance with regulations concerning asset and capital restrictions.

Prudential supervision or **bank supervision** is the oversight of how and who operates banks. Bank supervision helps to reduce the moral hazard and adverse selection problem. Bank examiners rate the health of banks according to the *CAMELS* system. *CAMELS* is an acronym for the six areas examined during a bank examination: capital adequacy, asset quality, management, earnings, liquidity, and sensitivity to market risk.

Banks are classified as either state banks or national banks. State banks receive their charters from a state banking authority, while national banks receive their charters from the Comptroller of the Currency. Once chartered, banks have to file periodic call reports that detail the banks' ownership, income and dividends, assets and liabilities, etc. If regulators find inappropriate activity, they are authorized to issue cease and desist orders to the bank. Nonmember state banks are examined by the FDIC, state banks that are members of the Federal Reserve System are examined by the Fed, and national banks are examined by the Office of the Comptroller of the Currency.

Assessment of Risk Management

On-site examinations have traditionally centered on the asset and capital requirements just mentioned. In recent years there has been a major change to examinations by adding a risk-assessment requirement. This extra review is directed toward seeing that management has in place adequate controls to monitor the riskier activities. For example, the amount of interest-rate risk has always been important, but managers are now required to monitor and report the extent of this risk. **Stress testing**, the calculation of losses under dire scenarios, and **value-at-risk (VaR)**, the size of a loss on a portfolio that happens X% of the time over a specified time period, are two important calculations.

Disclosure Requirements

These regulations are directed at the fair and consistent reporting of information. The content of publicly disclosed documents and the accounting principles that banks must follow are examples of attempts to provide adequate disclosure to stockholders, depositors, and creditors. These requirements come from Basel 2 for banks as well as the Securities Act of 1933 for publically traded institutions. **Mark-to-market accounting**, the valuing of assets on the balance sheet at market prices, has generated controversy as market prices may not be available during periods of extremely illiquidity as evidenced in the 2007–2009 financial crisis.

Consumer Protection

To see that consumers are treated fairly and receive the information needed to make intelligent borrowing decisions, several laws exist under this category. One frequently cited regulation is the **Consumer Protection Act of 1969**, which requires "truth in lending" about the costs of borrowing. All lenders must report the **annual percentage rate (APR)** and total finance charges to borrowers. Credit card issuers must provide information on how they assess finance charges as required by the **Fair Credit Billing Act of 1974**. The **Equal Credit Opportunity Act of 1974** and the **Community Reinvestment Act of 1977** are directed at eliminating discrimination in lending.

Restrictions on Competition

The objective here is to prevent banks from losing profits and then making higher risk loans to bring profits back up. These objectives are met by limitations on branching and preventing nonbank institutions from engaging in the banking business. A negative result of these restrictions is the possibility that banks can charge higher fees and that they can become less efficient due to the protection from competition.

The **Glass-Steagall Act** reduced risk taking by banks. This act, passed in 1933, separates commercial banking from the more risky investment banking. It also prevents investment banks from engaging in commercial banking activities. **The Gramm-Leach-Bliley Financial Services Modernization Act of 1999** eliminated this barrier.

The 1980s Savings and Loan and Banking Crisis

The **Depository Institutions Deregulation and Monetary Control Act of 1980** was the most significant piece of bank regulation since 1933. This regulation gave broader lending powers to Savings and Loans, approved NOW and ATS accounts, eliminated **usury** ceilings on loans, increased FDIC insurance to $100,000, and imposed **uniform reserve requirements** on all depository institutions. Increased competition from financial innovation of new securities and the greater moral hazard problem created by deposit insurance led banks to take on more risk, increasing the stress on the financial stability of the FDIC insurance fund. The result was passage of the **Federal Deposit Insurance Corporation Improvement Act of 1991 (FDICIA)**.

The FDICIA established needed changes in insurance coverage. It limited coverage on **brokered deposits** and put into place a system for banks paying risk-adjusted insurance premiums. It also redefined the "too-big-to-fail" philosophy making it possible for large institutions to fail that previously would have been bailed out. Other provisions require examiners to perform annual on-site examinations, restrict real estate lending, and require more reporting.

Banking Crises Throughout the World in Recent Years

One of the biggest problems facing bank regulators is the increased internationalization of banking. There is often confusion, conflict, and overlap among regulations of different countries for banks operating across international borders. The need for more uniform international regulation is demonstrated by the financial crisis in Latin America in 2001, the crisis in Russia and Eastern Europe in the mid 1990s, and in Japan also in the 1990s.

The Dodd-Frank Bill and Future Regulation

The Dodd-Frank bill represents the most comprehensive financial reform legislation since the Great Depression. The legislation created a new Consumer Financial Protection Bureau within the Federal Reserve. It expanded the ability to seize and unwind failing banks to those financial institutions deemed **systemic**. Limits on **proprietary trading,** called the Volcker Rule, were also included with the bill. The bill did not address capital requirements, compensation of bankers, government sponsored enterprises (e.g., Fannie Mae and Freddie Mac), credit rating agencies, or the unintended consequences of overregulation. There are doubts that the Dodd-Frank bill has dealt sufficiently with the too-big-to fail problem.

■ Exercises

Exercise 1: Terminology

Match the following terms from the left column with the closely related term from the right. Place the letter of the term from the right column in the blank provided next to the appropriate term on the left.

_____ 1. A proposed change to FDIC coverage that limits the portion of an account that is covered

_____ 2. The amount of bank capital divided by the bank's total assets

_____ 3. An important method for reducing adverse selection and moral hazard in the banking industry

_____ 4. The distribution of a large sum into smaller investments to meet FDIC coverage limits

_____ 5. When a bank is unable to meet its obligations to depositors

_____ 6. Activities that generate income from fees

_____ 7. A universal agreement on risk-based capital requirements

_____ 8. Size of a loss on a portfolio that happens X% of the time over a specified time period

_____ 9. Policy that allows no depositors or creditors to suffer losses in case of failure

_____ 10. Ratings bank examiners use to assess bank behavior in six categories

_____ 11. Concept where parties in a financial contract do not have the same information

_____ 12. Where FDIC reorganizes a bank and typically finds a willing merger partner to take over all of banks failed deposits

_____ 13. Most comprehensive financial reform legislation since the Great Depression

_____ 14. The calculation of losses under dire scenarios

_____ 15. The valuing of assets on the balance sheet at market prices

a. brokered deposits

b. too-big-to-fail

c. leverage ratio

d. value-at-risk (VaR)

e. off-balance-sheet activities

f. bank supervision

g. Basel Accord

h. bank failure

i. coinsurance

j. asymmetric information

k. purchase and assumption method

l. CAMELS

m. mark-to-market accounting

n. Dodd-Frank bill

o. Stress testing

Exercise 2: Problems of Deposit Insurance

Ironically, the existence of deposit insurance increases the likelihood that depositors will require deposit protection because the threat of withdrawals no longer constrains the managers of banks and thrifts from taking on too much risk. List some of the problems that deposit insurance creates or makes worse.

1. _____

2. _____

3. _____

Exercise 3: The "Too-Big-To-Fail" Policy

A. Justification of the Policy

    1. Describe the intended purpose of the "too-big-to-fail" policy.

        _____

        _____

B. Implications of the Policy

    1. When Continental Illinois became insolvent in 1984, the FDIC guaranteed all deposits, even those exceeding $100,000. The Comptroller of the Currency defended this action, arguing that the largest 11 banks were too big to fail. In 1990, however, the FDIC argued that the Bank of New England was too-big-to-fail, though it was only the thirty-third largest bank in the United States. What are some of the implications of this regulatory policy?

        _____

        _____

        _____

    2. Of the 169 banks that failed in 1990, 149 were resolved through "purchase and assumption" transactions, whereby all deposits—including those in excess of the $100,000 limit—were assumed by the healthy banks. How were the other 20 banks handled?

        _____

        _____

    3. How are uninsured deposits handled in these types of transactions?

        _____

        _____

Exercise 4: Calculating Capital Requirements

Use the financial statements below for Your National Bank of America to obtain the capital measure required by the Basel Accord.

Your National Bank of America			
Assets		**Liabilities and Capital**	
Reserves	$4	Checkable deposits	$30
Treasury Securities	15	Nontransaction deposits	80
Government agency securities	10	Borrowing	15
Municipal bonds	15	Loan loss reserves	5
Residential mortgages	15		
Real estate loans	20		
Commercial loans	50		
Fixed assets	11	Bank capital	10
Total assets	$140	Total liabilities & capital	$140

A.   The bank's leverage ratio is _____.

B.   Is Your National Bank of America well capitalized based on the leverage ratio? _____

Exercise 5: What Can Be Done about the Too-Big-to-Fail Problem?

List three approaches to solving the too-big-to-fail problem.

1.   _____

2.   _____

3.   _____

■ Self-Test

Part A: Fill in the Blanks

1.   In the United States, most depositors hold their funds in accounts insured by the _____.

2.   Because deposits up to $100,000 are completely insured, depositors lose their incentives to _____ their funds when they suspect that the bank is taking on too much risk.

3.   The attenuation of depositors' incentives exacerbates _____ and _____, encouraging bank managers to take on excessive risk.

4.   Restrictions that prevent banks from holding risky assets, such as common stocks and junk bonds, and requirements that banks hold minimum levels of _____ reduce moral hazard problems by increasing the cost to owners of bank failures.

5. Regular bank _____ help to ensure that banks comply with asset restriction and capital requirements.

6. The rationale for the _____ policy is that the failure of a large bank increases the likelihood that a major economic disruption will occur.

7. Once a bank has been chartered, it is required to file periodic _____ that reveal the bank's assets, liabilities, income, dividends, ownership, and other details.

8. Banks are examined regularly by _____ who represent the bank regulatory agencies.

9. The Consumer Protection Act requires that lenders disclose the cost of borrowing using a standardized interest rate called _____.

10. Consumer protection regulations are administered by the _____ system under Regulation Z.

11. When lenders do not lend to people living in a particular area of the community they serve, it is called _____ and is illegal under the Community Reinvestment Act.

12. One way regulations are able to reduce bank competition is to place restriction on the opening of new _____.

13. The Federal Deposit Insurance Corporation Improvement Act now places banks into one of five categories based on the amount of _____.

14. The FDICIA instructed the FDIC to come up with a(n) _____ method of determining insurance premiums.

15. In many bank crises throughout the world when there is lack of regulatory supervision the _____ problem becomes worse and leads to a banking crises.

16. _____ is a challenge to banking regulation because the increased size of banks increases the "too-big-too-fail" and exposes the financial system to systemic risk.

17. A bank's capital divided by its total assets is known as _____.

18. The practice known as _____ is when banks keep assets on their books that have equal risk based capital requirements but are relatively more risky.

19. The Dodd-Frank bill expanded the ability to seize and unwind failing banks to those financial institutions deemed _____.

20. The Volcker Rule placed limits on _____.

Part B: True-False Questions

Circle whether the following statements are true (T) or false (F).

T F 1. When a bank is well-capitalized (i.e., has a large amount of equity capital), the bank has less to lose if it fails and is thus more likely to pursue more risky activities.

T F 2. Actions taken by regulators to reduce moral hazard by preventing banks from taking on too much risk (such as regular bank examinations) also help to reduce adverse selection problems by discouraging risk-prone entrepreneurs from entering the banking industry.

T F 3. The FDIC argues that the too-big-to-fail policy protects the soundness of the banking system because the failure of a very large bank makes it more likely that a major financial disruption will occur.

T F 4. One problem with the too-big-to-fail policy is that it increases the incentives for moral hazard by big banks.

T F 5. Large banks are actually put at a competitive disadvantage relative to small banks as a result of the FDIC's too-big-to-fail policy.

T F 6. A financial innovation that made it easier for high-rolling banks to raise funds was brokered deposits.

T F 7. In the purchase and assumption method of handling a failed bank the FDIC purchases the bank and operates it until it is healthy again then sells it to the public.

T F 8. The Basel Accord made it so that off-balance-sheet activities will now be taken into consideration is setting bank capital requirements.

T F 9. The CAMEL rating given to banks by bank examiners includes an evaluation of the bank's marketing program, which is what the M in CAMEL stands for.

T F 10. The Glass-Steagall Act of 1933 prevented banks from opening branches across state lines.

T F 11. The FDIC now maintains separate insurance funds for insurance on banks and on thrifts.

T F 12. The most important feature of the FDICIA is that bank regulatory agencies are now required to be more vigorous in stepping in and taking corrective action when needed.

T F 13. Of the five groups that banks are placed into based on their capital, it is best to be in group 5, which is defined as being "well capitalized."

T F 14. The problem with historical-cost accounting is that changes in the value of assets and liabilities because of changes in interest rates or default risk are not reflected in the calculation of the firm's equity capital.

T F 15. The Federal Reserve has been highly supportive of requests to consolidate regulation and use a single joint agency in place of the multiple agencies currently in use.

T F 16. The FDIC insures depositors up to $100,000, but only if you apply for coverage.

T F 17. The Basel Accord requires that banks hold as capital at least 9% of their risk-weighted assets.

T F 18. The six areas assessed by the CAMELS rating are: capital adequacy, asset quality, management, earnings, liquidity, and sensitivity to market risk.

Part C: Multiple-Choice Questions

Circle the appropriate answer.

1. Moral hazard is an important feature of insurance arrangements because the existence of insurance
   (a) reduces the incentives for risk taking.
   (b) is a hindrance to efficient risk taking.
   (c) causes the private cost of the insured activity to increase.
   (d) does all of the above.
   (e) does none of the above.

2. Deposit insurance
   (a) attracts risk-prone entrepreneurs to the banking industry.
   (b) encourages bank managers to take on greater risks than they otherwise would.
   (c) increases the incentives of depositors to monitor the riskiness of their banks' asset portfolios.
   (d) does all of the above.
   (e) does only (a) and (b) of the above.

3. Regular bank examinations help to reduce the _____ problem but also help to indirectly reduce the _____ problem because, given fewer opportunities to take on risk, risk-prone entrepreneurs will be discouraged from entering the banking industry.
   (a) adverse selection; adverse selection
   (b) adverse selection; moral hazard
   (c) moral hazard; adverse selection
   (d) moral hazard; moral hazard

4. If the FDIC decides that a bank is too big to fail, it will use the
   (a) payoff method, effectively covering all deposits—even those that exceed the $100,000 ceiling.
   (b) payoff method, covering only those deposits that do not exceed the $100,000 ceiling.
   (c) purchase and assumption method, effectively covering all deposits, even those that exceed the $100,000 ceiling.
   (d) purchase and assumption method, covering only those deposits that do not exceed the $100,000 ceiling.

5. The too-big-to-fail policy
   (a) puts small banks at a competitive disadvantage relative to large banks in attracting large depositors.
   (b) treats large depositors of small banks inequitably when compared to depositors of large banks.
   (c) ameliorates moral hazard problems.
   (d) does all of the above.
   (e) does only (a) and (b) of the above.

6. Bank examiners now do a risk assessment of management. Which of the following criteria is *not* used in the management analysis?
   (a) The quality of oversight provided
   (b) The quality of how management measures and monitors risk
   (c) The existence and completeness of the bank's code of ethics
   (d) The adequacy of internal controls to prevent fraud or unauthorized activities

7. One method for helping to identify the amount of interest-rate risk a bank has is
   (a) disclosing the amount of loans the bank has outstanding.
   (b) having regulators estimate and report an interest-rate-risk measure for each bank.
   (c) to use a risk-based insurance premium method.
   (d) market-based accounting.

8. The government safety net for bank protection includes all of the following actions except
   (a) FDIC protection.
   (b) the lender-of-last resort role of the central bank.
   (c) quicker action by regulatory agencies to monitor bank managers.
   (d) all of the above.
   (e) (a) and (b) of the above.

9. Which of the following bank actions would be considered off-balance-sheet activity?
   (a) A bank entering into futures contracts
   (b) The ownership of government agency bonds
   (c) Making a loan to a friend of the president of the bank
   (d) Both (a) and (c)
   (e) None of the above is an off-balance-sheet activity.

10. Eliminating deposit insurance has the disadvantage of
    (a) reducing the stability of the banking system due to an increase in the likelihood of bank runs.
    (b) not being a politically feasible strategy.
    (c) encouraging banks to engage in excessive risk taking.
    (d) all of the above.
    (e) only (a) and (b) of the above.

11. The result of the too-big-to-fail policy is that big banks will take on _____ risks, making failures _____ likely.
    (a) fewer; less
    (b) greater; less
    (c) fewer; more
    (d) greater; more

12. The primary difference between the "payoff" and the "purchase and assumption" methods of handling failure banks is
    (a) that the FDIC guarantees all deposits, not just those under the $100,000 limit, when it uses the "payoff" method.
    (b) that the FDIC guarantees all deposits, not just those under the $100,000 limit, when it uses the "purchase and assumption" method.
    (c) that the FDIC is less likely to use the "payoff" method when the bank is large and it fears that the depositor losses may spur business bankruptcies and other bank failures.
    (d) both (a) and (b) of the above.
    (e) both (b) and (c) of the above.

13. Which of the following pieces of legislation provided for recapitalization of the FDIC to bring its insurance fund back to acceptable levels?
    (a) Depository Institutions Deregulation and Monetary Control Act of 1980
    (b) Competitive Equality in Banking Act of 1987
    (c) Financial Institutions Reform, Recovery, and Enforcement Act of 1989
    (d) Federal Deposit Insurance Corporation Improvement Act of 1991

14. Which of the following pieces of legislation phased out interest rate ceilings on bank deposits?
    (a) Depository Institutions Deregulation and Monetary Control Act of 1980
    (b) Competitive Equality in Banking Act of 1987
    (c) Financial Institutions Reform, Recovery, and Enforcement Act of 1989
    (d) Federal Deposit Insurance Corporation Improvement Act of 1991
    (e) Riegle-Neal Interstate Banking and Branching Efficiency Act of 1994

15. Which of the following pieces of legislation instructed the FDIC to set risk-based premiums on its insurance coverage?
    (a) Depository Institutions Deregulation and Monetary Control Act of 1980
    (b) Competitive Equality in Banking act of 1987
    (c) Financial Institutions Reform, Recovery, and Enforcement Act of 1989
    (d) Federal Deposit Insurance Corporation Improvement Act of 1991
    (e) Riegle-Neil Interstate Banking and Branching Efficiency Act of 1994

16. _____ occurs when a bank replaces a relatively low risk asset on its balance sheet with a relatively high risk asset which has the same risked based capital requirement.
    (a) Risk avoidance
    (b) Prudential supervision
    (c) Off-balance-sheet financing
    (d) Regulatory arbitrage

17. Which of the following is not a focus of the CAMELS system?
    (a) Capital adequacy
    (b) Management
    (c) Asset transformation
    (d) Earnings

18. Prudential supervision is the oversight of
    (a) how and who operates banks.
    (b) capital adequacy.
    (c) regulatory arbitrage.
    (d) insurance arrangements.

Part D: Short Answer Questions

1. Traditionally, bank examiners review the quality of a bank's balance sheet and its compliance with capital requirements and asset restrictions. Due to changes in the financial markets, examiners have expanded into a new area of review. Briefly explain this new trend in bank supervision.

   _____

   _____

2. What special problems exist with the regulation and examination of international banking?

   _____

   _____

3. The FDICIA reduced the scope of the deposit insurance coverage. What scope changes were made and what changes in bank management decisions are expected?

   _____

   _____

4. Who examines banks?

   _____

   _____

5. Describe regulatory arbitrage.

   _____

   _____

6. What are the forms of capital requirements?

   _____

   _____

■ Answers to Chapter 18

Exercise 1

1.	i	7.	g	13.	n
2.	c	8.	d	14.	o
3.	f	9.	b	15.	m
4.	a	10.	l		
5.	h	11.	j		
6.	e	12.	k		

Exercise 2

1. Banks with deposit insurance are likely to take on greater risks than they otherwise would. This is the moral hazard problem.

2. Deposit insurance attracts risk-prone entrepreneurs to the banking industry. This is the adverse selection problem.

3. Deposit insurance reduces the incentives of depositors to monitor the riskiness of their bank's asset portfolios. This is the free-rider problem (see Chapter 14).

Exercise 3

Part A

1. The failure of a large bank could lead to greater uncertainty in financial markets, potentially causing a major financial crisis that could result in adverse macroeconomic consequences. The too-big-to-fail policy is intended to prevent greater financial market instability and adverse economic conditions.

Part B

1. One implication is that individuals holding deposits in excess of the $100,000 insurance limit are fully protected. This suggests that depositors with uninsured deposits in large banks get a better deal than those in banks that are not-too-big-to-fail. It is also evident that the policy is not limited to the 11 largest banks and may indicate that banks, which are even smaller than the Bank of New England, could be too-big-to-fail, no matter how poorly they are managed. Bank performance may suffer as a result of the increased incentives for moral hazard by big banks.

2. The alternative to the purchase and assumption method for dealing with failed banks is the payoff method.

3. These banks are liquidated, implying that uninsured depositors usually suffer some loss, as happened to depositors of Freedom National Bank (see Box 2 in the text).

Exercise 4

A. Leverage ratio $= \dfrac{\text{bank capital}}{\text{total assets}} = \dfrac{10}{140} = 7.14\%$

B. Yes. A leverage ratio above 5% is needed for a bank to be considered well capitalized.

Exercise 5

1. Break up large, systemically important financial institutions

2. Higher capital requirements

3. Leave it to Dodd-Frank

Self –Test

Part A

1. FDIC	7. call reports	14. risk based
2. withdraw	8. bank examiners	15. moral hazard
3. moral hazard, adverse selection	9. annual percentage rate	16. Consolidation
4. capital	10. Federal Reserve	17. the leverage ratio
5. examination	11. red lining	18. regulatory arbitrage
6 too-big-to-fail-policy	12. branches	19. systemic
	13. Capital	20. proprietary trading

Part B

1. F	7. F	13. F
2. T	8. T	14. T
3. T	9. F	15. F
4. T	10. F	16. F
5. F	11. T	17. F
6. T	12. T	18. T

Part C

1. e	7. d	13. d
2. e	8. e	14. a
3. c	9. a	15. d
4. c	10. e	16. d
5. e	11. d	17. c
6. c	12. e	18. a

Part D

1. Bank examiners are now placing far greater emphasis on evaluating the soundness of a bank's management processes with regard to controlling risk. They have added a separate risk rating that feeds into the overall management rating as part of the CAMELS system.

2. Domestic regulators often do not have the knowledge or ability to keep a close watch on bank operations in other countries or on foreign bank offices in the domestic country. When a bank operates in multiple countries, it is unclear as to which regulator has examination responsibility. Problems extend from the lack of standardized regulatory requirements.

3. Changes include limitations on the coverage of brokered deposits and on use of the too-big-to-fail policy. These changes should encourage big depositors to monitor banks more closely. Bank managers should reduce their investment in excessively risky activities due to concerns of large deposit withdrawals.

4. Nonmember state banks are examined by the FDIC.

   State banks that are members of the Federal Reserve System are examined by the Fed. National banks are examined by the Office of the Comptroller of the Currency.

5. Regulatory arbitrate is when a bank replaces a low risk asset on its balance sheet with a higher risk asset which has the same risked based capital requirement.

6. The three forms of bank capital requirements are:
   1) the leverage ratio,
   2) off-balance sheet activities, and
   3) proposed risk based capital requirements by Basel 2.

Chapter 19
Banking Industry: Structure and Competition

■ Chapter Learning Goals

By the end of this chapter, you should

1. Have an understanding of the history of banking in the United States and how the current complex regulatory structure developed.
2. Know which regulatory agency regulates which bank.
3. Know the major provisions of recent banking regulations.
4. Be able to discuss the thrift industry.

■ Chapter Summary

This chapter provides a brief overview of the development of the banking structure of the United States. In addition, it examines the major regulations that have evolved, how these regulations are changing, and what future changes may occur.

Historical Development of Banking

The government chartered the first commercial bank (Bank of North America) in 1782 and the first central bank in 1791 (Bank of the United States). Congress did not renew the central bank's charter, and the country operated without a central bank until the second national bank was chartered in 1816. This was also a failure, and the government allowed its charter to expire in 1836. The United States did not have a central bank until the current Fed was created in 1913.

The United States has a **dual banking system**. This means that there are banks that are chartered and regulated by the states, called state banks, and banks that are chartered and regulated by the federal government, called **national banks**. Until 1863, only state chartered banks were allowed to exist. As a result, no national currency existed, and each state issued **banknotes**, which served as currency and could be exchanged for gold. The National Banking Act of 1863 created federally chartered national banks, resulting in the current **dual banking system**.

Between 1930 and 1933, the Depression led to the failure of around 9,000 banks. Bank regulation in 1933 established the **Federal Deposit Insurance Corporation (FDIC)** to prevent depositor losses and to reestablish confidence in the banking industry. This regulation (known as the Glass-Steagall Act) also separated commercial banking activities from investment activities.

The dual banking system and the federal government's role in establishing safety and trust in the banking system results in a hybrid of regulatory agencies. The **Office of the Comptroller of the Currency** has primary supervisory responsibility for the 1,700 national banks. The Federal Reserve and the state banking authorities jointly have responsibility over the 900 state banks that are members of the Federal Reserve System. The Federal Reserve (the Fed) also has regulatory control over bank holding companies. The FDIC and the state banking authorities jointly supervise the 4,800 state banks that have FDIC insurance but are not members of the Fed. This complicated supervisory and regulatory structure developed piecemeal over two centuries and has withstood many attempts at overhaul.

There are about 7,500 commercial banks in the United States. This is many more than in any other country. The primary reason is that early law restricted banks from opening branches across state lines. Some states passed even more restrictive laws that limited banks to only one branch. Restrictive state banking regulations and the **McFadden Act,** which prohibits interstate banking, should be viewed as the most anti-competitive force in commercial banking. These laws have been allowed to exist so long because the American public has historically been against banks gaining too much power.

Bank holding companies have developed as a means to circumvent some of the restrictive regulations. A bank holding company has ownership in several different banks or companies. The companies they own must be "closely related to banking" as defined by the Fed. Many states now let banks owned by holding companies purchase banks in their state. Electronic banking facilities have also been allowed to cross state borders.

Financial Innovation and the Growth of the Shadow Banking System

Changes in the financial environment stimulate a search by financial institutions for innovations that are likely to be profitable. An example of this is the growth of the **shadow banking system**. Many of the current banking practices are a direct result of economic conditions. Banks had to **financially engineer** processes to stay profitable when market conditions became unfavorable or unpredictable. There are three basic types of innovations: responses to supply, responses to demand, and avoidance of regulation.

Response to Changes in Demand Conditions

The volatility of interest rates has caused banks to respond to changes in demand conditions. In the 1970s, adjustable rate mortgages (ARMs) became available to lessen the interest-rate risk to financial institutions. The interest rates on ARMs change when market interest rates (typically the T-bill rate) change. ARMs are popular with consumers because they are usually offered at lower rates than fixed rate mortgages. In 1975, financial derivatives became available as demand for lower interest-rate risk increased. Financial derivatives are basically **futures contracts**, where a seller agrees to provide a certain standardized commodity to a buyer on a specific date at a specific price, offered through financial instruments. Derivatives help investors and financial institutions hedge, or protect themselves from interest-rate risk.

Response to Changes in Supply Conditions

Improvements in computer and telecommunications technology have given rise to many innovations in the banking industry. These improvements have given rise to products such as credit cards and debit cards. More recently electronic banking in the form of **automated teller machines (ATM)** have become widely accessible and allow for 24 hour access to a variety of services. Customers can now also bank from home using the Internet or phone and can conduct many common transactions electronically (often called **electronic money** or **e-money**). These innovations help banks lower costs and make banking more convenient for customers. The widespread use of these systems effectively lowers the need to keep currency on hand as most transactions exist in electronic form.

The rapid improvements in information technology have potential significant benefits to banks. A paperless society would lead to major cost reductions from elimination of the costs of processing paper checks. In some European countries, primarily Finland and Sweden, the use of electronic payment systems is the dominant form of transacting business. The United States lags in the use to electronic funds transfer methods. Improvements in technology have also increased markets for junk bonds and commercial paper due to the improvement in the availability of information used to evaluate these instruments. Previously these two instruments were considered prohibitively risky.

Prior to the widespread adoption of telecommunication, the lack of information made bond issuance for questionable borrowers very difficult due to information problems. The **junk bond** market emerged to fill this void for less well-known firms due in large part to Michael Milken of Drexel Burnham Lambert. Similarly, the **commercial paper** market has benefitted from better information sharing and allows many corporations to opportunity to issue short-term notes. One of the most important financial innovations is **securitization**. This is the process of transforming otherwise illiquid financial assets, such as mortgages and auto loans, into marketable capital market securities.

Avoidance of Existing Regulation

Government regulation leads to financial innovation by creating incentives for firms to skirt regulations that restrict their ability to earn profits. Two major restrictions have significant affects on financial innovation. Reserve requirements act as a tax on deposits because the Fed does not pay interest on reserves. This is money that financial institutions could otherwise earn interest on by lending it out. Also, restrictions on interest paid on deposits have been an innovative force. Until 1980 there was a deposit rate ceiling on time deposits. If market conditions forced rates higher, customers would withdraw funds to seek higher yields. The fast growth of money market funds and sweep accounts is a result of these restrictions.

Two banking innovative have been successful attempts to reduce the cost of holding required reserves and the interest rate restrictions. The creation of **money market mutual funds** allow the bank to accept funds that function similar to deposits, but they are not technically deposits, so reserves do not have to be maintained against these funds. The second innovation is **sweep accounts**. Sweep accounts allow the bank to take end-of-day excess funds that are in a corporation's checking account and "sweep" the funds into an overnight account that earns interest. These overnight investments do not require reserves.

Financial Innovation and the Decline in Traditional Banking

Improvements in technology have led to the creation of assets and markets that were previously unavailable or limited in their availability. Money market mutual funds, junk bonds, commercial paper, and securitization are four securities that have benefited from technology. These securities have led to the elimination of cost advantages that banks use to enjoy in both the raising of funds and the making of loans. They offer low cost alternatives to lenders and borrowers that were not previously available. Banks have responded in order to survive by taking riskier loans and increasing off-balance-sheet activities to increase revenues and profits.

The Structure of the U.S. Commercial Banking Industry

Most industries in the United States have far fewer firms than the commercial banking industry. The never-ending pursuit by banks to find loopholes in regulations results in major gradual changes in where banks do business. The gains from economies of scale and diversification are too large for banks to ignore. Many states have formed their own compacts allowing interstate branching between those states. Permission to branch across state lines was approved by the federal government in 1994 through the passage of the Riegle-Neal Interstate Banking and Branching Efficiency Act. The number of banks fell dramatically since the mid-1980s as many banks consolidated and others failed. This period has seen the rise of superregional banks, which are bank holding companies the size of money center banks but headquartered outside of New York, Chicago, and San Francisco. This period has also seen financial firms expand their product mix and develop into large, complex bank organizations (LCBOs).

Separation of the Banking and Other Financial Service Industries

Since the Great Depression, the Glass-Steagall Act separated commercial and investment banking. Repeal of the Glass-Steagall Act provision has increased competition in the banking industry. Banks were initially permitted to provide some nontraditional banking financial services. The Gramm-Leach-Bliley Financial Services Modernization Act of 1999 allowed securities firms and insurance companies to purchase banks and allowed banks to underwrite insurance and securities and engage in real estate activities. Another implication of these acts is the increased complexity of the newly merged financial firms. The process was accelerated during the 2007–2009 financial crisis as all five of the largest, free-standing investment banks ceased to exist in their old form. Bear Sterns was bailed out and forced into a sale to J.P. Morgan. Lehman Brothers declared bankruptcy. Merril Lynch was purchased by Bank of America. Goldman Sachs and Morgan Stanley concerted into bank holding companies, so they could access insured deposits.

Thrift Industry: Regulation and Structure

Savings and Loans Associations

Savings and Loans (S&Ls) were authorized by Congress in 1816 in the same legislation that permitted the existence of mutual savings banks. Their express purpose was to have the majority of their assets in mortgage loans. A significant distinction of S&Ls is that they were not permitted to offer demand deposits and the interest rate on their savings accounts was fixed at a rate slightly higher than that offered by commercial banks. By the 1920s, mortgage loans accounted for about 85% of their total assets.

The Great Depression caused many financial hardships for the industry, much like it did for commercial banks. Congress passed the **Federal Home Loan Bank Act** of 1932, creating the **Federal Home Loan Bank Board** and giving the thrifts the choice of being state or federally chartered. In 1934, Congress created the **Federal Savings and Loan Insurance Corporation (FSLIC)**, which served the same function as the commercial bank's FDIC.

Mutual Savings Banks

Mutual savings banks were first authorized in the United States in 1816. These institutions had the unique characteristic of being owned by their depositors. A disadvantage of mutual savings bank is being owned by a large number of depositors magnifies the agency problem because there are a large number of owners with each owning only a small part of the company. A main attraction was that they paid a little higher rate on deposits than did commercial banks.

Credit Unions

Credit unions are relatively small institutions, are owned by their depositors who obtain funds, and make loans to their members who are "bonded together" by a common interest. Credit unions have cost advantages over other institutions because they often use volunteers as employees, they are nonprofit and thus tax exempt, and they often receive support from an employer or other group representing the common interest. One disadvantage of Credit Unions is their common bond requirement. This requirement keeps many of them quite small. The industry accounts for only 10%t of all consumer deposits and 15%of all consumer loans.

Federally chartered and state chartered insured credit unions are under the regulation of the **National Credit Union Administration (NCUA)**. Deposits are insured up to $100,000 by the **National Credit Union Share Insurance Fund (NSUSIF)**. Their small size has led to the creation of organizations to help credit unions deal with economies of scale and liquidity problems.

International Banking

International banking has grown rapidly since 1960. This is because international trade has expanded. American banks can pursue activities that are prohibited in the United States, and banks also want to tap into the Eurodollars market. Eurodollars are U.S. dollar denominated accounts held in foreign banks. Most Eurodollar accounts are interest bearing, and they are not subject to reserve requirements. Because Eurodollars now exceed $5 trillion, they are one of the most important financial markets in the world economy.

Edge Act Corporations and international banking facilities (IBFs) are legal means to circumvent restrictive laws so that American banks can compete more effectively with foreign banks. Foreign banks have been growing at a faster pace than their U.S. counterparts. Japanese-owned banks have a U.S. market share of 25% in California and more than 15% nationwide.

Foreign bank activities in the United States have been extremely successful. Foreign banks now have more than 20% of total U.S. banking assets, and they make more than 50% of all loans to U.S. corporations. They operate in the United States by opening agency offices, by establishing subsidiary banks in the United States, and by opening branch offices of the foreign bank.

■ Exercises

Exercise 1: Definitions and Terminology

Match the terms on the right with the definition or description on the left. Place the letter of the term in the blank provided next to the appropriate definition.

_____ 1. Dollar denominated deposits in banks outside the Untied States

_____ 2. Bank subsidiary engaged primarily in international banking

_____ 3. Has some regulatory authority over banks that it insures

_____ 4. Limited service banks that either do not make commercial loans or alternatively do not acquire deposit liabilities

_____ 5. System of bank regulation in which banks supervision by both federal and state regulators

_____ 6. Permitted to own banks and other businesses related to banking

_____ 7. Regulatory body that charters national banks

_____ 8. The process of turning illiquid assets into marketable securities.

_____ 9. If not federally insured, only 0.2% of all commercial bank deposits

_____ 10. Prohibited banks from branching across state lines

_____ 11. Excluded from reserve requirement on time deposits received from foreigners

_____ 12. Permitted the creation of federally chartered banks

_____ 13. The Gramm-Leach-Bliley Act completely abolished this act

_____ 14. Banks supervised by the federal government and banks supervised by states operate side by side

_____ 15. Offering where seller agrees to provide commodity on specific date at agreed upon price

_____ 16. Banking location that provides ATM, Internet access, and customer service phone link.

_____ 17. Large bank located outside of money centers

_____ 18. Nonbank lending via the securities market

a. international banking facilities (IBFs)

b. dual banking

c. Comptroller of the Currency

d. McFadden Act

e. Edge Act corp.

f. Eurodollars

g. securitization

h. nonbank banks

i. Banking Act of 1863

j. bank holding companies

k. FDIC

l. Glass-Steagall Act

m. state banks

n. ABM

o. dual banking system

p. futures contract

q. superregional bank

r. shadow banking system

Exercise 2: Multiple Regulatory Agencies

In the left-hand column are listed types of financial institutions. In the right-hand column are the regulatory agencies that determine the extent of permissible activities of these institutions. Write the appropriate letter from the right-hand column after the financial institution on the left in the space provided. More than one letter may be used to indicate overlapping regulatory activities.

Financial Institution		Regulatory Agency
National banks	_____	a. FDIC
State banks	_____	b. Office of Thrift
Supervision		c. Comptroller of the Currency
Bank holding companies	_____	d. Federal Reserve System
Savings and loan associations	_____	e. NCUSIF
Mutual savings banks	_____	f. NCUA
Credit unions	_____	g. State banking regulators
International banking facilities	_____	

Exercise 3: Branch Banking

A. California law permits statewide branch banking. As a result, the California banking market is more concentrated than most other states. Despite the high level of concentration, many economists believe that the California banking market is highly competitive. Do these facts contradict one another? Explain.

_____

_____

_____

B. Nationwide branching is permitted in Canada, yet many economists suggest that competition is limited due to entry restrictions. Using the information from part A, suggest what this implies about competition in banking markets.

_____

_____

C. The savings and loan industry is more concentrated than the commercial banking industry (that is, there are a relatively small number of small savings and loans). What explains this fact?

_____

_____

D. Why have regulations restricting branching arisen?

_____

_____

E. How have banks responded in general to branching restrictions?

_____

_____

■ Self-Test

Part A: Fill in the Blank

1. The Federal Reserve regulates _____ and state banks that are members of the Federal Reserve System.

2. The Comptroller of the Currency regulates _____ banks.

3. The FDIC and state banking authorities jointly supervise the 5,700 _____ banks that are not members of the Federal Reserve System.

4. Ironically, today's _____ banking system is the result of the federal government's attempt to eliminate state banks during the Civil War.

5. The attempt to eliminate state banks failed because state-chartered banks were able to substitute checking account deposits for _____ as a source of bank funds.

6. There were more bank failures in the 1980s than in any decade since the _____.

7. Despite the problems facing banking today, few would trade today's conditions for those of the 1920s and early 1930s before the introduction of _____ insurance.

8. The plethora of small banks is best explained by the restrictions of both the federal government and many state governments to _____.

9. Although the growth of _____ companies has provided a traditional loophole around the McFadden Act, the use of this traditional method may soon be unnecessary.

10. Significant changes have occurred in international banking, where the growth of _____ and the desire of domestic banks to obtain additional funds are evident by the rapid expansion of overseas offices.

11. Congress passed the _____ of 1978, which prevented interstate branching of foreign banks.

12. One of the early ways that banks worked around the restrictions on branch banking was to use electronic _____ owned by someone else.

13. The passage of the _____ and _____ effectively permitted interstate branching thus overturning the McFadden Act.

14. Of the three frameworks for separation of banking and the securities industry the one that provides no separation is the _____ framework.

15. Junk bonds that were initially investment grade bonds are referred to as _____.

16. A corporation that owns controlling interest in several different banks is known as a(n) _____.

17. The ability to use one resource to provide many different products or services is _____.

18. Special subsidiary engaged primarily in international banking is _____.

Part B: True-False Questions

Circle whether the following statements are true (T) or false (F).

T F   1. The U.S. banking system is similar to that of most other industrialized countries by having a large number of banks that compete vigorously for business.

T F   2. The existence of federal deposit insurance is just one indication of the government's desire to promote a sound banking system.

T F   3. The purchase by bank holding companies of banks in different states was one of the first ways that banks were able to "branch" across state lines.

T F   4. Dual banking refers to a system composed of both commercial banks and thrift institutions.

T F   5. The Comptroller of the Currency has been granted the sole responsibility for supervising bank holding companies.

T F   6. Regulations that restrict competition in the banking industry are often justified by the desire to prevent bank failures.

T F   7. The U.S. banking industry has suffered a decline partly because the cost of funds has increased.

T F   8. Permitting banks to increase their participation in investment banking activities is likely to result in higher costs to consumers because banks are less efficient at this activity.

T F   9. The majority of U.S. bank branches in foreign countries are in Canada and Mexico due to their close proximity to the U.S. border.

T F 10. Foreign banks in the United States are extremely successful and currently hold more that 20% of total U.S. bank assets.

T F 11. The first money market mutual fund in the United States was not particularly successful because the interest return on these was not much higher than the return on bank deposits.

T F 12. It has been argued that the large number of banking firms in the United States can be seen as an indication of the absence of competition rather than the presence of competition.

T F 13. Securitization cannot be applied to assets such as automobile loans because the loan amounts are usually of too small a dollar amount to justify the cost of securitization.

T F 14. Technological advances are the main driving force that has led to the decline in the role of banks in the U.S. financial system.

T F 15. Eurodollars are European currencies held in U.S. banks.

T F 16. Some small banks are called *community banks* because elected community representatives run them.

T F 17. Financial innovation is often a product of avoidance of government regulation.

T F 18. Financial derivatives can be used to hedge against risk and are considered conservative investment vehicles.

T F 19. Information technology raised the cost of financial transactions but made it easier for investors to acquire information.

Part C: Multiple-Choice Questions

Circle the appropriate answer.

1. Which of the following is a bank regulatory agency?
   (a) Comptroller of the Currency
   (b) Federal Reserve System
   (c) Federal Deposit Insurance Corporation
   (d) All of the above

2. The main purpose of federal deposit insurance is
   (a) to drive state deposit insurance funds out of business.
   (b) to drive private deposit insurance funds out of business.
   (c) to help assure depositors that their deposits are safe, thereby preventing bank panics.
   (d) none of the above.

3. Although bank regulations have been highly successful in preventing bank failures during the last 50 years, they have had the adverse side effect of
   (a) limiting competition.
   (b) encouraging the growth of very large banks.
   (c) significantly reducing the number of banks in our economy.
   (d) doing all of the above.

4. Although the National Bank Act of 1863 was designed to eliminate state-chartered banks by imposing a prohibitive tax on banknotes, these banks have been able to stay in business by
   (a) issuing credit cards.
   (b) ignoring the regulations.
   (c) issuing deposits.
   (d) branching into other states.

5. An argument against banks being permitted to enter the securities business is that
   (a) they will be increasing their risky activities leading to a potential increase in the moral hazard and adverse selection problems.
   (b) there is an increase in the likelihood of conflicts of interest between the bank and security issuers.
   (c) the overall costs of the bank will increase resulting in higher costs and lower returns to depositors.
   (d) both (a) and (b) are arguments against this activity.

6. The large number of small banks that characterize the U.S. banking structure is probably best explained by
   (a) the McFadden Act.
   (b) restrictive state branching regulations.
   (c) the National Bank Act of 1863.
   (d) all of the above.
   (e) only (a) and (b) of the above.

7. Which of the following is not a reason for the spectacular growth in international banking?
    (a) An increase in international trade
    (b) The creation of the United Nations resulting in national banking accords
    (c) An increase in the number of multinational corporations
    (d) The ability of U.S. banks to engage in activities abroad that are prohibited in the United States
    (e) All of the above are reasons for this growth.

8. All of the following assets have benefited from securitization except
    (a) commercial paper.
    (b) collateralized mortgage obligations.
    (c) credit card receivables.
    (d) pass-through securities.

9. When economists argue that banking regulations have been a mixed blessing, they are referring to the fact that
    (a) bank regulations foster competition at the expense of banking system safety.
    (b) bank regulations foster banking system safety at the expense of competition.
    (c) branch banking, while desired by consumers, leads to less competition.
    (d) bank regulations foster competition by limiting branching.

10. The U.S. banking system has been labeled a dual system because
    (a) banks offer both checking and savings accounts.
    (b) it actually includes both banks and thrift institutions.
    (c) it is regulated by both federal and state governments.
    (d) it was established during the Civil War, thus making it necessary to create separate regulatory bodies for the North and South.

11. Before 1863,
    (a) federally chartered banks had regulatory advantages not granted to state chartered banks.
    (b) the number of federally chartered banks grew at a much faster rate than at any other time since the end of the Civil War.
    (c) banks acquired funds by issuing bank notes.
    (d) all of the above occurred.

12. Which of the following statements concerning bank regulation in the United States is true?
    (a) The Office of the Comptroller of the Currency has the primary responsibility of the 1,700 national banks.
    (b) The Federal Reserve and the state banking authorities jointly have responsibility for the 900 state banks that are members of the Federal Reserve System.
    (c) The Fed has sole regulatory responsibility over bank holding companies.
    (d) All of the above are true.

13. Bank holding companies are permitted to do all of the following except
    (a) own more than one bank even if the banks are in different states.
    (b) serve the investment banker function for issuing equity securities even if the bank is restricted from doing so.
    (c) engage in activities that are related to banking.
    (d) issue commercial paper and allow the bank(s) they own to use this money as a source of funds.
    (e) Bank holding companies are permitted to do all of the above activities.

14. The main reason the number of banks declined by 1,500 between 1992 and 1996 is
    (a) the failure of many small banks that were unable to compete with the larger banks.
    (b) an increase in the number of international banks entering the U.S. market by buying U.S. banks.
    (c) many banks in the United States have consolidated to form larger banks.
    (d) the failure of many banks due to the recession of the early 1990s.

15. The breaking down of barriers to interstate banking has led to
    (a) increased asset diversification by banks resulting in lower risk.
    (b) reduced economies of scale due to the need to maintain banks in multiple states.
    (c) a decrease in competition for the large money center banks because they are able to do more interstate branching than other banks.
    (d) All of the above have been attributed to increased interstate banking.

16. The Gramm-Leach-Bliley Financial Services Modernization Act of 1999 permitted
    (a) securities firms and insurance companies to buy banks.
    (b) banks to underwrite insurance and securities.
    (c) banks to engage in real estate transactions.
    (d) all of the above.
    (e) Only (a) and (c) of the above are true.

17. The Gramm-Leach-Bliley Financial Services Modernization Act of 1999 eliminated
    (a) the National Banking Act of 1863.
    (b) the McFadden Act of 1927.
    (c) the Glass-Steagall Act of 1933.
    (d) the Federal Reserve System's Regulation Q.

18. Developing new products and services to meet customer demand and prove profitable is known as
    (a) financial innovation.
    (b) financial engineering.
    (c) financial evolution.
    (d) none of the above.

19. Adjustable rate mortgages were created as a response to what type of condition?
    (a) Supply
    (b) Demand
    (c) Restriction
    (d) All of the above

20. What type of account enables banks to avoid "tax" from reserve requirements?
    (a) Money Market
    (b) Zero Balance (ZBA)
    (c) Sweep
    (d) Demand Deposit

Part D

1. In what direction is banking structure likely to go over the next decade in relation to the current number of banks and their size?

   _____

2. If banks enter the securities industry, there is expected to be at least one major benefit to the average investor from the increased competition. What is that expected benefit?

   _____

3. What are the reasons for the decline in commercial banks as the major source of funds to nonfinancial borrowers?

   _____

4. Are bank consolidation and nationwide banking good or bad for consumers and the economy?

   _____

5. Describe the negative effects of the Glass-Steagall Act and identify possible good that will come as a result of its repeal.

   _____

■ Answers to Chapter 19

Exercise 1

1.	f	7.	c	13.	l
2.	e	8.	g	14.	o
3.	k	9.	m	15.	p
4.	h	10.	d	16.	n
5.	b	11.	a	17.	q
6.	j	12.	i	18.	r

Exercise 2

National banks	a, c, d
State banks	a, d
Bank holding companies	d
Savings and loan associations	a, b, g
Mutual savings banks	a, b, d
Credit unions	d, e, f
International banking facilities	d

Exercise 3

A. A high degree of concentration does not imply an absence of competition, as long as entry is allowed. Competition may therefore be enhanced as banks open up branch offices in new markets. The largest three banks in a state may hold 70% of all bank deposits, yet any individual may have the option of choosing between seven or eight banks. Thus concentration and competition need not be related if entry is allowed.

B. The experiences of Canada and California suggest that entry is more important than branching in determining the competitiveness of banking markets.

C. The higher concentration of the savings and loan industry is explained by the more liberal branching regulations for savings and loans; almost all states permit statewide branching, and since the early 1980s, branching across state lines has been permitted through acquisitions of troubled thrifts.

D. The American public has historically been untrusting of large banking institutions. States with the most restrictive branching regulations were ones with populist anti-bank sentiment. Usually these were large farming communities where banks would periodically have to foreclose on farms or other property. Small banks were seen as easier to deal with.

E. They created bank holding companies, nonbank banks, and ATM locations.

Self–Test

Part A

1. bank holding companies
2. national
3. state
4. dual
5. bank notes
6. Great Depression
7. FDIC
8 branch banking

9. bank holding
10. international trade
11. International Banking Act
12. automated teller machines
13. Riegle-Neal Interstate Banking + Branching Efficiency Act

14. universal banking
15. fallen angels
16. bank holding company
17. economic of scope
18. Edge Act corporation

Part B

1.	F	8.	F	15.	F
2.	T	9.	F	16.	F
3.	T	10.	T	17.	T
4.	F	11.	T	18.	F
5.	F	12.	T	19.	F
6.	T	13.	F		
7.	T	14.	T		

Part C

1.	d	8.	a	15.	a
2.	c	9.	b	16.	d
3.	a	10.	c	17.	c
4.	c	11.	c	18.	a
5.	a	12.	d	19.	b
6.	e	13.	b	20.	c
7.	b	14.	c		

Part D

1. The fact that nationwide interstate banking is virtually a reality means that the banks in the United States will continue to consolidate. This consolidation will result in both a decline in the total number of banks to perhaps 4,000 or so and in the surviving banks being generally much larger.

2. The spread between the price paid for the security and the price it can be sold for should decrease. This decline should result in lower total costs of trading for investors and thus higher total returns.

3. They lost the cost advantage on deposits when Regulation Q was abolished. They also lost the income advantage because technology allows other firms to issue securities directly to the public with higher returns.

4. In general, bank consolidation is positive due to the economies of scale and geographical diversification that banks could not achieve previously. Economies of scale should help banks to reduce expenses, allowing them to put the saved capital to more productive uses.

5. The Glass-Steagall Act prevented commercial banking institutions from competing in the securities and investment banking industries. Consequently, commercial banks could not further diversify their investments. The increased competition of banks in the investment banking industry could lead to lower investment banking fees, allowing issuing companies to retain more of the funds raised for productive purposes.

Chapter 20
The Mutual Fund Industry

■ Chapter Learning Goals

By the end of this chapter, you should

1. Know why mutual funds have become popular.
2. Know the types of mutual funds.
3. Understand how mutual funds are regulated.
4. Understand how conflicts of interest affect the mutual fund industry.

■ Chapter Summary

Mutual funds have become popular since 1970. By allowing small investors to pool their resources to buy securities, investors benefit through lower transaction costs and enhanced portfolio diversification opportunities by purchasing mutual funds. The growth of the industry has led to increased product offerings that create further diversification opportunities. However, without adequate regulatory oversight, the mutual fund industry has been riddled in scandal the past few years.

The Growth of Mutual Funds

About half of all U.S. households own mutual funds. The amount invested in mutual funds has grown from about $50 billion to $11 trillion during the last 40 years.

Mutual Fund Structure

Although mutual funds date back to the 1800s, the industry's growth really began with the Investment Company Act of 1940. The Investment Company Act required increased disclosure requirement of fees and investment policies.

The text identifies five primary benefits of mutual funds: (1) liquidity intermediation, (2) denomination intermediation, (3) diversification, (4) cost advantages, and (5) managerial expertise. Liquidity intermediation is defined as the ability to convert an investment into cash quickly with low costs. Denomination intermediation enables small investors to purchase securities they would otherwise not be able to purchase without pooling their resources together. Mutual funds provide small investors access to diversified portfolios of securities both domestically and internationally. Because mutual funds purchase large numbers of shares, they are able to significantly reduce transactions costs for small investors. Many investors do not understand the fundamentals of investing and are comforted by having an experienced fund manager select the securities in the portfolio for them.

Eighty percent of mutual fund shares are owned by households with the median investor being 49 years old, married, and owning about $200,000 in financial assets. Mutual fund investment into retirement accounts is broken down between individual retirement accounts (IRAs) and defined contribution plans, primarily 401(k) plans.

Most mutual funds companies offer different types of funds and are called mutual fund complexes. Investors in that family of funds can usually transfer money across funds in the family.

Mutual funds are structured either as open-end funds or closed-end funds. Open-end funds are the most common structure and are structured such that individuals can invest at any time or sell the shares back to the mutual fund company at any time. Open-end funds are priced at the end of each day by determining the net asset value (NAV). Closed-end funds are sold to the public through an offering and trade in the secondary market like a regular corporate stock. Although the price per share is related to the value of the assets owned by the fund, the price per share can deviate from the value of the underlying assets.

Organizational Structure

The shareholders in mutual funds are the investors. The shareholders receive the earnings after expenses of the mutual fund. The fund's Board of Directors sets the investment policy and reviews the funds activities. The Board also selects the investment adviser, which is typically a separate company. The investment adviser manages the fund according to the fund's stated policies and objectives.

The NAV of a fund is calculated as a fund's new worth divided by the number of shares outstanding. The net worth is the assets of the fund minus the liabilities of the fund.

The four primary classes of mutual funds are (1) stock or equity funds, (2) bond funds, (3) hybrid funds, and (4) money market funds. More than half of all mutual fund assets are invested in equity funds.

Equity funds can be further categorized into capital appreciation funds, world funds, and total return funds. Capital appreciation funds pursue fast increasing share prices or rapid growth without concern for dividends. World funds invest primarily in stocks of foreign companies. Total return funds seek capital appreciation and current income via dividends.

The primary types of bond funds are corporate, high yield, world, government, strategic income, state municipal, and national municipal. The automatic reinvestment and liquidity intermediation features of bond funds make them popular. Strategic income and government bond funds are the two most popular bond fund groups.

Hybrid funds invest into both bonds and stocks. These funds provide diversification across asset classes.

Money market funds are open-end funds that invest in money market securities. These funds have no sales charge and typically have check writing privileges.

Index funds track the performance of a specific index. Relative to other equity or bond funds, these funds have low expenses. The low expenses often result in higher returns relative to managed funds with similar investment objectives.

Fee Structure of Investment Funds

There are three general types of fee structures for mutual funds: (1) load funds, (2) deferred load funds, and (3) no load funds. Load funds have front-end sales charges that are paid upon initial purchase of the fund. Deferred load or back-end load funds impose a sales charge if the mutual fund is sold within a certain period of time. The deferred sales charge declines over time. No-load funds do not impose sales charges. Load funds and deferred load funds are called Class A and Class B shares, respectively. Class C shares are often referred to as no-load funds, but they often impose a 1% deferred sales charge if the fund is sold within 12 months of purchase.

Other fees which funds may charge are (1) contingent deferred sales, (2) redemption fees, (3) exchange fees, (4) account maintenance fees, and (5) 12b-1 fees. Contingent deferred sales charges are declining back-end sales charges. Redemption fees are back-end sales charges for redeeming shares. Exchange fees may be charged when moving money from one fund to another within a family of funds. Account maintenance fees may be charges for low balances or account inactivity. 12b-1 fees are charges to pay marketing and advertising expenses.

Regulation of Mutual Funds

Four federal laws regulate mutual funds. The Securities Act of 1933 established certain disclosures. The Securities Exchange Act of 1934 initiated antifraud rules for the sale and purchase of fund shares. The Investment Company Act of 1940 mandates that mutual funds meet specific operating standards and register with the SEC. Fund advisers are regulated by the Investment Advisers Act of 1940.

Mutual funds must provide to shareholders a shareholder report and a prospectus that describes the funds investment strategies and risks, fees and expenses, and the funds goals. Federal tax status of distributions is also sent to shareholders annually. In January 2001, the SEC adopted new rules to improve the independence of investment company directors. In particular, the rules require that independent directors comprise at least a majority of the fund's board of directors. In addition, independent directors must select and nominate other independent directors and legal counsel for the fund's independent directors.

Hedge Funds

Hedge funds are more difficult to classify than other funds because they pursue so many different investment strategies. Some hedge funds attempt to be market neutral. Hedge funds seek pricing anomalies between related securities around the world. Hedge funds also set up lines of credit to leverage their investment positions.

Several features distinguish hedge funds from traditional mutual funds. First, the minimum investment ranges from $100,000 to $20 million. Most hedge funds are set up as limited partnerships and cannot have more than 99 limited partners with steady incomes of $200,000 or more or a net worth of $1 million, excluding home residence. Hedge funds typically require that investors commit their capital for long periods of time. One issue of concern is that hedge funds often charge large fees to investors. For example, a 1% annual asset management fee plus 20% of the funds profits.

Conflicts of Interest in the Mutual Fund Industry

The governance structure of mutual funds creates a situation where the principal's and agent's interests are not closely aligned. Unsurprisingly, given that most fund shareholders own only a small percentage of the mutual fund shares, in the absence of active monitoring, the structure of the investment adviser relationship does not lead to the goal of maximizing shareholder wealth.

Most of the mutual fund abuses reported in 2003 and 2004 were related to late trading or market timing. Late trading occurs when mutual fund orders that are received after 4:00 p.m. are allowed to trade at the 4:00 p.m. NAV price. Late trading enables investors to look back in time and trade securities after prices are already known. Late trading is an illegal practice. Market timing takes advantage of time zone differences by enabling investors to buy foreign securities at prior stale prices that are computed in a fund's NAV but do not reflect information that has been released since that stale price was established. Thus, arbitrage opportunities arise from the NAV prices not reflecting all publicly available information.

The government is responding to the mutual fund scandals by pushing for enhanced oversight and regulation. One proposal would require a higher percentage of mutual fund directors to be independent from management and fund ownership. Another proposal would strictly enforce trades received after 4:00 p.m. to be traded at the next day's NAV. A third proposal would require funds to charge a redemption fee if an investor sells shares within 60 or 90 days of purchase. Other ideas are to increase transparency of relationships between fund owners and investment managers, how fees are charges, investment manager compensation arrangements, and compensation arrangements between mutual funds and sales brokers.

■ Exercises

Exercise 1: Definitions and Terminology

_____ 1. Required increased disclosure of fees and investment practices

_____ 2. Funds with a fixed number of nonredeemable shares

_____ 3. Funds that have up-front sales charges

_____ 4. Equity funds that seek a combination of capital appreciation and current income

_____ 5. Funds that invest in both stocks and bonds

_____ 6. Mutual funds that have declining sales charges when investors take out funds.

_____ 7. The ability to convert an investment into cash quickly at low cost

_____ 8. Mutual funds that individuals can buy or redeem shares through the fund at any time

_____ 9. Equity funds that primarily invest in foreign company stocks

_____ 10. Provides access for small investors to securities requiring large investments

_____ 11. Mutual funds that do not have a direct sales charge

_____ 12. Funds which only invest in money market securities

_____ 13. Reduces portfolio risk by holding many different securities

_____ 14. Funds that track the performance of some index

_____ 15. Funds that seek fast increases in share prices with no concern for dividends.

a. diversification

b. denomination intermediation

c. index funds

d. world equity funds

e. open-end funds

f. load funds

g. capital appreciation funds

h. Investment Company Act of 1940

i. total return funds

j. deferred load funds

k. money market funds

l. closed-end fund

m. hybrid funds

n. no load funds

o. liquidity intermediation

■ Self-Test

Part A: Fill in the Blanks

1. The _____ for a fund is computed at 4:00 p.m. of each trading day.

2. _____ fees are charged to pay for marketing and advertising expenses.

3. Funds that seek fast increasing share prices with no income concerns are _____.

4. Equity funds that invest primarily in stock of foreign companies are _____.

5. About _____ of all U.S. households own mutual funds.

6. A mutual fund's _____ establishes the fund's investment policy.

7. NAV is computed as _____ divided by the number of shares outstanding.

8. Funds that invest in both stocks and boards are _____ funds.

9. A(n) _____ manages a mutual fund according to the fund's objectives and policies.

10. Funds that do not have any direct sales charges are called _____ funds.

11. _____ is the ability to convert an investment into cash quickly with low costs.

12. Some _____ funds seek pricing anomalies between related securities around the world.

13. The _____ initiated antifraud rules for the sale and purchase of fund shares.

14. A(n) _____ describes a fund's investment strategies and risk and fees and expenses.

15. _____ enables small investors to access securities requiring large initial investments.

Part B: True-False Questions

T F 1. Late trading takes advantage of time zone differences by allowing investors to buy foreign securities at stale prices.

T F 2. A fund's net worth is the value of its assets.

T F 3. NAV is computed as net worth divided by the number of shares outstanding.

T F 4. Denomination intermediation is the ability to convert a security to cash quickly with low costs.

T F 5. The board of directors establishes a fund's investment policy.

T F 6. Hedge funds seek pricing anomalies between related securities around the world.

T F 7. Redemption fees are back-end sales charges for redeeming shares.

T F 8. Account maintenance fees are declining back-end sales charges.

T F 9. Closed-end funds have a fixed number of nonredeemable shares.

T F 10. High yield funds are a type of bond fund.

T F 11. Strategic income funds are a type of equity fund.

T F 12. Money market funds do not have check writing privileges.

T F 13. The shareholders in mutual funds are the owners.

T F 14. Money market funds invest only in money market securities.

T F 15. Mutual funds do not provide cost savings to small investors.

Part C: Multiple-Choice Questions

1. Which of the following is not a primary benefit of mutual funds?
    (a) Liquidity intermediation
    (b) Cost advantages
    (c) Late trading
    (d) Diversification

2. Which of the following is one of the four primary classes of mutual funds?
    (a) Hybrid
    (b) Money market
    (c) Bond
    (d) Stock
    (e) All of the above

3. Class B shares are also known as
    (a) deferred load funds.
    (b) front load funds.
    (c) no load funds.
    (d) all of the above.

4. A prospectus provides all of the following about a fund except
    (a) the strategies and risks.
    (b) fees and expenses.
    (c) goals.
    (d) forecasted returns.

5. Index funds are popular investments because
    (a) they have low costs.
    (b) they provide diversification benefits.
    (c) they ensure performance close to that of the relative benchmark
    (d) of all of the above.

6. If an investor wants to diversify her stock portfolio globally, then she should invest into a
_____ fund.
   (a) capital appreciation
   (b) hybrid
   (c) world
   (d) national municipal

7. Which of the following is not a characteristic of money market funds?
   (a) Check writing privileges
   (b) No sales charge
   (c) FDIC insured
   (d) Only invest in money market securities

8. Which of the following is not a type of equity fund?
   (a) Hedge fund
   (b) Capital appreciation fund
   (c) World fund
   (d) Total return fund

9. If an investor wanted a mutual fund that produces income that is free from federal taxation, then she
should buy a(n) _____ fund.
   (a) national municipal fund
   (b) state municipal fund
   (c) high-yield fund
   (d) government income fund

10. _____ enables small investors to invest in securities that have high initial investments.
   (a) Liquidity intermediation
   (b) Denomination intermediation
   (c) Diversification
   (d) Market timing

11. _____ is the ability of a security to be converted to cash quickly at low cost.
   (a) Liquidity intermediation
   (b) Denomination intermediation
   (c) Diversification
   (d) Market timing

Part D: Short Answer Questions

1. Describe why mutual funds have become critical investments for small investors.

   _____

   _____

2. What is the difference between market timing and late trading?

   _____

   _____

3. Describe how the governance structure of mutual funds has led to conflicts of interest in the mutual funds industry.

   _____

   _____

■ Answers to Chapter 20

Exercise 1

1.	h	6.	j	11.	n
2.	l	7.	o	12.	k
3.	f	8.	e	13.	a
4.	i	9.	d	14.	c
5.	m	10.	b	15.	g

Self-Test

Part A

1.	net asset value	6	board of directors	11.	Liquidity intermediation
2.	12b-1	7.	net worth	12.	hedge
3.	capital appreciation funds	8.	hybrid	13.	Security Exchange Act of 1934
4.	world equity funds	9.	investment adviser	14.	prospects
5.	half	10.	no-load	15.	Denomination intermediation

Part B

1.	F	6.	T	11.	F
2.	F	7.	T	12.	F
3.	T	8.	F	13.	T
4.	F	9.	T	14.	T
5.	T	10.	T	15.	F

Part C

1.	c	7.	c
2.	e	8.	a
3.	a	9.	b
4.	d	10.	b
5.	d	11.	a
6.	c		

Part D

1. Mutual funds have become critical investments for small investments because funds allow them to obtain instant diversification, which they would not be able to achieve with small dollar investments into individual stocks. Furthermore, transaction costs can be a serious drag on portfolio returns for small investors who place small dollar amounts into individual stocks.

2. Late trading is where mutual fund companies accept orders from certain customers after 4:00 p.m., but still give the customers the 4:00 p.m. NAV. This enables those certain customers to trade on new information that is not priced into the closing NAV but can affect prices tomorrow. In general, market timing also takes advantage of stale prices but through different mechanisms. Market timing uses the different trading times around the globe to find stale security prices that have not reflected information that has been released since that market closed. Investors will buy a fund that owns these stale price stocks knowing that tomorrows NAV will reflect the new information.

3. The governance structure of mutual funds exacerbates the principal-agent problem. In particular, most mutual fund shareholders only own a small percentage of all outstanding shares. Consequently, without sufficient monitoring, the structure of the investment adviser relationship is not consistent with maximizing shareholder wealth.

Chapter 21
Insurance Companies and Pension Funds

■ Chapter Learning Goals

By the end of this chapter, you should

1. Know the different types of insurance available.
2. Understand the various features of the main types of life insurance policies.
3. Know why pension plans exist and the various features of different types of plans.
4. Know where insurance companies and pension funds place the majority of their investment funds.

■ Chapter Summary

Insurance plays a major role in the lives of most people. Insurance companies are very instrumental as a source of funds in the capital markets. This chapter looks at why insurance exists and the various sources of funds provided to insurance companies. This chapter also looks at the types of capital market financing that insurance companies engage in. Chapter 21 also looks at pension plans. These entities accumulate large sums of money as individuals save for their post-employment years. The accumulation of funds by pension programs is huge and provides a major source of financing to capital borrowers.

Fundamentals of Insurance

The limited wealth of most consumers and their unwillingness to take on excess risk opens the door for the insurance industry. Life insurance, property insurance, and health insurance are all designed to transfer all or part of the risk of loss to these firms. Consumers are usually willing to pay a fixed amount over time, called a **certainty equivalent**, in order to avoid the possible loss of a large unknown amount in the future. The insured party pays a **premium** to the insurance company in return for the promise that the company will pay a contractual amount should the insured event occur.

Not all risks are insurable. The insurance company must be able to compute the probability of a particular loss over a large group of people and be able to quantify the expected amount of the loss before it can be insured. Thus, the company must insure a large number of people to be able to rely upon the probability estimate to predict their future costs.

Not everyone can buy insurance. There must be a relationship between **insured** and the **beneficiary**. The beneficiary must be someone who would suffer loss if the insured event occurs. The insured party will be reimbursed or paid only for the amount of the loss. There is to be no profit potential built into the insured risk. This last condition includes that an insured cannot receive compensation for the same loss from more than one source.

One significant problem insurance companies face is the risk of moral hazard. This risk exists because the person most willing to transfer the risk of loss is someone who is the most likely to suffer the loss. One way to reduce the moral hazard problem is to have a **deductible** included in the policy. A deductible is the portion of the loss that the insured must pay before the insurance company becomes liable for payment.

Adverse selection is also a concern for insurers as those with a greater need for coverage should be more likely to apply. In practice, insurers deal with this problem by requiring examinations for health insurance or denying coverage based on pre-existing conditions.

Insurance is usually sold through agents for the company. If an agent sells insurance for only one company, they are an **exclusive agent**, whereas if they can sell a policy for a variety of firms, they are **independent agents**. Whichever sales approach is taken, the insurance company employs **underwriters** who review each application for coverage and determine if the company is willing to undertake the risk of that client.

Growth and Organization of Insurance Companies

Insurance companies are either organized as stock or mutual firms. A **stock company** is owned by stockholders and has the objective of making a profit. Policyholders own **mutual insurance companies**. The objective of mutual companies is to provide the lowest possible cost to the insured. Policyholders are paid dividends that reflect a surplus of premiums over cost. Dividends received from mutual companies are treated as refunds of overcharges on insurance premiums. Most insurance companies are organized as stock firms.

Types of Insurance

Life Insurance

Life insurance companies generally sell several types of policies. In addition to regular life, they may also sell disability insurance, annuity contracts, and health insurance. Life insurance coverage per se comes in three general types of policies: term life, whole life, and universal life. The law of large numbers states what when large numbers of people are insured, the distribution of losses will be normally distributed. The normal distribution allows insurance companies to better forecast expected losses and thereby price policies more accurately. **Term life** means the insured purchases only protection against untimely death. If the insured stops premium payments, the coverage terminates, and the insured has nothing left from the policy. With term life, the premium usually increases annually or at some fixed interval as the insured ages. With **whole life** coverage, the insured pays a fixed premium for as long as they want the coverage. In addition, should the insured terminate coverage, the policy will return some amount, called a **cash value** to the insured. Whole life contains a small savings component, which belongs to the insured. Because of the savings, the whole life policy is more expensive than term life. **Universal life** is like whole life except the cash value can be invested in assets that have the potential of earning higher returns than those of whole life.

Annuities are also very popular products for insurance companies. The insured will pay a premium for the annuity during their working years. Upon retirement, the insurance company promises to pay the insured a fixed payment for as long as they live. This contract provides security to the insured against running out of money to live on between retirement and death.

The liabilities of insurance companies come from the premiums paid by insured clients and from pension funds that the insurance company manages for clients. Both sources are long term, which allows the insurance company to invest in long-term assets. These companies invest in stocks, corporate and government bonds, mortgages, and real estate.

Health Insurance

Most health insurance is provided through company-sponsored plans. This approach makes the coverage affordable. Individual coverage is subject to the adverse selection problem and as a result is very expensive. For retired persons or those on welfare, the government provides coverage through Medicare and Medicaid, respectively. The rapidly increasing cost of medical care is driving firms to a new form of health insurance called **managed care**, which is where the coverage provider requires approval of services before they are provided, and the provider restricts service providers to those on a pre-approved list. After contentious debate, the Patient Protection and Affordable Care Act of 2010 expanded coverage to an additional 32 million Americans.

Property and Casualty Insurance

Property insurance protects the insured against losses from fire, theft, storm, explosion, and even neglect. The policy may be an **all-risk policy** covering the loss of property from almost any cause, or a **named-peril policy** covering losses associated with specific named perils. Most homeowner policies are all-risk policies.

Casualty insurance, also called **liability insurance**, protects the insured against loss in the event they are liable for injury or loss to other parties. If someone slips on ice on your property you may be liable for expenses and losses they incur due to injury. Casualty insurance covers this financial liability.

Due to the high losses that potentially could occur from property and casualty coverage, most insurance companies will share the risk of riskier perils with other insurance companies. This risk sharing is called **reinsurance**. Without this sharing of risk some higher-risk clients would not be able to obtain coverage.

Terrorism Risk Insurance Act of 2002

The Terrorism Risk Insurance Act of 2002 was passed on November 26, 2002. It limits the amount insurance companies are required to pay out in the event of international terrorism where losses exceed $5 million. The government will pay 90% of the losses in the event of a terrorist attack. However, losses greater than $100 billion are not covered under the act.

Administration and Regulation of Insurance Coverage

The insurance industry is not subject to direct federal regulation, but they must comply with the state regulations of every state in which they do business. State regulations are generally intended to protect the insured clients against loss from insolvency of the company and also to require a minimum level of knowledge by insurance agents by requiring a license to sell insurance.

The adverse selection and moral hazard problems are so great with insurance coverage that firms have developed a number of ways to reduce these problems. The agents and underwriters take many steps to screen high-risk from low-risk clients. Insurance companies may limit the dollar amount of the coverage, they will charge higher-risk clients a higher premium for the coverage, have clients pay part of the losses through **coinsurance**, or pay the first part of the loss through a deductible, or restrict them from engaging in certain risky activities. The insurance company has the right to investigate any claims to determine if fraud exists and to cancel the policy under certain conditions.

A **credit default swap (CDS)** is insurance against default on a financial instrument. Though useful as a way to hedge risk for holders that also own the underlying instrument, speculators may purchase a CDS without an insurable interest. A credit insurance alternative to CDS, monoline insurance companies specialize solely in credit insurance, as regulations do not permit other types of insurers to underwrite credit insurance. The use of such insurance allows a borrower to achieve a higher rating on its bond than could be possible without the backing of the monocline insurer.

Pensions

Pension plans are retirement accounts to which an employer, and perhaps the employee also, makes contributions during their working years and receives payments from after retirement. The amount of the retirement payment can be known in advance, as with a **defined-benefit plan**, or the amount may depend on the sum of money accumulated in the pension by retirement, called a **defined-contribution plan**. One risk the employee takes is if enough money has accumulated in the pension account to make the promised payments. If the exact amount of money needed is available the fund is **fully funded**, but if funds are inadequate, it is **underfunded**. If excess funds are in the account, it is **overfunded**.

Both **private pension plans**, sponsored by employers, groups, and individuals, and **public pension plans**, sponsored by a governmental body, exist. The best-known public plan is Social Security, which faces severe underfunding in the not too distant future as the "baby boomers" start to retire. This plan will be faced with the task of increasing payments into the plan or reducing benefits to retirees. The federal government is also considering privatization of all or part of the Social Security fund, which means that the contributions will be invested in private sector corporations and other assets.

Employee Retirement Income Security Act (ERISA)

Passed in 1974, ERISA provides the major regulations with which pension plans must comply. The most important provisions are that employees can transfer their plans when they change employers and they must become vested within seven years. However, most plans allow for vesting in less time. Vesting is the provision that makes it so that the employee cannot be denied benefits from the plan even if they leave employment with the sponsoring company. ERISA also improved what must be disclosed to the employee about the plan. ERISA created the **Pension Benefit Guarantee Corporation (PBGC)**, which functions much like the FDIC by providing employees protection against loss of benefits should the pension plan face financial failure. The amount of protection is capped at $49,500 per employee.

Individual Retirement Plans

Individual Retirement Accounts (IRAs) are tax deferred savings accounts initially created by the Pension Reform Act of 1978. These accounts allow individuals to set aside retirement assets up to a certain dollar amount depending on income and marital status. Keogh plans give retirement fund tax benefits to self-employed individuals and their employees. The Small Business Protection Act of 1996 created simplified retirement accounts called SIMPLE IRAs and 401(k) plans for businesses with fewer than 100 employees.

■ Exercises

Exercise 1: Definitions and Terminology

Match the following terms in the column on the right with the definition or description in the column on the left. Place the letter of the term in the blank provided next to the appropriate definition.

_____ 1. The payment that is substituted for the potential and unknown loss that could occur

_____ 2. Insurance against default on a financial instrument

_____ 3. The amount of the loss that the insured must pay before the insurance company makes any payment

_____ 4. Specifies the amount of retirement benefits the employee will receive from the pension plan

_____ 5. When an insurance company shares part of the risk with another company

_____ 6. When only certain listed risks are covered by a property insurance policy.

_____ 7. When the insured pays part of any loss with the insurance company paying the remainder

_____ 8. A contract that promises the insured a fixed payment over the remaining life of the insured.

_____ 9. Provides protection against loss should the insured become liable for another person or property

_____ 10. Provides protection against losses from fire, theft, storms, explosion, and neglect

_____ 11. An insurance company whose shares are owned by outside stockholders, like regular corporations

_____ 12. When the employee/employer make fixed deposits into a pension plan

_____ 13. An insurance company that is owned by its policy holders

_____ 14. A retirement account for anyone not covered by an employer sponsored plan

_____ 15. The party who receives payment should a loss occur in an insurance contract

_____ 16. People who review insurance contracts to determine if coverage should not be extended due to risk

_____ 17. Insurance policy that pays a death benefit and can accumulate cash value.

_____ 18. Insurance company that only underwrites credit insurance

a. annuity

b. casualty insurance

c. certainty equivalent

d. coinsurance

e. deductible

f. defined-benefit plan

g. defined-contribution plan

h. individual retirement account

i. credit default swap

j. mutual insurance company

k. named-peril policy

l. property insurance

m. reinsurance

n. stock company

o. whole life

p. underwriters

q. beneficiaries

r. monocline insurer

Exercise 2: Insurable Risks

For each of the following situations place an X in the appropriate column for the type of insurance that could be used to protect again this loss.

	Type of Insurance			
Risk	Life	Property	Casualty	Health
To be sure you are able to pay for your children's college	____	____	____	____
A neighbor slips on your porch steps	____	____	____	____
You wreck your car	____	____	____	____
You accidentally hit another car with your car	____	____	____	____
You get food poisoning	____	____	____	____
You want a guaranteed annuity payment at retirement	____	____	____	____
Your house catches on fire	____	____	____	____
Your car catches on fire	____	____	____	____
Your house is damaged in a hurricane	____	____	____	____
You are injured from flying debris in a hurricane	____	____	____	____

Exercise 3: Asset Allocation

For the following table of financial intermediaries place an X in the appropriate column for each intermediary if they are more likely to hold short-term or long-term assets.

Financial Intermediary	Long-term Assets	Short-term Assets
Life Insurance Company	____	____
Property and Casualty Insurance Company	____	____
Private Pension Fund	____	____
Individual Retirement Account	____	____
Money Market Mutual Fund	____	____

Exercise 4: Life Insurance and Private Pension Fund Assets

Place the percentage distribution of aggregate assets for each of the following asset categories of life insurance company at the beginning of 2005 and private pension fund assets as of the end of 2006.

Insurance Company	Pension Plan	
_____	_____	Corporate bonds
_____	_____	Mortgages
_____	_____	Stocks
_____	_____	Government securities

■ Self-Test

Part A: Fill in the Blank

1. The fixed payment that an insurance company charges its clients is called a(n) _____ and is the amount of the certainty equivalent.

2. The _____ is the party who receives the payment from the insurance company should a loss occur.

3. Insurance companies suffer greatly from _____ creating a problem with adverse selection and moral hazard.

4. The fact that the person more likely to suffer a loss is the one more likely to apply for insurance creates a(n) _____ problem.

5. A(n) _____ agent may sell insurance for a number of different companies.

6. _____ insurance companies only underwrite credit insurance and are prohibited by regulation from underwriting life, property, or health insurance.

7. Life insurance contracts are _____ term, while property and casualty coverage is _____ term and subject to frequent renewal.

8. _____ insurance replaces your income should you not be able to work due to an illness or an accident.

9. Insurance companies rely upon the _____, by insuring a large number of people, to make their loss predictions fairly accurate.

10. The government is involved in health care insurance through the _____ program that provides coverage to the elderly and _____ that covers those on welfare.

11. By providing coverage against many types of perils, property insurance losses are _____ difficult to predict than life insurance claims.

12. When one insurance company shares the risk of loss with another insurance company, they are engaging in _____, which is insurance for the insurance company.

13. Defined-contribution plans are becoming more popular. One reason for the popularity is that they place responsibility on the _____ for the pension plan's performance.

14. _____ plans are like Individual Retirement Plans except that they are for the benefit of the self-employed.

15. The Pension Benefit Guarantee Corporation is facing a potential crisis due to _____ of many private pension plans.

16. The major benefit of a(n) _____ policy is that cash value accumulates at a much higher rate than more traditional types of insurance.

17. _____ protects individuals from outliving their retirement funds.

18. _____ policies insure against loss only from perils that are specifically named in the policy.

Part B: True-False Questions

Circle whether the following statements are true (T) or false (F).

T F   1. Insurance companies and pension funds are considered financial intermediaries because they take in payments and then invest the funds in return-generating assets.

T F   2. Joe Smith can take out life insurance on his best friend's life because of their close friendship.

T F   3. Due to adverse selection, the loss probability statistic gathered for the entire population may be lower than the same statistic from people who actually buy insurance policies.

T F   4. Due to moral hazard, an insured person is less likely to take precautions against loss than an uninsured person.

T F   5. Insurance companies are regulated by the states in which they are chartered.

T F   6. Term insurance premiums usually decline as the insured gets older because the cumulative premiums paid is larger.

T F   7. Some term insurance policies can maintain a level premium by decreasing the amount of coverage as the insured ages.

T F   8. The interest earned on the savings portion of a universal life insurance policy is exempt from taxes until the money is withdrawn.

T F   9. Most people buy individual health insurance policies to insure themselves against losses due to medical problems.

T F 10. In HMO plans, the risk is shifted to the provider from the insurance company because the company pays the HMO a fixed fee for the services provided.

T F 11. Over the past decade, health care costs have risen at a faster rate than the general cost of living and real wages.

T F 12. The first fire insurance company was founded in Chicago after the Great Chicago Fire.

T F 13. Liability insurance is the same thing as casualty insurance.

T F 14. Most employees are familiar enough with investments to effectively manage their defined-contribution plans.

T F 15. Unless the Social Security system is modified, it is projected that the plan will be bankrupt by the year 2041.

T F 16. Defined Contribution Funds promises to pay employees a specific benefit when they retire.

T F 17. Individuals may contribute up to 100% of earned income to IRA plans.

T F 18. Keogh Plans are primarily used by large corporations to supplement pension plans

Part C: Multiple-Choice Questions

Circle the appropriate answer.

1. For someone earning about $53,400 per year, Social Security benefits will replace about _____ of their pre-retirement income.
   - (a) 15%
   - (b) 72%
   - (c) 24%
   - (d) 42%

2. Without insurance, individuals would have to do all of the following except
   - (a) accumulate a reserve fund for emergencies.
   - (b) keep reserve funds in highly liquid low-risk investment.
   - (c) invest reserves in short-term assets.
   - (d) depend on an insurance company to help them out in an emergency.

3. Insurance companies battle the adverse selection problem through
   - (a) risk-based premiums.
   - (b) restrictive provisions.
   - (c) cancellation of insurance.
   - (d) deductibles.

4. Insurance companies battle moral hazard problem through
   - (a) risk-based premiums.
   - (b) coinsurance.
   - (c) screening customers.
   - (d) All three of these are used to reduce moral hazard.

5. A person who has the responsibility of accepting or rejecting the issuance of a policy is an
   - (a) independent agent.
   - (b) underwriter.
   - (c) exclusive agent.
   - (d) insured.

6. The premium on a life insurance policy will be higher, everything else the same,
   - (a) the higher their life expectancy.
   - (b) the healthier the insured.
   - (c) if they have skydiving as a hobby.
   - (d) the younger the insured.

7. Property insurance would *not* protect the insured against a loss due to
   - (a) someone stealing a CD player out of their car.
   - (b) losing control of a car and running it into a neighbor's house.
   - (c) damage to the roof of a house from hurricane winds.
   - (d) accidentally falling through the ceiling of your house while in the attic.

8. Term life insurance does not
   (a) provide protection against death.
   (b) provide the least expensive form of life insurance protection.
   (c) have the premiums increase as the insured gets older.
   (d) have a savings component in the premium.

9. Whole life insurance does *not*
   (a) provide protection against death.
   (b) provide the least expensive form of life insurance protection.
   (c) have the premiums remain constant as the insured gets older.
   (d) have a savings component in the premium.

10. Which of the following is *not* true about annuity insurance contracts?
    (a) They face the adverse selection problem because people who are healthy are more likely to purchase an annuity.
    (b) The insured purchases the annuity by making payments during their working years.
    (c) The insured faces the risk of outliving the annuity payment.
    (d) Most annuities are purchased by pension plans for the plan participants at retirement.

11. The majority of an insurance company's assets are invested in
    (a) ownership of real estate.
    (b) mortgage.
    (c) corporate stocks and bonds.
    (d) government bonds.

12. Which of the following is a principal feature of ERISA?
    (a) All employees must be vested in the company pension plan by the end of seven years.
    (b) Employees must keep their pension plan with their old employer if they change jobs.
    (c) The pension plan is insured against bad investments by the Pension Benefit Guarantee Corporation (Penny Benny).
    (d) Individual employees must pay a premium to have their account insured by Penny Benny.

13. The life insurance policy with the greatest potential to accumulate savings is
    (a) term life.
    (b) whole life.
    (c) universal life.
    (d) disability.

14. An attempt to control rising medical costs is through
    (a) regulation of the pricing of medical services.
    (b) the creation of HMOs that negotiate prices with care providers.
    (c) charging higher premiums for health insurance coverage.
    (d) encouraging insured persons to use government medical facilities.

15. Which of the following is *not* true about the regulation of insurance companies?
    (a) They are regulated by the McCarran-Ferguson Act of 1945.
    (b) They are subject to the insurance regulations of each state in which they do business.
    (c) Most regulation of insurance companies is designed to protect the insured from losses due to insolvency of the insurance company.
    (d) Insurance agents are required to obtain a license for each type of insurance they sell.

16. What type of investment is designed for self-employed people?
    (a) Keogh Plan
    (b) IRA
    (c) Pension Plan
    (d) SIMPLE IRA

17. In what type of contract does an insurance company agree to pay a fix sum of payments to the beneficiary for a fee?
    (a) Whole Life
    (b) Universal Life
    (c) Annuity
    (d) Term Life

18. A main drawback to term life policies is that
    (a) coverage options are typically not as high.
    (b) as the insured grows older the cost increases.
    (c) there is no savings element or residual benefits.
    (d) Both (b) and (c)
    (e) All of the above

Part D: Short Answer Questions

1. In recent years, insurance companies have reduced their investment in mortgages and increased their participation in the corporate and government securities. What events triggered this shift?

    _____

    _____

2. How does the adverse selection problem add to the cost of insurance?

    _____

    _____

3. What is the benefit to the insurance company and to the insured of being part of a group plan instead of having individual coverage?

    _____

    _____

4. The government is considering several alternative privatization approaches to overcoming the looming Social Security crisis. Briefly discuss the biggest obstacle to privatization.

   _____

   _____

5. What are the benefits of investing in an IRA?

   _____

   _____

6. What is the main reason people buy life insurance?

   _____

   _____

7. Explain how insurance companies make profits when they are contractually required to pay benefits.

   _____

   _____

■ Answers to Chapter 22

Exercise 1

1. c	7. d	13. j
2. i	8. a	14. h
3. e	9. b	15. q
4. f	10. l	16. p
5. m	11. n	17. o
6. k	12. g	18. r

Exercise 2

	Type of Insurance			
Risk	Life	Property	Casualty	Health
To be sure you are able to pay for your children's college	X			
A neighbor slips on your porch steps			X	
You wreck your car		X		
You accidentally hit another car with your car			X	
You get food poisoning				X
You want a guaranteed annuity payment at retirement	X			
Your house catches on fire		X		
Your car catches on fire		X		
Your house is damaged in a hurricane		X		
You are injured from flying debris in a hurricane				X

Exercise 3

Financial Intermediary	Long-term Assets	Short-term Assets
Life Insurance Company	X	
Property and Casualty Insurance Companies		X
Private Pension Fund	X	
Individual Retirement Account	X	
Money Market Mutual Funds		X

Exercise 4

	LIC	PPP
Corp. Bonds	43.6%	10.8%
Mortgages	7.4%	0.0%
Stocks	23.4%	70.3%
Gov. Sec.	14.2%	8.2%

Self-Test

Part A

1. premium
2. beneficiary
3. asymmetric information
4. adverse selection
5. independent
6. Monoline
7. long, short
8. Disability
9. law of large numbers
10. Medicare, Medicaid
11. more
12. reinsurance
13. employee
14. Keogh
15. underfunding
16. universal life
17. Annuities
18. Named-peril policies

Part B

1. T
2. F
3. T
4. T
5. T
6. F
7. T
8. T
9. F
10. T
11. T
12. F
13. T
14. F
15. T
16. F
17. F
18. F

Part C

1. c
2. d
3. a
4. b
5. b
6. c
7. a
8. d
9. b
10. c
11. c
12. a
13. c
14. b
15. a
16. a
17. c
18. d

Part D

1. During the 1980s, the competition for funds between insurance companies and mutual funds intensified. In order to increase their returns, insurance companies took on higher risk investments, such as real estate and junk bonds. Both of these assets deteriorated in value, causing large losses to many insurers. These losses encouraged the shift to less-risky securities.

2. Adverse selection is a major concern to insurance companies because the consumer who is most interested in the risk transfer is more likely to incur this risk than is the general population. Insurers recognize that they are taking on more risk than the general population average and thus increase the cost of coverage.

3. Group coverage provides insurance to everyone in the group. The group is more likely to reflect the general population in risk. This similarly eliminates the adverse selection problem and allows the insurance company to charge a lower per person premium.

4. Funds placed in private accounts will be under the control of the individual and not accessible by the Social Security Administration. This makes funds needed to pay current retirees inaccessible and adds to the shortage of funds problem.

5. The benefits of investing in an IRA are they allow earnings to grow tax deferred and contributions may be tax deductible.

6. The main reason people buy life insurance policies is to protect the wealth of risk-averse people who prefer to pay an insurance premium than accept the risk that they may lose their wealth.

7. Insurance companies make profits when they are contractually required to pay benefits by accurately forecasting losses and pricing policies appropriately.

Chapter 22
Investment Banks, Security Brokers and Dealers, and Venture Capital Firms

■ **Chapter Learning Goals**

By the end of this chapter, you should

1. Understand investment banks and the underwriting process.
2. Know the roles of securities brokers and dealers in the markets and the services they provide.
3. Know how securities firms are regulated.
4. Understand the role of venture capitalists in the economy.

■ **Chapter Summary**

Securities dealers, brokers, investment banks, and venture capitalists all help to move funds from savers to borrowers. Venture capital firms raise investment capital for firms that are not ready to go public. Investment banks help to bring companies public in the primary market. Securities dealers assist investors to trade securities in the secondary market.

Investment Banks

Investment banks are participants in the primary market. They are involved with firms and governments that desire to raise capital by issuing new shares of stock or new issues of bonds. They are involved with the issuer early in the process and provide the client with advice on such items as the type of security to issue, filing of required documents, when to sell the security, and most important, the expected price for which the security will sell.

Investment banks also act as intermediaries in mergers and acquisitions by helping to buy and sell firms. Investment banks are paid fees for their services that range from 3% to 10% of the amount of the sale, depending on the size of the offering. In general, the larger the deal, the lower the percentage fee charged.

Background

The failure of about 10,000 banks during the Great Depression caused distrust in the banking system, leading to a number of regulatory reforms. These reforms were designed to stabilize the banking industry and improve savers perceptions of banks. One of the reforms was the separation of commercial banking from investment banking via the **Glass-Steagall Act**. The Glass-Steagall Act prohibited commercial banks from buying or selling securities for their customers. It was believed that investment banking was more risky than commercial banking. The gradual elimination and ultimate repeal of Glass-Steagall has led to mergers of commercial and investment banks.

Underwriting Stocks and Bonds

Investment banks are hired by firms to assist in the issuance and sale of securities on behalf of the firm. Essentially, the underwriter will purchase the securities from the company and sell the securities to investors. Important services that investment banks provide are (1) giving advice to the customer such as when and at what price to issue the securities, (2) filing documents with the Securities and Exchange Commission, and (3) underwriting options.

Setting an appropriate price for an **initial public offering (IPO)** is difficult to determine and is an important contribution by the investment bank in the underwriting process. However, if a company already has securities outstanding, then it is easy to determine the price for the **seasoned issue** offering.

Investment bankers also help their clients to file information with the Securities and Exchange Commission before the offering can proceed. The SEC was created by the Securities Exchange Acts of 1933 and 1934 to increase and monitor information provided to investors. Companies going public must file a **registration statement** with the SEC that details the firm's financial condition, the industry in which the company competes, the management of the firm, competitors, and the intended uses of the proceeds from the offering. Once the statement is filed, the company enters a 20-day period during which the SEC reviews the filings to ensure their completeness. A **prospectus**, part of the registration statement, must be provided to potential investors. For debt issues, the investment banker will also obtain a credit rating for the bonds, hire bond counsel to confirm legality, pick a trustee to ensure the company meets its stated obligations, and have the securities printed.

Once the required paperwork is accepted, the issuer will set a time, date, and price to sell the securities to the investment bank. The investment bank will increase or mark-up the price of the securities to earn its fees. If the investment bank wants to reduce its exposure of risk to the offering, it may form a **syndicate** with other investment banks that agree to purchase part of the offering. Each member of the syndicate is responsible for selling the shares it purchased. Often, investment banks publicize upcoming offers by placing **tombstones** ads in the *Wall Street Journal.*

Prior to that issuance, investment banks or brokerage houses gauge the demand for the upcoming offering by asking clients the number of shares they intend to purchase. If customers request all of the shares of the issuance then the offering is called **fully subscribed**. When demand is less than the size of the offering, the issue is **undersubscribed**. When the number of shares requested is greater than the number of shares to be sold the issue is **oversubscribed**.

Investment banks can substantially reduce the risk associated with an offering by agreeing to offer the securities on a **best efforts** basis. In a best efforts agreement, the investment bank does not purchase the securities from the issuer, but rather agrees to sell the securities on behalf of the issuer for a commission. Customers state the price they are willing to pay for the securities for best efforts offerings.

Some companies choose to offer their securities via a **private placement**. A private placement is an offering to a small number of investors which meet certain financial criterion. Because these are not public offerings, the securities do not have to be registered with the SEC.

Equity Sales

Investment banks also assist firms with the sale of specific divisions or the entire firm in some cases. The investment bank will assess the value of the business to be sold in an equity sale. Once the value is determined, a **confidential memorandum** is provided to prospective buyers detailing the financial status of the company. Interested prospective buyers will submit a **letter of intent** that outlines the preliminary terms of the offer to buy. When the letter of intent is accepted by the seller, the prospective buyer has 20 to 40 days to evaluate the accuracy of the information provided in the confidential memorandum. This is called the due diligence period. Ultimately, a **definitive agreement** will be drawn up detailing the negotiated and final terms of the sale.

Mergers and Acquisitions

Investment banks compete in the mergers and acquisitions market, too. When two companies join to form one company, a merger has occurred. Most mergers are friendly, but sometimes they become hostile because a company does not wish to merge with a particular company. Investment banks help both acquiring firms and target firms to identify suitable merger partners. They also solicit shareholders to sell their shares through the tender offer process.

Securities Brokers and Dealers

Brokers serve the purpose of bringing together investors who desire to buy or sell securities in the secondary market. Investors call brokers and give them instructions on the type of order they want carried out. Dealers buy and sell securities by quoting bid prices and ask prices. The bid price is the price at which the dealer is willing to buy, and the ask price is the price at which he is willing to sell. The difference between the two prices is called the spread. A **Market order** means they want the security bought or sold immediately at the best price available. A **limit order** instruction specifies the lowest price the investor will sell for or the highest price they are willing to pay. If the broker cannot immediately complete the limit order it is kept on record and will be completed if and when the security price reaches the limit price specified by the investor. Another common instruction is a **short sell**, which instructs the broker to borrow shares for the investor and sell them. The investor will buy the shares back later and replace the borrowed shares. A short sell is transacted when the investor believes the stock price will decline. By buying back the shorted security at a lower price than it was initially sold for will result in a profit.

Another order type is the **stop-loss order**. As the name implies, a stop-loss order is designed to reduce losses or protect profits. The investor chooses a price for the stop-loss order that is below the current stock price. If the price of the stock drops to that price, then the broker enters an order to sell the stock immediately.

Brokers also provide other services for the investor. **Margin credit** is a popular service. This credit is when the brokerage firm lends money to the investor to purchase the security. The investor can only borrow a maximum of 50% of the value of the securities. The Federal Reserve Board sets the margin percent. Another service created by Merrill Lynch is the **cash management account (CMA)**. This account has many services associated with it, such as check writing and credit cards that competed directly with services offered by commercial banks. The CMA was the catalyst in the gradual breakdown of the barriers between commercial and investment banking.

Brokerage firms are usually identified as being either **full service** or **discount.** The distinction between the two is that full-service firms provide their clients with a number of services, such as personalized investment advice, frequent reporting of performance, and research information. Discount brokers generally only take buy and sell orders and do not provide the other services. Both types will complete any transaction in a similar manner. For the investor the big difference comes in the commissions charged. Due to the multiple services provided, the highest commissions are from full-service brokers. Discount broker commissions are as much as 50% less, but then you have to make all the decisions without input from a broker.

A securities **dealer** also carries out trades for investors. The difference is that dealers will buy and sell the security themselves. They maintain inventories of securities they trade, so they will always have some to sell and will add to the inventory whenever someone wants to sell. Dealers are extremely important for maintaining liquidity of smaller firms' securities that do not trade on an exchange. Dealers are also called **market makers** because of the requirement that they buy and sell as desired by investors.

Regulation of Securities Firms

The importance of well functioning financial markets has led to security firms and markets being among the most highly regulated. The main legislation governing them is the Securities Act of 1933 and the Securities and Exchange Act of 1934. The main provisions of these acts are to require public firms to file documents with the Securities and Exchange Commission (SEC). In addition to regulating investment banking operations, the SEC also prohibits brokers and dealers from both trading on insider information, which is nonpublic information only known by a company's management, and misrepresenting securities. In general, the primary goals of securities laws were to restrict competition between securities firms to reduce the likelihood of failure and to protect the integrity of securities markets. Important provisions of the 1933 and 1934 acts are (1) to establish the SEC to administer securities laws, (2) to require the registration of new securities offerings disclosing all relevant information, (3) to require publicly held companies to file semiannual and annual reports to the SEC in addition to significant corporate events, (4) to require insiders to report purchases and sales of company stock, and (5) to prevent market manipulation. Before most securities can be issued the firm must file a **registrations statement**. Other significant legislation includes the Glass-Steagall Act of 1933, which separated commercial and investment banking; the Investment advisers Act of 1940, which required investment advisers to register with the SEC; and the Securities Protection Corporation Act of 1970, which insures investors against losses in their accounts from the financial distress of their brokerage firm. More recently, the Gramm-Leach-Bliley Act repealed the Glass-Steagall Act.

Private Equity Investment

Venture Capital Firms

Venture capital firms (VCs) provide capital to young or start-up firms that are not ready to go public. The money invested by a venture capital firms is normally raised by a limited partnership and invested by the general partner. Venture capital firms only invest into companies that they expect to produce high returns in the future.

Venture capital firms reduce information asymmetry between the investors in the venture capital fund and the firms that are funded by the venture capitalists. Venture capitalists take an equity position in funded firms with the expectation that it will stay invested into each firm for several to 10 years. Venture capitalists typically take seats on the board of directors of the funded firm and actively provide business advice and contacts. To help oversight of funded firms, VCs invest in funded companies in stages as the firms progresses.

Although venture capital grew from its initiation in 1946, it was not until 1979 when the U.S. Department of Labor stated that although the **prudent man rule** restricted pension funds from making risky investments, some pension funds could be invested into high-risk assets. Consequently, pension fund investment into venture projects jumped dramatically.

The life cycle of venture capital investments has three main phases: (1) a limited partnership is created and money is raised, (2) the capital is invested into start-up companies, and (3) the VC exits the investment. Not all of the capital is invested at once. The VC will contact its limited partners for capital as needed. These investments are referred to as **takedowns** or **paid-in-capital**.

The firms funded by VCs are also classified by life cycles. **Seed investing** occurs before a company has a product. **Early-stage** investing occurs when a firm has developed a product. **Late stage** investing occurs when funds are provided to help the company grow to a point at which it could go public.

VCs can exit an investment through two ways; taking the company public after 7 to 10 years or through merging the funded company with some interested buyer.

Over the long term, venture capital firms have been extremely profitable with a 20-year average return of 16.5%. Seed investing is the extremely profitable earning an average annual return of 20.5%. The average annual returns are time dependent with returns in the 1990s being extraordinarily high.

Private Equity Buyouts

A **private equity buyout** is the reverse of an IPO that is, a public company goes private. Private companies are not subject to costly reporting requirements under legislation like Sarbanes-Oxley. CEOs of private firms may feel less short-term pressure and often take large ownership stakes. Often, after the private buyout, the firm is then sold to another firm or taken public through an IPO.

■ Exercises

Exercise 1: Terminology

Match the following terms from the left column with the closely related term from the right. Place the letter of the term from the right column in the blank provided next to the appropriate term on the left.

_____ 1. When demand for an offering is less than the size of the offering

_____ 2. Funds borrowed from a broker

_____ 3. Group of underwriters that sell a primary market issue of securities

_____ 4. Order to trade the security at the current price

_____ 5. Order to trade the security at this price or better

_____ 6. Provided to each potential investor in the primary market

_____ 7. Selling securities borrowed from the broker

_____ 8. Restricted pension funds from making risky investments

_____ 9. Filed with the SEC before issuing primary

_____ 10. An order to sell a security if it drops to or below a specific price

_____ 11. When more investors want to purchase the issue than there are shares available

_____ 12. When the shares available and the shares demanded are equal

_____ 13. Selling new shares of a stock for a firm that already has stock outstanding

_____ 14. A securities dealer

_____ 15. Limited partner capital contributions to a venture capitalist as needed

_____ 16. Venture capital investments that help a company grow to a point at which it could go public

_____ 17. Venture capital investments occur before a company has developed a product.

_____ 18. A security offering in which an investment bank does not purchase the securities from the issuer

a. late-stage investing
b. fully subscribed
c. limit order
d. best efforts
e. margin credit
f. market maker
g. market order
h. under subscribed
i. seed investing market securities.
j. oversubscribed
k. prospectus
l. registration statement
m. seasoned issues
n. short sell
o. syndicate
p. prudent man rule
q. takedowns
r. stop-loss order

■ Self-Test

Part A: Fill in the Blanks

1. Investment banks assist in the sale of securities in the _____ market; brokers and dealers assist in the trading of securities in the _____ market.

2. Commercial banking and investment banking were separated in the Banking Act of 1933, more commonly known as the _____ Act.

3. When a firm sells securities in the primary market for the first time the security sale is called a(n) _____.

4. Investment banks place _____ advertisements in the *Wall Street Journal* to publicize an upcoming security offering.

5. When a merger attempt is resisted by the management of the firm that is being bought it is called a(n) _____ takeover.

6. The price that dealers pay to buy securities for their inventory is the _____ price, while the price they charge investors to sell from their inventory is the _____ price.

7. Merrill Lynch was the first brokerage firm to offer the _____, which provided investors with a package of services that competed directly with products traditionally offered by commercial banks.

8. The abolishment of fixed commissions after May 1, 1975, led to the creation of _____ brokers and increased competition in the securities brokerage industry.

9. A company that wants to go public must file a(n) _____ with the SEC that details the firm's financial condition.

10. An offering of new securities for a company which already has securities outstanding is known as a _____ offering.

11. Companies going public must issue a(n) _____ with the SEC.

12. When a company issues new securities, it must provide a(n) _____ to potential investors.

13. A(n) _____ is an offering of securities which does not have to be registered with the SEC and is sold to a small number of investors.

14. After an investment bank has determined the value of a business to be sold in an equity sale, it will provide a(n) _____ to potential investors detailing the financial status of the business.

15. The _____ rule restricted pension funds from making risky investments.

16. Calls for capital by a venture capital from its limited partners are known as _____.

17. When investors request to purchase all of the shares of a securities offering, the offering is said to be _____.

18. When demand for an offering is less than the size of the offering then it is _____.

19. An interested prospective buyer to the sale of a division of a company will submit a(n) _____ outlining the preliminary terms of the offer to buy.

20. In a(n) _____ , a public company goes private.

Part B: True-False Questions

Circle whether the following statements are true (T) or false (F).

T F   1. If an investor wants to buy some shares of outstanding common stock of General Motors Corporation, they can do so by placing an order with an investment bank.

T F   2. The amount of money an underwriter pays to the issuer of securities will depend upon the amount of money the investment bank receives for the shares.

T F   3. Probably the most difficult advice the investment bank gives the issuer of securities is the type of security they should issue.

T F   4. Once a registration statement is filed with the SEC, the issuer can sell the security after 20 days if the SEC has not objected to the content of the statement.

T F   5. Tombstone advertisements are offers by the investment bank to sell the security listed.

T F   6. The investment bank is not necessarily pleased when an issue is oversubscribed because it risks displeasing their clients.

T F   7. In a best-efforts offering, the price the issuer actually receives is not guaranteed by the investment bank.

T F   8. A stop-loss order is designed to reduce losses or protect profits.

T F   9. Brokerage houses generally do not charge interest on margin loans because they receive commissions for the trade.

T F   10. Persons considered "insiders" must file reports with the SEC whenever they buy or sell stock in their firm.

T F   11. The Security Investors Protection Corporation insures investor accounts against losses if the broker gives bad advice to the client.

T F   12. Private placements must the registered with the SEC.

T F   13. An undersubscribed offering is one in which the number of shares requested is greater than the size of the offering.

T F   14. Full-service brokers charge higher commissions than discount brokers because of the advice and assistance they provide to clients that discount brokers do not provide.

T F   15. The SEC prohibits brokers and dealers from trading on inside information.

T F   16. Publicly held companies must only file annual reports to the SEC.

T F   17. A hostile merger is one in which one of the companies does not wish to merge.

T F   18. When an investor places a limit order, she wishes to buy or sell immediately at the best possible price.

T F   19. Seed capital is provided by a venture capitalist to a company when it is making final preparations to go public.

Part C: Multiple-Choice Questions

Circle the appropriate answer.

1. One reason companies hire investment banks to help with the issuance of securities is
   (a) the SEC requires investment banks to be part of the issuance process.
   (b) only investment banks are permitted to deal in the primary market.
   (c) investment banks have expertise in this area that companies do not have.
   (d) All of the above are reasons investment banks are used.

2. An investment bank will help with all of the following except
   (a) audit the financial statements for inclusion in the registration statement.
   (b) secure a credit rating on bond issues.
   (c) filing the registration statement with the SEC.
   (d) have the securities printed for distribution.
   (e) The investment banks help with all of the above items.

3. The registration statement filed with the SEC contains
   (a) the firm's financial information.
   (b) information about the managers of the firm.
   (c) what the funds being raised will be used for.
   (d) management's assessment of the risk of the securities.
   (e) all of the above.

4. The actual offer to sell securities in the primary market is made through the
   (a) registration statement.
   (b) prospectus.
   (c) tombstone advertisement.
   (d) syndicate's brokers.
   (e) Any of the above can be used to offer to sell the securities.

5. For the investment bank and the issuer, the best supply/demand condition is a(n)
   (a) oversubscribed issue.
   (b) fully subscribed issue.
   (c) undersubscribed issue.
   (d) best-effort issue.

6. Which act repealed the Glass-Steagall Act?
   (a) The Securities Act of 1933
   (b) The Securities and Exchange Act of 1934
   (c) The Investment advisers Act of 1940
   (d) The Gramm-Leach-Bliley Act

7. When an investment bank purchases a new issue of securities in the hopes of making a profit, it is said to _____ the issue.
    (a) pawn
    (b) backstock
    (c) underwrite
    (d) syndicate

8. The agency that helps ensure that potential security purchasers are well informed is the
    (a) FCC.
    (b) FTC.
    (c) NRC.
    (d) SEC.

9. Brokers are distinguished from the dealers in that brokers do not
    (a) hold inventories of securities.
    (b) make profits.
    (c) incur losses.
    (d) deal directly with the public.

10. The legislation separating investment and commercial banking is known as the
    (a) Humphrey-Hawkins Act of 1978.
    (b) Monetary Control Act of 1980.
    (c) Federal Reserve Act of 1913.
    (d) Glass-Steagall Act of 1933.

11. A buy order that allows investors to specify the maximum price they are willing to pay is
    (a) a market order.
    (b) a priced order.
    (c) a short sell limit order.
    (d) a limit order.
    (e) both (c) and (d).

12. Important services that investment banks provide are
    (a) giving advice to customers.
    (b) filing documents with the SEC.
    (c) underwriting services.
    (d) all of the above.

13. When demand for an offering equals the supply of an offering, then the offering is
    (a) undersubscribed.
    (b) fully subscribed.
    (c) limit subscribed.
    (d) oversubscribed.

14. Which of the following details the negotiated and final terms of an equity sale of a division of a corporation?

   (a)   A prospectus

   (b)   A confidential memorandum

   (c)   A letter of intent

   (d)   A definitive agreement

15. What ways can a venture capital firm exit an investment?

   (a)   Sell the company in the secondary market

   (b)   Merge or sell the company

   (c)   Take the company public

   (d)   Both (b) and (c)

16. A firm that plans to raise new money through a primary market offering may look to an investment banker for all of the following except

   (a)   setting up a network of brokers, called a syndicate, to help market the security.

   (b)   helping the firm set the price that investors are willing to pay for the security.

   (c)   adding credibility to the issuance process because of the expertise provided.

   (d)   helping decide the amount of money the firm needs to raise.

17. Which of the following statements is correct about private placements?

   (a)   Under certain conditions, the SEC will waive the registration requirements.

   (b)   Most private placements are completed by selling securities to other financial intermediaries directly.

   (c)   To be considered a private placement by the SEC, the investor must agree to hold the security for a minimum of 10 years.

   (d)   Institutional investors have decreased their participation in private placements due to the recent decline in the liquidity of these types of issues.

Part D: Short Answer Questions

1. The Glass-Steagall Act was passed during the Great Depression. What factors motivated the passage of this act separating commercial and investment banking?

_____

_____

2. What is a private placement and what is the main advantage of the private placement?

_____

_____

3. Provide four important provisions of the Securities Act of 1933 and the Securities Exchange Act of 1934.

_____

_____

_____

_____

4. Detail the life cycle of firms funded by venture capitalists.

_____

_____

_____

_____

5. Describe how the underwriting process works in regard to the flow of funds from investors to the issuer of the security.

_____

_____

_____

6. What are the different types of orders that investors can use to buy or sale securities in the secondary market?

_____

_____

_____

■ Answers to Chapter 22

Exercise 1

1. h	6. k	11. j	16. a
2. e	7. n	12. b	17. i
3. o	8. p	13. m	18. d
4. g	9. l	14. f	
5. c	10. r	15. q	

Self-Test

Part A

1. primary, secondary	8. discount	15. prudent man
2. Glass-Steagall	9. registration statement	16. takedowns or paid-in-capital
3. initial public offering	10. seasoned issue	17. fully subscribed
4. tombstone	11. registration statement	18. undersubscribed
5. hostile	12. prospectus	19. letter of intent
6. bid, ask	13. private placement	20. private equity buyout
7. cash management account	14. confidential memorandum	

Part B

1. T	6. T	11. F	16. F
2. F	7. T	12. F	17. T
3. F	8. T	13. F	18. F
4. T	9. F	14. T	19. F
5. F	10. T	15. T	

Part C

1. c	7. c	13. b
2. a	8. d	14. d
3. e	9. a	15. d
4. b	10. d	16. d
5. b	11. d	17. b
6. d	12. d	

Part D

1. About 10,000 banks failed during the Depression. Congress attributed the failure to investment banking activities that were permitted prior to this act. They felt that the securities industry was too risky for banks to engage in. There were concerns about conflicts of interest between securities marketers and other banking departments and that excessive margin lending could result in huge defaults.

2. A private placement is when securities are sold to a limited number of investors rather than to the public at large. A major advantage is that the security does not need to be registered with the SEC. Avoiding registration saves significant amounts of money and avoids disclosure of information to competitors.

3. Four important provisions of the Securities Act of 1933 and the Securities Exchange Act of 1934 are
   1. to establish the SEC to administer securities laws,
   2. to require the registration of new securities offerings,
   3. to require company insiders to report purchases and sales of company stock, and
   4. to prevent market manipulation.

4. The life cycle of firms funded by venture capitalists is as follows:
   (a) Seed investments are investments into start-up companies before they have products.
   (b) Early stage investments are made after companies have developed products but are not ready to go public.
   (c) Late stage investments are made to prepare companies to go public or be sold.
   (d) Venture capitalist exit investments by either taking companies public or selling them to interested buyers.

5. In an underwriting arrangement the investment bank purchases the issue from issuer for an agreed upon amount. The investment bank now owns the entire issue. They sell the issue to outside investors at the offering price. The offering price should be higher than the price given the issuer. The difference in these prices will be the underwriter's compensation. If the offer price is less than the amount paid, the issuer the investment bank will experience a loss.

6. Investors can use the following types of orders:
   (a) market orders to buy or sell securities immediately.
   (b) limit orders to buy below the current ask price or sell above the current bid price.
   (c) stop-loss orders to sell if the stock price drops to some price below the current bid price or buy if the stock rises above some price above the current ask price.

Chapter 23
Risk Management in Financial Institutions

■ Chapter Learning Goals

By the end of this chapter, you should

1. Recognize the adverse selection and moral hazard risks faced by financial institutions due to asymmetric information.
2. Understand the actions that can be taken to reduce the asymmetric information problems.
3. Know how GAP analysis and duration GAP analysis help manage interest-rate risk.

■ Chapter Summary

In this chapter, we deal with two types of risk that are of significant concern to bank managers. Both interest-rate risk and credit risk must be faced and managed to avoid facing a financial crisis. How bank managers control the amount of interest rate and credit risk in their portfolio is dealt with in this chapter.

There are two types of risk that financial institutions face that, if not managed correctly, could prove to be fatal for the business. Because interest is the main revenue source for financial institutions, the managers must control the amount of interest-rate risk the firm faces. The potential for default on loans creates another area of serious concern. Managers deal with credit risk to mitigate the damage that could result from excessive loan defaults.

Managing Credit Risk

Credit risk is associated with the problems of adverse selection and moral hazard. The highest credit risk borrowers are the ones that are going to push the hardest to get their loans. Once the loan is received, the borrower is often able to spend the money for activities that were not disclosed to the bank. Managing credit risk involves functions that reduce these two problems down to an acceptable level for making the loan. That is, the managers attempt to reduce the amount of asymmetric information between the borrower and lender.

Managers will incur both **screening** and **monitoring** costs to reduce the amount of credit risk. In the screening process, they will gather information about the loan applicant to determine whether the bank should extend credit. The loan officer may visit the business to gain firsthand knowledge of the firm's operations. Banks often specialize in certain types of loans. By gaining expertise in a particular type of business, the institution can more effectively screen loan applicants. Management must weigh the benefits of specialization against the benefits of a diversified loan portfolio. Once the loan is made, the managers will continue to monitor the actions of the borrower to observe any indications of moral hazard behavior.

There are several arrangements the bank can have for monitoring the customer's behavior. One is the fact that **restrictive covenants** will be written into the loan contract. Information is gathered on a regular basis from the company to verify that these restrictions have not been violated. If the financial institution establishes a **long-term relationship** with the customer, they will have current transactions and a long history of information that can be used to observe the financial behavior of the firm's managers. Borrowers also prefer a good long-term relationship so they can more easily access funds in the future. The bank can agree to a **loan commitment** where they promise to extend credit to the customer whenever they need it. This arrangement gives the customer easy access to funds, but it also reduces moral hazard because such behavior could cost them the availability of this commitment. The bank may also take some assets as collateral for a **secured loan** to provide protection against loss in the event of financial problems by the borrower. Frequently a bank will require **compensating balances**. These balances are usually a percentage of the loan amount and must be placed in the borrower's checking account. These balances partially serve as **collateral** but also give the bank another piece of information to monitor the behavior of the borrower. A final approach is **credit rationing**. In such a situation the bank either refuses to make any loan to the customer or will lend the customer only part of the proceeds requested.

The refusal to make a loan is based on the adverse selection problem. Banks charge higher interest rates on loans that carry a higher degree of risk. The problem arises in that the customers willing to pay the highest interest rates are also the most likely to take greater risk than expected in order to earn the high return required to satisfy the cost of the loan. Making only partial loans reduces the moral hazard problem. A borrower is more likely to make some very risky decisions if they have a large amount of funds to work with than if they have a smaller amount.

Managing Interest-Rate Risk

When interest rates became more volatile, bankers became more concerned about their exposure to **interest-rate risk**, the riskiness of earnings that is associated with changes in interest rates. If a bank has more rate-sensitive liabilities, such as money market deposit accounts and variable rate CDs, than assets, such as adjustable-rate mortgages and commercial loans due within one year, a rise in interest rates will reduce the net interest margins and bank income. A decline in interest rates will raise bank income. There are two primary methods for managers to measure the sensitivity of bank income to changes in interest rates: (1) GAP analysis and (2) duration GAP analysis.

The income **GAP** is computed as the difference between the dollar amount of rate sensitive assets and rate sensitive liabilities. To compute the GAP, the banker will determine which assets and which liabilities will be subject to interest rate changes if market rates change in the next year. Multiplying the GAP by the change in interest rates immediately reveals the effect on bank income. A more complete picture of the bank's interest-rate risk can be computed if managers perform the same exercise for assets and liabilities that will be subject to interest rate changes over the next two years, three years, and so forth. The last refinement is called the **maturity bucket approach**.

An alternative method for measuring interest-rate risk is **duration GAP analysis**. The duration GAP method helps managers compute the change in the value of the bank's assets and liabilities that will result from interest rate changes. This is done by first determining the average duration of both bank assets and liabilities. The duration GAP formula is then used to calculate this value. This information will help managers make informed decisions about the amount of risk the bank should take based on the expected movement of interest rates in the future. The greater the duration GAP, the greater the interest-rate risk faced by the bank or other financial institution. New financial instruments, such as financial futures, options, and interest-rate swaps, have been developed, which help banks more easily manage their interest-rate risk without requiring them to rearrange their balance sheets.

Formally, the duration gap can be computed as:

$$DUR_{gap} = DUR_a - \left(\frac{L}{A} \times DUR_l \right)$$

where DUR_a is the average duration of assets, DUR_l is the average duration of liabilities, L is the market value of liabilities, and A is the market value of assets. For example, a bank that has $200 million in assets with an average duration 2.35 years and $175 million in liabilities with an average duration of 0.95 years has a duration gap of

$$DUR_{gap} = 2.35 - \left(\frac{175}{200} \times 0.95 \right) = 1.52 \text{ years.}$$

Managers can also estimate the affect of changes in interest rates on firm net worth. The change in the market value of net worth as a percentage of assets is:

$$\frac{\Delta NW}{A} = -DUR_{gap} \times \frac{\Delta i}{1+i}$$

where DUR_{gap} is the duration gap Δi is the change in interest rates and i is the original interest rate. So, the change in the market value of net worth as a percentage of assets from a rise in interest rates from 5% to 6% for the company with a duration gap of 1.52 is

$$\frac{\Delta NW}{A} = -1.52 \times \frac{0.01}{1 + 0.05} = -0.0145 \text{ or } -1.45\%.$$

Although income and duration gap analysis can be useful, advanced techniques like scenario analysis and value at risk are being increasing used by financial institutions.

Example of a Nonbank Institutions

Although all of the previous discussion centered on interest rate risk management for commercial banks, nonbank institutions, such as finance companies and savings and loans, face similar risks. An important distinction is that some financial institutions may face duration gaps that are opposite in sign to those of banks. This reverse gap can occur when the institution has a longer duration for liabilities than for its rate sensitive assets.

■ Exercises

Exercise 1: Definitions and Terminology

Match the terms on the right with the definition or description on the left. Place the letter of the term in the blank provided next to the appropriate definition.

_____ 1. Methods employed to measure interest-rate risk

_____ 2. The riskiness of earnings that is associated with changes in interest rates

_____ 3. A short-term source of funds for business that is arranged and approved before it is needed

_____ 4. GAP analysis extended to include different maturity intervals

_____ 5. An interest rate sensitivity analysis technique that tells the change in value that will result from a change in interest rates

_____ 6. A loan backed by collateral to reduce risk

_____ 7. Involves turning down a loan or reducing the actual amount lent below the requested amount

_____ 8. An account at a bank that is required as a condition for a loan

_____ 9. The average length of time over which the cash flow will occur for the asset or liability

_____ 10. A bank's agreement to provide a loan up to a given amount

_____ 11. The problem that bad credit risk borrowers are more likely to apply for loans

_____ 12. The risk that once borrowers obtain loans, they are more likely to invest in high-risk projects increasing the likely of default

_____ 13. The collection of information from prospective buyers to differentiate bad credit risks from good ones

a. loan commitment

b. secured loan

c. compensating balances

d. credit rationing

e. income GAP analysis

f. duration GAP analysis

g. line of credit

h. interest-rate risk

i. duration

j. maturity bucket approach

k. hazard of default

l. screening

m. adverse selection

Exercise 2: Interest-Rate Risk

Why is interest-rate risk of significant concern to banks?

_____

_____

Exercise 3: GAP Analysis

Suppose that the First State Bank has the following balance sheet.

Assets		Liabilities	
Variable-rate loans	$20 million	Variable-rate CDs	$30 million
Short-term securities	10 million	Money market deposit accounts	15 million
Reserves	10 million	Federal funds	5 million
Long-term loans	40 million	Checkable and savings deposits	30 million
Long-term securities	10 million	Long-term CDs	20 million

A. Calculate the GAP by subtracting the amount of rate-sensitive liabilities from rate-sensitive assets.

GAP = _____

B. If interest rates suddenly increase by two percentage points, will First State Bank's profits increase or decrease? _____

C. By how much do profits change?_____

D. If, instead, interest rates drop by three percentage points, what will be the change in First State's profit? _____

■ Self-Test

Part A: Fill in the Blanks

1. Banks face _____ due to the existence of adverse selection and moral hazard.

2. Adverse selection is reduced by the _____ of clients to identify good credit risks.

3. Specialization in certain types of loans by lenders is beneficial due to increased expertise, but there is a cost in terms of reduced _____.

4. An attempt is made to reduce the moral hazard problem by _____ the activities of the borrower.

5. Customers having long-term relationships with banks may benefit from _____ interest rates on their loans and will _____ the cost of monitoring for the bank.

6. Banks often obtain collateral to back up their loans by issuing _____ loans and also the use of _____ balances.

7. The refusal to make a loan to a client is called _____. This process can also result in a loan being made but not for the full amount requested.

8. If a restriction is not in a loan's restrictive covenants, a client with a long-term relationship with the lender is _____ likely to avoid risky activities thus reducing moral hazard.

9. With the increased volatility of interest rates in the early 1980s, banks have become more concerned about their exposure to _____.

10. If banks have _____ rate-sensitive liabilities than assets, a rise in interest rates will reduce bank profits, while a decline in interest rates will raise bank profit.

11. Under _____ analysis, the difference of rate-sensitive assets and rate-sensitive liabilities is multiplied by the change in the interest rate to obtain the effect on bank profits.

12. If the average duration of a bank's assets exceeds the average duration of its liabilities, then rising interest rates will _____ the bank's net worth.

13. Once a bank has calculated the _____ of its profits to fluctuations in interest rates, it can then consider alternative strategies for reducing its interest-rate risk.

14. The duration of a bank's total assets is the _____ of the duration of the individual assets.

15. _____ examines the sensitivity of net worth to changes in rates.

16. If a bank wants to reduce its exposure to interest-rate risk, then it should approve _____ variable-rate loans.

17. In general, the value of _____-rate loans are more sensitive to changes in interest rates.

18. Banks can manage credit risks by establishing _____ customer relationships.

Part B: True-False Questions

Circle whether the following statements are true (T) or false (F).

T F 1. If a bank has more rate-sensitive assets than liabilities, a rise in interest rates will reduce bank profits.

T F 2. Banks resist long-term relationships with customers because they obligate the bank to make loans.

T F 3. It is legal for a bank to review a customer's transaction history by looking at checks written on a compensating balance account.

T F 4. Asymmetric information leads to an adverse selection problem for banks.

T F 5. Monitoring activities reduces the amount of moral hazard.

T F 6. The cost of monitoring long-term customers is higher than with new customers due to the large volume of information available that can be reviewed.

T F 7. Restrictive covenants are good at covering every moral hazard problem that is likely to occur.

T F 8. One way that banks establish closer ties with corporate clients is to own some of the shares of the firm's common stock.

T F 9. Foreign banks are not allowed to own the stock of the client corporations.

T F 10. Banks will make loans to customers who are willing to pay very high interest rates because higher rates will increase the bank's income.

T F 11. Macaulay's duration is a measure of the average lifetime of a security's stream of payments.

T F 12. The higher the Macaulay's duration value, the greater the interest-rate risk.

T F 13. Calculation of the duration gap requires knowledge of the average duration of both the bank's assets and liabilities.

T F 14. Gap and duration gap analysis may give different conclusions about a bank's interest-rate risk.

T F 15. The maturity bucket approach to gap analysis is an improvement over basic gap analysis due to looking at interest-rate risk for longer than one year.

T F 16. Reducing the amount of screening will decrease the hazard of default.

T F 17. Variable-rate loans are more sensitive to changes in interest rates.

T F 18. If customers decide to leave deposits in the bank longer, then the duration of the bank's liabilities will increase.

Part C: Multiple-Choice Questions

Circle the appropriate answer.

1. When interest rates are expected to fall, a banker is likely to
    (a) make short-term rather than long-term loans.
    (b) buy short-term rather than long-term bonds.
    (c) buy long-term rather than short-term bonds.
    (d) do both (a) and (b) of the above.

2. If Bruce the bank manager determines that his bank's GAP is a positive $20 million, then a five-percentage point increase in interest rates will cause bank profits to
    (a) increase by $1 million.
    (b) decrease by $1 million.
    (c) increase by $10 million.
    (d) decrease by $10 million.

3. If a bank has more interest sensitive assets than liabilities, a rise in interest rates will
    (a) increase income.
    (b) reduce income.
    (c) leave income unchanged.
    (d) None of the above

4. Duration GAP analysis is useful for
    (a) measuring the change in the bank's net worth due to interest rate changes.
    (b) determining the change in net income due to interest rate changes.
    (c) determining the interest rate sensitivity of the bank.
    (d) Both (a) and (c) are true.

5. Identify the bank asset or liability that is not interest rate sensitive.
    (a) Marketable securities
    (b) Adjustable rate mortgages
    (c) Checking accounts
    (d) Federal funds

6. In monitoring the bank's loan customers, the bank is allowed to
    (a) review the activity of checking accounts the borrower has at the bank.
    (b) maintain the money at the bank and only allow checks to be written on items the bank approves.
    (c) require the borrower to maintain a percentage of the loan proceeds on deposit at the bank.
    (d) all of the above.

7. If interest rates are expected to rise within the next year, a bank manager would _____ in order to mitigate the impact on net income.
    (a) increase the number of adjustable rate mortgage loans
    (b) reduce borrowing federal funds from other banks
    (c) try to issue fewer long-term CDs and more short-term CDs
    (d) prefer to not take any of the above actions

8. If a rate sensitive asset has a Macaulay's duration of 2.6 and interest rates are expected to increase from 8% to 10%,t the expected change in the value of the asset is
    (a) a decrease of 5.2%.
    (b) a decrease of 4.8%.
    (c) an increase of 5.2%.
    (d) an increase of 4.4%.

9. In calculating the duration GAP, the bank manager would first need to know the duration of all of the following except the bank's
    (a) average asset duration.
    (b) average liability duration.
    (c) average equity duration.
    (d) The manager would need to know the duration of all three of the above.

10. GAP analysis as presented in the text requires several assumptions that weaken the accuracy of the results. These weaknesses include all except which of the following?
    (a) The cash account is rate-sensitive.
    (b) The yield curve is flat.
    (c) Loan prepayments must be accurately estimated.
    (d) Interest rates for all maturity assets and liabilities change by the same amount.

11. Which of the following is true about GAP analysis?
    (a) All financial institutions have the same degree of interest-rate risk.
    (b) Banks with a positive income GAP will have income decline when interest rates rise.
    (c) If finance companies raise most of their funds through the issuance of commercial paper and make long-term loans, their income GAP will probably be positive.
    (d) All of the above are true statements.

12. Increasing the amount of rate-sensitive liabilities, all else remaining the same, will
    (a) make a positive GAP smaller and result in increased interest-rate risk.
    (b) make a negative GAP larger and result in decreased interest-rate risk.
    (c) decrease the decline in profits that would occur if interest rates fall.
    (d) decrease the decline in profits that would occur if interest rates rise.

13. The maturity bucket approach to GAP analysis
    (a) is used primarily by credit unions because credit unions have more fixed-rate loans.
    (b) excludes short-term accounts that will be renewed before the end of the year.
    (c) does not include one-year maturity assets in the analysis.
    (d) looks at the rate-sensitive assets and liabilities beyond one year.

14. When a financial institution reviews the loan application of an existing customer, the lender knows that _____ relative to a noncustomer applicant.
    (a) they can ignore credit screening for their existing customer
    (b) the monitoring process will be less expensive
    (c) the moral hazard risk will be a little higher
    (d) the adverse selection risk goes away

15. The duration gap for a bank with assets of $400 million, liabilities of $300 million, an average duration of assets of 3.5 years, and an average duration of liabilities of 1.25 years is
    (a) 1.8 years.
    (b) 2.4 years.
    (c) 2.6 years.
    (d) 2.8 years.

16. The income gap for a bank with rate sensitive assets of $92 million and rate sensitive liabilities of $106 million, an average duration of assets of 2.7 years, and an average duration of liabilities of 1.1 years is
    (a) −$14 million.
    (b) $14 million.
    (c) 1.4 years.
    (d) 1.7 years.

17. If interest rates rise 2%, what will the change in income be for a bank that has an income gap of –$25 million?

    (a) –$500,000
    (b) –$250,000
    (c) $250,000
    (d) $500,000

Part D: Short Answer Questions

1. What are the advantages to a borrower and to the bank of making a loan commitment?

   _____

   _____

2. What is the difference between the ability of U.S. banks to own equity in client firms versus what is permitted in Japan and Germany?

   _____

   _____

3. What is credit rationing, and why would commercial banks engage in this activity?

   _____

   _____

4. Why should banks be concerned about the duration of their assets and liabilities?

   _____

   _____

5. What are four principles for managing credit risk?

   _____

   _____

6. Describe what will happen to a bank's net interest margin and income if interest rates rise and the bank has more interest rate sensitive liabilities than assets.

   _____

   _____

■ Answers to Chapter 23

Exercise 1

1.	e	6.	b	10.	a
2.	h	7.	d	11.	m
3.	g	8.	c	12.	k
4.	j	9.	i	13.	l
5.	f				

Exercise 2

Interest rates are the major sources of revenue and income to the bank and also a major expense incurred by the bank. If the bank has too many fixed-rate assets relative to the fixed-rate liabilities, an increase in rates will have a significant negative impact on income and returns. This matching of assets and liability rates must be managed to avoid financial distress by the bank.

Exercise 3

A. $30 million – $50 million = –$20 million

B. Profits will decline

C. –$400,000 (= –$20 million × 0.02)

D. Profits will increase by $600,000 (= $20 million × 0.03)

Self Test

Part A

1.	credit risk	7.	credit rationing	13.	sensitivity
2.	screening	8.	more	14.	weighted average
3.	diversification	9.	interest-rate risk	15.	Duration GAP analysis
4.	monitoring	10.	more	16.	more
5.	lower, lower	11.	GAP	17.	fixed
6.	secured, compensating	12.	reduce	18.	long-term

Part B

1.	F	7.	F	13.	T
2.	F	8.	F	14.	T
3.	T	9.	F	15.	T
4.	T	10.	F	16.	F
5.	T	11.	T	17.	F
6.	F	12.	T	18.	T

Part C

1.	c	7.	a	13.	d
2.	a	8.	b	14.	c
3.	a	9.	c	15.	c
4.	d	10.	a	16.	a
5.	c	11.	b	17.	a
6.	d	12.	d		

Part D

1. By receiving a loan commitment customers know that they have a source of credit available when they need it. For the bank the benefit is that they have started the foundation for a long-term relationship. This relationship facilitates the collection of information and reduces the asymmetric information problem. With such an arrangement, the borrower must continually supply the bank with information about the firm's income, financial position, and business activities.

2. Japanese and German banks both have ownership and voting rights for certain industry firms to which they make loans. This gives them access to information that U.S. banks would not have access to about their customers. U.S. banks are not permitted to own an equity interest in any non-affiliated company. The adverse selection and moral hazard problems are greater for U.S. banks than in Japan and Germany.

3. Credit rationing takes two forms. One, the bank refuses to make a loan regardless of the interest rate the borrower is willing to pay. This approach reduces the risk from adverse selection. Two, a loan is made but for less than the borrower requested. This method reduces the potential loss from moral hazard.

4. Banks should be concerned about the duration of their assets and liabilities because duration measures the interest rate sensitivity of assets and liabilities. In general, the greater the difference in duration between assets and liabilities, the more variable a bank's income and balance sheet will be to changes in interest rates.

5. Four principles for managing credit risk are (1) establish long-term customer relationships, (2) credit rationing, (3) collateral, and (4) loan commitments.

6. The rise in interest rates will reduce the bank's net interest margin and income.

Chapter 24
Hedging with Financial Derivatives

■ Chapter Learning Goals

By the end of this chapter, you should

1. Be able to distinguish between forward contracts, futures contracts, options and swaps.

2. Know the terminology to use with these contracts.

3. Know how to immunize a portfolio by either buying or selling futures, options, or swaps.

4. Understand why financial managers may want to eliminate interest-rate risk, systematic risk, or foreign exchange rate risk.

■ Chapter Summary

Hedging

In the 1980s and 1990s, interest rates and foreign exchange rates became more volatile. To combat this, financial institutions' managers have learned to use **financial derivatives** to reduce risk. Financial derivatives are securities that derive their value from some other security. In this chapter, we investigate the use of forward contracts, futures contracts, options, and swaps to reduce risk.

The Forward Market

Firms may desire to reduce interest-rate risk by forming a **hedge**. A hedge reduces risk because when the price of the underlying asset moves one way, the price of the forward or futures contract will move in the opposite direction. This reduces or eliminates any gains or losses. A **forward contract** is an agreement to exchange assets in the future. The price and date of the exchange are agreed upon up front. A **long contract** means the holder agrees to buy the asset in the future, while the **short contract** holder agrees to sell and deliver the asset in the future.

We should distinguish forward contracts from **future contracts**. Forward contracts are unregulated and not standardized. They are not traded on an organized exchange. Their advantage is that they can be very flexible. Forward contracts suffer from several problems, however. First, investors may find it difficult to locate a **counterparty** to their hedge. Counterparties are investors who will take the other side of the transaction. Second, forward contracts are subject to default if one or the other party chooses not to complete their end of the contract.

Interest-Rate Forward Contracts

An interest-rate forward contract is an agreement between two parties to trade a debt instrument. The terms of a contract are (1) identification of the actual debt instrument to be delivered at a future date,

(2) the amount of the debt instrument to be delivered, (3) the price or interest rate on the debt security at delivery date, and (4) the delivery date.

Financial Futures Contracts

Financial futures contracts also specify that a specific financial instrument will be delivered by one party to another on a specified date.

Futures contracts eliminate the two problems found with forward contracts. First, finding a counterparty is simplified through the fact that all futures contracts are standardized. It is not necessary to find a specific investor willing to take the other side of a unique contract because every investor gets the same contract. Finding a counterparty is also simplified by the fact that all transactions are handled through a **clearinghouse** that guarantees the contract against default. Also, all futures contracts are traded through an exchange, which enhances liquidity. To protect the exchange from loss, they are **marked to market** every day. This means that at the end of every trading day, the change in the value of the futures contract is added or subtracted from a margin account. If the margin account falls too low, the investor must replenish it. A final advantage that futures have over forward contracts is that most futures contracts do not result in delivery of the underlying asset on the expiration date, while forward contracts do. A trader who sells short a futures contract can avoid making delivery on the expiration date by making an offsetting purchase of a long futures contract.

An example of a financial futures contract is the Treasury bond futures contract traded on the Chicago Board of Trade (CBOT). The contract's par value is $100,000 with prices being quoted in points of $1,000 and minimum trading increments of 1/32nd of a point or $31.25. The CBOT specifies that the bonds to be delivered on a T-bond contract and must have at least 15 years until maturity at delivery date. The amount of bonds to be delivered will vary if the coupon rates on the bonds to be delivered are different from 6%. Suppose on Feb. 1, you sell one June contract at 115 or $115,000. By shorting the contract, you are agreeing to deliver $100,000 face value of long-term Treasury bonds in June for $115,000. If interest rates rise such that the price of the contract drops to 110, then you will gain $5,000 ($115,000 – $110,000) because you could buy back the futures contract at a lower price. The price of the futures contract will be the same as the price of the underlying asset on expiration date. Otherwise, a riskless profit or arbitrage opportunity will exist. Of course, if an **arbitrage** opportunity did exist, market participants would trade the two assets until the prices adjusted to eliminate the arbitrage opportunity.

Hedging with Financial Futures

To hedge the interest-rate risk on a portfolio of bonds one needs to determine how many futures contract to sell. The number of contracts (NC) is the value of the asset (VA) divided by the value of the futures contract (VC). Suppose you own $10,000,000 of 20-year Treasury bonds and there is a T-bond futures contract maturing in one year that is priced at face value of $100,000. Thus the number of contracts that should be shorted to eliminate the interest-rate risk for the portfolio is 100 contracts ($10,000,000/$100,000). The net gain or loss on the hedged position is the change in the value of the futures position plus the change in the value of the portfolio of bonds.

Types of Hedges

Financial institutions to hedge their interest-rate risk often use financial futures. Two types of hedges are a **micro hedge** and a **macro hedge**. A micro hedge occurs when a futures contract is purchased or sold to hedge one particular security. Macro hedges occur when futures contracts are purchased or sold to offset an entire portfolio.

A perfect hedge means that any loss on the hedged asset is exactly offset by the gain on the future. Because fractional futures do not exist, a perfect hedge is hard to obtain in practice, so managers will usually settle for a partial hedge, which eliminates most of the risk exposure.

The Market for Financial Futures

Futures contracts trade on organized exchanges such as the Chicago Board of Trade, the Chicago Mercantile Exchange, and the New York Futures Exchange. These exchanges and the trading of futures are regulated by the **Commodity Futures Trading Commission (CFTC)**. The most widely traded futures are listed daily in the *Wall Street Journal*. The popularity of futures has led other countries to develop their own trading. England, Japan, and France, as well as other countries, all have major activity in futures trading. One reason for the overall popularity of futures is that the futures contract is a standardized document, unlike the forward contact, which can vary from one contract to the next. The contract has the added feature that it can be traded in the secondary market any time prior to the delivery date. A third benefit of the futures contract is the virtual elimination of default risk. This task is accomplished by having both the buyer and the seller contract with a third party that has very little likelihood noncompliance. This third party is a clearinghouse and introduced further in the next paragraph.

Futures trade a little different from stocks. First is the fact that when investors take either a long or short position in a futures contract, they are actually marking a contract with a future **clearinghouse**, not the person taking the other side of the transaction. When a contract is entered into, both the buyer and the seller must put up a deposit, called a **margin requirement**, with the clearinghouse. This deposit provides some financial security to the clearinghouse. At the end of each day, the clearinghouse will transfer funds from the buyer's to the seller's margin account or visa versa based on how the contract price changed to favor one of the two participants. This daily margin account adjustment is called marked to market. The number of contracts outstanding for a specific futures contract is called the **open interest**.

Hedging Foreign Exchange Risk with Forward Contracts

Firms can control their **foreign exchange rate risk** by using either futures or forward contracts. A firm selling goods to another country may want to protect itself from losses due to exchange rate fluctuations that may occur between the time the goods are sold and the time the goods are paid for. A firm that will receive foreign funds in the future hedges by entering into a contract that obligates the firm to sell the foreign funds in the future. The contract will lock in the current exchange rate. When the firm receives the funds, they sell them at the old exchange rate regardless of what current rates have become.

You may find that you have trouble determining whether to buy or sell a futures contract. One way to figure this out is to use Long/Short Analysis. To do this, first determine whether the investor is long or short originally, then take the opposite position. If you currently own the asset, you are long. For example, if you have Treasury bills that you want to hedge or if you will have Japanese yen in two months, you are long. To hedge your position, sell a futures contract (go short). If you do not own the asset but must buy it in the future, you are short. To hedge your position, go long. For example, if you have made a commitment to make a loan in six months, you are short. To hedge your position, you will need to buy futures contracts (go long). If you must pay a foreign supplier with foreign currency in the future, you are short that currency, so you must go long.

Hedging Foreign Exchange Risk with Futures Contracts

Suppose your company is due 20 million euros in two months for $20 million worth of goods that it has sold to Germany. To protect the $20 million against adverse exchange rate movement, you should sell euros futures contracts. Each March euro futures contract has a contract amount of 125,000 and in this example, a price of $1 per euro. Thus, the number of contracts to hedge is 80 contracts (20,000,000 euros/ 125,000 euros).

Alternatives to using forward and future contracts to hedge risk are options and swaps. These derivatives have certain advantages that make them preferable in some situations. Options and swaps are popular because they can overcome problems faced when using futures or forward contracts.

Stock Index Futures

Banks reduce interest-rate risk by hedging with financial futures. Some financial institution managers also are concerned about stock market risk, the risk that occurs because stock prices fluctuate. **Stock index futures** can be used to control this risk. Index futures first appeared in 1982 and have become one of the most widely traded of all futures contracts.

Financial managers can use stock index futures to reduce **systematic risk**. This type of hedging is called **portfolio insurance**. Although portfolio insurance removes the possibility of losses when the market falls, it also removes the chance for gains when the market rises. Managers will want to hedge their portfolios when they believe the market is going to fall or if they believe they can pick individual stocks that will out perform the market.

Financial managers can also use stock index futures to lock in current stock prices if they expect funds to arrive in the future that will be invested in stocks. To lock in current prices, the managers will go long and buy stock index futures. If the market rises, the gain on the futures will be used to add to the expected incoming funds. The incoming funds and the futures gain will provide enough money to purchase the stocks at the price that existed at the time the futures contract was entered plus any increase in price due to movement of the market.

Stock Index Futures Contracts

The most traded equity futures contract is the Standard & Poor's 500 Index (S&P 500) futures contract. Stock index futures are settled with cash, not securities. At expiration, the cash delivery is 250 times the index value. For example, if the S&P 500 index is 1,189 on expiration date, then the cash delivery is $297,250. If you had gone long the futures contract when the S&P 500 was 1,150, then your gain is $9,750 [(1189 − 1150) * 250]. For a naïve S&P 500 stock index futures hedge, the number of contract to sell is the portfolio value divided by (250 × index value).

Options

Options are contracts that give the purchaser the right to buy or sell the underlying financial instrument at a specific price, called the **exercise price** or **strike price**, within a specific period of time. Although the purchaser of an option is not obligated to buy or sell, the writer, or seller, of the option *is* obligated should the buyer choose to exercise the option. A pizza coupon is a simple example of an option. The coupon will state that the holder can buy pizza at a stated price until a given **expiration date**. The pizzeria is obligated to honor the coupon, but the holder has the option of exercising it or not. An option to buy, like the pizza coupon, is called a **call option**. An option to sell is called a **put option**. To help remember that a call gives the right to buy, think about *calling* to order a pizza.

The text describes two types of option contracts: American options and European options. American options can be exercised anytime prior to expiration date, but European options can only be exercised on expiration day. Options on individual stocks are called **stock options,** while option contracts on financial futures are called **financial futures options** or **futures options**.

Pizza coupons are usually free, but you usually must pay a **premium** to buy an option. In the options markets, the price of the option is called the premium. The premium is dependent on several factors. First, as the exercise price rises, the premium on call options falls, and the premium on put options rises. This is rational because increasing the exercise price lowers the probability the call option will be exercised. For example, the higher the price offered on the pizza coupon, the less likely it is that you will use it. Second, as the term to maturity of the option increases, the premium will increase because it is more likely that the option will move **into the money** the more time available. An in-the-money call option is one where the price of the underlying asset is greater than the exercise price. If the buyer decides to exercise the in-the-money call option, they will be able to buy the security at the exercise price and then sell it at the higher market price. For a put option in-the-money is when the exercise price is above the security price and again exercising the option will be profitable for the buyer of the put. As can be determined, in-the-money options should be exercised, while **out-of-the-money** options will expire unexercised. Finally, premiums increase as the **volatility** of the underlying financial instrument increases. This is because increased volatility increases the chance of the security moving into the money.

One problem with futures and forward contracts is that although they do limit losses on hedged portfolios, they also limit the potential for gains. By purchasing options on futures, you can control losses while preserving the potential for gains. The premium you pay for the option represents the cost of this loss insurance and is the maximum loss that the option buyer can have. The buyer of futures does not have this known floor on the amount of their potential loss.

Factors Affecting the Price of Options

Three factors are instrumental in determining the size of the premium the option buyer pays for the option. First is the value of the exercise price relative to the current price of the underlying security. The further the exercise price is from the security market price, the greater the premium. Another way of saying this is that the lower (higher) the exercise price of the call (put) the higher the premium, everything else remaining the same. A second factor is the length of time remaining until the option expires. For both put and call options, the longer the time till expiration the greater the premium. The final point is the variability of the price of the underlying asset. The greater the variability, for both puts and calls, the higher the option price.

Interest-Rate Swaps

Interest rate **swaps** are important tool's for controlling interest-rate risk. In a plain vanilla swap, one firm agrees to pay a fixed rate of interest on a stated sum and another firm agrees to pay a floating interest rate on the same sum, called the notional principal. The advantage of this arrangement is that it effectively converts fixed rate assets into floating rate assets and vice versa. A bank that finds that it has more interest rate sensitive liabilities than assets can protect itself from an increase in interest rates by agreeing to pay a fixed rate on a swap in exchange for receiving floating rate payments. What this does is convert fixed-rate assets into floating-rate assets.

The use of swaps to eliminate interest-rate risk can be cheaper than rearranging a bank's balance sheet. Swaps have an advantage over futures because swaps can be written for long periods of time. The disadvantage of swaps is that they suffer from the liquidity and default risk that plague the forward market. Intermediaries have set up markets in swaps that help alleviate these problems. For example, Citicorp will match firms together, and each firm will deal exclusively with the bank.

Credit Derivatives

In recent years a new form of derivative has surfaced and has grown at an astounding rate to where there is currently a market for these derivatives that reaches trillions of dollars. There are three types of credit derivatives: (1) credit options, (2) credit swaps, and (3) credit-linked notes.

A credit option is just like other options covered earlier except that the underlying asset is a specific security, such as a company's bonds, or an interest rate spread, such as the spread between the rate on a U.S. Treasury bond and the rate on a corporate bond. A credit swap is an agreement for the exchange of loan payments between parties. Two banks may agree to have the loan payments on equal dollar amounts of a loan go to the each other. This approach allows of each bank to share in the loans of the other bank and thus increase diversification. Another type of credit swap is called the credit default swap and is an arrangement where one firm pays another party a regular payment in exchange for the second party making payment to the firm in the event the underlying security owned by the first firm is downgraded or defaults. A credit-linked note is a combination of a bond and a credit option. This derivative gives the issuer of a bond the right to reduce payments to the lender in the event certain market event occurs.

■ Exercises

Exercise 1: Definitions and Terminology

Match the following terms in the column on the right with the definition or description in the column on the left. Place the letter of the term in the blank provided next to the appropriate definition.

_____ 1. A security that derives its value from another security	a.	micro hedge
_____ 2. A nonstandardized agreement where one party agrees to sell an asset and another party agrees to buy the asset in the future	b.	marked to market
	c.	hedge
_____ 3. A standardized agreement where one party agrees to sell an asset and another party agrees to buy the asset in the future	d.	derivative
	e.	macro hedge
_____ 4. A method of reducing risk where the change in contract value just offsets the change in asset value	f.	futures contract
	g.	long contract
_____ 5. The contract holder agrees to buy the asset in the future	h.	forward contract
_____ 6. The contract holder agrees to sell the asset in the future	i.	short contract
_____ 7. The change in the value of the future contract is added or subtracted from the margin account	j.	option
	k.	premium
_____ 8. A futures contract designed to hedge one particular asset	l.	European option
_____ 9. A futures contract designed to hedge an entire portfolio	m.	call option
_____ 10. An option that gives the holder the right to sell an asset in the future	n.	notational principal
	o.	strike price
_____ 11. An option that gives the holder the right to buy an asset in the future	p.	currency swap
_____ 12. The price at which an option permits the holder to buy or sell an asset	q.	swap
	r.	American option
_____ 13. The price of an option	s.	put option
_____ 14. An arrangement where one party pays a fixed interest rate and another pays a floating rate.	t.	futures options
	u.	interest-rate swap
_____ 15. An option that can be exercised any time up to maturity	v.	arbitrage
_____ 16. An option that can be exercised only at maturity	w.	open interest
_____ 17. The amount of funds on which the interest is being paid	x.	interest-rate forward contract

_____ 18. A contract that gives the purchaser the right to buy or sell an underlying security

_____ 19. An arrangement where one currency is exchanged for another

_____ 20. Gives the buyer the right to buy a futures contract

_____ 21. A contract to exchange interest or currency payment commitments

_____ 22. An agreement between two parties to trade a debt instrument

_____ 23. A riskless profit opportunity

_____ 24. The number of outstanding futures or options contracts

Exercise 2: Taking a Hedge Position

For each of the following situations determine whether the manager should go long (L) (buy the security in the future) or short (S) (sell the security in the future) if a hedge is desired.

_____ 1. A bank commits to make a loan for $1 million three months from now.

_____ 2. Second National Bank holds $50 million in Treasury securities.

_____ 3. Second National Bank has a portfolio of $100 million of mortgage loans.

_____ 4. A mutual fund manager believes the stock market will fall.

_____ 5. A pension fund manager wants to lock in current stock prices and knows he will have a net inflow of $10 million in two months.

_____ 6. A firm sold $1 million in tires to Japan with payment due in yen in three months.

_____ 7. A firm must pay $1 million in pounds to an English firm in two months.

Exercise 3: Futures versus Forward Contracts

List four features that distinguish futures contracts from forward contracts.

1. _____

2. _____

3. _____

4. _____

Exercise 4: The Type of Financial Derivative

Identify the type of transaction that a financial manager should initiate in each situation.

1. A bank has $20 million of mortgage securities and wishes to protect against rising interest rates.

   _____

2. A bank has more rate sensitive assets than rate sensitive liabilities.

   _____

3. A firm will engage in monthly transactions that will involve the receipt of foreign currency.

   _____

Exercise 5: Option Pricing

Explain how each of the three variables below influences the size of the option premium.

Exercise Price _____

Time to expiration _____

Asset price volatility _____

Exercise 6: Swap Markets

Explain how the use of an intermediary reduces the liquidity and default problems of swaps.

_____

_____

■ Self-Test

Part A: Fill in the Blanks

1. A firm with a portfolio of Treasury notes may _____ by _____ future contracts.

2. A(n) _____ is where the investor agrees to sell an asset at some time in the future at an agreed upon price.

3. One problem with forward contracts is that it may be difficult to find a(n) _____, someone to take the other side of the transaction.

4. Forward contracts are subject to _____ because the counter party could go bankrupt.

5. The futures exchanges and trading in financial futures are regulated by the _____ _____, which was created in 1974.

6. The elimination of riskless profit opportunities in the futures markets is referred to as _____, and it guarantees that the price of the futures contract at expiration equals the price of the underlying asset to be delivered.

7. Because futures contracts are _____, it is easier for an investor to find a counter party.

8. Each day futures contracts are _____, helping to reduce the chance of losses to the clearinghouse.

9. If you will receive $1 million at the end of the month and want to lock in the current market prices then you should _____ stock _____.

10. A firm that will receive $10 million in francs in two months could reduce its exchange rate risk by _____ foreign exchange forward contracts.

11. Futures contracts that are linked to debt securities are called _____ because their purpose is to protect against interest rate movements.

12. Both the buyer and seller of a futures contract must meet a(n) _____ by depositing money at the futures clearinghouse.

13. The *Wall Street Journal* reports futures trades on a daily basis including the _____, which is the number of contract outstanding.

14. A contract that gives the purchaser the right to buy or sell an asset is a(n) _____.

15. A(n) _____ gives the holder the right to buy an underlying asset.

16. The price that the holder of a call option can demand from exercising the option is the _____.

17. An option that cannot be exercised until maturity is call a(n) _____.

18. When the price of common stock exceeds the exercise price of the call option on that stock the option is referred to as being _____.

19. The buyer of an option can have a loss no greater than the option _____.

20. The most common type of interest-rate swap is often referred to as a(n) _____.

21. The amount on which interest is being paid in a swap is called _____.

22. A major advantage of hedging with swaps instead of futures is that swaps can be written for _____ time horizons.

23. If you go long one S&P 500 futures contract when the S&P 500 is 1,075 and close out the contract when the S&P 500 is 1,100, then you will have a(n) _____ of _____.

24. When an equity portfolio manager wants to hedge against a broad market decline, he should _____ equity futures.

25. A portfolio manager which wants to hedge a portfolio of $100 million of Treasury bonds against rising interest rates should short _____ T-bond futures contracts.

Part B: True-False Questions

Circle whether the following statements are true (T) or false (F).

T   F   1.   Interest rate futures can be used to reduce the risk of selling goods overseas.

T   F   2.   Forward contracts are more flexible than futures contracts because they are not standardized.

T   F   3.   A micro hedge could be used to immunize a portfolio of securities.

T   F   4.   To remove exchange rate risk, a firm that must pay in a foreign currency should sell futures contracts.

T   F   5.   To mark a contract to market involves adding or subtracting funds from a margin account.

T   F   6.   A counter party will go short when you sell a forward contract.

T   F   7.   The stock index futures market has not grown in the last few years because of uncertainty about future stock prices.

T   F   8.   To corner a market means that someone has purchased the bulk of a particular asset so that high prices can be charged when forward contracts are settled.

T   F   9.   Open interest refers to the number of futures contracts that have not been settled.

T   F   10.   A pension fund manager who believes stock prices will rise will likely sell stock index futures.

T   F   11.   Call option premiums are generally higher the greater the exercise price.

T   F   12.   Option premiums are higher the greater the volatility of the underlying asset.

T   F   13.   A put option gives the buyer the obligation to sell the underlying asset.

T   F   14.   Options can be written on futures or directly on the underlying asset.

T   F   15.   Swaps are derivatives.

T   F   16.   A bank with a negative GAP might sell call options on futures contracts.

T   F   17.   The SEC is the only agency that regulates options trading.

T   F   18.   An option that is in-the-money would be unlikely to be exercised.

T   F   19.   The main difference between a futures and an options contract is that the profit curve for the options contract is nonlinear.

T   F   20.   One problem with options is that accounting rules may require that losses be reported unnecessarily.

T   F   21.   If you need to sell 20 futures contracts short to hedge your portfolio, then buying puts on 20 futures contracts will also prevent losses.

T   F   22.   A swap is a financial contract that obligates one party to exchange a set of payments it owns for another set of payments owned by another party.

T   F   23.   The CFTC regulates trading in financial futures.

T   F   24.   The multiplier for the S&P 500 futures contract is 500.

T   F   25.   Investors who want to protect the value of their portfolios by using financial derivatives are called speculators.

T   F   26.   A company about to engage in a new bond issue to the public is concerned that market rates may change before they go to market with the bonds. Buying a credit option would be beneficial to this firm.

Part C: Multiple-Choice Questions

Circle the appropriate answer.

1.   An investor who chooses to hedge in the futures market
    (a)   gives up the opportunity for gains.
    (b)   reduces the opportunity for losses.
    (c)   increases his earnings potential.
    (d)   Both (a) and (b) are true.

2.   A portfolio manager with $100 million in Treasury securities could reduce interest-rate risk by
    (a)   selling financial futures.
    (b)   going long on financial futures.
    (c)   buying financial futures.
    (d)   Both (b) and (c) are true.

3.   A mutual fund manager who expects $100 million to be received in two months and who believes the market will fall should
    (a)   sell stock index futures.
    (b)   buy stock index futures.
    (c)   buy financial futures.
    (d)   stay out of the futures market.

4.   If a bank sold a futures contract that perfectly hedges its portfolio of Treasury securities and interest rates then fall,
    (a)   the bank suffers a loss.
    (b)   the bank has a gain.
    (c)   the bank's income is unchanged.
    (d)   none of the above occurs.

5. The main reason why futures contracts are marked to market every day is because
   (a) it makes the accounting simpler.
   (b) it allows each party to recognize gains or losses.
   (c) it reduces the chance of loss for the exchange.
   (d) it is required by law.

6. When an investor agrees to buy an asset at some time in the future, he is said to have gone
   (a) long.
   (b) short.
   (c) ahead.
   (d) back.

7. The main advantage of a forward contract is that it
   (a) is standardized and reduces search cost.
   (b) is default risk free since the contract is between the exchange and the investor.
   (c) is flexible because it can be written any way the parties desire.
   (d) Both (a) and (b) are true.

8. At the expiration date of a futures contract, the price of the contract is equal to the
   (a) price of the underlying asset to be delivered.
   (b) price of the counterparty.
   (c) hedge position.
   (d) value of the hedged asset.

9. Futures markets have been successful and have grown rapidly because of
   (a) standardization of the futures contract.
   (b) the ability to buy or sell the contract up to the maturity.
   (c) the reduced risk of default in the futures market.
   (d) all of the above.

10. The Hunt brothers suffered a loss of more than $1 billion after
    (a) hedging in the financial futures market.
    (b) trying to corner the market for silver.
    (c) selling futures contracts on silver.
    (d) buying futures contracts on silver.

11. If you thought the stock market was going to increase in the near future and you wanted to make some money in the futures market, you could _____ an index future and wait for the market to rise then _____ the same contract.
    (a) sell, buy
    (b) hedge, arbitrage
    (c) buy, sell
    (d) You cannot trade the stock index futures unless you owned a portfolio of stock.

12. Put and call option premiums are increased when
    (a) time to maturity increases.
    (b) volatility is lower on the underlying asset.
    (c) strike price is lower.
    (d) Both (b) and (c) are true.

13. An option that lets the holder sell an asset in the future is a
    (a) put option.
    (b) call option.
    (c) swap.
    (d) premium.

14. A put option on Treasury bonds with a strike price of 100 is selling for $1.00. If the bonds are currently selling for 102, then the option is
    (a) in-the-money.
    (b) worthless.
    (c) above the money.
    (d) not yet in-the-money.

15. When an investor holds both a security and a put option on a short futures contract he has
    (a) limited his gains.
    (b) limited his losses.
    (c) arbitrage.
    (d) Both (a) and (b) are true.

16. An important tool for managing interest-rate risk that requires the exchange of payment streams on assets is a
    (a) futures contract.
    (b) forward contract.
    (c) swap.
    (d) cross hedge.

17. Call option premiums are lower, all other things held constant, when
    (a) the time to maturity is shorter.
    (b) the volatility of the underlying asset is lower.
    (c) the strike price is lower.
    (d) None of the above affect option pricing.

18. Which of the following is a disadvantage of the swap as a method for controlling interest-rate risk?
    (a) Swaps are more complex.
    (b) Swaps are more expensive than simply restructuring the balance sheet.
    (c) Swaps lack liquidity.
    (d) Swaps may not accomplish the goal.

19. Which of the following is an advantage of interest rate swaps?
    (a) Swaps lower interest rate costs more cheaply.
    (b) Swaps are more complex.
    (c) Swaps are very liquid.
    (d) Swaps are short term.

20. One major disadvantage of using futures options in place of futures contracts is
    (a) futures options only work if rates are expected to decline.
    (b) gains from option must be recorded in the financial statements before they are received.
    (c) options do not allow the buyer to receive any gains.
    (d) premiums must be paid for the option contracts.

21. The multiplier for the S&P 500 futures contract is
    (a) 50.
    (b) 250.
    (c) 500.
    (d) 1,000.

22. Equity futures contracts are settled in
    (a) shares of the stocks in the underlying index.
    (b) shares of the index.
    (c) cash.
    (d) both (b) and (c).

23. If a portfolio manager shorts 10 S&P 500 futures when the index is 1152 and the S&P 500 index is 1178 at expiration, then the gain or loss from the futures position is
    (a) −$65,000.
    (b) −$6,500.
    (c) $6,500.
    (d) $65,000.

24. Which of the following credit derivatives would allow General Motors to tie their payments on a credit instrument to an event such as the sales of SUVs dropped below a specified level?
    (a) credit option
    (b) credit swap
    (c) credit default swap
    (d) credit-linked notes

Part D: Short Answer Questions

1. What system does the futures market have in place that is absent in the forward market that eliminates the concern with default risk?

_____

_____

2. Some financial market analysts believe that index futures were a major factor in the "Black Monday" stock market crash in 1987. What role do these critics believe index futures contracts had in this crash?

_____

_____

3. Why must the price of a futures contract and the price of the underlying asset be the same on the expiration date of the contract?

_____

_____

4. Why do many risk managers prefer to buy an option on a interest-rate futures contract than writing an option directly on the debt instrument itself?

_____

_____

5. With the current price of a stock at $80, an investor buys a call option on that stock with an exercise price of $85, for a premium per share of stock of $3. Explain the profit position of the investor as the price of the stock increases from the $80.

_____

_____

6. What are the advantages and disadvantages of using interest-rate swaps versus hedging with other derivatives (futures and futures options)?

_____

_____

7. Suppose that you are an insurance company that has $50 million invested in a mutual fund the tracks the performance of the S&P 500 and are concerned that market might decline over the next six months. Consequently, you short 25 S&P 500 futures at 1,085. Six months later, the contracts expire with the S&P 500 at 1,115. What is the net gain or loss from the equity portfolio and the futures contracts?

_____

_____

8. What would the net gain or loss would have been if the contracts would have expired with the S&P 500 at 1,060?

_____

_____

9. Why did the portfolio lose money in (8) even though the portfolio manager sold 25 S&P 500 futures contracts and the market declined?

_____

_____

■ Answers to Chapter 24

Exercise 1

1.	d	6.	i.	11.	m	16.	l	21.	q
2.	h	7.	b	12.	o	17.	n	22.	x
3.	f	8.	a	13.	k	18.	j	23.	v
4.	c	9.	e	14.	u	19.	p	24.	w
5.	g	10.	s	15.	r	20.	t		

Exercise 2

1. L
2. S
3. S
4. S
5. L
6. S
7. L

Exercise 3

1. Futures are standardized contracts.

2. Futures can be bought or sold up until maturity.

3. Futures can be satisfied with any similar security.

4. Futures are marked to market daily.

Exercise 4

1. Put option on short futures contract.

2. Swap—pay floating rate and received fixed rate.

3. Swap—receive dollars and pay foreign currency.

Exercise 5

Exercise price—the further the exercise price is from the current price of the underlying asset the smaller the premium.

Time to expiration—the longer the time the larger the premium due to the fact that there is more time for the asset price to eventually rise (call) or fall (put) to make the option in-the-money.

Asset price volatility—the greater the price movement the more likely the price will move to the point of making the option in-the-money and thus a higher premium.

Exercise 6

An intermediary can match counterparties to the contract, which enhances the ease of marketing swap contracts. They also guarantee payments to each counter party and thus reduce the credit risk to only that of the intermediary.

Self-Test

Part A

1. hedge, selling
2. short contract
3. counterparty
4. default risk
5. CFTC
6. arbitrage
7. standardized
8. marked to market
9. buy, index futures
10. selling
11. interest-rate forward contracts
12. margin requirement
13. open interest
14. option
15. call option
16. strike price
17. European option
18. in-the-money
19. premium
20. plain vanilla
21. notional principal
22. long
23. gain, $6,250(1,100 - 1,075) \times 250$
24. short
25. $1,000(\$100,000,000/100,000)$

Part B

1. F	10. F	19. T
2. T	11. F	20. F
3. F	12. T	21. T
4. F	13. F	22. T
5. T	14. T	23. T
6. F	15. T	24. F
7. F	16. F	25. F
8. T	17. F	26. T
9. T	18. F	

Part C

1. d	9. d	17. c
2. a	10. b	18. c
3. a	11. c	19. a
4. c	12. a	20. d
5. c	13. a	21. b
6. a	14. a	22. c
7. c	15. b	23. a
8. a	16. C	24. d

Part D

1. Traders in the futures market do not transact with a specific counterparty because all contracts are essentially with a futures clearinghouse. The clearinghouse guarantees the completion of the contract, thus eliminating concern about the counter party not completing the contract.

2. The market was more volatile during this period. The increased volatility caused portfolio managers to become concerned about a fall in the market. To hedge this event, the managers sold index futures. This selling pressure pushed futures prices down. To keep stock prices in line with the index price decline, traders began selling large blocks of stock, thus driving stock prices lower and contributing to the crash.

3. If the futures contract allowed the buyer to purchase the asset for less than its current market value, the investor could do so and immediately turn around and sell the asset for the higher price. The futures contract buyer thus made a riskless profit. If the futures price was higher, the investor could sell the contract, collect the high price, then buy the asset at the lower price and keep the difference, again for a riskless profit.

4. The benefit of the option on futures is the liquidity of the futures contract. Futures are generally more liquid than the underlying debt instrument. Most investors prefer the contract written on the more liquid instrument.

5. As long as the stock price is less than $85, the investor has a loss of $3 per share. As the price exceeds $85, the investor's loss decreases until the stock price reaches $88 ($85 + $3). From that point on, the profit becomes positive and increases almost dollar for dollar with the stock price.

6. Swaps have two main advantages. One, they are long term. Second, they allow firms to exploit their comparative advantages in borrowing and share the benefits with the counterparty. The disadvantages are the lack of liquidity and the risk of default on the interest payments agreed to.

7. The S&P 500 increased by 2.76% [(1,115 −1,085)/1,085]. Thus, the equity portfolio gained $1,380,000 (0.0276 × $50 million). However, the futures position lost $187,500 because you short the futures but the market went up [(1,115 −1,085) × 250 × 25]. The net gain is $1,192,500.

8. The gain from the short futures position is $156,250 [−(1,060 − 1,085) × 250 × 25]. The S&P 500 declined by 2.36% [(1,060 − 1,085)/1,060], so the equity portfolio lost $1,180,000 (0.0236 × $50 million). The net loss is $1,023,750.

9. The portfolio manager did not fully hedge the portfolio against possible losses. She only partially hedged the portfolio. To fully hedge the portfolio, she would need to sell 184 contracts [$50 million/ (250 × 1085)].

Chapter 25
Financial Crises in Emerging Market Economies

■ Chapter Learning Goals

By the end of this chapter, you should

1. Be familiar with the causes of financial crises in emerging market economies.
2. Define and explain the stages of a financial crisis in emerging market economies.

■ Chapter Summary

This chapter describes the causes and dynamics of financial crises in emerging market economies. Building on the framework established in Chapter 7, the analysis of how asymmetric information can generate adverse selection and moral hazard, called **agency theory**, provides the basis for defining a **financial crisis**—a disruption in the financial system that prevents the efficient transfer of funds from savers to households and firms with productive investment opportunities. Unlike Chapter 8, the coverage in this chapter focuses on emerging economies.

Dynamics of Financial Crises in Emerging Economies

In **emerging market economies**, those economies that are in the early stage of market development and only recently opened up to the rest of the world, the dynamics of financial crises have many similarities to crises in advanced economies, but they also have a few key differences.

Stage One: Initiation of Financial Crisis

Unlike the host of triggers in advanced economies, in emerging market economies, a financial crisis is usually triggered by financial liberalization/globalization or severe fiscal imbalances. The elimination of restrictions on financial institutions and markets domestically, accompanied by opening up the economy to flows of capital from other nations, is called **financial globalization**. Even if existing fiscal policy is sound, such globalization often leads to a lending boom due to a weak "credit culture" and new access to global capital markets. Capital inflows are often stimulated by currency policies that peg to the dollar, giving foreign investors a sense of lower risk. As in advanced economies, risk taking grows unchecked and eventually the risk taking causes loss to mount and loss of asset value to lenders. In emerging economies, the effect of these losses are more severe as there are fewer alternatives to banks. Although these boom-bust cycles can be prevented by prudent regulation, local politicians often lack the proper incentives. Examples of this scenario include Mexico in 1994 and East Asia in 1997.

Another trigger for emerging markets is government fiscal imbalances that lead to substantial budget deficits. Faced with a lack of buyers for their debt, governments often encourage or outright force banks to purchase government debt. When investors lose confidence in the government's ability to repay, this causes the value of the debt to drop weakening the balance sheets of the banks. Examples of this scenario include Argentina in 2001–2002 and Russia in 1998.

Stage Two: Currency Crisis

As speculators become aware of the impending financial crisis, they begin to take positions to profit on the depreciation of the local currency. **Speculative attacks**, in which speculators engage in massive short sales of the currency, can cause the value of the currency to collapse as supply grows and demand shrinks.

If the government attempts to defend the currency by raising interest rates, this action further weakens the banks. If not, the central bank must intervene by selling foreign currency reserves until exhausted. With no other options, the government must devalue the currency.

Stage Three: Full-Fledged Financial Crisis

In typical practice, debt contracts in emerging markets are typically denominated in foreign currency (e.g., dollar). This exacerbates the debt burden for domestic firms after a currency devaluation. The firms' assets do not rise in terms of local currency; however, the value of the debt rises as it is denominated in foreign currency. A concurrent currency crisis and financial crisis is called a "twin crisis." Another consequence of the collapse of the currency is the potential for higher inflation. This leads to higher interest rates, which can heighten adverse selection and moral hazard concerns.

Preventing Emerging Market Financial Crises

To prevent crises, therefore, governments must improve prudential regulation and supervision of banks to limit their risk taking. Government regulations to promote disclosure by banking and other financial institutions of their balance sheet positions, therefore, are needed to encourage these institutions to hold more capital because depositors and creditors will be unwilling to put their money into an institution that is thinly capitalized. Regulations to promote disclosure of banks' activities will also limit risk taking because depositors and creditors will pull their money out of institutions that are engaging in these risky activities. Moving to a flexible exchange rate regime in which exchange rates fluctuate can also discourage borrowing in foreign currencies because there is now more risk in doing so. To avoid financial crises, policy makers need to put in place the proper institutional infrastructure before liberalizing their financial systems.

■ Exercises

Exercise 1: Definitions and Terminology

Match the terms on the right with the definition or description on the left. Place the letter of the term in the blank provided next to the appropriate definition.

_____ 1. Reduction in lending in response to lender's weaker balance sheets

_____ 2. Disruption in the financial system that prevents the efficient transfer of funds

_____ 3. The elimination of restrictions on financial markets and institutions

_____ 4. Occurs when debt contract denominated in a foreign currency

_____ 5. The bundling together of small loans into standard debt securities

_____ 6. Structure credit product that paid out cash flows into a number of tranches of unequal risk

_____ 7. Example of advanced economy experiencing a crisis like an emerging economy

_____ 8. Economies that are in the early stage of market development

_____ 9. Massive short-sales of a currency intended to cause a decline in the currency's value

_____ 10. Significant unanticipated decline in asset values accompanied by increased indebtedness

a. debt deflation

b. Iceland

c. currency mismatch

d. speculative attack

e. deleveraging

f. mortgage-backed security

g. emerging market economies

h. securitization

i. financial liberalization

j. financial crisis

Exercise 2: Dynamics of Financial Crisis

List the three stages of a financial crisis in an emerging market economy.

1. _____

2. _____

3. _____

Exercise 3: Preventing Emerging Market Financial Crises

List the four ways to prevent a financial crisis in an emerging market economy.

1. _____

2. _____

3. _____

4. _____

■ Self-Test

Part A: Fill in the Blanks

1. When emerging market economies face large _____ that they cannot finance, they often force banks to purchase government debt.

2. The process of liberalizing restrictions on financial institutions and markets while opening up to flows of capital and financial firms from other nations is called _____.

3. _____ is an example of an advanced economy that suffered a crisis like an emerging market.

4. The development of new, sophisticated financial instruments and products called _____ includes innovations like structured credit products.

5. During a(n) _____, prices of assets may be driven far above their fundamental values.

6. A(n) _____ is characterized by multiple banks failing simultaneously.

7. Although financial liberalization promotes financial development in the long run, in the short-run, it can lead to a(n) _____.

8. Unlike the Mexican and East Asian crises, Argentina has a(n) _____ banking sector.

9. The East Asian crisis of 1997 was initiated by the mismanagement of _____.

Part B: True-False Questions

Circle whether the following statements are true (T) or false (F).

T F 1. Financial crises have largely been eliminated due to advances in financial innovation.

T F 2. The stages of a financial crisis are identical in advanced and emerging economies.

T F 3. Although usually beneficial in the long run, in the short run financial liberalization can cause credit booms.

T F 4. Asset-price bubbles occur when prices rise far above fundamental values.

T F 5. Agency problems occurred in the mortgage market because originators of loans always hold the loan.

T F 6. In emerging markets, financial liberalization and severe fiscal imbalances are the primary triggers for crises.

T F 7. The 1998 crisis in Russia was an example of fiscal imbalances causing a crisis in an emerging market.

T F 8. "Twin crises" happen when a currency crisis and a financial crisis occur simultaneously.

Part C: Multiple-Choice Questions

Circle the appropriate answer.

1. Which of the following can NOT initiate a financial crisis in an emerging market economy?
   (a) Financial liberalization
   (b) Financial globalization
   (c) Stronger lender balance sheets
   (d) Severe fiscal imbalances
   (e) All of the above can initiate a financial crisis.

2. Which of the following is not a stage of financial crisis in an emerging market economy?
   (a) Initiation of the financial crisis
   (b) Currency crisis
   (c) Full-fledged financial crisis
   (d) Debt deflation

3. Which of the following is an example of globalization causing an emerging market financial crisis?
   (a) The Great Depression in the United States
   (b) Mexico in 1994
   (c) East Asian in 1997
   (d) All of the above.
   (e) Only (b) and (c) of the above.

■ Answers to Chapter 25

Exercise 1

1. e   6. c
2. j   7. b
3. i   8. g
4. f   9. d
5. h   10. a

Exercise 2

1. Initiation of the crisis due to mismanagement of financial liberalization or globalization OR severe fiscal imbalances

2. Currency crisis

3. Full-fledged financial crisis

Exercise 3

1. Beef up prudential regulation and supervision of banks

2. Encourage disclosure and market-based discipline

3. Limit currency mismatch

4. Sequence financial liberalization

Self-Test

Part A

1. fiscal imbalances
2. financial globalization
3. Iceland
4. financial engineering
5. asset-price boom
6. bank panic
7. credit boom
8. well-supervised
9. financial globalization

Part B

1. F   5. F
2. F   6. T
3. T   7. T
4. T   8. T

Part C

1. c
2. d
3. e

Chapter 26
Savings Associations and Credit Unions

■ Chapter Learning Goals

By the end of this chapter, you should

1. Know the different sources of funds for mutual savings banks, Savings and Loan associations, and credit unions.
2. Be familiar with the principle customers and types of loans that mutual savings banks, Savings and Loan associations, and credit unions rely upon for their business.
3. Understand the principal factors that led to the thrift crisis and the current structure of the thrift industry.

■ Chapter Summary

This chapter introduces you to a few nonbank financial institutions. Specifically, the material will provide an introduction to the creation and development of mutual savings banks, Savings and Loan associations, and credit unions. All three institutions have their origin and much of their survival linked to the consumer market and rely less on commercial businesses.

Mutual Savings Banks

Mutual savings banks were first authorized in the United States in 1816. These institutions had the unique characteristic of being owned by their depositors. A disadvantage of mutual savings bank is being owned by a large number of depositors magnifies the agency problem because there are a large number of owners with each owning only a small part of the company. A main attraction was that mutual savings banks paid a little higher rate on deposits than did commercial banks. Currently there are about 367 savings banks primarily concentrated along the eastern seaboard part of the country.

The text identifies two advantages of the mutual form of ownership. First, depositors contribute all of the capital to mutual savings banks, which represents equity ownership. Consequently, mutual savings banks are safer because they have fewer liabilities than commercial banks. Second, managers of mutual savings banks are more risk averse than corporate managers because they do not gain from earnings growth but will lose their jobs if the institution fails.

Savings and Loan Associations

Savings and Loan (S&Ls) were authorized by Congress in 1816 in the same legislation that permitted the existence of mutual savings banks. Their express purpose was to have the majority of their assets in mortgage loans. A significant distinction of S&Ls is that they were not permitted to offer demand deposits and the interest rate on their savings accounts were fixed at a rate slightly higher than that offered by commercial banks. By the 1920s, mortgage loans accounted for about 85% of their total assets.

The Great Depression caused many financial hardships for the industry much like it did for commercial banks. Congress passed the **Federal Home Loan Bank Act** of 1932 creating the **Federal Home Loan Bank Board** and giving the thrifts the choice of being state or federally chartered. In 1934, Congress created the **Federal Savings and Loan Insurance Corporation (FSLIC)**, which served the same function as the commercial bank's FDIC.

Savings and Loans in Trouble: The Thrift Crisis

All went well for the industry until about the late 1970s when inflation increased significantly to more than 13% by 1979. The legislated low rate paid on S&L deposits encouraged depositors to seek higher return uses for their funds. The creation of **money market accounts** by securities firms provided the perfect outlet. These accounts paid close to current money market rates. Large numbers of depositors took their funds out of thrifts. To replace these withdrawals, the thrifts had to pay higher returns on CDs and borrowed money. The S&Ls now had their assets in low-rate long-term mortgages and their fund sources were primarily costly short-term securities. The stage was set for a crisis.

Financial innovation such as money market mutual funds and securitization also hurt the industry and drove firms to seek out new sources of profits. One approach was to take on riskier assets in hope of earning higher returns. This approach was enhanced by the near simultaneous creation of new markets for securities, such as junk bonds, swaps, and financial futures, as well as the approval of letting thrifts put a larger portion of their assets into riskier areas such as commercial real estate, consumer loans, and direct investments. Deposit insurance was increased from $40,000 or $100,000 in 1980, increasing the moral hazard problem, and deposit ceilings were phased out. Still higher rates had to be paid to attract funds. **Brokered deposits** were one source that was both attractive and expensive. Higher risks were taken in an attempt to generate adequate funds to make these interest rate commitments.

The high inflation of the late 1970s and early 1980s along with the recession in 1981–1982 were the two factors that brought the crisis to a head. The increasing interest cost for short-term fund sources and the fixed-rate returns on long-term mortgages led the thrifts head-on into a situation of fighting for their survival. Lack of appropriate action by the Federal Home Loan Bank Board and the FSLIC (both organizations have now been abolished) added to the bravery of thrift managers to take on higher risks. Lack of regulatory action magnified the moral hazard problem. The weight of the costly and escalating sources of funds and the lowering of rates on assets due to competition for customers led many thrifts into financial distress.

By 1987 the crisis was at the peak. A first attempt was made to bail out the S&Ls through the **Competitive Equality in Banking Act of 1987**. The inadequate funding of this Act doomed it to failure. In 1989 passage of the **Financial Institutions Reform Recovery and Enforcement Act (FIRREA)** was aimed directly at stopping and solving the thrift crisis. One FIRREA action was to create the **Resolution Trust Corporation** that has the responsibility of overseeing the S&L crisis. The final cost of this crisis to taxpayers is approximately $120 billion.

Political Economy of the Savings and Loan Crisis

To act in the best interest of taxpayers, regulators must set tight restrictions on holding assets that are too risky, impose high capital requirements, and not adopt a stance of **regulatory forbearance**, refraining from exercising their regulatory right to close insolvent savings and loans, that allows insolvent institutions to continue to operate.

The Savings and Loan Industry Today

Between 1986 and 2009, the number of S&Ls declined from around 3,600 to 1,173. This reduction in numbers came about through consolidations with other S&Ls and conversions to commercial banks and credit unions. Currently, nearly 70% of all S&L loans are secured by real estate. Though the industry suffered losses between 1987 and 1990, the industry returned to health by 2001 and posted steady profits until the 2007–2009 financial crisis.

The Future of Savings and Loan Industry

Since the creation of the Savings and Loan primarily for the purpose of making mortgage loans, the market place has generated other institutions and sources of mortgage lending. The question arises as to whether Savings and Loan are needed any more. Given the return to profitability of the S&Ls and the fact that the total assets have increased since 1993, the market place seems to indicate that they still play an important role in the U.S. financial markets.

Credit Unions

Credit unions are relatively small institutions, owned by their depositors that obtain funds and make loans to their members who are "bonded together" by a common interest. Credit unions have cost advantages over other institutions because they often use volunteers as employees, they are nonprofit and thus tax exempt, and often receive support from an employer or other group representing the common interest. One disadvantage of Credit Unions is their common bond requirement. This requirement keeps many of them quite small. The industry accounts for only 10% of all consumer deposits and 15% of all consumer loans.

Federally chartered and state chartered insured credit unions are under the regulation of the **National Credit Union Administration (NCUA)**. Deposits are insured up to $100,000 by the **National Credit Union Share Insurance Fund (NSUSIF)**. Their small size has led to the creation of organizations to help credit unions deal with economies of scale and liquidity problems. These organizations are **central credit unions**, which provide administrative assistance, **U.S. central credit union**, which provides assistance to the 44 state central credit unions, and the **Central Liquidity Facility (CLF)** that provides services to credit unions similar to what the Federal Reserve provides to commercial banks. Credit unions also form **trade associations** that are made up of a number of credit unions that provide central services for all credit unions in the association.

Their primary source of funds (approximately 73%) is through deposit. Credit unions offer savings accounts, called **regular share accounts**, CDs, called **share certificates**, and checking accounts, called **share drafts**. Their assets consist primarily of small loans to their members (40%) with the balance in cash, government securities, deposits at other institutions, and fixed assets.

■ Exercises

Exercise 1: Terminology

Match the following terms from the left column with the closely related term from the right. Place the letter of the term from the right column in the blank provided next to the appropriate term on the left.

_____ 1. Insures savings and loan deposits for up to $100,000 per account

_____ 2. The funds in these accounts can have checks written on them

_____ 3. Created the Federal Home Loan Bank Board and permitted S&Ls to be federally chartered.

_____ 4. Credit unions are distinguished from other banks by this rule

_____ 5. A commercial bank that serves as a central bank for credit unions

_____ 6. Created to allow credit unions to take advantage of economies of scale

_____ 7. Charged with regulating and supervising federally chartered credit unions

_____ 8. "Lender of last resort" for credit unions

_____ 9. The credit union equivalent of a commercial bank savings account

_____ 10. Refraining from exercising regulatory rights by regulators is called this

_____ 11. A CD at a credit union

_____ 12. The organization responsible for managing the S&L crisis

_____ 13. Some thrifts were initially organized as such banks

_____ 14. Groups that have organized together to provided services to large numbers of credit unions

_____ 15. Product offered by credit unions where customer agrees to leave funds on deposit for a specified period of time in exchange for a higher rate of return

_____ 16. Practice where regulatory institutions refrain from exercising regulatory duties

a. Federal Home Loan Bank Act of 1932

b. regulatory forbearance

c. Savings Association Insurance Fund

d. National Credit Union Administration

e. U.S. Central Credit Union

f. Central Liquidity Facility

g. Resolution Trust Corporation

h. common bond membership

i. mutual

j. Credit Union National Association

k. share certificates

l. regular share accounts

m. share draft

n. regulatory forbearance

o. share certificates

p. trade associations

Exercise 2: The Thrift Crisis

How did financial innovation contribute to the savings and loan crisis by S&L managers, increasing the risk of the firm's asset portfolio?

_____

_____

_____

■ Self-Test

Part A: Fill in the Blanks

1. Mutual saving banks, Savings and Loan associations, and credit unions are referred to collectively as _____.

2. Most mutual savings banks are _____ because they were not permitted at the federal level unit 1978.

3. The agency problem is accentuated at some thrifts by the _____ form of ownership.

4. The managers of thrifts under the mutual form of ownership are _____ risk averse because they are not owners and thus gain nothing from great performance but can lose everything if firm fails.

5. Mutual savings banks are concentrated in the _____ portion of the United States.

6. The amount of insurance provided on accounts at Savings and Loan was increased in 1980 to _____ from $40,000.

7. Regulatory forbearance by regulatory agencies increases _____.

8. The average size of Savings and Loan is _____ than the average size of commercial banks.

9. Credit unions are designed to meet the needs of _____ and not businesses.

10. The first credit unions in the United States were established in the state of _____ in 1910.

11. Credit unions are organized under the _____ form of ownership.

12. The single most important feature of credit unions that distinguishes them from other depository institutions is the _____ membership rule.

13. Credit unions are classified as _____ and are thus exempt from _____.

14. Credit union operating costs are generally considered to be _____ than those of banks.

15. _____ help credit unions by providing educational services, investing excess funds, holding clearing balances, as well as other services.

16. The _____ was established to manage and resolve insolvent thrifts following the S&L crisis.

17. The _____ passed by congress in 1934 allowed federal chartering of credit unions in all states.

18. The _____ idea says that only members of a particular association, occupation, or geographic region are permitted to join the credit union.

Part B: True-False Questions

Circle whether the following statements are true (T) or false (F).

T F   1. Congress created Savings and Loan and mutual savings banks for the express purpose of making it easier for individuals to purchase homes.

T F   2. In the early years of the savings and loan industry their main assets were consumer loans for items such as cars, furniture, and appliances.

T F   3. The deposits of mutual savings banks and S&Ls are both insured by the Federal Savings and Loan Insurance Corporation.

T F   4. When the S&L industry hit a crisis in the late 1970s and early 1980s, the Federal Home Loan Bank Board was quick to step in and take action to minimize the problems.

T F   5. The Financial Institutions Reform, Recovery, and Enforcement Act, passed in 1989, created the Resolution Trust Corporation that was given the responsibility of cleaning up the S&L crisis.

T F   6. Although the number of S&Ls is less than the number of commercial banks, the average asset size of S&Ls is significantly larger.

T F   7. One advantage of S&Ls over commercial banks is that S&Ls do not have to meet the reserve requirements to which commercial banks are subject.

T F   8. Credit unions were created primarily to provide loan needs not met by commercial banks and other thrifts.

T F   9. The first credit unions were created in Germany in the 1900s.

T F 10. Because credit unions are nonprofit organizations, they do not have earnings to distribute to their owners.

T F 11. To be able to make deposits and borrow from a credit union a person must be associated with other customers through a "common bond."

T F 12. Credit unions are able to diversify the risk of their assets because the customers they lend to purchase a wide variety of items.

T F 13. Regular share accounts at credit unions are like savings accounts at commercial banks.

T F 14. Share draft accounts are the credit union's equivalent of CDs at commercial banks.

T F 15. Credit unions are small relative to banks and S&Ls primarily due to the fact that they are limited in their customer base by the common bond requirement.

T   F   16.   The Central Liquidity Facility (CLF) is an agency that is usually the primary lender for credit unions in need of day to day funds.

T   F   17.   Shares are insured by up to $50,000 at state charted credit unions by the National Credit Union Share Insurance Fund (NCUSIF).

T   F   18.   Regular share accounts are essentially savings accounts that permit checks to be drawn against them.

Part C: Multiple-Choice Questions

Circle the appropriate answer.

1.   Of the following financial intermediaries, which is the largest in terms of aggregate assets?
   (a)   Commercial banks
   (b)   Savings and Loan
   (c)   Mutual savings banks
   (d)   Credit unions

2.   Which of the following thrifts has the lowest potential for principal-agent problems?
   (a)   Savings and Loan
   (b)   Mutual savings banks
   (c)   Credit unions
   (d)   Both (b) and (c) face low potential principal-agent problems.

3.   The mutual form of ownership has all of the following features except
   (a)   no stock is issued or sold.
   (b)   all deposits represent equity capital.
   (c)   managers of mutuals are more inclined to look out for the welfare of the owners than are managers of the corporate form of ownership.
   (d)   the threat of a takeover by another firm is not a threat to managers of mutuals.

4.   In the early 1900s, the number of S&Ls reached approximately
   (a)   8,000.
   (b)   20,000.
   (c)   10,000.
   (d)   12,000.

5.   One example of regulatory forbearance by the S&L regulators during the early years of the S&L crisis was that
   (a)   they failed to put insolvent S&Ls out of business.
   (b)   they failed to take control of the money supply to reduce interest rates.
   (c)   they paid depositors too much from the S&L insurance fund.
   (d)   they lent too much to S&Ls that were having financial difficulties.

6. Regulatory forbearance resulted in many S&Ls doing all of the following except
   (a) taking riskier loans in an effort to increase earnings.
   (b) offering extremely high interest rates to attract depositors from other S&Ls.
   (c) lowering the rate they charged on loans to increase revenues.
   (d) increasing their equity capital to reduce the risk of bankruptcy.

7. Charles H. Keating is best known in the financial markets for
   (a) being chairman of the Federal Home Loan Bank Board.
   (b) his involvement with Lincoln Savings and Loan of Irvine, California.
   (c) his involvement with the bankruptcy of the California Pension Fund.
   (d) serving as a financial advisor to President Reagan during the S&L crisis.

8. The Financial Institutions Reform, Recovery, and Enforcement Act (FIRREA)
   (a) eliminated deposit insurance for S&Ls.
   (b) did away with the Federal Home Loan Bank Board.
   (c) eliminated the opening of any new S&Ls.
   (d) allowed S&Ls to purchase junk bonds to increase interest earned on their assets.

9. After passage of FIRREA in 1989, S&Ls increased their relative loans for _____, reducing their portfolio risk.
   (a) business purposes
   (b) consumer mortgages
   (c) commercial real estate loans
   (d) household products

10. Federal chartering of credit unions was authorized by the
    (a) Financial Institutions Reform Act.
    (b) National Credit Union Act of 1970.
    (c) Federal Credit Union Act.
    (d) None of the above apply; credit unions are all charted at the state level.

11. Service fees charged by credit unions are lower than those of commercial banks because credit unions enjoy all of except which of the following advantages?
    (a) Credit unions pay lower interest rates on deposits.
    (b) Credit unions are nonprofit organizations.
    (c) Credit unions are tax-exempt.
    (d) Their costs are lower due to using some volunteer labor.

12. The lender of last resort for credit unions is the
    (a) National Credit Union Insurance Fund.
    (b) Credit Union National Association.
    (c) Credit Union National Extension Bureau.
    (d) Central Liquidity Facility.

13. The largest source of funds for credit unions is/are
    (a) equity capital.
    (b) share draft accounts.
    (c) share certificates.
    (d) regular share accounts.

14. Depositors at credit unions can write checks against their
    (a) regular share accounts.
    (b) demand deposit accounts.
    (c) share draft accounts.
    (d) share certificate accounts.

15. The main disadvantage of credit unions is
    (a) the common bond requirement keeps them relatively small reducing the range of services they can provide.
    (b) the use of volunteer workers keeps them from having adequate professional managers.
    (c) their average costs are higher due to having to be located near their depositors.
    (d) the lack of support they get from common groups associated with employers.

16. Credit Unions were created primarily to
    (a) skirt governmental regulations.
    (b) provide financing for the ultra wealthy.
    (c) provide small consumer type loans to the middle class.
    (d) None of the above

17. Mutual Saving banks and Savings and Loan associations are different in which of the following ways?
    (a) Mutual savings are concentrated in the northeast, while saving and loans are located throughout the country.
    (b) Mutual savings may insure their deposits with state or with the Federal Deposit Insurance Corporation.
    (c) Mutual savings are not as heavily concentrated in mortgages and have more flexibility in investment practices.
    (d) All of the above

18. Which of the following is not an advantage of the mutual form of ownership?
    (a) Mutual Savings banks are safer because they have fewer liabilities.
    (b) Managers of savings bank tend to be more risk averse than corporate managers.
    (c) Mutual Savings banks eliminate the principal-agent problem.
    (d) Each owner possesses a small percentage of the bank.
    (e) Both (c) and (d)

Part D: Short Answer Questions

1. How does the mutual ownership structure of financial institutions influence the agency problem?

   _____

   _____

2. What are the three main reasons the regulatory authorities did not properly address the S&L crisis in the early stages of the problem?

   A) _____

   B) _____

   C) _____

3. What is the main distinction between commercial banks and thrifts in terms of the customers they serve?

   _____

   _____

4. How does the principal-agent problem encountered by the savings and loan industry differ from the agency problem faced by corporations?

   _____

5. Briefly describe what regulatory actions were taken to help to solve the S&L crisis.

   _____

   _____

6. What are the advantages that Credit Unions have over traditional banking organizations?

   _____

   _____

   _____

7. What are the main functions of the National Credit Union Administration?

   _____

   _____

■ Answers to Chapter 26

Exercise 1

1.	c	7.	d	13.	i
2.	m	8.	f	14.	p
3.	a	9.	l	15.	o
4.	h	10.	b	16.	n
5.	e	11.	k		
6.	j	12.	g		

Exercise 2

The creation of new products, such as money market mutual funds and securitization, put pressure on Savings and Loan associations to find new ways to generate profits. The existence of deposit insurance, along with the relatively new availability of junk bonds, swaps, and financial futures, enticed S&L managers to take on higher risk in an effort to enhance their profitability.

Self-Test

Part A

1.	thrifts	7	moral hazard	13.	non-profit, federal taxes
2.	state-chartered	8.	greater	14.	lower
3.	mutual	9.	consumers	15.	central credit unions
4.	more	10.	Massachusetts	16.	Resolution Trust Corporation
5.	northeast	11.	mutual	17.	Federal Credit Union Act
6.	$100,000	12.	common bond	18.	common bond membership

Part B

1.	T	7.	F	13.	T
2.	F	8.	T	14.	F
3.	F	9.	T	15.	T
4.	F	10.	F	16.	F
5.	T	11.	T	17.	F
6.	T	12.	F	18.	F

Part C

1.	b	7.	b	13.	d
2.	c	8.	b	14.	c
3.	c	9.	b	15.	a
4.	d	10.	c	16.	c
5.	a	11.	a	17.	d
6.	d	12.	d	18.	e

Part D

1. Having a large number of shareholders where each only owns a very small part of the total encourages the agency problem since none of the shareholders have a large enough stake in the firm to perform the monitoring function.

2. A) The amount of money in the insurance fund was inadequate to close the insolvent S&Ls.

    B) The organizations were established to encourage S&L growth and thus did not want to shut them down.

    C) To avoid admitting that they were in trouble, the agencies preferred to wait and hope the crisis ended.

3. Thrifts direct their attention to servicing the loan needs of consumers. They lend primarily to middle-class working households. Banks concentrate more on lending to business firms.

4. The agency problem is based on the condition that the managers of a business may have personal interests that are different from the shareholders and may make decision based on their personal preference and not in the best interest of the owners. The S&L principal-agent problem arises when the government regulators of S&Ls do not take actions that are in the best interest of the taxpayers.

5. The Savings and Loan bailout was accomplished through the Financial Institutions Reform, Recovery, and Enforcement Act of 1989 (FIRREA). The regulatory oversight was taken from the Federal Home Loan Bank Board and given to the Office of Thrift Supervision within the U.S. Treasury Dept. The FDIC assumed the regulatory responsibilities of the FSLIC and became the sole administrator of the federal deposit insurance system. Last, the Resolution Trust Corporation was created to manage and dispose of insolvent thrifts in receivership.

6. The text identifies three primary advantages of credit unions: (1) they receive employer support, (2) they are exempt from paying taxes, and (3) they are part of large trade associations, which increases the services they can offer and lowers their costs.

7. The National Credit Union Administration is an independent federal agency that supervises and regulates federally chartered credit unions and state-chartered credit unions that receive federal deposit insurance.

Chapter 27
Finance Companies

■ Chapter Learning Goals

By the end of this chapter, you should

1. Understand the purpose of finance companies.
2. Know the types of finance companies.
3. Know how finance companies are regulated.
4. Know important parts of finance companies' balance sheets.

■ Chapter Summary

This chapter discusses finance companies, detailing the purpose and types of finance companies. It also provides how finance companies are regulated and how their balance sheets are different from other industries.

History of Finance Companies

Installment credit agreements represented the first type of finance offering by companies in the United States, retailers in particular. An **installment credit** agreement is a loan to a customer that requires the customer to make fixed payments over specified term. Comparatively, a **balloon loan** is a loan that requires one payment on the maturity date. Installment loans spread the payments out to help borrowers to better manage their finances. Auto manufacturers were the first to establish **finance companies** to support product sales through installment loans.

Purpose of Finance Companies

Finance companies are a type of money market intermediary. The money markets are wholesale markets with minimum required investments of $100,000. Finance companies allow small businesses and individuals to access the money market by loaning the proceeds of large commercial paper offerings to them in small increments. Because finance companies are not regulated to the extent of commercial banks, they can hold and raise assets in ways commercial banks cannot. This difference allows them to be flexible in meeting customer needs. Specifically, they accept higher risk loans than banks and can provide favorable loan terms to customers who are purchasing goods from affiliated companies.

Risk in Finance Companies

Finance companies are susceptible to two types of risk: default risk and liquidity risk. The **default risk** of a loan is the likelihood that the customer will not pay. Customer rates of default are often higher for finance companies than banks because they provide loans to customers who are considered higher risk or more likely not to repay the loan. **Liquidity risk** for a finance company is the risk that it will not be able to borrow funds if it has a cash shortfall. The secondary market for finance company assets is not well developed, so finance companies have to search for alternative sources of finding when they need capital. This is more of an issue for small finance companies than large finance companies. If the risk of a finance company increases, then renewing debt when it matures or **rolling over** the debt may become more difficult. Because finance companies hold shorter-term assets than banks, they are less concerned about interest-rate risk.

Types of Finance Companies

There are three general types of finance companies: (1) business, (2) sales, and (3) consumer. Business loans are more common than consumer loans. In 2013, the aggregate distribution of loans by finance companies is 60% for consumer loans, 12% for real estate loans, and the remaining 28% are business loans.

Business (Commercial) Finance Companies

Business finance companies provide a type of credit called **factoring,** which is where the finance company purchases a firm's account receivables at a discount. The finance company is known as the factor. The finance company takes on the responsibility of collecting the accounts receivables that it purchases. Alternatively, the finance company may loan funds to a company and assume the responsibility of collecting the accounts receivables but not actually purchase the receivables. However, if the firm does not pay its loan or fails, then the finance company may take possession of the accounts receivables. Finance companies that specialize in these types of loans are able to achieve economies of scale in billing and collections of receivables.

Some finance companies specialize in **leasing** equipment. The finance companies purchase equipment and lease it to users. If the lessee fails to make the lease payments, then the finance company will **repossess** the equipment. The owner of the equipment, i.e. the lender, depreciates the equipment for tax purposes. If the finance company is a subsidiary of a manufacturer that is experiencing losses, as long as the finance company is profitable, it can still benefit from reduced tax expense arising from the depreciation expense. Lessees often benefit from smaller up front payments compared to purchasing the asset.

Floor plan loans are loans where a finance company will pay for a business' inventory and place a lien against each item in inventory. As each item is sold, the borrower pays off the lien against the inventory item and receives a clear title. Car dealerships are good examples of the type of businesses that borrow using floor loans.

Consumer Finance Companies

Consumer finance companies make loans to consumers to purchase items, such as home appliances, or to refinance small debts. Some consumer finance companies are owned by banks. Consumer loans are typically higher risk loans with the exception of home equity loans that are secured by second mortgages of homes. A home equity loan against a primary residence benefits from the tax deductibility of interest. Thus, the **effective interest rate** for a home-equity loan is the interest rate times (1 minus the tax rate). For example, the effective rate for an individual with a marginal tax rate of 28% and a home equity at 7.5% is 5.4% [7.5% × (1 − 0.28)].

Sales Finance Companies

Finance companies that make loans to consumers to purchase from a particular manufacturer or retailer are known as sales finance companies. Sales finance companies are also known as **captive finance companies** and are owned by the manufacturer or retailer to whose customers it makes loans. Rates on these loans may be lower than from other lenders because the loans are subsidized by the manufacturer's earnings.

Regulation of Finance Companies

If a finance company is owned by a bank or bank holding company, then it is subject to federal regulation. All other finance companies are regulated at the state level. The few regulations imposed on finance companies are designed to protect consumers.

One of the few federal regulations that finance companies must follow is **Regulation Z**, also known as the truth-in-lending regulation. It requires finance companies and banks to provide in an understandable and prominent fashion the annual percentage rate (APR) charged on loans and the total interest costs on loans. The homestead exemption, part of federal bankruptcy law, allows consumers declaring bankruptcy to keep possession of many assets while eliminating the debt associated with those assets. **Usury** statutes prevent excessively high interest rates from being charges on loans. The interest rates are determined by each state. Other regulations restrict finance companies' ability to collect on defaulted or delinquent loans.

Finance Company Balance Sheet

Assets

Loans are the primary assets of finance companies. The **reserve for loan losses** account enables finance companies to allocate a portion of income to offset losses from loan defaults each reporting period. The reserve for loan losses account helps companies to smooth losses out instead of having to take large losses as they arise.

Liabilities

Finance companies liabilities include commercial paper, bank loans, and debts owed to the parent company.

Income

The main source of income for finance companies is interest income from the loan portfolio. Other sources of income are origination fees charged for making loans and credit insurance sold to customers to pay off the loan if the customer becomes disabled.

Growth of Finance Companies

The expansion of finance companies usually follows the growth of the economy, increasing during expansions and stabilizing during downturns. As of 2009, finance companies have around $2 trillion in assets.

■ Exercises

Exercise 1: Definitions and Terminology

Match the following terms from the left column with the closely related term from the right. Place the letter of the term from the right column in the blank provided next to the appropriate term on the left.

_____	1. A loan where the borrower makes equal payments over a specific time period	a. balloon payment
_____	2. Problems that arise from a finance company running out of cash	b. default risk
_____	3. Renewing debt each time it matures	c. repossession
_____	4. A loan that requires the borrower to make one payment at maturity of the loan	d. captive finance
_____	5. A chance that a customer will not repay his loan	e. roll over
_____	6. Purchasing accounts receivable at a discount	f. consumer finance
_____	7. When a lender takes an asset back because the borrower failed to make payments on time	g. business finance
_____	8. Finance companies that buy receivables at a discount	h. installment credit
_____	9. Finance companies that make loans to individuals to purchase items or to refinance small debts	i. factoring
_____	10. Finance companies owned by the manufacturer or retailer to whose customers it makes loans	j. liquidity risk

■ Self-Test

Part A: Fill in the Blanks

1. A(n) _____ finance company makes loans to refinance small debts and to individuals to purchase items.

2. A(n) _____ loan against a primary residence benefits from the tax deductibility of interest.

3. _____ loans are the most common type of business loan.

4. Finance companies are a type of _____ intermediary.

5. _____ risk is the risk that a borrower will not repay a loan.

6. The primary assets of finance companies are _____.

7. _____ is the main source of income for finance companies.

8. A(n) _____ finance company is one that is owned by a retailer or manufacturer to whose customers it makes loans.

9. When a finance company renews debt each time it matures, it is said to _____ the debt.

10. A(n) _____ loan requires the borrower to make one payment at the maturity of the loan.

Part B: True-False Questions

T   F   1.   Commercial paper is a type of liability on a finance company's balance sheets.

T   F   2.   Origination fees are the main source of income for finance companies.

T   F   3.   The reserve for loan losses account enables finance companies to smooth out their bad loan losses.

T   F   4.   Repossession is the chance that a borrower will not repay a loan.

T   F   5.   Default risk is when a lender takes an asset back because the borrower has not made payments on time.

T   F   6.   Rolling over debt is when a company renews debt each time it matures.

T   F   7.   Factoring is the name for finance companies buying accounts receivable at a discount.

T   F   8.   The effective interest rate for a 10% home equity loan taken out by a person in the 28% tax bracket is 7.2%.

T   F   9.   An installment loan requires a borrower to make equal payments over a specific time period.

T   F   10.   A consumer finance company makes loans to individuals to purchase items or refinance small debts.

Part C: Multiple-Choice Questions

1.   Which of the following is the risk that a finance company will not be able to borrow funds if it has a cash crunch?
    (a)   credit risk
    (b)   default risk
    (c)   interest-rate risk
    (d)   liquidity risk

2.   Which of the following is true about loans that finance companies make?
    (a)   The loans are lower risk than bank loans.
    (b)   The loans are higher risk than bank loans.
    (c)   Less regulation gives finance companies more flexibility in making loans that meet customer needs.
    (d)   Finance companies can provide favorable loan terms to customers from an affiliated or parent company.
    (e)   Only (b), (c), and (d) are true.

3. Which of the following is not a type of finance company?

    (a) Business

    (b) Captive

    (c) Consumer

    (d) Sales

    (e) None of the above

4. The main source of income for finance companies is

    (a) interest income.

    (b) origination fees.

    (c) referral fees.

    (d) sales of repossessed assets.

5. The types of risk that finance companies typically face include

    (a) default risk.

    (b) exchange rate risk.

    (c) liquidity risk.

    (d) prepayment risk.

    (e) both (a) and (c).

6. _____ requires finance companies and banks to report the annual percentage rate charged on loans.

    (a) Glass-Steagall

    (b) Regulation T

    (c) Regulation Z

    (d) The Securities Act of 1933

7. _____ prevent(s) excessively high interest rates from being charged on loans.

    (a) The Federal Reserve

    (b) The Securities and Exchange Commission

    (c) Regulation Z

    (d) Usury statutes

8. The effective interest rate on a 9% home equity loan for an individual with a marginal tax rate of 28% is

    (a) 2.52%.

    (b) 5.50%.

    (c) 6.48%.

    (d) 7.36%.

9. The reserve for loan losses account
    (a) exists for the allocation of income to offset losses from loan defaults.
    (b) is a liability on a finance company's balance sheets.
    (c) smoothes out losses from loan defaults.
    (d) Both (a) and (b)
    (e) Both (a) and (c)

10. Sales finance companies are also known as
    (a) captive finance companies.
    (b) commercial finance companies.
    (c) consumer finance companies.
    (d) business finance companies.

Part D: Short Answer Questions

1. Why are finance companies important?

    _____

    _____

2. What are three types of finance companies and to whom do they provide credit?

    _____

    _____

3. What are the important assets and liabilities on a finance company's balance sheets?

    _____

    _____

■ Answers to Chapter 27

Exercise 1: Definitions and Terminology

1. h   6. i
2. j   7. c
3. e   8. g
4. a   9. f
5. b   10. d

Self-Test

Part A

1. consumer
2. home equity
3. Equipment
4. money market
5. Default
6. loans
7. Interest income
8. captive
9. roll over
10. balloon

Part B

1. T   5. F   9. T
2. F   6. T   10. T
3. T   7. T
4. F   8. T

Part C

1. d   5. e   9. e
2. e   6. c   10. a
3. e   7. d
4. a   8. c

Part D

1. Finance companies are important because they provide individuals and small businesses access to the money markets. In addition, they provide credit to high risk borrowers who cannot obtain loans from commercial banks.

2. The three types of finance companies are as follows:

   a. Commercial finance companies provide loans to businesses for equipment, motor vehicles, securitized business assets, and other items.
   b. Consumer finance companies make loans to individuals to refinance small debts or to purchase specific items.
   c. Sales finance companies make loans to consumers to buy from a particular retailer or manufacturer.

3. Important assets are loans and reserves for loan losses. Important liabilities include commercial paper, bank loans, and debts to a parent company.